THE VITALITY
OF THE CHRISTIAN TRADITION

Contributors

VIRGINIA CORWIN, Associate Professor of Religion and Biblical Literature, Smith College

ERNEST R. HILGARD, Professor of Psychology and Education, Stanford University

HOWARD B. JEFFERSON, Professor of Philosophy, Colgate University

JOHN KNOX, Professor of Sacred Literature, Union Theological Seminary

JOHN MOORE, Associate Professor of Ethics and Religion, Hamilton College

JAMES MUILENBURG, Professor of Old Testament Literature and Semitic Languages, Pacific School of Religion

ALBERT C. OUTLER, Associate Professor of Historical Theology, Divinity School, Duke University

DOUGLAS V. STEERE, Professor of Philosophy, Haverford College

GEORGE F. THOMAS, Professor of Religious Thought, Princeton University

HENRY P. VAN DUSEN, Professor of Systematic Theology, Union Theological Seminary

LYNN D. WHITE, President, Mills College

AMOS N. WILDER, Professor of New Testament Interpretation, Chicago Theological Seminary

THE VITALITY
OF THE
CHRISTIAN
TRADITION

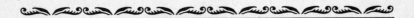

Edited by
GEORGE F. THOMAS

HARPER & BROTHERS
PUBLISHERS
New York and London

To

CHARLES FOSTER KENT

Woolsey Professor of Biblical Literature
in Yale University

and

Founder of the National Council on Religion
in Higher Education

1867-1925

CONTENTS

PREFACE

THE PURPOSE OF THIS BOOK IS TO STATE AS CLEARLY AS POSSIBLE THE major insights and values of the Christian tradition, to trace their development from their beginnings in the Bible to the present day, and to deal with some of the problems created by the widespread reaction against them in the modern world. The contributors have attempted to present these insights and values as accurately as possible, but with a minimum of detail. They have deliberately abstained as far as possible from footnotes and other scholarly apparatus, because they wished to reach the general reader as well as the specialized student of religion. For their deeper purpose was, not the academic one of expounding the history and meaning of Christianity for other scholars, but the practical one of arousing thoughtful men and women from all walks of life to the dangers involved in the neglect of the Christian tradition in our American life, its art, literature, education, and philosophy, as well as its business and politics. They are convinced that indifference to the Christian tradition has impoverished our whole culture and weakened our democracy in recent generations and that we must renew that tradition if disaster is to be prevented in the future.

As professors in colleges and universities, we have a special concern also for more adequate instruction in the historical development and achievements of Christianity as well as its implications for the modern world. We are convinced that few schools, colleges, and universities are meeting their responsibility to provide adequate religious instruction and counsel for their students. Chapters 7 and 8 illustrate our concern for this situation. Chapter 7 presents the possibilities of a college course in devotional classics for the religious development of students; chapter 8 indicates some of the causes of the widespread religious illiteracy and indifference in academic circles and among educated people in general. It is our hope that the book as a whole may point to the rich treasure of ideas and ideals that is to be found in the Christian tradition and remove some of the difficulties which prevent so many educated men and women from taking Christianity seriously in their thinking and living.

Though full responsibility for each chapter is taken by its author alone, the book was planned as a whole. It has been our purpose to secure as comprehensive treatment as possible. It will be obvious to the reader, however, that there are omissions in each chapter which prevent it from being an exhaustive treatment of its period or topic. This was inevitable if the development of the Christian tradition as a whole and something of its many-sided influence upon Western civilization were to be presented in a single volume. The book, therefore, makes no pretension to completeness in its treatment of the history and impact of Christianity. We have, however, attempted to be as inclusive as space permitted.

The book was also planned to insure as much unity as possible. There has been no attempt to impose a single interpretation of Christianity upon all the chapters. There is, however, a significant degree of unity in the points of view of the contributors. Despite the differences between us at certain points, we are all united by the conviction that the essentials of the Hebraic-Christian world view and way of life, when interpreted intelligently and with the help of modern scholarship, have a strong claim upon our faith and loyalty. We do not believe that the truth of a belief can be measured by its newness; and we are not afraid of a belief because it is old. We are not persuaded, for example, that the scientific method is the only way of arriving at truth, that naturalism is the only respectable philosophy, or that humanism is the last word in religion. We believe that there are significant truths and values in the traditional Christian view of the world and of man. We are not concerned to defend all aspects of traditional Christianity, institutional, theological, or otherwise. But we reject the idea that the liberal and critical mind must be forever undecided on the great issues of life and uncommitted to any definite position with respect to them. And we believe that a reasoned faith in the essentials of Christianity is both compatible with the critical attitude of the seeker after truth and necessary to the recovery of meaning in personal and social life.

The contributors have been drawn together by their association as Fellows of the National Council on Religion in Higher Education founded in 1922 by Charles Foster Kent, Woolsey Professor of Biblical Literature in Yale University. The primary purpose of the National Council is to stimulate more adequate religious instruction and coun-

seling in colleges and universities. For twenty years it has appointed
Fellows dedicated to this purpose. It has not only enabled them by
the grant of stipends to pursue their graduate studies in religion and
other fields, but it has also helped to place them in responsible positions and has brought them together in annual meetings for fellowship and discussion of their common problems. It now has more than
130 Fellows in teaching, personnel, and administrative positions in
educational institutions of the United States and Canada, from Yale
to Stanford and from Toronto to Texas, as well as many in college
pastorates, in government service, and in other professions. This book
is in large part the fruit of the long friendship of the contributors as
Fellows of the National Council and of their common interest in
religion in higher education. We speak, of course, only for ourselves,
and not for the whole group of Fellows, who represent different points
of view. Finally, in gratitude to Professor Kent for his vision and his
service to the National Council we have dedicated this book to his
memory.

THE EDITOR

THE VITALITY
OF THE CHRISTIAN TRADITION

1

The Faith of Ancient Israel

HISTORICAL FORCES EXERT A PROFOUND INFLUENCE UPON ALL OF US. OUR lives are intimately bound up with the communities in which we live. What is happening in the present is deeply rooted in what has happened in the past. Time is a river upon which we live our lives. We cannot understand ourselves without knowing something about the river and its course, even though it roll on over thundering cataracts beyond us. We are a part of history, and history is a part of us. We cannot separate ourselves from history any more than we can separate ourselves from nature.

Other ages than our own have sought to weave a pattern out of the tangled skein of historical circumstance. In the second century before Christ, when the Jews were subjected to terrible persecution under the tyranny of a foreign conqueror, the writer of the Book of Daniel sought to explain the rise and fall of empires in the centuries preceding his own. He inspired his contemporaries with courage and faith by pointing to a supreme and controlling purpose at work in the midst of the tragedy of his times. History was for him a world court in which the nations of the world were judged and held accountable. In the fifth century of our own era, Augustine, faced with a world in which the vast and imposing structure of the Roman Empire was crumbling before his eyes, meditated upon the historical tradition in which the Christian community was rooted, and discovered in it the presence and activity of a divine intention. The result of his thought and reflection appears in his *City of God*, which was destined to influence Christian thought and faith for many centuries.

Both Augustine and the writer of Daniel were authentic interpreters of the Hebraic tradition. Nothing is so characteristic of that tradition as its concern with history. Israel sought in history an understanding of its existence and destiny. For this reason the authentic approach to the appreciation of the Hebraic genius and tradition in the world is historical. Other approaches always involve some distortion. Historical criticism has performed the revolutionary task of fitting the materials of the Bible, originally compiled in ways utterly alien to modern ideas, into the pattern of their historical setting of time, place, and occasion. He who reads the Bible in the light of this social and historical background is not only having a fresh and vivid experience but is at the same time following the ancient Hebrews themselves in seeing meaning in the immediacies of historical event. Thus a religion which expresses itself in terms of history and finds in history the most adequate vehicle of divine revelation must be read by modern men in its historical and social context. Our own contemporary search for coherence in history, our bafflement in the midst of a staggering historical crisis, and our profound concern for the fate of man are all closely related to the fundamental interests of the Old Testament, above all, to that central portion which we call prophecy. It is doubtful whether there is any other heritage which speaks so directly to the condition of modern men. The conviction of the author is that the modern world must recapture the essential insight and faith of Hebraic prophetic religion if it is to face the future with hope and confidence.

The little land of Palestine, the home of Israel, was strategically located in the ancient world. A narrow strip of land skirting the extreme eastern end of the Mediterranean Sea for about one hundred and fifty miles, it did not emerge into the full tide of Mediterranean civilizations until relatively late. The titanic forces that are today stirring in this area recall the glory that was ancient Greece, but they might well remind us also of the history of Semitic peoples from the dawn of Mediterranean civilizations to the time when the early Christian movement broke the confines of its Semitic origin and emerged into the broad expanse of three of the world's great continents. Palestine was also an international corridor occupied by minority peoples who seldom achieved sufficient military power to resist the advance of imperialisms like those of Egypt, Assyria, Babylonia, Persia, Greece, and Rome. The Old Testament is a precipitate of the international relations of a minority people living in a corridor between rival powers. Not only Asia and Africa but Europe also contributed to the history of the little land. Each time the tide of invasion swept over western Asia, Palestine was to feel its effect. The coming of the Philistines about 1170 B.C. was but part of a much more extensive invasion, but so great was the pressure that the Hebrew tribes were forced to unite and to establish a monarchy to resist this threat to their existence. When the whole of western Asia had been fashioned into the mold of Assyrian Empire, the Scythians, wild nomadic horsemen from the plains of Russia, broke through the mountain barriers to the north and contributed to the final destruction of one of the world's most ruthless powers. The coming of Alexander the Great in 332 B.C. and the arrival of Pompey in 63 B.C. were destined to have effects even more profound for the history of culture and religion. In short, Europe, Asia, and Africa all contributed significantly to the life of ancient Israel. Again, Palestine was an oasis in the northwestern part of the vast Arabian desert. The desert never ceased to be a source of stimulus and invigoration to her life. The prophets often appeal to the desert as the true home of Israel's faith. Elijah as a true son of the desert is a genuine expression of the nomadic Yahweh religion.

We should expect the history of a people occupying the Palestinian corridor to be of a peculiarly dynamic character. If the Hebrews were to maintain themselves in their world at all, they had to possess vitality sufficient to meet the forces that were threatening their existence. These threats were as much cultural and religious as they were political and military, though the two cannot be separated in Oriental antiquity. Israel had no choice but to exert herself against foreign encroachment and domination. The alternative would have been assimilation and destruction. One of the striking features of world history is that Israel never was completely absorbed. It was the function of the prophets to arouse their contemporaries to a realization that what was happening to them in their times was a threat not only to their national existence but to the foundation of their faith in God. The events of history were of supreme importance; God was speaking in them. And this speech was a proclamation of His will. But the prophets also provided a dimension of depth to their message by recalling the significance of crucial events in the past. It is no accident that on the eve of the institution of the Yahweh cult, immediately after the destruction of the Amalekites in an internecine desert encounter (Exod. 17:8-16), Moses with great solemnity inscribes a stone with a record that must be remembered. Similarly, in the dark days when the Assyrian power had devoured the little kingdom of Judah and times were heavy with tragedy, the prophet in one of the classical utterances of prophetic faith calls upon his contemporaries:

My people, remember now, what Balak, king of Moab, planned,
And what Balaam, the son of Beor, answered him,
From Shittim to Gilgal,
That ye may understand the righteous acts of Yahweh.
—*Mic. 6:5*

The words of Jesus, "This do in remembrance of me," in the most solemn moment of his life are genuinely Hebraic in this respect.

HISTORY AND REVELATION

It is against this background that the major features of Hebraic religion should be examined. In turning to the scriptural record we catch a view of the mountain peaks, but we must also survey the ranges that stretch before and behind us. We must identify ourselves with the crises of history and with the persons who emerge out of these crises, but with the men of the Old Testament and of the New we must see that history also involves continuity. Only by doing justice at one and the same time to the concreteness of historical vicissitudes and the total stream of tradition in which those vicissitudes fall are we able to appreciate what constitutes Israel's legacy to the world.

The historical orientation of Hebrew religion is reflected in the literature of the Old Testament. The first seventeen books are historical in form. The prophetic books are for the most part the response of the prophets to definite historical situations and are best understood when the social background to the passages is grasped. That Isaiah of Jerusalem saw his vision "in the year that King Uzziah died" (Isa. 6) and made a memorable appeal to faith in a severe international crisis (Isa. 7) helps us as nothing else can to appreciate these passages. Prophetic religion, both within and outside the prophetic books (e.g., II Sam. 9-20), sees God at work in historical crises. This explains the urgency of prophetic religion. The Exodus from Egypt is the supreme event of Israel's existence. It is the dramatic act of God in which he leads her from tyranny and oppression to the rigors of the desert, from slavery into freedom, from Egypt to Sinai, the mount of her covenanting. At the high moment of deliverance Miriam breaks out in a song of ecstatic joy:

Sing to Yahweh, for He hath triumphed gloriously,
The horse and the rider He has hurled into the sea.
—*Exod. 15:21*

In the trackless desert wastes Yahweh is the Leader of the tribes in cloud and fire (Exod. 13:21 ff.); in their weariness and thirst He heals the bitter waters (Exod. 15:22-26); in their hunger He is their Provider (Exod. 16); in the desperate conflict with Amalek He is their Conqueror (Exod. 17:8-16); amidst the thunders and earthquake and fire of Sinai He descends to become their Covenant God (Exod. 19:16-20:2). As He journeys with them in the desert, so He is with them in the invasion of the Palestinian corridor. When the tide of battle turns, they see His power still at work. Yahweh is not conquered by other more powerful deities; rather, His will is revealed to Israel even in her defeat. He gives victory to the enemy because His own people do not obey His will. Israel sees from the beginning that her God is not subservient to her own desires and needs. It is His righteous will upon which she is dependent for her existence and survival. This insight that God is a God of right before He is a God of a favored people made ethical development possible. Patriotism had always to be checked by a higher allegiance and power and will. For Israel history is not the arena of capricious forces where only the strong survive. It is not finally a battlefield where God prospers the big battalions. It is not a colossal tragedy in which small nations always fall before aggressive tyrannies. The issues of history are moral; justice and right and truth are victorious in the end.

If the past history of Israel is the theater of God's revealing, the present is the moment in which she stands under judgment. It is the moment in which something is demanded of her. The decisiveness of the present moment is sounded in all the prophets. In Amos (5:18-27), Isaiah (2:6-21), and Zephaniah (1) this is expressed in the proclamation that the Day of Yahweh is at hand. The present is the commanding moment in which Israel must see herself under obligation and responsibility. Man's will is challenged by the demand of God. But this demand for decision is not divorced from an awareness of the significance of past history. It is never sheer invasion. It does justice to the "invasive" character of the Divine Will, and it accentuates its urgency always. But it is the same Yahweh who leads Israel out of the house of bondage, who reveals Himself by sending prophets and Nazirites, who is known by what He does, has done, and will do, who speaks in the crucial moment of the present (Amos 2:9-16; Mic. 6:1-8; Jer. 25:1-14).

But the orientation in the classical period of Hebrew religion is not primarily toward the past but toward the future. In this respect it is like the early Christian movement, though the tensions with the historic past seem to be more freshly preserved in Hebraism than in early Christianity. Moreover, the orientation toward the future in the Old Testament is characteristically an historical orientation. As the events of history express the purpose of God, so Israel will be judged in the light of that purpose. As He creates the earth that men may experience community upon it (Isa. 45:18), so He will come to judge the earth with justice, and the peoples with His truth (Pss. 97-100). As He battles in the primeval deeps to bring the world into being out of chaos and dark night (Isa. 51:9 ff.), so He will, at the end of time, accomplish His purpose for the nations of the world. Israel lives her life in the midst of this awareness. The genius of Hebraism here is that it not only takes time seriously but conceives of it as involving the fate and destiny of men in terms of life and death, beginning and end, judgment and grace, creation and redemption.

The Hebraic attitude toward history is further understood by its relation to nature. To Hebraism nature is never the primary mode of the divine revealing. Passages which suggest that God reveals Himself through nature nearly always have their accent elsewhere. In the thunder and lightning of Sinai it is the historical context that is primary: "I am Yahweh who brought you up out of the land of Egypt." In the prophets nature is employed as the means of divine judgment upon the nation. In a series of powerful oracles Amos describes the catastrophes of nature which Yahweh has sent upon the land in order to make known to Israel His will and purpose, but each strophe ends tragically: "Yet have ye not returned unto me." In the poems of Second Isaiah creation is viewed as the work of God's power and wisdom, but this is made the basis for His judgment of the nations and the redemption of His people. Yahweh is seldom, if ever, identified with nature. His power is felt in various natural phenomena, but they are His instruments—the lightning His arrows, the earthquake and storm the work of His hands. The produce of the soil is the intentional gift of His goodness. Nature is subordinated to Yahweh. It shows forth His majesty and glory as we see in many of the Psalms (8, 19, 29, 104) and in the sublime nature poetry of the Book of Job. The progress of Hebrew thinking proceeds from the grace of God as seen in history to the activity of God in nature. In this respect it stands as an interesting contrast to the development of Greek thought from the natural to the spiritual.

Finally, history concretizes itself in the emergence of personalities who speak to the historical situation and make it luminous with meaning. The significance of the Aramean aggression in the ninth century B.C. would never have become apparent to us had it not been for the figure of Elijah, who understood the threat of Phoenician mercantile civilization to Israel's trust in Yahweh and His righteous will. The implications of Assyria's pressure upon the Palestinian corridor in the eighth century would never have concerned us had it not been for Amos and Hosea and Isaiah and Micah. The tumult of the closing decades of Judah's existence culminating in Jerusalem's destruction in 586 B.C. would never have revealed new dimensions of personal religious experience had it not been for the poignancy of Jeremiah's confessions (Jer. 11:18-23; 12:1-6, etc.). These men incarnate their times. They could even name their children after the burden of their messages—"Jezreel" (Hos. 1:3-5), "A remnant shall return" (Isa. 7:3), "Speed-spoil-haste-prey" (Isa. 8:1-4).

History, then, is the primary sphere of the divine revealing. In her experiences as a people and a nation Israel sees the purpose of God expressed. The events of the past are significant not only for their own time but for their disclosure of how Yahweh may work in the present and reveal Himself to Israel in the future. Since the will of Yahweh is righteousness and His purpose the solidarity of the community, we witness a profound moralization of the movement of history. It points to an end, to a culmination, to a Day of Yahweh when God will perform His purpose. Nature gradually emerges into the horizon of Hebraic thinking, but it never exists in its own right. At times the concern with nature is cosmic in its sweep, but even then it must obey the Divine Will:

> Hear, O heavens, and give ear, O earth,
> For Yahweh hath spoken:
> Sons have I reared and brought up,
> But they have rebelled against me!
> —*Isa. 1:2*

Of special importance is the emergence of great personalities in the midst of great historical crises. The stress of various periods in Israel's history is matched by the stature and grandeur of her prophets. The appearance of Hosea and Jeremiah and Jesus, each at the eve of a collapse of the nation, is suggestive of the essential genius of Hebraism and of the later Christian movement.

THE COVENANT OF ISRAEL WITH GOD

Israel's understanding of herself and the nature of her existence is expressed in the covenant relationship (Exod. 24:1-3). The purpose of the liberation of the Hebrew slaves from Egypt is "that they may meet God upon the mountain." The goal of the wanderings in the desert is the meeting with Yahweh. There the scattered clans gather in common allegiance to one God, Yahweh. There He reveals Himself to them. He discloses His name so that they may relate themselves to Him. His is the initiative; He finds them in the desert (Hos. 9:10). He descends upon the mountain and "it quaked greatly." But out of the cataclysm of nature comes the Voice which makes possible the relationship between these forlorn and disparate groups and Himself.

This meeting with Yahweh is for Israel an act of decision. The relationship between them is not a necessary one, so that the fate of God is not identified with the fate of the people. The bond between Israel and Yahweh is not first of all the bond of nature. Whatever His ultimate origin, Yahweh is not for the Hebrews a nature spirit; He is not bound to the soil; He is not a heavenly body or any phenomenon of nature. He is a free agent who wills and acts and reveals Himself to His people. The people on their part must decide for or against Him, and their decision is voluntary. No covenant relation is possible without this choice. And their choice is an act of dedication to their God, an act of loyalty and eager allegiance. "All the words that Yahweh hath spoken will we do" (Exod. 19:8; 24:7). This emphasis on an act of will, a decision and a choice, is characteristic of the Old Testament throughout. "Choose you this day whom you will serve" (Josh. 24:15). What is primary in Hebrew psychology is the will of man, in contrast with the Greek emphasis upon knowledge and harmony. The urgency of the ethical imperative of the Hebrew is characteristically absent from Greek thought. Man becomes what he is by the decisions he makes. Israel's first great historic act is her act of voluntary allegiance to Yahweh, and it determines her whole destiny.

The covenant relationship gave to Israel a loyalty that transcended every other. So long as the consciousness of the covenant continued alive, neither the nation nor any other instrument of power could demand an utter loyalty. It was only Yahweh who could demand that. Therefore, the nation Israel is always being subjected to radical criticism by the prophets. The prophets are the witnesses to the primary reality of the covenant allegiance. The word of Yahweh is characteristically "I am your destruction, O Israel!" (Hos. 13:9). That is the word that every nation and every historical community must understand. It is the word, too, that modern nations refuse to hear when they demand unqualified allegiance to the state, forbid criticism, and restrict freedom of speech and worship. The covenant with God is the charter of human liberty. It is the instrument that prevents Hebraism from becoming merely a national religion. The genius of prophetic religion is precisely that this transcendent reference always served to check the tyranny of nationalism.

But Israel's loyalty to Yahweh was also interpreted in terms of obligation and responsibility. The relationship is contingent upon Israel's obedience. The revelation is a revelation of an imperative. Whatever the character of the original decalogue may have been, the presence of the ten commandments (Exod. 20:3-17) and of the laws of the Covenant Code (Exod. 20:23-23:33) immediately following the opening words of revelation on the mountain is characteristically Hebraic. The Hebrews are a people chosen of Yahweh and therefore greatly privileged; but it is a relationship that is contingent on Israel's obedience.

Together the clans and tribes covenanted with Yahweh. Their act is one of solidarity. It binds them to Yahweh; it also binds them to one another. They had always known something of closely knit solidarity natural to desert tribes; now it was a solidarity with a historical content. It came later to be understood in terms of a common experience and a common voluntary choice and a common obligation for united Israel. It was destined to be of enormous consequence for her history.

The covenant relationship was mediated through a person, through Moses, "the man of God." Veiled in the mystery of a thousand years of living tradition, the ancient records yet reveal a figure whose personality is intimately interwoven through all the successive strata of narrative. The events do not merely center in him; it is Moses who gives color and warmth to them. Michelangelo's conception of him has an inner authenticity. Later Judaism did not err in attributing to him a central and commanding position. In the covenant Yahweh revealed Himself to Israel, but the revelation was made through the man Moses. The accretion of legendary materials about him, far from qualifying his importance, may be said to be a silent testimony to his grandeur and to the centrality of a person in the revelation.

To appreciate something of the meaning of the covenant relation for ancient Israel let us turn for a moment to the continuing history of the people. For the covenant relationship is the expression of Israel's understanding of herself. When Phoenician power encroaches upon the national independence of Israel, it is Elijah who sees the policy of King Ahab as defection from the covenant relationship. This is implicit in the story on Mount Carmel (I Kings 18); it is articulate in the theophany before the cave on the mount of the original revelation to Moses (I Kings 19:1-18). Israel has broken the covenant, and the prophets who witness to its demands have been destroyed. At a later period Hosea sees the cancer of corruption eating away the life of the nation; in the midst of the decline and collapse of national life he stands as a moving witness to the reality of the covenant. His figure of the marriage relationship between Yahweh and Israel, while not original with him, was destined greatly to deepen and enrich the significance of the covenant. In a passage of disputed authenticity, but in all likelihood from Hosea, he thinks of the future covenant:

> And I will betroth you to myself forever;
> And I will betroth you to myself in righteousness, and in justice,
> And in kindness and mercy.
> And I will betroth you to myself in faithfulness;
> And you shall know Yahweh.
> —Hos. 2:19-20

Jeremiah, like Hosea before him and Jesus and Augustine after him, lives at a time of the decline and destruction of his national community. The dominant question of Jeremiah's life is the nature of Israel's relationship to God. Throughout forty long and tumultuous years he struggles under the impulsions of the divine imperative which surge through him like a blazing fire. Yahweh tries the heart of Jeremiah, puts it constantly to the test. There is nothing in the Old Testament and little in the New to match the intimacy of the converse between God and Jeremiah. His final reflections concerning the covenant relationship are an inevitable outgrowth of his own conflicts and spiritual experiences. There is not a phrase in the account of the new covenant that does not reward patient study:

Behold! the days are coming, is the oracle of Yahweh, when I will make a new covenant with the household of Israel and with the household of Judah, not like the covenant which I made with their fathers on the day that I took them by the hand to lead them out of the land of Egypt—that covenant of mine they broke, so that I had to reject them—but this is the covenant which I will make with the household of Israel after those days, is the oracle of Yahweh: I will put my law within them, and will write it on their hearts; and I will be their God, and they shall be my people. And they shall teach no more every one his neighbor, and every one his brother, saying 'Know Yahweh'; for all of them shall know me, from the least of them to the greatest of them, is the oracle of Yahweh; for I will pardon their guilt, and their sin will I remember no more.

—Jer. 31:31-34

Such a statement not only represents the culmination of Jeremiah's thought and conflict but also summarizes in numerous ways the general movement of prophetic thought up to his time. The locus of religion has shifted from the nation to the individual, and the assurance of forgiveness in the closing words is the foundation upon which the whole passage rests. Second Isaiah continues the thought of Jeremiah and in a lyrical and climactic poem extends the covenant of love to all the nations of the earth (Isa. 55:3-5). Finally, on the eve of his death, Jesus returns to the covenant relationship, rich with suggestion and historic association, as an adequate instrument to express the meaning of his suffering and death: "This cup is the new covenant in my blood. Drink ye all of it."

The covenant relationship is the central feature of Israel's religion. It is the culmination of a series of historical events, the purpose of the deliverance from slavery, and the goal of the desert wandering. To Yahweh's disclosure of Himself Israel may respond voluntarily. His disclosure involves her in an act of fateful decision. In her voluntary allegiance to Him she determines her future course. The common act of allegiance bound the clans and disparate groups into an indissoluble community. But the relationship to Yahweh is contingent. It is not sealed once for all in a single act of decision. The covenant places Israel under the burden of an obligation. It is the structure which expresses her accountability to a reality higher than herself. She always found herself faced with the demands of the covenant relationship.

Her history was the record of a broken covenant, but her conception of herself as a people committed to God's will and ultimate purpose made possible a lofty ethical development. Finally, the covenant was mediated by a person whom legend and fancy have not effaced. God spoke to Israel through his servant Moses.

COMMUNITY

Israel's understanding of herself in terms of the events and vicissitudes of history on the one hand and in terms of the covenant relationship on the other provides us with an insight into the third great feature of her religious faith. For a people which takes its history seriously will naturally raise the question of the nature of its own community: What is it that constitutes its security, solidarity, and source of hope? The covenant relationship was such an expression of community. The experiences of the desert tested the bonds of community, and the many decades of invasion of the Palestinian corridor strained it to the breaking point. The Song of Deborah, the oldest fragment of any size in the whole Old Testament (Judg. 5), is a superb illustration of the divisive forces the Hebrew tribes encountered as they entered a broken land of hills and valleys. The problem of Israel's relations with the native Canaanites was even greater and was destined to have profound influence not only upon her own culture and traditions but also upon the very constitution of the nation itself.

The classical passage extending the scope of the Hebrew community beyond national bounds is to be found in the first two chapters of the Book of Amos. The prophet sees Yahweh's activity and power in the history of Aram and Phoenicia and Philistia and Moab as well as in Israel herself. The fate of these nations lies in the power and will of Yahweh. He determines what their future will be. His judgment is decisive. And His judgment is moral; it is concerned with community. Doom is pronounced upon Damascus "because they have threshed Gilead with threshing instruments of iron"; destruction awaits Moab "because he burned the bones of the king of Edom." If Yahweh has been active in Israel's history, He has also been active in bringing the non-Semitic Philistines to Palestine and the hated Arameans from Kir. The Hebrews may be a favored nation, but they are favored for an obligation and a responsibility (Amos. 3:2). When they refuse this burden, they automatically renounce the covenant relationship with Yahweh. They are in fact no more favored than the Ethiopians.

> Are ye not to me like the Ethiopians,
> O children of Israel, is Yahweh's oracle.
> Did I not bring forth Israel from the land of Egypt,
> And the Philistines from Caphtor, and the Arameans from Kir?
> Behold the eyes of the Lord Yahweh are upon the sinful kingdom,
> And I will destroy it from the surface of the ground.
> —*Amos 9:7-8*

In such a passage the existence of the nation is interpreted in profoundly moral categories. It is the classical statement that the ultimate meaning of history is to be found in moral purpose, above all, in justice. The natural bond between nation and God is here completely severed, and in its place appears the moral imperative of justice.

In Isaiah's vision in the Temple the prophet sees the whole earth filled with the presence of Yahweh. Yahweh is exalted in the earth, and His exaltation is His righteousness and justice. In the poems of Second Isaiah the nations are never very far from the center of the stage. It is Israel's function in history to be a light to the nations. Israel is to bring the nations to the recognition of the God of righteousness and mercy as the Lord of history and of nature. The uniqueness of Israel and of Israel's history is never forgotten, to be sure, for this would be to undercut the very significance of Israel in the life of the world. It is not impossible to defend the poet's fervent devotion to Israel and her place in history in the light of subsequent events even down to our own day. There are many men in our time who would eagerly assent to the poet's conviction that Israel has been in actual historical fact the instrument of divine revealing to the nations of the world.

In the little Book of Jonah we see the universalism, implicit in the general movement of Israel's religion, expressed in the form of a short story. The story has its setting at a much earlier time when the Assyrian Empire is at the height of its power. But the design of the writer, living in the third century B.C., is to counteract the orthodox and narrow piety of his own time. Jonah, a typical representative of that cloistered faith that gains its intensity by its provincialism, is commanded by God to go to Nineveh, the capital of the Assyrian power, to proclaim the prophetic message of imminent judgment. Surely this would be the last place to be included within the sphere of the divine concern. Yet, much to the prophet's disgust, Nineveh repents, and Yahweh's mercy and love include this plunderer of nations and ruthless monster within the embrace of His concern. For Nineveh is a city of men and women and children and even animals, and the universalistic faith of Hebraism could not tolerate the exclusion of any of these from the onward sweep of its community. Finally, the Book of Malachi, the last in our present Old Testament, though by no means the last in point of time, can express this universalism in the loftiest vein:

> For from the rising of the sun, even to its setting,
> My name is great among the nations;
> And in every place an offering is made, is brought near to my name,
> And a pure offering,
> For my name is great among the nations.
>
> —Mal. 1:11

The significance of this development from community based upon tribal loyalty to an all-inclusive human community needs scarcely to be underlined. That its realization is born out of the on-going history of the nation at the crossroads of the world's nations and continents, in the teeming Mediterranean area which has such profound political importance in our own time, makes it especially illuminating. For, given the basic presuppositions of Israel's conception of herself as a covenant people whose God expressed His will for her in and through the events of history, the presence of all that was human in the community of God's people could ultimately never be alien to her.

THE NATURE OF GOD

But in all that has been said thus far we have not yet sufficiently stressed what was primary in Israel's consciousness throughout the centuries of her historical existence, that is, the portrait of the God whom she knew as the Sovereign and the Sustainer of her life. That Israel believed earnestly and even passionately in God is not the supreme fact about her. Belief in the existence of God was universal in Oriental antiquity. Atheism is seldom or never a problem in the Old Testament. The existence of God is always assumed, never denied. But what is really important is that God is always present. He is always accessible and available. His presence is the primary factor in man's existence and man's understanding of his function as a person. He must always be reckoned with. What lends particular force to the situation in which man finds himself before God is that He is energetically active. He is known to Israel by His acts in her behalf. It is His purpose for man that is revealed in the events of life and experience. His word is event. When the prophet received a message from God, it was to him an overwhelming event, an event in which the purpose of God was directed to his own life and to the community of Israel. He is for all Israel the living God. He is not like the dying and rising nature gods who repine and pass away with the approach of winter and revive with the resuscitation of natural life in spring amid the tears of their devotees. And this ever-living God of Israel is the source of all life. "They that wait upon the Lord shall renew their strength."

All the resources of human speech are taxed in the attempt to express what God means to Israel. Every conceivable image seems to be applied to Him. But the characteristic language throughout is language that is personal. Yahweh is a Judge, a King, a Potter, a Mother, a Father, a Husband. The language is frequently anthropomorphic, and, strange as it may seem, very often the most deeply rewarding and revealing passages are the most anthropomorphic in character. Nor can it be said that the progress of religion has sloughed off these anthropomorphisms. The Book of Psalms is testimony that this is not so. He is a God who can be pained at the heart, who can fashion with His hands, and breathe the breath of life into man.

The God of the Hebrews is both far and near. The tension between His remoteness and His presence is preserved. Both are affirmed again and again. The holiness of God in the sense of His remoteness and distance, his far-offness, is a primary characteristic of God. This is often expressed in primitive forms, as in the command to Moses not to violate the tabu by approaching the bush or in Uzzah's violation of the tabu by touching the ark. There is something over-powering, dreadful, awe-inspiring, dangerous in God. Man cannot see Him and live. He is the Wholly Other. When He is felt to be near, it is something to strike terror or fear into one. The term "holy" never loses this connotation. The feeling of God's separateness is a constant element in the conception of God's holiness.

But the striking thing about the holiness of God in ancient Israel is that God's remoteness ceases to be merely remoteness. Holiness is more than His transcendent power, more than a demonic quality, more than utter difference. It is His moral nature that separates Him from man. The vision of Isaiah is notable for its lofty expression of the moral element in God's holiness. The seraphs hovering about the throne of the Divine Presence cry out in antiphonal response:

> Holy, holy, holy, Yahweh of hosts,
> The whole earth is full of his glory.

The immediate response of the prophet is one of overwhelming humility and personal unworthiness:

> Woe is me, for I am undone, for a man of unclean lips am I,
> For the King Yahweh of hosts mine eyes have seen.

Yahweh is here transcendent in the majesty of His righteousness. As Isaiah says elsewhere:

> The Lord of hosts is exalted through justice,
> The holy God shows himself holy through righteousness.
> —*Isa. 5:16*

Yet the remoteness of God as expressed in the experience of His holiness is balanced by the equally profound sense of His nearness and presence. The psalmist may cry out in poignant longing, "O that I knew where I might find him," but his cry is real just because Israel is so aware that He is never very far from any one of us. Another poet expresses this sense of His constant presence in words that find their echo in one form or another in many passages:

> Whither shall I go from thy spirit,
> And whither from thy presence shall I flee?
> If I ascend to the heavens, thou art there,
> And if I make Sheol my bed, behold thou (art there);
> If I bear the wings of dawn
> And dwell in the very end of the sea,
> Even there shall thy hand guide me
> And thy right hand hold me secure.
> —*Ps. 139:7-10*

The prophet Amos is just as aware of the presence of God as our poet. But with Amos it is the judgment of God that is inescapable and pursues men through heaven and Sheol. (Amos 9:2-4).

While absolute monotheism appears relatively late in the development of Hebrew religion, there is a direct line which seems to lead in that direction even from the time of Moses. Some realization of the significance of Yahweh's act in delivering His people from the power of Egypt and its gods seems present even in the early forms of the Exodus narrative. But in general the growth of monotheism parallels fairly closely the expanding historical relationships of Israel. That Yahweh is Israel's God and that the Hebrews have only Yahweh as their God are brilliantly affirmed in the work of Elijah. Amos' thought of Yahweh seems at times to include the whole earth. It is certain that his is at least a practical, ethical monotheism. With Assyria's advance and the historical situation facing Judah in the latter part of the eighth century B.C., it is not surprising to have Isaiah claim the whole earth for Yahweh's province. But in the poems of Second Isaiah from the time of the Exile the existence of other gods than Yahweh is spurned with contempt, and the prophet's scornful satire is matched by repeated lyrical outbursts on the creative activity and active rule of one God as Lord of heaven and earth. Yet one is never permitted to forget in the writings of Second Isaiah that his thought is directed to the world of nations as well as to Israel:

> Who hath measured the waters in the hollow of his hand,
> And ruled off the heavens with a span?
> Who has held the dust of the earth in a measure,
> And weighed the mountains with a balance,
> And the hills in scales?
>
> Who hath directed the mind of Yahweh,
> And instructed him as his counselor?
> With whom took he counsel for his enlightenment,
> And who taught him the right path?
> And showed him the way of intelligence?
>
> Behold! the nations are like a drop from a bucket,
> Like fine dust in the scales are they counted.
> Behold! the coast-lands weigh no more than a grain;
> And Lebanon is not enough as fuel for sacrifice,
> Nor are its beasts enough for burnt offering.
> —*Isa. 40:12-16*

If the existence of Israel was to achieve any coherence and meaning in the international setting of her scattered community after the Exile, the divisiveness of that world must be overcome by the unity expressed in the conviction that there is one God of history and of nature for all the peoples of the world.

MAN

The Hebraic portrait of man emerges inevitably from the portrait of God as active in the life and experience of the Hebrew community. Nowhere is man considered as an abstraction; it is always the living community of persons or the individual person with which the Old Testament concerns itself. There is such a thing as a Hebrew anthropology, but it is always derivative, always implicit in the stories, poems, and oracles which are addressed to specific situations. Thus in the second chapter of Genesis we have the classic statement of Hebrew anthropology, but the account is an exceedingly naïve and primitive story of the creation of man. God fashions man of dust and breathes into his nostrils the divine breath. Both are essential to his being. When the breath returns to God who gave it, he ceases to exist (Eccles. 12:7). The physical body is good, not evil, for God fashioned it and made it into a living being (Jer. 1:5; Ps. 139:13-15; Job 10:1-18). When belief in a future life developed, it was the body that experienced resurrection, not the soul separated from the body.

Man is a member of a community. He is a social being. Isolation from the community is cause for grievous lament as with Jeremiah and Job. The sense of communal solidarity is rooted in the tribal organization of the desert. The individual Hebrew understood his nature by the fact that he was one of the children of Israel. He belonged to a community, and separation from it meant a loss of his true character. For the most part, it is the social group which is the object of the divine interest and revelation. The individual does emerge from time to time throughout the ancient records, but such emergence is always something exceptional, something of tremendous consequence. It is this which makes the prophetic call so significant. Yet even here the individual is used as an instrument for the divine purpose and work in the community of Israel.

Man's creaturehood is for the Hebrew a sign of his greatness, for he is the created work of a good and gracious God who is Lord and Creator of the world. Both creation accounts (Gen. 1:1-3:24) show clearly this lofty estate of man. In the one he is the goal of God's creation. He is made in the very image of God as the culmination of His creative work. In the other, man is created first; but all the effort of the creative activity is directed to his comfort and felicity. A poet of another age, contemplating the wonder and sublimity of this representation in a mood more exalted than Milton's, can cry:

> Thou has made him but little lower than God,[1]
> And dost crown him with glory and honor.
> —*Ps. 8:5*

Such an outburst may not be characteristic of the whole of Hebraism, but it is of great importance to recognize that profound pessimism about man and preoccupation with the fall of man are almost completely absent from the Old Testament. The sharp prophetic invectives are nowhere motivated by any a priori assumption of man's fallen estate.

But Hebraism recognizes the evil in man. If he is made for community, for sharing in the covenant relationship with his fellow-men and with God, he is constantly destroying this relationship by which he may alone find his true nature. He finds himself faced with the will of God, and his own will is always awakened by the demand for a response. It is characteristic that his existence is made up of concrete situations in which he can and must decide. His choices are genuine. It is more correct to say that man sins and sins often than to generalize with the dogma that he is a sinner. The prophetic message is directed for the most part to Israel's sins, not to her sin. It was inevitable, of course, that with the fall of the state and the radical social disintegration that attended it reflection should be centered on the habitual sinning of Israel. Out of this preoccupation the dogma of man as a sinner later developed. But classical Hebraism does not generalize in this manner. That man is commanded by God and is called to obey the divine commands is, indeed, an indication of his greatness. He sees life under the burden of a duty and an allegiance that is rooted in the divine relationship to him. The compilation of prophetic materials in the Book of Isaiah expresses this thought in its opening:

> Hear, O heavens, and give ear, O earth,
> For Yahweh hath spoken:
> Sons have I reared and brought up,
> But they have rebelled against me!

The first word of the divine oracle, contrary to the normal order of the Hebrew sentence, is "sons." The Old Testament as a whole speaks not merely of "sons of Israel," but of Israel as God's son.

---

[1] The Hebrew word rendered "angels" in the King James Version is properly rendered in the American Revised Version as "God." The Hebrew is *Elohim*.

In times of darkness and tragedy like our own it is not surprising that theologians like Karl Barth and Emil Brunner should follow the lead of Ezekiel in accentuating the sin of man. We in our time are shaken by the terrible tidal wave of evil engulfing the world and our own inevitable participation in it. We are stricken with a sense of guilt that was only too foreign to our fathers, and that guilt is both personal and corporate. But Hebraism with all its emphasis upon God's judgment and the Day of the Lord, which is darkness and not light, maintains the responsibility of the will and the choice of man before God. It is not daunted by a hopeless pessimism nor by any doctrine of man's utter depravity. There is ample reason for believing that the representation of man as made in the image of God stamps the mentality and faith of Israel much more consistently than the representation of his fall. Critical handling of the materials even accentuates this conviction.

This conception of man as a creature responsible for his decisions and acts to a God who is both his Creator and his Judge requires further elaboration. In no respect is Hebrew religious faith more distinctive than in the urgency and energy of its moral imperative. Prophetic religion is an expression of this compelling demand. In the idyllic story of man's existence in the garden it must be observed that the forbidden trees are placed in the midst of the garden; of these man must not eat. In other words even the primitive utopia is conceived realistically. Similarly, as we have already seen, the covenant relationship is defined in terms of obligation. Amos sees this perfectly:

> You only have I known
> Of all the families of the earth;
> Therefore will I visit upon you
> All your iniquities.

The confrontation of Hebrew persons with God is a confrontation with an absolute command. The experience of Moses on the mountain and the wrestling of Jeremiah in his call are classical instances of what is everywhere encountered in only a lesser degree (Exod. 3-4; Jer. 1).

And these men who have felt the pressure of an absolute and ultimate "must" are themselves the embodiments of divine imperatives. The presence of power, whether of the state or of the privileged group or of entrenched priesthood, is always threatened and challenged by the prophetic word. Moses stands before Pharaoh with his immortal words, "Let my people go," and we in our time read them with a new sense of their profound import. The striking thing about it is that the more we learn of the historical details involved in his situation, the grander the picture becomes. Nathan stands before the power and brutality of David in behalf of a wronged alien and points his finger in solemn judgment, "Thou are the man!" The conscience of the world burns in those four words (two in Hebrew). Elijah with all his severity meets Ahab and denounces him as the enemy and troubler of Israel, and the sympathy of the world still reaches out to Naboth and the human rights and freedoms we associate with him. Amos faces Amaziah, entrenched priest of Bethel; so Isaiah faces King Ahaz; so Jeremiah, Zedekiah; and so Jesus of Nazareth, the Roman judge. With some exaggeration, perhaps, Lord Acton said, "All power corrupts. Absolute power absolutely corrupts." Prophetic religion knows that and does something about it. It judges and condemns all the pretensions of men. For its allegiance is to a Power transcendent to all others. But this power wills justice and mutuality and mercy. It wills man's freedom. Allegiance and commitment to such a God is the guarantee of human freedom.

Here we encounter the very basis of our democratic faith in the essential dignity of all men. The authentic sources of the century of the common man and, indeed, for our hopes and visions of a just social order and an enduring peace are here exposed to full view.

THE PROBLEM OF SUFFERING

For any nation to conceive of itself in the categories that have been briefly sketched it was inevitable that the presence of suffering and tragedy should arouse great perplexity and kindle reflection. In this respect, too, we today read the biblical record with fresh minds. For millions of men in our generation are echoing the ancient lines:

> Deep calleth to deep at the sound of thy waterfalls;
> All thy waves and thy billows pass over me.
> —*Ps. 42:7*

The great germinating moments in Israel's religious faith are moments of suffering and pain and tragedy. It is no coincidence that the initial experience of Moses and the first words of Yahweh to him are burdened with this concern:

I have seen the plight of my people who are in Egypt, and I have heard their cry under their oppressors; for I know their sorrows, and I have come down to rescue them from the Egyptians.

Out of the tyranny and power of what has been described as the world's first great territorial imperialism comes this word, and it appears at the historical beginning of Hebraic-Christian faith. Its beginning was of infinite presage for the future.

Similarly, Hosea sees in his own tragic experience with a faithless wife a reflection of God's experience with Israel. Hosea was able to diagnose the fatal disease of his own time with such clarity and force because of his capacity for identification with the hurt of his own people. His perception of the nation's sinning as infidelity to its Covenant Lord, his passionate sensitiveness to all the moods and colors of nature and to all the feelings and dispositions of men—all these make of him one who learned obedience by the things that he suffered. On the eve of his nation's destruction he penetrates more deeply into the nature of national existence and the relation of the nation to God than does any other prophet of his time or country.

Jeremiah is spiritually akin to Hosea. There is an intimate affinity between the two prophets. Jeremiah's earliest oracles quiver with the vitality and heartbreak of Hosea's oracles. He witnesses his nation approaching the dark and inevitable abyss. Always he sees her before the Covenant God; always he sees her as a traitor to her historic trust. In chapters 11-20 of his book we have the record of his confessions, and they are full of the sorrow and pain of one who shared his people's tragedy and suffered more deeply than they because he could see it as their defection from their God, their refusal to see the hand of judgment in their fate, their passionate and stubborn heedlessness amidst the divine persuasion, their persistent taunting of the prophet and his deep humiliation. He was a man of sorrows and acquainted with grief.

In the strange linking of prophetic personality with prophetic personality Second Isaiah lays hold of the message flung out by Jeremiah in his hour of darkness. His borrowing from Jeremiah is of such an intimate sort, so inwardly revealing, the habit of a great poet who remembers lines that will not be forgotten, his portrait of the suffering servant of the Lord (Isa. 52:13-53:12) so much like Jeremiah, that some have thought the latter to be in the mind of the rhapsodist. But Second Isaiah views the suffering of Israel for the first time in the range of her entire history. He sees what living in the little international corridor has been like through all the centuries. He remembers as no other, and the genius of his poetry is that with all his remembering he has caught a vision of the God of Israel's history, of all the nations, and of the significance of Israel's faith for the world that finds its parallel nowhere else in Hebraic-Christian thought. His supreme poem begins and ends with a strophe from Yahweh, but the poem proper is the confessional of the nations in which they recognize that Israel's sufferings were vicarious for them. It was with her stripes that they . were healed.

> Surely it was our pain that he bore,
> The sorrows he carried were ours,
> But we considered him stricken,
> Smitten of God and afflicted,
> But he was wounded for our transgressions,
> Bruised for our iniquities;
> On him fell the chastisement to make us whole,
> All of us like sheep had gone astray,
> Each had turned to his own way.
> But Yahweh caused to fall on him
> The guilt of us all.
> —*Isa. 53:4-6*

These are the highest peaks of Israel's pain. But there are others too. Job and his immortal cry tower with them. Some of the psalms reach into the clouds and break into sunlight at their crests. But it is characteristic of many of them that they brood over the enormity of the problem before they come to their affirmations. The seventy-third Psalm seems as much troubled by the apparent moral neutrality of God as Job is, yet its ancient author can trust even where he does not see and can find support in the consciousness of fellowship with God:

> Nevertheless I am always with thee;
> Thou holdest my right hand.
> By thy counsel thou leadest me,
> Thou shalt guide me with thy counsel,
> And afterward receive me gloriously.
> Whom have I in heaven but thee?
> And there is none on earth that I desire above thee;
> My flesh and my heart fail;
> But God is my heart's rock and my portion forever.
> —*Ps. 73:23-28*

Only twice in the Old Testament does the prospect of a life beyond the grave suggest itself with clarity as a possible solution to the problems of suffering. Judaism and early Christianity took that direction. But the men of the Old Testament—men like Hosea and Jeremiah and Second Isaiah and Job—had probed the problem to its depths. And their solutions have sustained their suffering people through more than two thousand years, not least in the dark trials of our day.

JUDAISM

The religious faith of ancient Israel which sought to interpret the will of God in the life of the nation we have called "Hebraism"; the religious faith that emerges from this long development after the fall of the nation in 586 B.C. we may call "Judaism." Fixed dates for the beginning of Judaism are always precarious. One might argue that Judaism is an outgrowth of the Reformation of 621 B.C., which finds its classical expression in the Book of Deuteronomy; he might contend that Judaism is a product of the Babylonian Exile; or he might see in the work of Ezra and Nehemiah its true origin. A good case might be made for each of these dates as the proper beginning.

Our problem is further complicated by the circumstance that Judaism, like Hebraism, is not one religion but many. The first impression that one wins from a study of Judaism, as of Hebraism, is its diversity. In both we encounter the most obvious contradictions and want of cohesion. Moreover, little attempt is made to overcome this lack of homogeneity. The religious strands intertwine and overlap, and there is nowhere any suggestion of a unified system of thought. Attempts to state the philosophy of Israel's religion are, therefore, always doomed to less than success. In the Judaism of the centuries before Christ we encounter the glowing faith of the Psalmist, the tempered wisdom of the "sages," the passionate hope of the apocalyptist, the authoritarian demands of legalism, the ritual and cult of the Temple, the strong confidence that history adheres to a "logical" pattern, and, not least of all, the persistence of prophetic religion. All of these "religions" must be viewed and understood together. Failure to understand this means failure to understand the continuity between Hebraism and early Christianity on the one hand and between Hebraism and Judaism on the other.

Nowhere in the whole Old Testament do we get a more vivid and comprehensive picture of the nature and many-sidedness of Judaism than in the Book of Ezekiel. Ezekiel has often been called the "father of Judaism." That he appears during the riven years before and after the fall of Jerusalem and the destruction of the nation in 586 B.C. makes him all the more significant for our purposes. With him Israel becomes a holy community. In its center is the Temple. Its sanctity must be preserved by careful observance of cult and its ritual. Institutions are revived and deepened with a priestly sense of their venerability. A vision of an ecclesiastical utopia provides a blueprint for the emerging Judaism. Expiation for sin becomes a central function of sacrifice. Not least of all Ezekiel meets the crisis of the nation's disintegration and the growing problem of theodicy by resort to a pronounced emphasis upon the individual. Every man experiences the consequences of his own conduct. "The soul that sins shall die."

The destruction of the national community had had a profound effect upon the religion of Israel. It meant that a religious faith that had authenticated itself primarily in terms of history and the continued life of the nation had received what seemed an irreparable blow to its major conviction. The destruction of nations and the responses of communities to their falls are of great interest to us, for many nations of the modern world are confronting survival in the world without the support and security of their national matrix. The fall of the Greek city-states in the fourth century B.C., of the Roman Empire in 476 A.D., and of the medieval structure in the fifteenth century are illuminating to thoughtful persons in our day. But the response of ancient Israel to the loss of her national existence has an even greater significance. For Israel was forced to raise afresh the central question of her existence, what God was doing in the world and what it was He was saying, in the light of a fundamental trust that it was He who was Creator and Ruler and Judge of history. The urgency of this concern prompted a revision of her historical writings to show that there was a moral logic involved in the past,[2] or if not a moral logic, a theocratic will at work.[3] Nostalgia for tradition and the security of institutions and law brought about a deepening exclusivism. The failure of history to confirm her trust kindled a passionate faith that God's will would nevertheless be done despite all appearances. The hopelessness of the present

---

[2] Cf. the frameworks of our present Books of Judges and Kings.
[3] As in the Priestly history of the Pentateuch and Chronicles.

was more than matched by the fiery hope in the future when God would reveal Himself supernaturally and miraculously to vindicate His people. Such a passionate faith is common after great national catastrophe and frequently takes on tragic forms even in our day.

It was only natural that the main ecclesiastical institution should assume greater importance with the fall of the Holy City and its Temple. The fervid imagination of Jews scattered to the four corners of the ancient world and stricken by the destruction of the Temple built by Solomon would aggrandize the place and significance of the Temple in the life of Israel. With the growing recognition that the national community would not be restored the Temple became the center of Israel's communal life. Israel became an ecclesiastical community. To Jerusalem gathered the faithful from all over the Dispersion. The Second Temple, built between 520 B.C. and 516 B.C., did not bear the aspects of grandeur and venerability associated with the idealized name of Solomon, but it became nonetheless the center of an active and fervent cult. The sacrificial worship assumed deeper meaning in the lives of individuals, and opportunities for individual worship were greatly increased. Hymns and prayers and ritualistic cries, many of them preserved in our Psalter, attended the various stages of the sacrificial offering. The ceremonial law, much of it of great antiquity, was now carefully codified and adapted to the new ecclesiasticism. The ancient rite of circumcision was followed with scrupulous propriety. Sabbath observance became a central feature of the faith. The creation of the world as recounted in Genesis 1 culminates in this great institution, and the prophetic books were revised to include a new emphasis upon it. The festivals were observed with increasing devotion to ritualistic nicety and propriety. Men could explain their own dark and somber years in terms of their failure to give Yahweh the best of the flock. The Book of Psalms is perhaps our best index to the life of the Temple community; the chief impression we receive from it is of joy and peace and deep gratefulness to Yahweh (Ps. 84). Such experiences as those arising out of the celebrations of the Day of Atonement and the Passover doubtless proved for many a source of spiritual power and re-enforcement.

We know only too little of the origin and development of the synagogue. But when we first encounter it, it is already the center of spiritual life in every city and village where Jews were gathered in any number. It was an institution both for Sabbath services and for the education of the faithful in biblical and doctrinal knowledge. Twice a week and on other special occasions portions of the Torah or Law were read in Hebrew. On the Sabbath and days of festival additional readings were given. These were followed by an Aramaic translation. The Shema was recited as the central creed of Judaism:

Hear, O Israel: the Lord our God, the Lord is one. And thou shalt love the Lord thy God with all thy heart, and with all thy soul, and with all thy might. And these words, which I command thee this day, shall be upon thy heart; and thou shalt teach them diligently unto thy children, and shalt talk of them when thou sittest in thy house, and when thou walkest by the way, and when thou liest down, and when thou risest up. And thou shalt bind them for a sign upon thy hand, and they shall be for frontlets between thine eyes. And thou shalt write them upon the doorposts of thy house, and upon thy gates.

—Deut. 6:4-9

Prayers of praise, thanksgiving, and intercession were offered, and a doxology was sung. The synagogue, called into existence by the absence of the Temple, proved to be the great carrier of the Jewish faith throughout the Mediterranean world. Its emphasis on religious training gave Judaism a stamp of its own, and proved an effective means of communicating the faith to many thoughtful and religious men in the Hellenistic world. Since sacrifice could only be offered in the Temple, the synagogues succeeded in perpetuating Jewish piety—indeed, in deepening it—by dispensing with sacrifice and in enriching it by their emphasis on prayer and Scripture. The forms of its worship were largely transmitted to the early Christian community.

Central as the synagogue became in the social life of the community, it is possible that the Law came to assume an even more significant role. As in the case of the Greeks with the loss of the city-state and the authority of its law, so in ancient Israel after the fall of the nation with its attendant institutions there doubtless arose a widespread sense of forlornness, confusion, and uncertainty. A powerful authoritarian force was necessary to withstand the internal forces of deterioration and the external forces of imperialistic coercion. The dimension of historical depth, so sought for in times of social stress, was recovered by the priests of the Second Temple. Traditions were gathered and assigned a position of distinction and sanctity. Ancient practices and customs were codified and given a status of dignity by being assigned to Moses, the great Lawgiver of the past. The cultic celebrations of the Temple were expanded, refined, and deepened. Great attention was devoted to minutiae. In these and other ways the life of the individual was closely regulated.

The Priestly Code of the Pentateuch, found especially in the Book of Leviticus, is a monument to the work of the priests in the fifth and sixth centuries before Christ. The process of canonization, which had begun even before the Exile, came to a head in the canonization of the Torah, usually rendered "Law" but more appropriately translated as "Instruction" or "Teaching." But the legalistic tendencies were not checked by such canonization, for men soon realized that a developing society demands continuing legal interpretation and refinement. The precepts of the Torah were explained and illustrated by the scribes and eventually, after centuries, were embodied in the Mishna.

Ezra the Scribe became the focal figure in this whole legalistic development. The later rabbis could scarcely find language lofty enough to describe the contribution of Ezra to Judaism. What function the historical Ezra performed it is not easy to say, but the book which bears his name has the genius of Judaism in one of its major phases stamped upon it throughout. But if we wish to know something of the meaning of the Law for a pious Jew of the second century B.C., we may turn to the dying words of Mattathias, the father of the Maccabean brothers:

Arrogance and reproach have now grown strong; it is a time of disaster and hot anger. Now, my children, you must be zealous for the Law, and give your lives for the agreement (covenant) of our forefathers. Remember the deeds of our forefathers which they did in their generations, and you will win great glory and everlasting renown. Was not Abraham found faithful when he was tried, and it was credited to him as uprightness? . . . My children, be manful and strong for the Law, for by it you will obtain glory. . . . And you must gather about you all who observe the Law, and avenge the wrongs of your people. Pay back the heathen for what they have done, and give heed to what the Law commands.
        —*I Macc.* 2:49-52, 64, 68 (Goodspeed's translation)

It has been common for us to speak of the Jewish Law as a great burden to its adherents. Doubtless there were occasions and situations in which the Law proved onerous and harsh. But we must always be careful to balance adverse judgments of this kind with other judgments drawn from the great treasury of Jewish religious devotion, the

Book of Psalms. One need but read such Psalms as 1, 19, and 119 to
appreciate what the Law meant to the average pious Israelite. The
Law was divine revelation, and it was the supreme evidence of God's
graciousness to Israel that He gave her the Torah as a lamp to guide
her through her historic pilgrimage:

> The law of Yahweh is perfect, renewing the soul,
> The testimony of Yahweh is trustworthy, making wise the simple;
> The precepts of Yahweh are right, making the heart glad;
> The commandment of Yahweh is pure, enlightening the eyes;
> The fear of Yahweh is clean, enduring forever.
> The judgments of Yahweh are true, and they are also right;
> They are more valuable than gold, and much fine gold;
> And sweeter than honey, and the droppings of the honeycomb.
> —*Ps. 19:7-10*

On the other hand, one must not discount the very real perils of
literalistic interpretation, preoccupation with ritual, and an exaggerated
emphasis on the written word.

The Book of Psalms is the best mirror we possess for catching a
reflection of authentic Jewish piety. It does not have the penetration
and passionate drive of the prophetic books, but it does show us the
soul of man in the presence of God. Almost every human emotion is
reflected in it. Samuel Taylor Coleridge once wrote of the Psalter:
"I have found words for my inmost thoughts, songs for my joy, utterances for my hidden griefs, and pleadings for my shame and feeble-
ness." This universality of appeal has been the discovery of worshipers
for two thousand years and more. It is not, of course, all on the same
level. The presence of a few imprecatory passages, which invoke bitter
curses on enemies, is illustrated in the terrible lines against the "daugh-
ter of Babylon" at the close of Psalm one hundred and thirty-seven:

> Blessed be he who seizes your little ones,
> And dashes them to pieces on a rock.

But what is striking is the relatively small number of such passages
in a history which was characterized by many centuries of foreign
domination and cruelty. We may not condone such hatred, but millions
of men in our time find no difficulty in understanding or even echoing
it. Perhaps the most common tribute to the genius of this ancient
devotional literature is the way men have turned throughout the
centuries to such Psalms as 23, 121, 90, 91, and 46 in hours of darkness

and grief, to such Psalms as 51 in times of contrition, to such Psalms as 8, 19:1-6, 29, and 104 in the contemplation of nature, to such Psalms as 24, 27, 103, 42, 43, and 84 in periods of deep devotion. Where in literature is there anything to surpass this cry from the depths:

> Out of the depths I cry to thee, O Yahweh!
> O Lord, hear my voice!
> Let thine ears be attentive
> To my supplicating voice.
>
> If thou, O Yahweh, shouldst record iniquities,
> O Lord, who could stand?
> But with thee there is forgiveness,
> That thou mayest be revered.
>
> I wait for Yahweh, my soul waits,
> And for his word I hope.
> More than watchmen for the dawn,
> Watchmen for the dawn.
>
> Hope, O Israel, in Yahweh,
> For with Yahweh there is mercy.
> And with him is plenteous redemption.
> For he will redeem Israel
> From all its guilt
>   —*Ps. 130*

If we want to understand how the Jews managed to face their world with a degree of serenity and peace in the years of oppression between 586 B.C. and the fall of Jerusalem in A.D. 70, one avenue is the songs, hymns, and prayers of the Book of Psalms. Here again, as so often, other strands of Judaism wove their way into the fabric of personal religion, such strands as wisdom, law, eschatology, history, and prophecy. The devotional poems of the Book of Psalms are never far from the heart of Judaism; and in this the Christian Church has followed almost without reserve.

We have dealt thus far with three of the main elements of Judaism: the ecclesiastical, legal, and devotional. The fourth element, wisdom, has its affinities with both the legal and the devotional elements. It is true that the Wisdom Literature serves in many respects as a foil to the others. Yet the Law came to be identified with wisdom, and the wisdom motif recurs from time to time in our Psalter in what may be called "wisdom poems." The sages of Israel had their colleagues in other lands, notably in Edom, Egypt, and Babylonia, but they are nonetheless authentic interpreters of the Jewish mind. The history of Jewish wisdom utterance may be as ancient as legal precept or cultic hymn, but its classical period is without doubt after the Exile. Wisdom was a healthy corrective to the tendencies toward legalistic orthodoxy on the one hand and apocalyptic enthusiasm on the other, for it was more related to the experiences of everyday life than the first and more restrained and realistic than the second. It was a major product of the decline of prophecy as the result of the fall of the state. Not that prophetic activity disappeared; on the contrary, it discovered new avenues of expression. But the sages could not share without reservation all the ardor of the prophets and their passionate assertion of Yahweh's moral control of history.

Indeed, they were profoundly troubled by the problem of evil and hence were occupied with questions of theodicy. The Book of Job is their most eloquent statement of the problem. The friends of Job propose the orthodox answer to the problem of suffering, the answer that is given by the larger part of the Old Testament: God rewards righteousness and punishes sin. Prosperity is God's reward, adversity and suffering His retribution. But these complacent answers do not content Job. He hurls question after question before the very presence of God. Nowhere do we receive what the modern man would call a solution to the problems raised by Job, yet the book does show us a figure of epic stature wrestling with this deepest of human problems. One is conscious as the drama moves on that this man is never very far from God. This sense of his own fellowship with God seems to grow on him, and when finally the Voice comes out of the whirlwind, Job is aware of the solace that comes from communion with God.

> I had heard of thee by the hearing of the ear,
> But now mine eye seeth thee.
> —*Job 42:5*

He has not received the answer he sought, but he has received that for which he had forgotten to ask, the courage "to grasp life's nettle" and to walk humbly with his God. The book is one of the world's superb monuments to the integrity and dignity of a man.

The construction of the Book of Job suggests that it is not the work of an isolated thinker. There were obviously many like the author who shared his problems and perplexities. Koheleth, the author of Ecclesiastes, has some of the same questions, though his mood is one of world weariness and of boredom at the emptiness of things and the moral neutrality of the universe. He discerns no divine government of the world, no reward for virtue or punishment for evil, no life beyond the present. His is a plaintive cry of futility and an almost thorough-going skepticism. The opening words strike the keynote of the book:

Futility of futilities, all is futility.

Ecclesiastes is the most non-Hebraic book of the Old Testament. The authors of the Book of Proverbs, too, know the questions involved in the working of God's justice, but the book answers them relatively simply. In general it is the doctrine of rewards and punishments, the answer, perhaps, of the majority of men. Despite the wide usage of its observations and the diversity of point of view in it, the book inculcates a utilitarian morality of simple homespun common sense and sagacity, of self-discipline and enlightened self-interest. Maxims concerning everyday conduct are frequent, covering moderation, buying and spending, friendship and marriage—indeed, the whole gamut of human relations. The religion of the wise men is a far cry from the passionate faith of the prophets.

But two more questions occupy the thought of the sages: the future life and wisdom. The major contributions to each lie outside the scope of the Old Testament canon. If a man dies, he is gathered unto his fathers. Such existence as there is beyond death has no attractiveness; man has lost his personality. Sheol is a land of darkness and of death. The significant survival of the personality suggests itself to Job, but he cannot imagine its possibility. Koheleth denies it. In the late Book of Daniel, however, we finally get a clear and unquestionable affirmation that man's personality survives death. The body is preserved as is consistent with Hebraic anthropology:

And many of those who sleep in the land of dust shall awake, some to everlasting life, and others to everlasting reproach and contempt. Then those who are wise shall shine like the brightness of the firmament, and those who have led the multitude to righteousness like the stars forever and ever.

—*Dan. 12:2-3*

Outside the Old Testament personal survival continues to be affirmed; the intertestamental period devotes itself to the thought with great assurance.

Wisdom is not only personalized as the agent of the Divine Will but becomes intimately related to God. Proverb 8:22 ff. is a notable landmark in the process toward complete hypostatization. Here wisdom, present before the creation of the world, is represented as a child sporting before God. Ben Sirach and Wisdom of Solomon carry the process to its culmination.

> For wisdom is more mobile than any motion,
> Yea, she pervadeth and penetrateth all things by reason of her pureness.
> For she is a vapour of the power of God,
> And a clear effluence of the glory of the Almighty;
> Therefore nothing defiled findeth entrance into her.
> For she is a reflection from (the) everlasting light,
> And an unspotted mirror of the working of God,
> And the image of his goodness.
> Though being (but) one she can do all things,
> And (though) abiding within herself she reneweth all things,
> And from generation to generation passing into holy souls,
> She maketh men friends of God and prophets.
> For nothing doth God love save him that dwelleth with wisdom.
> —*Wisd. of Sol. 7:24-28*

Such speculation was to be of significance to the Christian theologians who speculated on the nature of Christ, as it was easy to see in Him the embodiment in time of the eternal Wisdom of God.

The fifth and final feature of historical Judaism to command our attention is the messianic expectation. The orientation of Hebraic prophetic religion was, as we have already seen, towards the future. Yahweh was about to act in some decisive way in the midst of Israel's national life, and it was the function of the prophets to declare God's will and intention for His people. The prophetic message was chiefly one of judgment and imminent doom, but the hope that Israel might yet return was never completely lost. As for the great majority of Israelites, the expectation of a great and decisive day in which God would intervene in behalf of His own people inspired much of their religious activity. With the defeat of the nation and the passing of the years, the passionate trust and firm conviction that Yahweh was still Lord of history reasserted itself in fresh and vivid ways. However strong the nations might prove to be and however inconsequential Israel's place in the world might appear externally to men's eyes, Yahweh would intervene to correct the distortions and inequities of history and bring about a new age in which Israel would be vindicated and the nations would receive the punishment due them. But these hopes took on an almost infinite variety. Their most characteristic literary vehicle was the highly imaginative writing known as the "apocalypse" (e.g. Isa. 24-27 and Dan. 7-12). But the period in which these hopes found their classical expression was from 200 B.C. to about the end of the first century of the Christian era.

Nationalistic messianism was deeply rooted in the Old Testament Scriptures. It had received its noblest expression in the messianic oracles of Isaiah of Jerusalem (Isa. 2:2-5; 9:1-7; 11:1-9), which portrayed an era of universal peace, prosperity, justice, and felicity. The messianic leader would spring from the line of David, and there is nothing supernatural about him. Indeed, it is doubtful if the title of "Messiah" in its later Christian sense is ever to be found in the Old Testament Scriptures. The culmination of nationalistic messianism appears in the Books of Haggai and Zechariah. In the late Maccabean period this type of expectation is revived and receives its perfect expression in the Psalms of Solomon:

> Behold, O Lord, and raise up unto them their king, the son of David,
> At the time in which thou seest, O God, that he may reign over Israel, thy servant,
> And gird him with strength, that he may shatter unrighteous rulers,
> And that he may purge Jerusalem from nations that trample her down to destruction.
> . . . .
> And he shall not suffer unrighteousness to lodge any more in their midst,
> Nor shall there dwell with them any man that knoweth wickedness.

Over against this-worldly messianism of this sort must be set the apocalyptic messianism which conceived of a miraculous intervention of God. The great event is not explicable in terms of the continuity of history but of discontinuity and crisis. The whole is clothed in mystery. The time and the manner of the kingdom no man knows. A cosmic cataclysm will break in the midst of world history; the end will come in which doom will fall upon the wicked and a golden era of happiness dawn for the righteous. The Parables of Enoch, with their vision of judgment by a heavenly "Son of Man," give us the best and most complete description of this type of messianism. The following passages merely illustrate something of the quality of this literature.

On that day mine Elect One shall sit on the throne of glory,
And make choice of their works . . .
. . . .

And I will transform the heaven, and make it an eternal blessing and
    light;
And I will transform the earth and make it a blessing,
And I will cause mine elect ones to dwell upon it,
But the sinners and evildoers shall not set foot thereon.

—*En. 45:2-6*

And at that hour the Son of Man was named
In the presence of the Lord of Spirits,
And his name in the presence of the Head of Days.
Before the sun and the signs were created,
Before the stars of heaven were made,
His name was named in the presence of the Lord of Spirits.

—*En. 48:2-3*

And the congregation of the elect and holy shall be sown
And the elect shall stand before him on that day.
And all the kings and the mighty and the exalted, and those who rule
    on earth
Shall fall down before him on their faces,
And worship and set their hope upon, that Son of Man,
And petition him and supplicate for mercy at his hands.

—*En. 62:8-9*

There are other passages where ethical and universalistic elements
emerge with greater clarity. Amos' ethical interpretation of the Day
of Yahweh as a day of darkness because of the sins of Israel and her
neighbors was never completely forgotten. Yet, despite the pessimism
of this literature about the present, the optimistic faith in a God who
was Lord of men and nations dominated, and the fervent hopes and
expectations of the pious triumphed over all the tragedy of their times.
Even the characteristic historical emphasis was overcome in order to
make place for belief in the resurrection of the body and enjoyment
of rewards in a Kingdom beyond history.

In a world where men's thoughts were centered on such themes
with eager expectancy, John the Baptist came preaching, and Jesus
of Nazareth came to hear the message of the prophet. It is to the new
religious movement thus initiated that the next chapter is devoted. But
the message that both John and Jesus proclaimed was deeply rooted in
the religious past of classical Hebraism and its successor, Judaism, and
the Christian Church has always recognized with deep gratitude its
immense debt to ancient Israel.

2

The Beginnings of Christianity

THE NEW TESTAMENT AND WESTERN CULTURE

ERNEST RENAN ONCE CALLED THE GOSPEL OF MATTHEW THE MOST important book ever written, meaning presumably that it has had an influence upon the thought and life of the West more considerable and more significant than that of any other book. The historian, however secular his interests, will not be disposed to dismiss such a remark as a mere pious sentiment. If it falls short of being altogether convincing, this is only because for nearly eighteen centuries Matthew has circulated not by itself but as the first book in the New Testament and has made its impact upon our culture only in the closest association with the twenty-six other writings which belong to that collection. It is difficult to estimate the influence of any single book because it is artificial to separate it from the rest. But if the collection is regarded as one book, there can be no doubt that the New Testament is the most important item in our literary heritage. It has had incalculably more to do with the formation of Western culture than any other book —indeed, one is tempted to say, than all other books combined.

The only exception likely to be taken to this statement has to do with the propriety of speaking of the New Testament as a single book. The question is twofold, involving, on the one hand, the relation of the New Testament to the Old Testament—the question of independence of the older literature—and, on the other, the relation of its several books to one another—the question of its unity within itself. We must thus ask: Is the New Testament a coherent whole? And is there any true and important sense in which it can be considered as a complete whole, independent of the Hebrew Scriptures with which it has always been so closely associated?

The answer to both of these questions lies in the fact that the New Testament is the creation of the Christian Church during the first two centuries of its existence. From the middle of the first century, when

Paul wrote his letters in response to the needs of his churches, to the middle of the third, when the process of canonization was virtually complete, the New Testament grew with the Christian movement. It has, therefore, as much unity as had the Church of the first century; it is as independent of the Old Testament as early Christianity was of Judaism. Both this unity and this independence have frequently been exaggerated. The connections of the new movement with Judaism were so intimate and important that neither its practices nor its ideas are intelligible apart from that background; there was, moreover, within the movement itself great diversity of theological belief and of religious experience. Nevertheless, for all its debt to Judaism, Christianity was a new teaching and a new way; and both teaching and way, whether met with in Rome or Ephesus, in Antioch or Alexandria, were recognizably its own. A new religious community had emerged whose distinctness from Judaism and whose inner organic unity became constantly more manifest. The New Testament was created by this community, truly and intimately reflects its life and thought, and thus shares both its unity and its distinctiveness. To be sure, a few of its books could have been omitted without great loss— as, for example, Jude, or II Peter, or II and III John, or even the epistles to Timothy and Titus—and several books which were considered for membership in the canon but were rejected might have been included without altering substantially the character of the collection, but the number of books in each of these categories is surprisingly small. By whatever official actions the New Testament reached its final form, its contents by and large were developed by the sure and inevitable processes of organic growth. It is not a mere collection. It is a living book because it sprang directly out of the experience of a living community.

A recognition of this intimate relation between the New Testament and the life of the Christian Church during its first and most creative epoch is necessary to an understanding not only of the New Testament itself but also of the important part it has played in the formation of our culture. At many points in this volume the importance of Christianity as a factor in the creation of Western culture is discussed. Here it is enough to say that its importance is greater than that of any other factor. By "Christianity" I mean, needless to say, not a hierarchy nor any formal organization or institution as such but the Christian community in the most general sense, with its body of ideas, its accumulation of symbols, its treasures of art and literature, its ethic, its sacraments and its practices of worship—in a word, its life as a concrete historical community. Christianity so defined has not only helped to form our culture; it would hardly be too much to say that it *is* our culture if culture is thought of as communal spiritual life, that, except as the West is Christian, it has no culture in the true sense at all. Such a statement does not discount the importance of Judaism and of Greek and Roman civilization in the formation of Western culture. Both classicism and Judaism have made contributions of supreme significance; many of these contributions, especially since the Renaissance, have been direct, but the most significant of them have been indirect. Both classicism and Judaism have entered most creatively into the life of the West as Christianity was able to appropriate them and make them a part of itself. The Christian tradition has been the organizing, synthesizing factor in Western civilization.

The New Testament owes its own great importance in Western life largely to this same fact. Regarded as a factor in culture, the New Testament is most significant not because it is great literature in the sense of belles-lettres nor even because of the truth *in abstracto* of its ideas, though it contains great literature and supremely important ideas; it is culturally most significant because it puts us into touch with the historic roots of our cultural life. The New Testament, simply because it was produced by the Church in its most creative epoch, has served as both norm and resource, has sustained and nourished the life of the Church—and therefore the culture of the West—in every century since.

This service of sustaining and nourishing the life of the Church and the culture of Christendom the New Testament has accomplished in two ways: (1) It has brought to each generation a living portrait of Jesus, around whom the Christian movement came into being, and (2) it has enabled the Church perpetually to renew itself through contact with its own past in its most creative period. These two functions are discharged together and cannot, even in discussion, be neatly separated. Offhand, one might think of the Gospels, especially the first three, as discharging the first function and the rest of the New Testament—Acts, epistles, Revelation—as discharging the second. But the case is not so simple. Gospels, no less than epistles, sprang out of the experience and were addressed to the needs of the Christian community and therefore speak to us quite as much about the faith and life of the early Church as about Jesus himself. And, on the other hand, the epistles, which seem to tell us scarcely anything about Jesus, make us vividly aware of how much Jesus meant to those who had known him and to their successors and thus actually tell us something of the greatest importance about him. Here again the New Testament must be taken as a whole. As a whole, it brings us into the presence of Jesus and into touch with the life of the earliest Christian churches. In doing so, it serves, as sacraments also serve, constantly to restore and renew the nature of the Christian community, which has been the principal maker of Western culture and is now the best hope of its redemption.

CHRISTIANITY AND JUDAISM

The close historical connection between Christianity and Hebrew-Jewish religion has been referred to more than once in this and the preceding chapter. So close and intimate is that connection and so important is the Hebrew element in our cultural heritage that we often speak of our religious tradition as the "Hebraic-Christian tradition." The study of Christianity must begin with the study of Hebraism and Judaism, and any understanding of Jesus must wait upon an understanding of the life and thought of the Jewish community. Jesus was not simply an individual; he was a Jew. And the Church was in the beginning a Jewish community and carried into every subsequent phase of its history a profoundly Jewish character. It is not by accident that what is Scripture for the Jew is also Scripture for the Christian. The presence and importance of the Old Testament in the Church is a symbol of a relationship so intimate and essential that no phase of the experience or theology of the Church is free from its influence.

The preceding chapter has been devoted to a discussion of the religion of the Old Testament and to the character of Judaism in the period several centuries long which immediately preceded the Christian era. Three strains in Jewish thought during this period are particularly important and even in this brief summary need to be distinguished: the rabbinic, the wisdom, and the apocalyptic. These strains flow together, and only in degree and proportion of emphasis can they be separated. All three represent in their distinctive features elaborations of particular aspects of the religion of the prophets. Rabbinism, taking its start from the prophets' demand for obedience to the will of God, concerned itself with the interpretation of the Law (the Torah) and with the application of it to new and changing situations. The wisdom writers, although the origin of their movement was independent of and antedated the prophets, emphasized another and equally important element in the prophetic message, namely, the idea that the will of God is grounded in the nature of God and that righteous conduct is thus ultimately the only rational conduct, the true wisdom. Apocalypticism was a development of the prophetic hope, the hope of a redeemed Israel and sometimes of a redeemed humanity, although a growing pessimism about the possibilities of redemption under the evil conditions of history led to the interpretation of God's victory over His enemies in largely otherworldly terms.

None of these developments kept consistently to the high levels which the greater prophets had set. Rabbinism often descended to a dry legalism, preoccupied with the merest minutiae of external behavior. Wisdom sometimes took the form of a merely prudential and quite unimaginative moralism. Apocalypticism, despite its despair of history, was often materialistic and nationalistic in its conception of the Kingdom of God. But these are only the baser manifestations of essentially noble strains in Jewish thought: God is righteous and He is One. God created man in His image, and man's true life consists in obedience to God's will. God requires righteousness and has made known the meaning of righteousness in the Torah. God's justice is not mere justice but is compassion also; He is slow to anger and plenteous in mercy. He will eventually destroy evil, which has corrupted His good creation, and will establish His rule, His Kingdom, among men; and all who belong to that Kingdom shall know and love Him and His law will be written on their hearts.

Such were the ideas on which Jesus was nourished and which became the breath and blood of his personal life; and the teaching of Jesus, for all its originality and power, was in large measure determined by them. The distinction of Jesus lies not in the novelty of his ideas, taken formally and abstractly, but in the clarity and sureness with which he distinguished between the more and the less important elements in his religious inheritance, in the depth of meaning he found in the central affirmations of Judaism, and in the power with which both in word and act he expressed that meaning.

JESUS' MESSAGE: THE KINGDOM OF GOD

Jesus summed up his message in a phrase we have already had occasion to use, the Kingdom of God. A glance at the Synoptic Gospels (the first three Gospels) will show how constantly that phrase was on his lips. It is not too much to say that it was the text of all his preaching. This very fact should put us on guard against ascribing too narrow a meaning to the words. In its primary meaning the phrase is undoubtedly to be understood within the context of apocalypticism as an allusion to the final victory of God over His enemies and to His reign over His redeemed creation. The expectation of this victory and reign was, as we have seen, an essential part of the faith of Judaism. It is expressed, whether in cruder or finer forms, in prophets, teachers, apocalyptists, and psalmists. Jesus believed that the moment for the realization of this agelong expectation had come. He began his public teaching career with the proclamation: "The Kingdom of God is at hand." These words express Jesus' fervent faith in the triumph of God in history, the eventual accomplishment of His righteous purpose among men. God's will would shortly be done on earth as it is done in heaven. But this would happen as the result, not of the moral efforts of men nor of the working out of the natural processes of history, but of a mighty act of God which would bring history as it had been to an end, an act of judgment and creation—judgment upon the old order, creation of the new.

This so-called "eschatological" message had an inescapable ethical meaning. The Kingdom of God is the rule of God, and the rule of God involves men's doing the will of God. This will is for Jesus completely sovereign and of ultimate authority. More than that, the goodness which God requires of men is also absolute and complete. Many of the most memorable of Jesus' sayings convey this understanding of God's demands: One must love even one's enemies just as God does; one must purge one's self of all selfishness and pride; one must utterly lose one's life in devotion to God's righteous purpose. The love which God requires of us is no mere sentiment or natural affection. It is moral good will. It is actual self-denial—not mere self-restraint for the sake of occasional services to others but ruthless repudiation of self as the center of one's world. Not the strong and proud, the self-assertive, but the poor in spirit and the humble, the self-forgetting and self-giving, are those whom God approves. The really great are those who become the slaves of all. And this slavery must be willing, free, and without reservation. Nothing less than a complete reassessment of values and a complete reorientation of life was demanded.

Jesus yields in no measure to the temptation to adjust God's demands to our human weakness. Various attempts have been made to soften Jesus' harder sayings. It has been said by some that his ethic was an "interim ethic," that is, it was meant to apply only in the brief period before the end of the present age, and by others that it was a "Kingdom ethic" in the sense that it was intended to apply only after the present age should have ended and the eschatological Kingdom of God should have fully come. Neither of these attempts has been successful. Both presuppose that Jesus is trying to state what men can do either now or later; actually he is saying what God demands both now and later. He means that men even now stand under the obligation of an absolute righteousness.

But one who carefully reads the Synoptic Gospels cannot resist the conclusion that both of the terms, "ethical" and "eschatological," together fail to exhaust the meaning of Jesus' phrase, the Kingdom of God. Underneath both is what, for lack of a better name, must be called the "religious" meaning of the words. The Kingdom of God is the kingship of God, the sovereignty of God, eventually (and, Jesus believed, soon) to be established within a transformed history but eternally actual and operative. One might by repentance and trust even now know the inner meaning of the rule of God. One could not perfectly obey, but one might be perfectly submissive. God stood ready to receive not only the righteous (no one was righteous) but also the penitent; or, rather, the attitude of penitence, humility before God, and trust in His goodness *is* the righteousness which God the Father asks. A broken and a contrite heart He will not despise. Such belong already to His Kingdom.

This meaning of the Kingdom of God follows from Jesus' understanding of the nature of God. No reader of the Synoptic Gospels can miss how unutterably important to Jesus was God's reality. Life had for him no meaning apart from God. God was the Lord of life, the Ruler of history, the Judge of the nations, the Creator and Lover of every living thing, ever and everywhere present and known to those who called upon Him in faith and truth. Man's only duty was the service of God; his highest joy, the love of God.

I have said that Jesus' great distinction as a teacher lay in his bringing home to men's minds and hearts the truth and surpassing significance of religious ideas with which they were in the formal sense already familiar. Consider, for example, this matter of his apprehension of God. His conception was essentially the prophetic idea of one absolutely righteous Will, consistent and ultimately decisive in human history, which meant wrath for those who persisted in being rebellious, but which by virtue of the same righteous character meant forgiveness and renewal for those who repented and turned to God in trust and submission. Jesus' thinking always conforms to this definition and can hardly be said to go beyond it. But so vivid was his awareness of the Reality to which this definition applies, especially in His character as forgiving and sustaining love, and so complete was his devotion, that the term "God" had in his words a peculiar meaning and value. Many who heard him felt not so much that they were hearing a man talking about the love of God as that the love of God was actually being poured out in him. His words conveyed not so much new ideas about God as the living God Himself; and what had been for many an abstract idea became, as they listened, an infinitely precious reality. This fact about Jesus, as far as any human explanation is possible, accounts for the tremendous impact he made upon his associates and, more than any other single fact, lies back of the emergence and growth of the Christian movement. "God was in Christ reconciling the world unto Himself"—this sentence in which Paul comes near to expressing the substance of his faith was nothing more or less than a statement in theological terms of what Jesus himself had actually meant to those who had known and loved him.

THE HISTORICAL SIGNIFICANCE OF JESUS

Jesus is historically important because of what he meant to his own generation—a meaning mediated and perpetuated through the life of the Church—and because of what he has said directly to every generation since his own. The larger part of the rest of this chapter will be devoted to the first of these two points; the second of them, however, should be considered briefly now.

A considerable part of the historical significance of Jesus lies in the fact that he has spoken, through the pages of the New Testament, directly to the minds and consciences of Western men ever since the Gospels became widely published in the Mediterranean world. He has spoken not merely through his recorded words but also through the entire impression of his personality which the Gospels convey. It would be difficult to find in our part of the world a single person who has not at some time felt his appeal; and in art, literature, and song, as well as in common speech, he has for centuries been the symbol of the highest conceivable nobility and beauty in human life. His moral character as it appears in the Gospel stories—his sincerity and truth, his disinterestedness, his refusal to be anxious about himself, his compassion for all men, especially the poor, the sinner and the outcast, his bold disregard of convention when it stood between himself and another, his hatred of all injustice and oppression, his courageous facing of temptation, loneliness, and death—this character has become the ethical ideal of Western man, however unfaithful to it he has been.

In the same way, Jesus' vivid apprehension of the reality and the nearness of God, of God's transcendence of, but activity within, nature and history; his uncompromising demand for obedience to God's absolute will; his recognition that God's power to create good and destroy evil is even now mightily operative in the world and his confidence that it will eventually be triumphant; his joyous sense of the utter goodness of God, of the tenderness and universality of God's care for his creatures, of God's readiness, even yearning, to forgive and restore the repentant sinner—these insights of Jesus, expressed in the Gospels in words and acts which merge into one another, have entered into the warp and woof of our cultural life. For us Western men, whether we know it or not, or want it to be so or not, the deepest significance of life is connected indissolubly with events which happened in Palestine twenty centuries ago. It is impossible for most of us to think seriously about ourselves, our fellow men, or God, without also thinking of Jesus. If we are asked what God means to us, we are almost certain to answer, in effect, "The God and Father of Jesus." We may add, "I am not sure that such a God exists, but it is only such a God in whose existence I am interested." And if we are asked the same question about ourselves and our fellow-man, we are likely to answer, "Both he and I are men for whom Christ died." To each generation since his own, Jesus has spoken directly and freshly and, for all our infidelity, persuasively. And he has thus spoken through the pages of the New Testament.

But the major importance of Jesus in the history of the West lies not in what the reports of his words and acts have meant to subsequent generations but in what he himself meant to his own and to later generations. The principal historical significance of Jesus lies in the emergence of the Christian Church.

The question of Jesus' relation to the early Church has been the object of vigorous controversy. Some students have not hesitated to regard Jesus as being in the fullest sense the founder of the Church. According to this view, Jesus not only called a community into being but also established an institution and laid down the lines of its organization. Such a view of Jesus' relation to the Church goes back very early and is expressed in some of the Gospel materials themselves, as, for example, in the saying attributed to Jesus, "Thou art Peter; and on this rock I will build my church," and, even more clearly, in the promise to the disciples, "What soever ye shall bind on earth shall be bound in heaven, and what soever ye shall loose on earth shall be loosed in heaven."

Others, however, have argued that Jesus had little, if anything, to do with the creation of the Church, either consciously or unconsciously. In this view the Christian community came into existence only after Jesus' death and sustained only a very casual and accidental connection with his life. Jesus' career was significant only because it served to bring together the group which became the primitive Church. Whatever solidarity the group had was based, not upon any memory of, or response to, the career and character of the man Jesus, but almost entirely upon a fervent faith that the apocalyptic expectations of many in Israel were about to be fulfilled, a faith only rendered more vivid by the conviction that Jesus had been raised from the dead and would return as the Messiah.

Both of these extreme views are worse than dubious. If by "the Church" is meant an organized society, a formal institution, then it is certain that Jesus cannot be said to have "founded" it. The sayings in the Gospel of Matthew which were quoted above—sayings virtually unique in the Gospel tradition—are almost certainly to be interpreted as examples of how the early Church's faith affected its way of remembering and transmitting Jesus' words. If Jesus used the word "Church" at all, he undoubtedly meant the congregation of Israel, the existing Jewish community to which he belonged, not what later became recognizable as the Christian community. But if those who think of Jesus as the conscious creator of a new religion are in error, those who deny any real or important connection between Jesus and the Church are even more mistaken.

Two remarks may be made by way of objection to this second extreme. The first is that although Jesus did not establish an institution, it is by no means clear that he did not consciously form a community. Certainly it appears that he called disciples around him and that he devoted himself particularly to teaching them. He may even have sent them out on teaching missions of their own. If Jesus said, "Fear not, little flock: it is your Father's good pleasure to give you the kingdom" (and there is no good reason for questioning such a saying), he must have thought of the little band of his disciples as being in some special sense the community of the Kingdom, the point of its appearance, and the center of its life—the faithful "remnant" of Israel which was destined to be the core of a transformed society.

The second remark is that whether or not it was Jesus' intention to form a community, there can be no doubt that the community was formed around him. It was because Jesus was what he was that the Church came into being and came into being as precisely the thing it was. The content of the early Christian message was not faith only; it was also memory, memory able to support and nourish faith. Back of the belief in Jesus' messiahship, back of the conviction of the resurrection, lay the remembrance of a man—a man morally worthy of being the kind of Messiah he was now believed to be, a man whose resurrection from the dead not only could be believed (other resurrections were believed) but also could make itself felt as a supremely significant event, a mighty act of God for man's redemption.

The vigorous and distinctive life of the early Church, its universalism as regards nation, race, and class, its exalted ethical standards, its indomitable confidence in the triumph of God's righteous purpose, its joyous awareness of Jesus as alive after his passion and as present in the Church forevermore—these and other features of the first Christian communities point to the mystery of Jesus' greatness. They remind us, too, that Jesus speaks to us not only directly through the Gospels but also through the continuing life of the historic Church, of which the New Testament—Gospel and Apostle—is a product and apart from which it cannot, except in the most meager sense, be understood.

For this personal meaning of Jesus was the central fact in the experience of the early Church and, as I have already said, lies back of the development of its theology. We have seen that Jesus expected the advent of the Kingdom of God, a divinely created and sustained order of righteousness and peace. This Kingdom was so near as to be also in some sense or measure present. The powers of the Kingdom were already at work within the world: "If I by the finger of God cast out demons, then is the Kingdom of God come upon you." This Kingdom was God's Kingdom, not his own, although it is probable that he thought of himself as standing in some special relation to it. No problem in the life of Jesus is more difficult than that of determining what that relation was. According to the Gospels Jesus regarded himself as the Messiah or as the Son of Man, an apocalyptic figure corresponding to the Messiah of earlier prophecy. This representation may, of course, be true; but many critical students of the Gospels are inclined to see here another case where a later belief of the Church has been read back into Jesus' mind. This seems quite likely not only because of the evidence of the Gospels (Jesus' consciousness of being the Messiah is more conspicuous in the later than in the earlier Gospels) but also because of the inherent improbability that Jesus could have thought of himself as being either a messianic king or a supernatural judge and redeemer. At the same time, it is difficult to understand the rise of the messianic faith of the primitive community unless Jesus thought of himself as sustaining some unique relation to the Kingdom.

The truth of this matter we can probably never know. What we do know is that with Jesus' death and resurrection the eschatological hope, as it prevailed in the community of his followers, underwent important modification. Jesus himself became the center of it. He was thought of as the Messiah, and his early second advent to inaugurate the Kingdom of God was ardently expected. His earthly career, especially his death and resurrection, were brought into the closest possible connection with this expected "fulfillment of all things."

The first believers did not merely look forward to the *eschaton*, the last age; they thought of themselves as actually living within it. The last age had already begun. We are likely to think of the career of Jesus as marking the center of history; the early Church thought of it as marking the beginning of the end of history. God had already "visited and redeemed his people." A new epoch in history had begun, the last short epoch, in which the new and the old existed for a moment side by side—the new, present but not consummated; the old, judged but not destroyed. The God of all nature had manifested Himself in mighty acts of which the earliest believers had themselves been witnesses. The life of Jesus, his death, his resurrection, the coming of the Holy Spirit, the creation of the Church, the second advent—all were parts of one mighty eschatological event. The first Christians thought of themselves as literally standing in the very midst of the saving act of God. The life of the Spirit had already begun although the sentence of death against the flesh had not yet been executed. But God would soon bring His saving act to completion, utterly destroying the flesh, its works, and its world, and releasing those to whom "the earnest of the Spirit" had been given into the glorious freedom of the sons of God. It was not simply something God would do which the first Christian preachers proclaimed; it was something, the final consummating thing, which God had already begun to do. The Church regarded the *eschaton* as having already begun and looked upon itself as the divine community belonging even now to the new order which was yet fully to be revealed. This sense of belonging to eternity as well as to time, to the Kingdom of God as well as to history, has been one of the permanent and essential features of the Church.

In a word, the earliest Christians found God in Christ or, rather, knew that God had sought out and found them there, and realized that among themselves a new kind of human community had miraculously come into existence. As Paul expressed it, they were the body of Christ. Within that fellowship Jesus meant more than a man can mean. He came to represent to those who belonged to it nothing less than the whole meaning of life; he was the disclosure of the ultimate character and purpose of God. The death of Christ became the symbol of a new apprehension of God—a God who suffers with, and because of, man that He may redeem him from the powers of evil which have him in their grasp. Christ's continued presence in the fellowship after his death became the promise of the final fulfillment of this redemption, the sure token of the realization of the Kingdom of God. Many of the terms in which this faith is expressed in the New Testament belong to an ancient epoch, but Christians of all generations since then have known that in some way beyond their understanding the events of which the life of Jesus was the center come close to laying bare the very heart of life.

THE ACHIEVEMENT OF PAUL

Second only to the name of Jesus in the history of the beginnings of Christianity is the name of Paul, and even a brief discussion of the New Testament cannot close without giving some special attention to this man, who, although he never saw Jesus in the flesh, became, in understanding, in devotion and in influence, the greatest of all his disciples. Paul was a Hellenistic Jew, loyal to the Torah and to the traditions of Judaism, who, meeting with the expanding Christian movement, perhaps in Syria, became first the persecutor and then the protagonist. It is sometimes said that he was responsible for the spread of Christianity to non-Jews. This is not true; the movement had included Gentiles before Paul became identified with it, and many important gentile Christian churches, as, for example, those at Rome and Alexandria, were not of his founding. But no other single participant in this critical transition of Christianity from a Jewish to a largely gentile environment approaches Paul in importance.

Not only is it true that the churches which he established in various parts of Asia Minor and Greece were the most influential part of gentile Christianity for nearly a century after his death, but also he himself bore the brunt of the attack of those who around the middle of the first century made a supreme effort to bring the gentile Church within the Jewish fold. Had Paul lost his fight for the liberty of the Christian from the yoke of socio-religious Judaism, the subsequent history of the West would have been profoundly different, since it is impossible to suppose that any large number of non-Jews would have been willing to accept such burdens as circumcision and the Jewish Sabbath and food laws. As a matter of fact, the fight would almost certainly not have been lost even if Paul had not been there to win it, because important social forces were involved on his side and would eventually have had their way. Still, it was Paul's great destiny to stand at a crucial point in this epochal struggle, to receive and to accept the challenge of the enemy, to suffer his bitterest assault, and by uncompromising and effective resistance to turn the tide of battle. The letters of Paul, especially those to the Galatians and the Romans, are monuments of this moment in the history of the Church; and it is because of the importance of that moment that thirteen of the twenty-seven writings of the New Testament carry Paul's name and that a fourteenth, the Book of Acts, is largely concerned with his career.

But Paul is important in this critical period of transition, not only because he was the great protagonist of the freedom of the members of the community of Christ from the traditional requirements of membership in the Jewish socio-religious community, but also because he had a decisive part in the reformulation of the Christian message under the impact of the gentile mission. Although Paul was primarily a Jew and in considerable part thought, spoke, and understood as a Jew, nevertheless, he was by temperament and experience eminently fitted to interpret the significance of Christ in terms congenial to the first-century Hellenistic world. That world was seeking a savior. Between Alexander the Great and Augustus the old national and racial securities and the accompanying religious sanctions of the peoples around the Mediterranean had been in large part destroyed. Men had become suddenly and vividly aware of themselves as individuals, and, as such, intolerably alone. Moreover, they were burdened with an increasing sense of guilt and with a growing despair as to the meaning of life. As the prevalence of the mystery cults of salvation attests, there was never a time when the need for a disclosure of the love of God was more desperately felt. Into this world Paul came preaching "Jesus Christ and him crucified."

Paul's preaching began with the human situation. Man had been alienated from God, and thus every man had been set against his brother and divided against himself. It was not a part of man's original nature to be thus alienated and divided: God had made man in His own image, and man could know his true life only in fellow-ship with God. But sin, which Paul conceived, not abstractly, but as a real, almost personal power, had entered the world and had brought human life under subjection, corrupting God's good creation and separating man from his Father. Man's difficulty was not that he did not know what he should do; the Jews had the Torah, and even the Gentiles, in virtue of their creation, had something of God's law written on their consciences. The difficulty was rather that both Jew and Gentile, "delighting in the law of God after the inward man," found also within themselves a power which "warred against" the law of God and prevented their fulfilling it: "What I would do, that I do not; what I would not do, that I do." Man is unable to keep the law of God, which he realizes is also the law of his own true life. He lacks the power to throw off the sin which has fastened itself upon him. He cannot restore the created harmony within himself and between himself and others which sin has overthrown. He is thus confused, impotent, lost: "O wretched man that I am! Who will deliver me from this body of death?"

To man in this tragic situation God comes in Christ. Christ was the divine Son of God, dwelling with Him in heavenly places and sharing His nature. To save man Christ becomes man. He "empties himself," taking on our flesh with all its limitations, in order that he may encounter and defeat the evil powers, which have men in their control. He suffers the cruelest assault of these powers on the cross. His resurrection is the seal of his victory over them. He thus becomes the "new man." He gives the race a new start: "As in Adam all die, even so in Christ shall all be made alive." God has inaugurated in Christ the new age of the Spirit, the Kingdom of God.

To this new age every man is called to belong, whether Jew or Greek, slave or free. The condition of being admitted is simply faith. This faith is not mere intellectual assent but a personal acceptance of God's free gift. A man has only to recognize his desperate sinful plight and his inability to extricate himself from it, to trust in the power of God to help him, and to yield himself without reservation to the unspeakable love of God which is disclosed in Christ's sacrifice. He cannot hope to deserve God's favor; he must recognize that God wishes to bestow it upon him without his deserving it: "God proves His love for us that while we were yet sinners Christ died for us." Ethical goodness was for Paul, as for Jesus, not the condition of salvation, but the fruit of it. Through penitence and trust one becomes incorporated in the society of the new age, the "colony of heaven," the "body of Christ." The estrangement which sin has wrought is overcome; one realizes the forgiveness of one's sins and the power of a new life—a new life in one but not one's own: "I live, yet not I, but Christ lives in me."

This message of redemption swept like a flame around the Mediterranean Sea and melted the heart of the ancient world. It was based upon facts of history to which, at the beginning, hundreds of living persons could testify and was confirmed in the personal experience of other thousands. Paul's theology is often described as being alien both to Jesus' mind and to ours—as being both unintelligible and irrelevant outside of his own narrow world. Such a description is true neither to Paul nor to our own experience. Although we do not habitually think in terms of demonic powers, Paul's understanding of the human situation is permanently valid: we are in the grip of sin and we do lack the power to extricate ourselves. And though we may not find altogether congenial all the terms in which Paul stated his doctrine of salvation, we do know that when salvation comes to us, it comes not as something achieved but as something bestowed, a gift of God's grace, which we find ourselves simply accepting with wonder and joy, knowing nothing so well as that we do not in the least deserve it. This love of God, offering forgiveness and moral renewal, is at the heart of all that Jesus, as well as Paul, tried to say. For the story of the Son of God who loved us and gave himself for us is the early Church's way of expressing and conveying the love of God which had actually made itself known in the words, the life, and the death of Jesus.

THE TRUTH OF THE NEW TESTAMENT

This chapter began with a discussion of the importance of the New Testament in the cultural tradition of the West. In the preceding paragraph, and occasionally throughout, I have raised a more fundamental question—the question of the truth of the New Testament and therefore of its importance in a truly ultimate sense. The answer we can give to that question depends largely upon our conception of the significance of the events in which the Christian community, and therefore the New Testament, arose; and our understanding of these events depends in turn upon what they have actually meant to us. Was God, in a supreme sense, present and active in the events of which the life of Jesus was the center and of which the Church, in so far as it is truly the Church, is the continuation? If this is true—and belief that it is true comes near to being the heart of Christian faith—the New Testament, which gives us our only written record of these events, is also true and is incomparably important. In its pages the events happen, as it were, again and again. And as we read, we know that in Christ God is still reconciling the world unto Himself.

3

The Early Centuries of the Church

THE NEW TESTAMENT PERIOD OF THE CHURCH WAS NOT REALLY SEPARATED from the succeeding decades. In the eyes of Christians of the later generations who looked back to the beginning the figures of the apostles seemed to tower above men of their own day, but from the vantage point of the twentieth century one is impressed by the vitality and resourcefulness shown throughout the early centuries. It is true that the genius of a Paul was not easy to match. Polycarp remarks soberly, "For neither am I, nor is any other like me, able to follow close upon the wisdom of the blessed and glorious Paul. . . ."

The Church, nevertheless, raised up men fully capable of solving the new problems. The world was already filled with competing cults and controlled by a state whose emperors had claimed for themselves divine authority and status, yet within three centuries Christianity grew from being the hope of an insignificant little group in the provinces into one of the controlling influences in the Roman Empire. The vitality of faith of the anonymous men of the churches is demonstrated by that growth, for their missionary conviction and enthusiasm stood up against both the erosion of their neighbors' contempt or hatred and the torture of martyrdom under official persecution. The Church was able not only to strengthen its own members so that they lived a puritan existence in the midst of communities of laxity or licentiousness. It was able, also, to make that puritan standard and the conviction from which it sprang persuasive, so that more and more critics became Christians. The pagan world had not lacked moralists of high purpose, but they had been unable to make their influence widely felt in the secular life of their time. It is the more significant that Christianity succeeded where they failed.

All this can be understood only as we recognize that the Church never wavered in its certainty that it knew the eternal gospel. It was not interested in problems of organization or ethics or philosophy for their own sake, but because these became essential to the preaching of that gospel. In the consciousness of being the bearer of eternal meaning the Church turned its attention to the problems that succeeding centuries presented. Three were fundamental: first, the practical one of fashioning a body for the spirit, of creating an institution that could maintain unity and prevent the gospel from being dissipated by diverse interpretations; second, that of finding ways of living in and transforming a hostile world; and, finally, that of developing clarity in affirmations of faith originally expressed in terms inherited from different cultures and never intended to fit into a systematic structure of thought.

BUILDING THE CHURCH

In the earliest years there was no actual uniformity in organization and no need for any. The churches were created, in the first place, by traveling apostles, who went from one city to another, leaving behind them groups held together by a strong sense of the new meaning which life had taken on. Leadership was spontaneous and informal. The interest of some individual might impel him to offer his resources to the little group, as Philemon encouraged the church to meet in his home; but in the early years there were no local church officers except teachers and prophets (Acts 13:1), whose position depended on inspiration rather than appointment. There was no central core other than apostles who might or might not be members of the Twelve, and even they were chiefly sources of guidance and inspiration rather than of formal authority. But as the generation of those who had known the Lord began to die out, the need for local control became clear. Traveling preachers were no longer sure guides, for, as the *Didache* shows, there were unscrupulous men among them who were battening on the simplicity of the churches by ordering meals and money for themselves under the supposed command of the Holy Spirit.[1] Resident bishops and presbyters and deacons gradually took over the guidance of the little churches to which they belonged, and local experiments developed freely. The Church, for example, had different patterns for its ministry at different times and places. In some churches it seems likely that there were several bishops all at once;[2] at other times authority over the congregation

[1] *Didache* xi, 3-12.
[2] *Ibid.* xv, 1; cf. Iren. *Adv. Haer.* IV, 26, 2.

was shared by the bishop and a college of presbyters.[3] In such a case the bishop differed from the presbyters by distinctions not of order but only of function.

Such diversity inevitably led to uncertainty as to where authority lay. Presbyters, recalling the old dignity of their office and their early equality with the bishops, were sometimes disposed to take the initiative. Confusion resulted within individual churches and even in larger units. Some means had to be devised of getting decisions on matters of universal concern, such as the problems of membership, which were becoming acute. What was the distinguishing mark of a Christian, and who had the right to answer that question? The early dependence on the guidance of inspired persons no longer sufficed.

An interesting example of this can be seen in the case facing Cyprian, Bishop of Carthage, during the great Decian persecution in 250. Under the fury of the testing process an alarming number of Christians had fallen away from the Church. When the persecution let up, many of these repented bitterly of their weakness and implored the Church to receive them again as members. Some asked pardon and received letters of amnesty from those who had confessed their Christianity and were waiting in prisons for their approaching deaths. Presbyters in some churches received the "lapsed" back into communion without consulting Bishop Cyprian, who was himself in hiding. Here was a case where divided authority might lead to serious consequences. Cyprian roundly rebuked the presbyters on the ground that they had no right to decide such a question. That power, he said, rested only with bishops, each acting independently of the others on cases arising in his own diocese, checked by the joint decisions of the bishops in council. He held that the bishop was not an isolated individual but was, on the contrary, integrally united with all the others by the action of the Holy Spirit. Such a view in his eyes insured agreement even when bishops had to act without consultation with one another. "The episcopate is one, each part of which is held by each one for the whole." The principle implies the equality of all bishops and shows that however influential the Roman church had been from early days, the Roman bishop was not *ipso facto* the supreme head of the Church. From the latter part of the second

[3] *Apos. Constit.* 16. Cf. A. Harnack, *Sources of the Apostolical Canons,* London, 1895.

century on the authority of bishops speaking through councils and synods had been an important practical means of meeting the problems presented. The thought of Cyprian finally expressed a principle which justified the practice and clarified the way by which in the future the Church could speak with authority to her members, to the "lapsed," and to the heretics cast out from membership.

The fact that it was not until the third century that the churches finally agreed on the persons who had the right to speak on controversial issues must not obscure the existence from the beginning of a very real sense of unity. They held themselves to be members of the one Church of God. Ignatius, so far as we can tell from the literary remains, is the first to speak, early in the second century, of the "catholic" or "universal" Church,[4] but he does not really go further than does the New Testament letter to the Ephesians, which sees the Church everywhere "filled by him who fills the universe entirely" (Eph. 1:23). Irenaeus proclaimed against the heretical teachers that the faith of the Church throughout the world was one, "as if she possessed only one mouth," and the other Fathers commented in similar vein. It was Cyprian, again, who made the classical statement that only in the Church could salvation be found.

He can no longer have God for his Father who has not the Church for his mother. If anyone could escape who was outside the ark of Noah, then he also may escape who shall be outside the Church.[5]

He even went so far as to insist that heretics who died confessing the name of Christ were not martyrs. Separation from the Church implied an individual pride that was insupportable, and therefore he declared that "the inexpiable and grave fault of discord is not even purged by suffering."[6]

Here we come on an aspect of the thought of the Church that is most puzzling and alien to modern Protestants, who are loathe to accept exclusiveness in religion. It is difficult to understand how the Church became so intolerant, so absolute in its claims. A study of the history of Christianity in the second century shows that, however regrettable it may have been, such a development was inevitable if the Church was to live. It was a century when the minds of many

---

[4] *Smyr.* 8
[5] *De Unit.* 6, ANF V.
[6] *Ibid.* 14.

Christians were not occupied with the gospel of the early years but were turned with peculiar fascination to philosophical speculation about the relation between God and the world, the problem of evil, the secrets of creation, and the real nature of man and non-human spiritual forces. This absorption in philosophy and mythology did not mean that Christians were perverse. They simply shared the interests of many of their contemporaries, who were caught up in this sort of speculation. But schools formed around influential teachers, and the impact of their teaching upon Christians became so strong that the Church was forced to do something to protect the simplicity of the gospel.

Even a summary statement of their beliefs shows why the Church set itself in sharp opposition to Gnosticism. Gnostics were so called because they offered to exclusive groups esoteric "knowledge" or *gnosis*. Their world-view was dualistic, sharply distinguishing between spirit, which was divine, and matter, which was evil. The explanation of the differentiation of spirit and matter began for most Gnostics with an unknown God who was the primary existence, and from whom came forth spiritual powers, who were in turn the progenitors of inferior powers. One of the last of many series of emanations, far removed from the Supreme God, created the material world. This world was utterly foreign in nature to the spiritual worlds of the powers. The pessimism of the Gnostics about the world of nature and of men is to be seen in their belief that the creation of the world was an act springing either from defiance of the Supreme God or from ignorance of Him. Men were described as particles of spirit imprisoned in matter, although many Gnostics believed that this was true only of some men and that perhaps the majority were grossly material and therefore incapable of salvation. The bondage of the spiritual men could be broken only by the act of a savior descending from the spiritual worlds to bring knowledge of the unknown God. Among Christian Gnostics that savior was Christ, who was often represented as one of the great powers, but in non-Christian systems other saviors were introduced. The fundamental dualism of the Gnostics affected not only their views of nature and man but also their Christology, for they refused to admit that Christ had so far humiliated himself as to be born as man, bound to a body. They offered various explanations of the relation of the spirit Christ to the human body which he inhabited, but the intent of all of these explanations was to show that there was an incarnation in appearance only. Thus the teaching of the Church about the importance of the humanity of Christ was imperiled. Many of the Gnostics were truly religious men, but in all of the systems the philosophical dualism and the taste for bizarre mythology threatened the very existence of the simple gospel. It was obvious that the Church could not remain silent before this perversion of its teaching.

Marcion, who was considered a Gnostic by the early Fathers, although he was in many ways not typical, was the most disturbing influence in the Church of the second century. He was one of the most moderate and high-minded of the heretics, but the difficulties he raised for Christianity were profoundly important in their effect on the Church. He was the son of a Christian bishop, and he first attempted to bring about a reform within the Church; when he was cast out from membership, however, he set up a church of his own. He was convinced that most men after Paul had been unable to understand the truth of his teachings and those of Jesus. His comparison of the Old Testament with the Gospels and letters which had grown up in the Christian churches led him to believe that there was no continuity at all between Judaism and Christianity. The Jews had worshiped the God revealed in their Scriptures, a Creator who could show towards his creatures justice but nothing more divine, and upon whom must be blamed the world with all its obvious evil. Christ came to declare a higher and very different God, hitherto unknown even to the Creator. The Supreme God was merciful and loving, and it was His will that men should be saved from the toils of their own sin and involvement in the material world. Like more orthodox Christians Marcion was interested in the saving work of Christ rather than in the esoteric "knowledge" of the Gnostics about intermediate spiritual powers. Nevertheless, in his conviction that Christ was in no way part of this material world—a conviction made necessary by his view of the creation as the evil work of an inferior God—Marcion denied the heart of the gospel that the Lord had lived a life in history. He held that the birth of Christ was only apparent and that his body was not made of matter. These beliefs he based chiefly on ten of the letters of Paul, and the Gospel of Luke. With judicious editing, free correction, and the addition of introductions he was able to prove his points from these books, and his followers read them, along with one of Marcion's own writing, in preference to the Gospels and epistles in their original form.

The Church was thus presented with an alarming problem. Marcion agreed with the majority on many points, but the points at which he diverged were crucial. Furthermore, he was collecting the Christian writings and making free use of them for his own purposes. The result was that the Church was forced to develop a strategy to meet him. It began both to define its beliefs and to decide which of its writings were orthodox, that is, which were to be read at services. The two movements went on simultaneously in the Church over a long period, but the content of a canon of Scriptures was generally agreed upon, except in the Syrian Church, by the early part of the fourth century, whereas the full working out of theology took longer.

In order to be sure that the Church read only the prescribed books, and those in their original, unmutilated form, the Church Fathers held that a book had either to have been written by an apostle or to be directly dependent upon the teaching of one of them. Irenaeus, for instance, declared that the apostles had received power and supernatural gifts from the Lord after the resurrection and that they therefore had perfect knowledge.[7] No revelation coming from a later period or from non-apostolic circles was sufficiently guaranteed. Whether or not the Church of the second century was correct in all of its traditional beliefs about authorship, there is no question but that this measure which it devised served well to rule out the fantastic writings of the Gnostics. The list in the Muratorian fragment probably represents the custom at Rome about the middle of the second century. It includes our present New Testament, with the exception of Hebrews, James, the third epistle of John, and the second epistle of Peter. Several books which were not finally included in the New Testament had their enthusiastic admirers at Rome, but the writer condemns them because they were not written by apostles. The fragment thus reveals early popular disagreement about what classes of books were worthy to be read at public worship, and perhaps opposition to making any restrictions. In the mind of the writer, however, the basis of choice was already clearly defined. Books written by or about apostles, and those only, should be placed in the canon. Early in the fourth century Eusebius of Caesarea drew up a list in

[7] *Adv. Haer.* III, 1, 1.

order to foster greater agreement among the churches and to curb laxity, and for the first time we find precisely the books that make up our New Testament. It was the same list that was adopted at a Council at Rome in 382, and from that time onwards it represents the custom of the west, although bishops in Asia Minor and Syria were slower in agreeing. By that time, however, the disagreement was in no way on the necessity of declaring a canon of books but simply on the admission or exclusion of certain ones. Both east and west had long since agreed that the Church must distinguish between books which ought to be read in public services and those which could have only private use.

The idea of having a creed is not the same thing as reaching agreement on the beliefs which it ought to contain. The latter concern was under discussion over a long period of time, whereas the idea of having a "rule of faith," as Tertullian called it, was recognized as desirable fairly early.[8] It goes back in essence to the simple confession made by a person about to be baptised into the Church and to the many personal confessions or doxologies such as we find in Paul's letters, but in the second century these were expanded and eventually used as definitions and tests of orthodoxy. The earliest expanded creeds probably differed in form from place to place and changed as the decades passed, for the Fathers do not quote identical confessions. Something like the following seems to have been in use at Rome shortly after the middle of the second century:

I believe in God, the Father Almighty, and in Christ Jesus, his son, who was born of Mary the Virgin, was crucified under Pontius Pilate, and was buried; on the third day he rose from the dead, ascended into the heavens, and sitteth on the right hand of the Father, whence he shall come to judge the living and the dead; and in the Holy Spirit, the resurrection of the flesh.[9]

In this we can see the emphasis placed on the beliefs which the Church most strongly affirmed over against the heretical denials of the Gnostics and Marcion. There was one God, not two, and that one God was to be recognized as Creator and Ruler of the world of nature. Against the denial by Marcion and others of the full humanity of Jesus it is affirmed that he had a real human birth from Mary and that he suffered. His resurrection and his return are likewise affirmed,

[8] Tert., *Praes. Haer.*, 12-14, 19.
[9] Cf. A. C. McGiffert, *The Apostle's Creed*, 1902, p. 100.

and the dualism of the Gnostics is again denied in the last article where the salvation of the whole man, and not simply of the spirit, is asserted. The relation between the beliefs which are by implication denied and the position of Marcion is too close to be accidental, although it is possible that the tenets of the more typical Gnostic schools are also refuted.

The creed was obviously meant to draw distinctions between what could be considered true Christianity and what must be repudiated. It would have been better in some ways for the later Church if the rule of faith had included all that the Church thought important, instead of emphasizing only those points on which there was disagreement. But when one reads the vagaries of Gnostic speculation, even with an understanding of the difficult philosophical problems with which the Gnostics were busying themselves, one must be grateful for the simplicity and directness of this earliest creed. By the beginning of the fifth century legend held that the apostles composed the creed before they separated to their preaching, each contributing a phrase. Far from being apostolic in origin, it was, as we have seen, a production in great measure of the second century, although it took on its final form in Gaul perhaps as late as the eighth century.

Thus, in the second century the Church set itself to define the limits of orthodox belief and usage. The books to be read, the beliefs to be affirmed, and the authority of the men ordained to guide the Church were all pointed out. It was a phase of development no doubt necessary if the Church was to continue to exist, but many Christians felt bitterly that such rigidity ignored the admonition of Paul to "quench not the spirit." Uniformity seemed to them deadening. The movement known as Montanism protested vigorously that the Spirit still spoke directly to the Church through inspired persons, not simply through the writings of the apostolic age. The Montanists thus criticized not only the growing reverence for a canon of sacred writings but also the ordained priesthood as a sufficient medium for the working of God. It is perhaps not strange that the main body of the Church felt this to be a dangerous tendency. But the refreshing openness of the heretics to new inspiration, their enthusiastic belief that Christ would soon return, and the challenge of their asceticism swept into the movement many members of the Church, the greatest of whom was Tertullian. The protest against tightening authority failed; but however necessary it was for the life of the Church that limits be set, from the point of view of the twentieth century we must regret the loss of the freedom and initiative that had operated so fully in the earliest years.

The sacraments alone escaped the growing tendency towards uniformity and regulation. They were destined in the Middle Ages to be made the subject of dogma, but in the early centuries interpretation of their meaning and use was freer, largely because they had not become closely involved with the heretical movements. In them was expressed the untrammeled devotional life of the Christian fellowship. The Church was, for the most part, content to define the circumstances under which they could be validly performed and then to allow marked liberty of thought with respect to their meaning.

Baptism was from very early years necessary for it was the initiation of every Christian into the Church. In it one declared his wholehearted loyalty to God in Christ and was purified of the sins of his old life. Originally it was held that the gift of the Holy Spirit was connected with baptism in the accompanying laying on of hands, but later the two were separated and by the third century the gift of the Spirit was made at confirmation in a wholly distinct ceremony. The central aspect of baptism remained the forgiveness of sins. Since it could be received only once, the Church declared that baptism in the name of the Trinity was valid even if it was performed by a heretic. But precisely because the purification came only once, a custom grew up of delaying baptism until late in life in order that sins committed during life might not nullify the cleansing. This practice marks a decline of wholehearted joy in the new loyalty to Christ and the development of that kind of superstition which is an ever-present danger to sacramentalism.

The other great sacrament was the Eucharist. From the beginning the Lord's Supper, repeated at dawn on Sunday mornings or forming the culmination of a real meal, had been the center of Christian piety. There was in the early years no single interpretation of what happened in the Supper, although all knew that the very life of the Church was there. Paul treated it as a memorial and a witness of the death of the Lord. Others followed the thought of the Fourth Gospel which seems to declare a "realistic" doctrine, that Christ is in some sense physically present in the elements. ". . . . The bread I will give is my flesh, given for the life of the world" (John 6:51). The language of still others suggests that their thought, like that of some other passages in the Fourth Gospel, was occupied wholly with the spiritual availability of Christ in the Eucharist. It is extremely difficult to find any fully developed theory of the nature of the Eucharist. During the early centuries men were concerned to show simply that in it the grace and power of God were offered.

Other sacred rites were gradually accepted as sacraments as the Church came to believe that in them grace was conferred. Agreement on the number of sacraments was neither asked for nor attained until the twelfth century. In some cases it is difficult to say just when a rite became a sacrament. Certainly from an early period the ordination of men to the ministry was considered sacramental. By the late second century it was held that only men ordained by the Catholic Church could validly perform the Eucharist. Obviously it was thought that some supernatural gift had been conferred on them in ordination, giving them powers beyond those of ordinary men.

Similarly, thought about penance developed over a long period. It came about because there had to be some way of meeting the appalling fact that even after baptism Christians could commit serious sins. The Church at first declared that for grave sins there could be no forgiveness. However, as time passed, the severity of discipline was relaxed, and it was no longer held that there were any sins which were unforgivable. The sacrament of penance, in which the grace of God is given in absolution to the repentant sinner, came to take the place of the rigorous practice of the earlier years. The culmination of this process goes far beyond the first centuries into the period of the Middle Ages. Indeed, the importance of the sacramental system as a whole is to be found only then, for in the early Church there was no insistence that the grace of God was mediated in sacraments alone. In the early centuries the warmth of devotion and the sense of joy in God dominated over the temptation to reduce the sacraments to institutional uniformity and to declare that in them the ways of God with men were narrowly charted and defined. As a result, the tendency towards formalism, which shows in the early development of the ministry, the canon, and the creeds became effective only later in the history of the sacraments.

CHRISTIANITY AND THE WORLD

However important for the eventual history of Christianity was this development of an institution to carry the preaching about the redemption of man and the eternal work of God, that was not all that the Church was concerned with in the early centuries. It was not even the concern that touched most directly the great mass of Christians in the churches. They needed to be strengthened to live in a pagan environment without losing their conviction, to be in the world yet not of it. The problem is a perennial one, although in our own day the accommodation of the Church to the world has progressed so far that many are not even aware of the existence of the problem.

It is not necessary to step outside the New Testament period to find the difficulty. Paul wrote in anguish of spirit to the Corinthian church where cases of sexual immorality had appeared among those who, he hoped, had already become "new men in Christ." Their conversion, although perhaps sincere enough, had not been thorough, and they found that weaning themselves from the world and the practices that they had known was not easy. In the Fourth Gospel the great prayer of Jesus expresses an unwillingness to ask that Christians should be "taken out of the world." In some way they must be one with the Father and the Son and yet live in the world. Here is an awareness of what the final goal must be and a great faith that it can be achieved without specific directions about the road to be followed.

In the earliest period the Church made rigorous ethical demands. "Love your enemies"; "be ye merciful even as your Father is merciful"; "whosoever is angry with his brother shall be in danger of the judgment." These sayings enjoin perfection. The Church was expecting of its members adherence to a standard that made no concessions to the world. The author of the epistle to the Hebrews first states the belief which in time came to plague the Church, that for sin after baptism there could be no forgiveness.

The rigorousness of these standards inevitably set the problem of the relation between the Church and the world. Isolation is no real problem for a small community afire with a sense of mission. "He who is not with us is against us." There is no middle ground. But as the number of Christians grew, the situation changed. Inevitably, not all understood Paul's belief in the new man—a veritable death and rebirth. Their righteousness was more pedestrian, and they hankered after the old ways. Compromise was easy. By the end of the first century, moreover, many of the factors which had encouraged strictness in the life of the primitive Church were passing away. The apocalyptic belief that the end of the world with its attendant judgment was at hand had weakened and was no longer held by the majority. As the generations succeeded each other, an ever larger number of people had come to take the Church for granted since they had been born and brought up in it. Recurrent persecutions tested their loyalty from time to time, but the decades between testing saw an inevitable relaxing of earnestness. There was conflict between those who held to the old perfectionism and those who were less heroic in stature.

From the beginning Christians had been engaged in the ordinary vocations of the world. As the Church became more closely related to the pagan world, its members had to decide the complex question of how far as Christians they could live as their neighbors did and at what points they must diverge. Tertullian declares early in the third century that Christians may not be teachers because the non-Christian literature which formed the core of the curriculum was too closely bound up with the recognition of the pagan gods. Likewise, he deplores the acceptance into membership in the Church of men having anything to do in their work with the pagan temples, and this might include the worker in gold-leaf or the plasterer or the cabinet worker. He holds that no Christian can enter the army, even in peacetime, since it involves the military oath of loyalty to Caesar whereas the Christian's sole loyalty is to Christ. A further reason is that the business of the soldier requires the shedding of blood. His prohibition suggests that Christians were in fact serving in the army, but it is clear that some members of the Church protested against such activity. Tertullian was probably more extreme on these matters than the Church as a whole, but there were many who agreed with him.

As wealthier groups were drawn into membership, a still more difficult question had to be faced: whether Christians could take any responsibility for the conduct of the general community or whether their principles precluded taking public office since in that capacity it might be necessary to condemn a man to death under the law.

Tertullian wrote sarcastically that if a man could hold office without officiating at the pagan sacrifices, presiding at the public shows and fights, taking oaths, acting in lawsuits when a capital penalty might have to be applied, and sending men to imprisonment and torture, then he might safely be an official. But his listing of the obligations associated with public office shows why Christians were slow to come forward as leaders in the general communities, even had there been no question of hostility towards them. The difficulty raised a profound problem about the strategy of the Church. Was it to witness to the work of God by staying aloof and maintaining standards higher than those of pagans, or was it to try to redeem the practices of the world, as well as the individuals in it, by entering the struggle? This is a matter on which people have always differed, so it is not surprising to find difficulty arising early in the Church's history.

Until the early fourth century the Church had to maintain itself in an environment always suspicious and often actively hostile. During persecutions men and women went to death or imprisonment in the mines, serenely confident that by witnessing to their faith to the end, they would go straight to the throne of God at their death. That the courage and devotion of Christians under torture produced compassion in the onlookers and were the source of new conversions is not strange. But the effect of persecution on the attitude of Christians towards the state which counted them such bitter enemies is interesting. For persecution was certainly the most difficult aspect of the relation of the Church to the state. Two different and contradictory views were held. One is that of the book of *Revelation*: Rome is Babylon, the harlot upon the seven hills, whose wickedness will be wiped out by the act of God. The other is the one maintained by Paul: since all authority is of God, anyone who opposes the rulers goes contrary to the divine plan (Rom. 13). It is the latter view that was held by the Apologists and most of the other early Fathers. It was most fully expressed in the epistle of Clement to the Corinthians:

Thou, Master, hast given the power of sovereignty to them [rulers and governors] through thy excellent and inexpressible might, that we may know the glory and honour given to them by thee, and be subject to them, in nothing resisting thy will. And to them, Lord, grant health, peace, concord, firmness that they may administer the government which thou hast given them without offence.[10]

[10] K. Lake, ed., *Apostolic Fathers, I*, ch lx.

Between these two poles of violent rejection and complete acceptance of the state the thought of the Church swung, now waiting for persecution to pass and holding that the reign of Christ must overthrow the rule of the emperor, now emphasizing the work done by the Church in praying for the emperor and in being, as one writer says, "the soul of the world."

The last great persecution occurred in the reign of Diocletian at the beginning of the fourth century. Within a decade the situation was completely reversed, for by an edict of Constantine and Licinius in 313 Christianity became a *religio licita*, a recognized cult, and thus enjoyed the religious toleration offered to all sects. From that time on the problem of the Church in relation to the world was a different one, for the Christian community was in danger of being absorbed by the world. It was no longer a "sect," in theory composed only of saints, but it had become a "church," counting within its membership many who had taken only the first stumbling steps towards eventual salvation. Christians themselves had to be persuaded of the glories of the new life into which they had already been initiated. Instead of having to nerve its members to face persecution with courage, the Church now had to devise means of education and discipline for the vastly larger group that came into it when there was no danger. The level of morality and enthusiasm inevitably fell, as, indeed, by contrast with the primitive community, it had been doing for a long time. But, in spite of the new problems, the influence of the Church grew throughout the fourth century, since, except during the pagan revival of Julian the Apostate, it was the imperial religion. And when the empire lost its hold in the fifth century, it was the Church that stepped into the breach and managed institutions of government and of public welfare which were carried on into the years of decline ahead. The chief reason why the Church could take over the function of maintaining order was that it had been accepted, nominally at any rate, by so large a group of men and women. It had, therefore, a chance of helping to mold their thought and action and thus of building a new society.

An important aspect of the relation between the Christian and the world is connected with the ownership of property. From the beginning there were two emphases, expressing different degrees of ethical rigorousness. One of these takes its rise from the deep conviction held by Jesus that wealth is a hindrance to the development of single-minded devotion to the things of God. The classical statement of this is the well-known judgment that "it is easier for a camel to go through the eye of a needle than for a rich man to enter into the Kingdom of God." Influenced by this side of the teaching of Jesus and also by the belief that the coming of the Kingdom with its complete overturning of this world's values was imminent, the members of the Jerusalem church lived for some time in community, having "all things in common." But if this side of the Church's attitude towards property rested on Jesus' preaching about the need to choose between God and Mammon, there was another aspect of it which arose from an examination of the Christian obligation to love. Surely it could mean nothing less than sharing one's property with anyone who needed help.

Whoso hath the world's goods, and beholdeth his brother in need and shutteth up his compassion from him, how doth the love of God abide in him?—*I John 3:7*

The conviction grew that Christians are to consider themselves stewards using for the common good property entrusted to them by God. Groups representing the two tendencies continued side by side in the Church, the one forming eventually the basis for the monastic renunciation of wealth, the other offering the basic philosophy on the use of wealth.

Clement, towards the end of the second century, writes that the criticism of the Church is not against the possession of wealth but only against wealth which is used selfishly:

So let no one do away with possessions, but rather the passions of the soul such as do not permit the better use of property, that becoming noble and good, he may be able to use nobly even these possessions.—*Who Is the Rich Man That Shall Be Saved?* xiv.

Lactantius, in the early part of the fourth century, develops to its logical conclusion the idea of stewardship when he says[11] that the love which expresses itself generously is not a mark of perfection in the one who loves but simple justice offered to men who are in all ways equal before God. He sees justice and equity as the goals toward which Christians must constantly strive and by this principle

[11] *Institutes* VI, 10-12.

actually interprets Christian virtue in such a way that it might become a revolutionary force in society. The intellectual basis for a real reform was laid, and it is interesting to speculate whether the interest in the social gospel which has marked our own time might not have been characteristic of the fourth century if the success of the Church had not dampened its reforming zeal and driven many of its finest spirits into monastic withdrawal.

From the beginning the Church had deprecated the strength of any interest that diverted men from their central devotion. Asceticism expressed not primarily a metaphysical dualism between spirit and matter but rather a deep religious devotion. Thus Paul advised against marriage, not because it was wrong in itself, but because he believed that the end of the world would come shortly and any man or woman who would serve God during the interval of crisis must be free from all ties of human affection. That conviction must have been shared by many, for in Paul's letters we find references to the virgins and widows who had set themselves apart to carry on the work of the gospel. But as the expectation of the immediate coming of the Kingdom faded, the emphasis on celibacy declined likewise. In the second century Montanism discouraged marriage for its members and attracted a large number of converts, but, as we have seen, the movement was repudiated as heretical by the Church as a whole. During the third century individuals here and there began to choose a life of solitude, and throughout the fourth century an ever increasing number chose to repudiate the normal life of the world and live the life of hermits as a way of showing their devotion to Christ and their willingness to sacrifice for his sake.

The movement led naturally to the development of religious communities. In the middle of the fourth century Pachomius founded a monastic community in Upper Egypt, and here for the first time there was worked out a rule of life which is the forerunner of the later great monastic rules, such as the order of St. Benedict. In such communities men and women lived apart from the world and its temptations but in closer touch with the Church and its sacraments than had the hermits. The monastic life satisfied the need that many felt for showing their heroic devotion to Christ in the face of the allurements of the world. Accommodation to worldly standards had gone so far in the Christianity of the fourth century that to many nothing short of a drastic separation of their lives from ordinary pursuits seemed adequate. Asceticism served both as a protest against the world and as a pattern within which the life of contemplation could be developed.

The Church had by the fourth century seen the full consequences of its own "success." It included within its ranks many who were merely nominal Christians, whose lives were not very different from those of their neighbors who acknowledged no Christianity. It is precisely the situation in which the Church of today finds itself. A long process of accommodation has blotted out the distinguishing lines between Church and world, both in ethics and theology. The solution which the Church of the fourth century devised was the development of groups who separated themselves from the world. That pattern is still used in the Catholic churches and may yet become useful to Protestants in some modified form. The other solution open to the Church is that of ranging itself on the side of active criticism and reform of society, openly doing battle with the forces of reaction and secularism, as the social gospel has urged. The future of the Church is bound up with the recognition of the seriousness of its predicament in the world.

EARLY THEOLOGICAL DISPUTES

The third of the great concerns of the Church was the clarification of its theology. Although this need was not widely felt before the second century, there was no time in the history of the Church when theology was wholly lacking. In the beginning Jewish thought about God was quite naturally taken over by the early Christians, many of whom were Jewish by birth or were Greeks who knew much about Judaism and were attracted to it. The rise of Christianity would be incomprehensible apart from its heritage from Judaism, which preached a God whose spiritual and moral power worked in the lives of men, inspiring and judging them. But when Christians tried to understand what place Jesus Christ held in their thought and life, they were forced to go beyond the ideas inherited from Judaism and to strike out into new territory.

In the process of dealing with these problems, Christians did what men have always done when they develop a theology which expresses the very heart of their life: they seized upon terms that already had richness of meaning and pressed them into service. It is difficult to say whether the fact that they were not forced to coin new concepts made their task harder or easier. A new vocabulary is usually regarded with suspicion, but familiar terms can often be interpreted in such a way as to carry the new insights and truths. The danger is that old associations will insensibly modify the new meanings. In any case, in trying to make clear what they believed about the saving work and the transcendent worth of Jesus, the crucified one, the Christians of the first hundred years described him successively as the Messiah, the Son of God, the Lord, the Logos or Word of God, and finally as God.

There were two problems especially on which the Church had to do much serious thinking. The first one to emerge was that of the nature of the *work* of Jesus Christ. What had he really effected by his life and death? Clarity in this matter was vital to the life of the Church, and the need for it was seen with particular sharpness by men like Paul who were concerned to interpret to those of other religions or of no religion their own experience of liberation through Christ. The second was the question of Christ's *relation to the Father*. Here the difficulty was primarily a matter of theological consistency. How was it possible to declare at the same time that there is only one God and yet that Christ is in some sense God? Monotheism could not be abandoned, for it was the very core of the Jewish-Christian tradition. But neither could one deny that Christ was uniquely related to the Father if redemption was to have any meaning. The Church had an inarticulate but sure sense that the wrong answer given to the second question would make all Christianity void. It is precisely because the issues at stake were so important that the clarification took so long and the castigation of heretics was so severe.

As we have already seen, Paul was concerned chiefly with the first of these problems, the saving work of Christ. He was convinced that his own experience of release and new freedom was the clue. For Christ had broken the hold of the Law, which had laid an obligation upon men without helping them to meet it, and in its place had given them new power to turn towards God in faith. He threw off the burden of sin which they had inherited from their erring father Adam, the first man. The coming of Christ was thus a sign of the mercy of God, who acted through His Son to free men. Thus the greatest wonder and glory in Paul's mind is that in Christ men have deliverance from bondage into new life.

Another answer to the problem of the work performed by Christ was that he had revealed God to men. The Fourth Gospel declares that without the Son no man could have known the Father. Justin Martyr was interested in a somewhat different aspect of the work of revelation. Wherever men have known the truth, he said, their minds have been illumined by the Logos. He had worked from the beginning, and the prophets and Socrates and Heraclitus were all dependent on him, but not until the Logos became incarnate in Christ, had the revelation become complete. Justin is thus less concerned to explore the relation between the Logos and God than he is to guarantee the fullness of the revelation in Christ and its continuity with all previous revelation.

Irenaeus, bishop of Lyons in the middle of the second century, had yet another view of the work of Christ. He believed that when men were saved by Christ, they were radically changed. God was different from man because by His very nature He was immortal, whereas man was tragically mortal, subject always to the ravages of sin and death. The great work of Christ had been that he brought eternal life to men. Like Justin, Irenaeus believed that Christianity enjoined obedience to the will of God revealed in Christ; but the gift of eternal life is also essential, and for that man is dependent on God. God became man in order that men might become gods. The Logos assumed perfect manhood and thereby made men capable of participating in divinity. For Irenaeus the belief that the Logos is fully God is essential because of his belief that this redemption effects a change in the very nature of man.

Most of the later writers on theology followed the path indicated by Irenaeus when he declared that Christ brought eternal life to men. They believed with him, therefore, that the saving work of Christ implied full deity. But they had also to solve the second major problem concerning Christ which faced the Church, his relation to the Father. How were they to reconcile monotheism with the growing conviction of Christ's deity? For this purpose the term "Logos" or "Word" was extraordinarily flexible. It seemed to avoid the pitfall of ditheism because the Word of God could never be said to have had a separate existence apart from God and was subordinate to Him. The dependence, moreover, was a relationship very different from that of the creatures to the Creator, for the Logos had been with God from the beginning and, indeed, could be said to be God. At the same time there was a real distinction between the Father and the Logos. It was primarily one of function, for the latter had done the work of creation and revelation, always working according to the purpose of the Father but, nevertheless, taking an active and distinct part. Finally, the Logos, in order to perform its unique functions, must have existed with God before the incarnation. It was this pre-existent Logos that took on flesh and redeemed man.

But the nature of the relation of the Logos to God the Father had to be defined. Origen, who wrote during the first half of the third century, advanced the argument by pointing out the implications of the term "Son." He said that there never was a time when the Son was not. Had that not been true, God would not always have been Father. The idea that the Son had come into existence at some time would introduce a principle of change into the Godhead and thus destroy its very meaning. Rather, the process of the generation of the Son, unlike human generation, was eternal. This was a way of saying that a dynamic relationship had existed between the Father and the Son from all eternity, and any belief that at the incarnation something novel had happened in the relationship between them was effectually blocked. Another of the important consequences of this theology was its success in showing that the Son had always been distinct from the Father. Finally, he maintained that if the Son was to act as revealer he must fully share the being or essence of the Father. The areas in which unity and distinctness could be said to subsist were becoming clearer. By a process of eternal generation the Son was at once distinct from the Father and of the same being or essence as the Father. A long step had been taken toward the Nicene Creed.

Tertullian, a somewhat younger contemporary of Origen, made a quite different attack on the problem, for instead of drawing out the implications of a philosophical concept such as the Logos or Word he began with an analogy from experience in the law courts. He pointed out that in law more than one *persona* or legal "party" could share *substantia* or title to property, so that one could rightly say there were two *personae* and yet one *substantia*. In an analogous way the *substantia* of God, which was divinity, could be shared by more than one *persona*, as in the case of the Father and the Son. The word *persona,* as Tertullian used it, however, did not mean exactly the same thing as our word "person," an independent, substantial individual. He meant by it a distinct character, but with no independent existence. The use of the term *substantia* seemed a very good way of expressing unity between Christ and the Father, because it indicated that they shared the same being; while the use of *persona* indicated that they were manifested to the world in different characters. When the Nicene controversy broke out in the fourth century, the Church found ready at hand the formulae which Tertullian had suggested a century earlier.

As we have seen, the prevailing trend was to declare that Christ and the Father were in some way one from all eternity. The Logos theology in the hands of Irenaeus, Origen's conception of the eternal generation of the Son, and Tertullian's insistence that they shared one *substantia,* all pointed in the same direction. But there was an important protest against this dominant and increasing trend. Paul of Samosata, writing in the latter half of the third century, was most deeply concerned that the humanity of Christ should not be undermined. Like the others he was willing to say that the Logos was with God from eternity, but he declared that the Logos was not a person; rather, it was a quality or power of God. This power descended upon the human person, Jesus, who achieved unity with God by identifying his will with the Divine Will. Paul taught that the only unity which is possible between persons is one of inner disposition and hence that the unity of Christ with the Father emerged only from the perfect love of Jesus for God. By this means it seemed to Paul that he had preserved the only kind of unity between God and man that is worth affirming and at the same time that he had prevented the loss of the real humanity of Christ. His view was condemned, but it was to appear again in the theology of Theodore of Mopsuestia. It is a kind of thought that is attractive in our own time to many who find difficulty with metaphysical explanations of the relation of Christ to God in terms of unity of nature.

THE GREAT CREEDS

The fourth century saw the struggle that ended in the general acceptance of the Nicene theology. The difficulty started when Arius, a presbyter of Alexandria, boldly declared that Christ was not coeternal with the Father but that he had come into existence by the creation of the Father and was therefore subordinate to Him. The Son was not to be classed with other creatures, but, although he could be called God, he was not *truly* God. In this Arius was apparently motivated as a strict monotheist by reverence for the Father. He was more outspoken in his readiness to assert the subordination of the Son to Him than even Paul of Samosata had been. The errors which the Council of Nicaea saw in his position are contained in the anathemas at the end of the Nicene Creed.

But those that say, "There was a time when he was not," and that "he came into existence from what was not," or who profess that the Son of God is of a different "subsistence" or "substance" or that he is created, or changeable, or variable, let them be anathema.

The chief thesis of Athanasius, the ground on which in the long run he defeated the Arian party, was his insistence that their teaching was religiously inadequate. Their position, he argued, undermined the full deity of Christ and hence man's hope for redemption. If the Son were not eternal, then the redemption of mankind would not have been secure; for if he had not always existed, then it would be true also that he might sometime pass away. Either contingency would have left man in his sin. Athanasius further criticized the weakness of the position of Arius in its use of the analogy of "creating" rather than "begetting" with respect to the Son. Arius had attempted to describe Christ as less than God but more than creatures, a kind of *tertium quid* somewhere between God and man. He was Godlike in that he was created before time, but he was, nevertheless, not one with the Father. To say that, Athanasius declared, was to reduce Him to the level of His own creation, since it meant that He, like it, had come from nothing. The Son must, on the contrary, be of the essence of the Father and utterly different from the dependent creation. Finally, if He had not been truly God, He would not have had the power to bring immortality, nor would He have been in a position to reveal God truly to men, who as a result of the sin of Adam had been darkened in their reason. Athanasius sums up the meaning of the divine redemption in a passage in the *De Incarnatione Verbi Dei*:

it was in the power of none other to turn the corruptible to incorruption, except the Savior himself, that had at the beginning also made all things out of naught; and that none other could create anew the likeness of God's image for men, save the Image of the Father; and that none other could render the mortal immortal, save our Lord Jesus Christ, who is the Very Life; and that none could teach men of the Father, and destroy the worship of idols, save the Word that orders all things and is alone the true Only-begotten Son of the Father.[12]

The history of the rejection of the Arian errors is a confused one because the Church as a whole was not theologically inclined and hence was suspicious of any statement of belief that was drawn up in unbiblical, philosophical terms. During the Council of Nicaea in 325 and at later councils various attempts were made to write creeds based on Scripture. They always proved unsatisfactory, however, because both the Arians and their opponents could agree on the words while reading into them quite different meanings. The creed of the Nicene Council, and also that of the Council of Constantinople in 381, at which agreement was finally reached, made use of unscriptural terms. The most controversial of these innovations was the Greek word *homoöusios*, "of one substance." The Eastern Church was long opposed to the use of this word, because it seemed to blot out all distinctions within the Trinity by emphasizing the unity of the Godhead. Eventually, however, they were persuaded that the word avoided the dangers which they feared, and it was written into the creed. The phrases of the creed that deal with the relation between the Son and the Father express belief in

. . . one Lord Jesus Christ the Son of God, begotten of the Father, the Only-begotten; that is of the essence of the Father: God of God, Light of Light, very God of very God, begotten, not made, being of one substance with the Father; by whom all things were made both in heaven, and on earth; who for us men and for our salvation came down and was incarnate, and was made man; he suffered, and on the third day he rose again, and ascended into heaven; from thence he shall come to judge the quick and the dead. . . .[13]

In later years the creed was enlarged, but on the point of the relation of the Son to the Father the earlier statement was not essentially changed.

With the close of the trinitarian controversy the Church had agreed on a formula stating its belief in the deity of Christ: he was one with the Father in essence, yet eternally distinct in person. But the declara-

[12] *NPNF* IV, ch. 20
[13] P. Schaff, *Creeds of Christendom*, Vol. I, New York, 1881.

tion of the Nicene Creed that he was fully God inevitably raised questions about his humanity. The danger was that theology would undermine history and sever Christianity forever from the human Jesus. The problem first became the concern of the whole Church in the fourth century. Apollinarius, working in the spirit of Athanasius, developed the view that the Logos had taken the place in Jesus of a human mind. The Logos was in no essential way changed by the incarnation, although He had accepted a limitation in form. The complete person resulting from the union was thus divine as to mind or spirit and human only as to soul and body. By this explanation Apollinarius tried to avoid both the contradiction involved in suggesting that there were in Jesus Christ two complete persons, one divine and one human, and the danger of introducing into the person of the incarnate Son the development and potential sinfulness inevitable in human mind. But in dodging these difficulties he presented a truncated picture of the humanity of Jesus, from which the chief element, that of human mind, was lacking. For this error his view was condemned at the Council of Constantinople.

Out of the historically minded school of Antioch developed a position which was much more successful in safeguarding the humanity of Jesus. Theodore of Mopsuestia held that the union of the divine and the human was not one of essence but one of moral nature. Union was not brought about by the addition of the divine essence to the human but was based on ultimate similarity of dispositions. God dwelt in Jesus because his nature was wholly worthy of the approval of God, and the two natures were held together in one person in a complete and indissoluble union. But these views, which were very similar to the beliefs of Paul of Samosata earlier, were, like his, doomed to be rejected. Nestorius, a student of Theodore, maintained that Mary could not be said without danger of error to be the Mother of God since of her was born the human nature only. The Church declared that his way of putting the matter indicated that the moral union of the two natures was insecure and hence that the person of Christ was not guarded against disunity. For this error Nestorius was condemned, but his views were dominant in a great part of the Syrian Church for centuries and became the form in which Christianity was first preached to Persia, India, and China. Apollinarius had not sufficiently established the humanity of Jesus Christ; Nestorius, it was thought, had failed to achieve unity between the divine and the human. But the historical and ethical concern of the school of Antioch with the humanity of Christ had lost out to the metaphysics of Alexandrian theology. Not until the late nineteenth century was there again in the Church a group that took as its point of departure the historical Jesus, accepting the reality of his human struggle, growth and limitation.

Finally, at Chalcedon in 451 a creed was accepted which affirmed the existence of the two natures, divine and human, in one person without making clear just how the two were related. The orthodox doctrine on the subject was defined in the following words:[14]

We . . . all with one consent, teach men to confess one and the same Son, our Lord Jesus Christ, the same perfect in Godhead and also perfect in manhood; truly God and truly man, of a reasonable soul and body; consubstantial with the Father according to the Godhead, and consubstantial with us according to the Manhood, in all things like unto us, without sin, begotten before all ages of the Father according to the Godhead, and in these latter days, for us and for our salvation, born of the Virgin Mary, the Mother of God, according to the Manhood; one and the same Christ, Son, Lord, Only-begotten, to be acknowledged in two natures, inconfusedly, unchangeably, indivisibly, inseparably; the distinction of natures being by no means taken away by the union, but rather the property of each nature being preserved, and concurring in one Person and one Subsistence. . . .

This affirms unlike Apollinarianism that Jesus Christ had a rational soul and was "perfect in manhood." Against Nestorianism it holds that the Virgin Mary is the Mother of God and that the two natures are indivisibly connected. Throughout, the creed denies the condemned positions of the heretics and affirms the orthodox position that Christ is both God and man. But in no sense does it answer the question on which theologians had been at work for a century, as to how the union between the divine and the human natures is to be understood.

The agreements reached in the Nicene and Chalcedonian creeds brought nearly to a close the age of controversies and creed-making. Until the end of the sixth century eastern theologians wrangled about the nature of the person of Christ, but the western Church remained unconcerned. The main body of orthodox doctrine had been defined and the limits marked out. The theologians of the Church had been

[14] P. Schaff, *op. cit.*, Vol. II, New York, 1881.

able to relate their thought to the philosophical heritage of their day and thus to justify the faith that the Church proclaimed. But the great majority of Christians never understood the subtleties of the creeds, and this fact involved the Church in real difficulty. As the tide of Christian understanding and classical education ebbed, the temptation grew to identify Christianity with intellectual assent to beliefs bearing little resemblance to a living faith. The creeds, however, remain impressive affirmations of the Christian faith and testimony to the fact that Christianity was able to express its profoundest convictions in terms which spoke to philosophically trained men as well as to the simple, holding in equilibrium the twin forces of reason and faith. For our own day full understanding of the creeds is made difficult because they are couched partly in the terms of dualistic Greek philosophy. This difficulty indicates the necessity that each generation of Christians must face anew of wrestling with the relation of their fundamental convictions to a perennially modern world.

The Synthesis of Augustine

Augustine began to serve as bishop in North Africa and to deal with theology shortly after the Council of Constantinople had reached an agreement about the nature of the Trinity, while the debates on the person of Christ were in full swing. A less independent mind might well have accepted as his own the problems then in the forefront of attention. But Augustine was not only a vigorous and independent thinker but also a Latin, and hence he shared the practical interests of the west as well as the metaphysical concerns of the east. He approached theology from a point of view different from that of his eastern contemporaries—one which in the long run brought about a new synthesis of the old material. One cannot pick up any of his writings without finding that in one way or another his mind is constantly returning to its central preoccupation, the relation of God to man not only in redemption but in all aspects of life. Neither the persons of the Trinity nor the eternity of the Son was his controlling idea. Rather, it was the working of one God in creation, in history, and in the cosmic drama of sin and salvation. This approach forced Augustine to discuss the nature of God as a unity in order to explain His relation to the creation, and also to examine the nature of man. It was the second part of the inquiry that was the most original contribution of Augustine to Christian thought.

Although man can have certainty of the existence of God, knowledge about 'God's nature must remain forever beyond the realm of reason and can be received only by revelation. However, man can rationally understand at least something of the mystery of the Trinity by analogies drawn from his own nature as a spiritual person. That there is unity in the soul, he is certain, for it is an analysis of himself that he is making. But that there is a kind of plurality is equally obvious. In saying that he is and that he delights in knowing that he is, he has analyzed the self as at once being, knowing, and loving or willing. Another analogy of the nature of the Trinity may be seen in the memory, the understanding, and the will. Love can be real only for an object which is known; knowledge of anything is meaningful only when present experience is linked with previous consciousness now remembered. So memory, understanding, and will must all be present simultaneously to make any one of the operations meaningful. In a similar way, the persons of the Trinity are one Being, manifesting His activity in a variety of ways. The unity of God is the dominating element in the thought of Augustine. In contrast, the Cappadocian Fathers like Gregory of Nyssa had the idea that the essence of deity is impersonal but manifested in three persons. This latter conception is dangerously near to tritheism, a pitfall ever present to popular thought and not always avoided by theologians even after Nicaea.

In his thinking about God, Augustine tried to effect a synthesis of ideas from several different sources, for he was influenced by Neo-Platonic and Hebrew thought, and he worked within the framework of the orthodox Trinitarian dogma. The Neo-Platonic idea of God was of an abstract ground of being, itself beyond ordinary existence and change. Hebrew thought, on the other hand, emphasized the active nature of God, the Creator and Judge. Neo-Platonism is grounded in metaphysics, which Hebrew thought completely ignores. The two conceptions are very different, and neither is identical with orthodox doctrine on the Trinity. Like Neo-Platonism Augustine's thought starts with the declaration that God is Being, and the only ground of finite being. When it is said that He is Creator, the dependence of all existence upon Him is meant. He is also the Good and the only Fountain of goodness. For goodness is inseparable from existence, all existence being good and nonexistence evil. Moreover, God cannot be said merely to *possess* being and goodness, for they *are* God. They are essence, not attributes. In this sense God is simple, since He has no attributes; He is therefore unchangeable in His nature. Even the fact that God is triune does not affect His simplicity, for the unity of Being is in no way altered by the existence of the three "persons," as Augustine conceives them by analogy with functions of the mind.

Yet, despite the strong influence of this Neo-Platonic conception of God, the way in which Augustine expresses his personal faith is clearer proof than any offered by his arguments that for him God was one Personal Will, as in the Hebraic tradition, and that he interprets the trinitarian doctrine in this sense. It is the work of the one God, in His creating, and loving, and judging activity that appears. But though the Hebrew and Christian conception of God as Personal Will at work in history thus supplements the Neo-Platonic idea of God as pure Being and Good, the two conceptions appear in juxtaposition without being genuinely fused.

God existed before time, but with the creation time began, for with it there came movement, succession, and plurality. God created the universe, angels, and men from nothing, and hence all are dependent on Him for their being and good. Indeed, He is always sustaining them since without His support they would lapse into nonexistence. He created men capable of immortality but with wills free to choose Him as the object of their ultimate loyalty. It was their nature to find completion only in the uninterrupted love and enjoyment of the unchangeable Good, which is God, and hence anything less is evil and misery for them. Into that misery men fell by virtue of the sin of the first man Adam who chose to set up his will against that of God, according to the story in Genesis.

At this point Augustine's thought follows a road which is not open to most modern thinkers, for he describes the plight of man to all generations as the inevitable result of the sin of Adam. Since Adam was the father of the human race, his descendants were bound up in unity with him, and all born subsequently bear the mark of his defection in that their wills are weakened and his guilt is theirs. Their wills are no longer free to love God, for by Adam's sin they are wholly turned towards evil. In most of his writings Augustine declares that there is nothing evil but the evil will, which is the turning away from God as true Being and Goodness to inferior things and values of the sensible world. In this interpretation of the will as the source of evil he avoided the Gnostic explanation of evil as a material principle in which the good became enmeshed. For Augustine human responsibility is central. It is not the flesh with its desires and passions that is the cause of evil. It is the wrong direction of the will expressed in the love of self and creatures above God. Since all men were and are involved in sin by reason of Adam's offense and their own repeated acts, they were all rightly under condemnation, and God would have been entirely just if He had deserted them all.

But here enters the love of God in redemption. Although Augustine was orthodox in his views, the work of Christ did not take central place in his thought. He even suggested that God might have found some other way of saving fallen humanity. The same explanations of the atonement that his predecessors had used appear in Augustine's writings, e.g., that Christ took away the wrath of God and that by the incarnation he endowed the whole human race with glory. Most important for Augustine was the idea that by his death Christ took from men the burden of original sin by opening to them the grace of God. All of this is usual enough. But when Augustine developed his belief that God was responsible for the redemption of men, he ran into difficulty. He had tried to make man wholly responsible for evil by saying that the only evil is that of the free will choosing self instead of God. But he did not quite succeed since he was loathe to make man independent. He would not admit that man's will even before the fall of Adam was sufficient to hold him to a life of righteousness. Hence he had to acknowledge that God must have withheld from Adam His saving grace. Only by this expedient could Augustine protect his belief that everything is utterly dependent upon God.

As a result, he was driven to a doctrine of predestination, which logically undermined his declaration that the rebellious will is the source of evil. For in a doctrine of predestination everything that happens in history and in the lives of men must be said to be not only foreknown but also purposed by God. He is the source of the grace that saves men; and because grace comes from Him, it is irresistible. But God is responsible not only for granting grace but also for withholding it and thus for leaving some men in their sin. Augustine interprets the saving of any men at all as proof of the mercy of God since all merit death for their sin. He simply brushes aside the question as to whether God could be said to be unjust in treating men unequally. The nearest he comes to answering it is his declaration that some of the aspects of evil in the world must be accepted on faith. For man sees things from a limited and therefore distorted point of view, whereas to God all things are good. In some mysterious way it is better on the whole that the world have sinners and that they be punished eternally to manifest God's justice.

To suggest, however, that because Augustine failed to present a wholly consistent or satisfactory explanation of the origin of evil, he is condemned as philosopher would be grossly to overstate the point. He held together in his own religious experience the two paradoxical truths which he was unable to reconcile intellectually: that man is utterly dependent upon God and finds his fulfillment in knowing and loving Him, yet that man is responsible for his own waywardness. In the *Confessions* he has shown movingly and frankly the life of a man who found his greatest joy in loving God, although he had not been able to silence in himself the temptations of a proud and dominant nature.

Too late I loved Thee, O Thou Beauty of ancient days, yet ever new! too late I loved Thee! And behold, Thou wert within, and I abroad, and there I searched for Thee; deformed I, plunging amid those fair forms, which Thou hadst made. Thou wert with me, but I was not with Thee. Things held me far from Thee, which, unless they were in Thee, were not at all. . . . When I shall with my whole self cleave to Thee, I shall nowhere have sorrow, or labour; and my life shall wholly live, as wholly full of Thee. But now since whom Thou fillest, Thou liftest up, because I am not full of Thee I am a burden to myself."[15]

Both here and elsewhere he acknowledges in the most realistic way the continuation of the power of sin even in the life of men of faith, so that their earthly pilgrimage must be full of temptation and struggle; but at the same time their hearts have been flooded by the love of God, and they have a freedom from sin such as the natural man does not possess, for all his boasted free will.

The Church never wholly accepted the consequences which Augustine drew from the doctrine of original sin. But it was immensely indebted to him for the conception, which he developed in the *De Civitate Dei*, of the conflict between the city of this world and the City of God. He wrote at a time when the invasions of the Germanic tribes

[15] *Confessions of Augustine*, E. B. Pusey, ed.

were demonstrating beyond doubt that the power of the Roman Empire was broken. Darkness was closing in. Pride in the power and civilization of Rome, nourished for centuries, no longer had any justification. But although the failure of Rome certainly did not leave Augustine unmoved, he saw in it only another act in a vast drama of history which had begun with the creation of the angels and which would go on until in the good purpose of God the elect should have filled the places left by the rebellion of the bad angels and evil men should have been cast out from His presence forever. The really significant events of history are not the human interests and ambitions of secular histories but the fall of Satan and Adam and his posterity into self-love, the redeeming love of God which sent the God-man to earth, and the working out of that love in the lives of His elect.

In the rebellion of the wicked angels appeared the first sign of a division which would run through all succeeding time. The city of this world is the outworking of the blind and evil will of selfish men who depend on themselves rather than on God. The citizens of the Heavenly City are the good angels and men, living and dead, whose treasure has not been in the world. The fall of the Roman Empire is thus not an ultimate tragedy, for the seeds of destruction of the earthly city have been in it from the beginning in the form of pride, injustice, and war. Its decline shows by contrast the permanence and glory of the continuing Heavenly City, represented by the Church. Some men who seem to belong to the City of God may not have staying power and will in the end show that their citizenship is in the city of the world; others may come late to a knowledge of the true values of the City of God. In either case the purpose of God is carried out. History has been permeated with meaning from the beginning because God has acted through it to school the souls of men. Its meaning is thus not natural but supernatural, for its ultimate values are those of God, not men.

Yet it was not wholly an otherworldly meaning that Augustine saw in history, for here in this world men could live as denizens of the City of God. The ambiguity of his thought at this point was at once a strength and a great weakness. For in so far as man could lay hold of eternal meaning in this life, the dramatic conception of membership in the Eternal City had a reforming power which had been the genius of Christianity from the very beginning. The Church was from that point of view no human institution but partook of divine power and grandeur. As the earthly representative of the Heavenly City, it was depicted as greater than the empire, which was waning as the Church was waxing. But in so far as the City of God was identified by Augustine with the Church, there was weakness in his thought; for that which was human and fallible in the Church could be revered along with that which was touched with greatness. The beginning of ecclesiastical rigidity can be seen here. He needed to recognize the human as well as the divine aspects of the Church, but he sometimes seemed to suggest that it was wholly the City of God rather than an earthly vehicle. But whatever its weaknesses, Augustine's conception had sufficient grandeur to lay hold on the imaginations of men. It provided a framework into which the history of succeeding centuries could be fitted, in which the Church could be seen as at once the heir of the Roman power in the temporal world and the possessor of the spiritual power granted to Peter.

With Augustine the early centuries of the Church came to a close. He was the heir of the generations who had struggled to meet successive problems: those of building a church, of clarifying its relations to the non-Christian world, and, finally, of expressing the meaning of its own faith. But by his genius the results of earlier years no longer appeared as independent interests but were presented to following generations in dramatic unity. He inherited the institutions of the Church—the ministry, sacraments, Scriptures, and creeds, which had been slowly developed by his predecessors—but he looked past the externals and saw it as the great company of men and women in all ages who had found rest in God. Again, he knew so vividly in his own experience the problems of the conflicting claims of the Church and the world that he recognized the conflict as ultimate and inevitable. Throughout the *Confessions* runs an unsparing analysis of the hold which the "lust of the eye and the vainglory of life" had upon him. And he dramatized it forever as the struggle of the City of God against the city of the world, a struggle the end of which was certain because God purposed it. Finally, he took the theology which had been carved out by successive generations of churchmen, developing one idea or another as the tides of controversy and the fortunes of heresy turned, and he fitted the blocks into a massive structure which could serve as the foundation for all men's thoughts about the work of God and the whole life of man, in this world and in the world to come.

4

The Significance of Medieval Christianity

THE COMPLEXITY OF THE MIDDLE AGES

ELEVEN OF THE NINETEEN CENTURIES SINCE GOLGOTHA ARE CUSTOMARILY grouped together as "medieval"; yet there is no agreement regarding the general implications of the term. From one point of view this span between Augustine and Luther is the Golden Age of Christendom, preceded by four hundred years of preparation for triumph and followed by four centuries of schism, scepticism, and disintegration. A contrary party holds that it is a valley of shadow between the pinnacles of the early Church and the Protestant Reformation. Both these views share the delusion that the so-called "Middle Ages" were a unified historical epoch. The Middle Ages as an entity is a fantasy which was originated by the neo-classicists of the Italian Renaissance who could see in the generations since the decay of Rome nothing save gothic degradation, a fantasy which was propagated by the reformers as well as by the philosophers of the Enlightenment who together identified such barbarism with popery and superstition. The same conception in inverted form was revived by nostalgic Catholic Romantics longing for an age unencumbered by either Protestants or illuminati.

The Middle Ages, however, have no significant unifying characteristics. They embrace a complex series of historical epochs and changes far more drastic than any which separate Merovingian France from Roman Gaul or Shakespeare's England from that of Chaucer. The notion of the Middle Ages as a single and static period is as fanciful as are the illustrations of children's books showing King Arthur, Richard Lionheart, and Joan of Arc all accoutered in the full plate armor of the sixteenth century. In the Middle Ages everything from village customs to styles of handwriting altered with almost every generation. The reputation of the Middle Ages for conservatism and changelessness may perhaps be understood by the analogy of our popular use of the adjective "Victorian." We all know that the Victorian age was one of radical experiment and mutation, yet because our grandfathers were Victorian, we use the expression to indicate the ultimate in moss-backism. Belaboring the past in the interest of present flexibility of mind may be socially salutary as well as pleasurable, but an historian must endeavor to keep his scientific activities uncontaminated by even the worthiest propaganda. He will recall that the newly invented windmill spread as rapidly in the late twelfth century as the railroad did in the middle nineteenth and will use the words "Victorian" and "medieval" without connotation of immutability, much less of atrophy.

Nor is medieval Christianity an entity; to discuss it as such is to produce a composite photograph corresponding to nothing which ever existed. Its thoughts, its emotional attitudes, and its institutions were in constant and often rapid flux. The river of the Christian tradition, rising in the high hills of antiquity, flows down to the modern world through broken country. Sometimes it is disturbed by rapids, sometimes serene, often muddied, often clear, receiving tributaries, gaining much, losing little, seemingly guided by the terrain through which it passes, yet, propelled by its own forces, in no small part responsible for the forms of the landscape.

Since the conventional limits of the Middle Ages are entirely arbitrary, one must trespass somewhat beyond them to gain any real understanding of the vicissitudes and significance of the various forms of medieval Christianity. The history of the Western Church since apostolic times has centered about three great crises: the Monastic Reformation, the Medieval Reformation and the Protestant Reformation. The early Middle Ages were dominated by the results of the first, the eleventh to thirteenth centuries by the accomplishment of the second, the later Middle Ages by preliminary symptoms of the third. Each of these three reformations marked a vigorous reaction of the Christian yearning for spiritual perfection to its changing environment and resulted in mutual adaptation between Christianity and the dominant social and intellectual forms. While none of these movements can be properly understood without reference to its general historical context, nevertheless, no purely secular economic or sociological interpretation of them is adequate. In each case the initiative towards change came from within the Church itself, arising out of deep spiritual discontent and concern lest the purity of religious life be sullied by worldly influences. Consequently, each of these reformations was essentially ascetic although, since each was dominated by a quite different view of religious perfection, each produced its characteristic type of ascetic in the monk, the friar, and the Puritan respectively.

THE MONASTIC REFORMATION: LABOR AND LEARNING

Despite the blood of martyrs and the ink of the Fathers, the early Church does not offer an entirely edifying spectacle. "Not many wise, not many noble" joined the new faith; the great mass of converts, however well-intentioned in their first enthusiasm, brought ignorant and tangled minds to the altars of Christ. As the decades passed, Ananias and Sapphira, those prototypes of the Christian-with-reservations, had much spiritual progeny. As early as the beginning of the third century Tertullian was so exasperated by the failure of Christians to live up to their professions that he left the main body of the Church and joined a small moralistic sect of heretics. Able and unscrupulous men, who may indeed have considered themselves devout believers, began to rise to positions of power in the Christian community. Hippolytus, a bishop of high repute, has left us an astonishing contemporary account of how a Christian slave named Callistus began his career by embezzling the deposits placed by his coreligionists in his master's branch bank in the slums of Rome. After conviction he tried to achieve eternal bliss by smashing up a synagogue, but in place of the lions he was condemned to the mines of Sardinia whence he was reprieved through the influence of Marcia, a Christian concubine of the Emperor Commodus. After his return to Rome he rose from humble posts to increasing responsibility in the management of church properties until at last, in the year 217, he became Bishop of Rome. The fact that Pope Callistus is revered as a saint admirably illustrates the breadth of Christian charity.

The recognition of the legality of Christianity by Constantine and the favors which he heaped upon the Church made the new religion fashionable and adhesion to it expedient. Opportunists flocked to baptism, although the wealthiest, who could afford to keep a priest constantly in attendance, followed the Emperor's prudent example of postponing that sacrament until the hour of death when, by expunging all sin, whether original or accrued, it made heaven inescapable. The Church was increasingly clogged with nominal Christians devoid of conviction or of more than the most conventional morality. By the fourth century it seemed to many that the pagan Empire, far from being Christianized, had on the contrary paganized the Church.

The more earnest critics of this degeneration saw no solution save retirement from a world doomed to damnation. Soon the waste places were sprinkled with hermits, severed from human conversation, seeking the single blessedness of solitude. "How fares the race of men?" asked one such recluse discovered after years of absolute isolation. The early leaders of this ascetic movement had little hope or expectation of reforming either the corrupt world or the corrupted Church: there was no time for that. They believed that the end of the drama of salvation was imminent; the part of wisdom was to flee the wrath to come. Yet in their flight they created the monastic pattern of life and the institution of the monastery, a reservoir of spirituality from which the arid world and the parched Church might be irrigated. Their abrupt break with all the elements and influences tending to weaken the apostolic faith and zeal, their fervid indictments of demi-Christians, led to a revitalization of the whole Christian movement. For at least seven centuries thereafter the monastery was the citadel of the City of God, the monk the criterion of sanctity. The Last Judgment having been indefinitely postponed, the ascetic reaction against worldliness, which had begun merely as a snatching of brands from the burning, became the Monastic Reformation.

In the Western or Latin-speaking Church this movement was molded and its impulses channeled by three great leaders of the sixth century: Benedict, Cassiodorus, and Pope Gregory the Great. The importance of their work can scarcely be exaggerated: it still influences the whole of the Occident and, not least, America.

The hermitic life, spent alone with God, has left us records revealing at times a profundity of religious insight, a humility of spirit, and a reticence concerning ultimate mysteries which cannot fail to stir all save the most impenetrably socialized modern reader. But these same accounts indicate that so lonely an existence might prove a path to psychosis as well as to salvation. Revulsion against the excesses of fanatics soon led to forms of corporate monasticism in which the vagaries of the individual were checked by the experience of other ascetics. Naturally such communities needed a constitution and laws of conduct. The *Rule* of Benedict was so practical, so moderate and so flexible that it quickly became universal in the Western Church.

As a youth Benedict had become a hermit, dwelling in a cave of the Apennines so inaccessible that his food is said to have been lowered to him in a basket by a kindly shepherd. His fame spread; disciples gathered; frictions developed. Benedict decided that in the interest of their spiritual development his followers needed organization and discipline. To this end he slightly modified the hermitic ideal of complete abandonment of the world: his was to be a withdrawn community. He founded his monastery on a mountaintop above Cassino, which as recently as the nineteenth century could not be reached by vehicles. To maintain its isolation and thus to fulfill its spiritual function such a community was of necessity completely self-supporting, a world in itself. This meant that Benedictine monks had to labor with their hands, hard and long.

His insistence on the spiritual value of manual work makes Benedict the pivotal figure in the history of labor. Greco-Roman society rested on the backs of slaves. Work was the lot of slaves and any free man who dirtied his hands with it, even in the most casual way, demeaned himself. Plato once sharply rebuked two friends who had constructed an apparatus to help solve a geometrical problem: they were contaminating thought. Plutarch tells us that Archimedes was ashamed of the machines he had built. Seneca remarks that the inventions of his time, such as stenography, were naturally the work of slaves since slaves alone were concerned with such things. In the classical tradition there is scarcely a hint of the dignity of labor. The provision of Benedict, himself an aristocrat, that his monks should work in fields and shops therefore marks a revolutionary reversal of the traditional attitude towards labor; it is a high peak along the watershed separating the modern from the ancient world. For the Benedictine monks regarded manual labor not as a mere regrettable necessity of their corporate life but rather as an integral and spiritually valuable part of their discipline. During the Middle Ages the general reverence for the laboring monks did much to increase the prestige of labor and the self-respect of the laborer. Moreover, since the days of Benedict every major form of Western asceticism has held that "to labor is to pray," until in its final development under the Puritans labor in one's "calling" became not only the prime moral necessity but also the chief means of

serving and praising God. The importance of frugal living and consecrated labor in building up fluid investment-capital and in fostering
the rapid expansion of capitalist economy in the regions of Europe
and America most deeply affected by the puritan spirit is a commonplace of the economic history of early modern times. The Benedictine
ancestry of the puritan attitude towards work is less often emphasized.

Besides communal worship and periods of labor, the Benedictine
Rule prescribes regular periods of devotional reading for the monks.
There is, however, no indication that Benedict expected his abbeys to
become centers of scholarship. It was his contemporary, Cassiodorus,
who made the monasteries the custodians of culture during the turbulence of the early Middle Ages.

Cassiodorus was a scion of the Roman nobility, a man of excellent
education who for many years dominated the bureaucracy of the
Ostrogothic kings of Italy. But his chief concern was to halt the rapid
decay of educational and cultural standards. Cassiodorus saw that the
Church was the one stable institution in that age of growing chaos
and realized that if anything of learning or of ancient literature was
to survive, it would be under the patronage and protection of the
Church. In 536 he proposed to Pope Agapetus the setting up in Rome
of a Christian university which should teach the entire range of the
liberal arts in preparation for the specifically religious studies of theology, scripture, and ecclesiastical history. Agapetus was impressed
but died shortly thereafter, and nothing came of the plan. Then Cassiodorus had an inspiration: the monastery, an ideal spiritual community being propagated from Monte Cassino by the now aged Benedict,
would offer the perfect institutional framework for a Christian university. In 540 Cassiodorus retired to his ancestral estate in Calabria
and there set up an abbey. To it he attracted scholars and pupils who
studied the pagan authors as an integral part of their education. He
established a library and a scriptorium for the copying of manuscripts
including heathen works. He encouraged translations from Greek into
Latin. Gradually he spread the idea that broad and deep learning was
a necessary attribute of the monk and that to treasure and multiply
books was a part of the monastery's religious function. As Benedictines
spread over Europe, they carried a zeal for learning with them which
was never entirely lost even in the most troubled centuries. It was
their ceaseless and laborious copying of manuscripts which preserved

for us all that we know of ancient Latin belles-lettres. None has reached us through translation into Greek, Arabic, or the lesser tongues. The barest fragments have been excavated at Pompeii, Herculaneum, or elsewhere. The rare extant Latin manuscripts of the premonastic period survived in abbey libraries. But for the enthusiasm of monks for the Latin pagans we should know as little about the writings of classical Rome as we do about the Mayan literature which once flourished in the jungles of Yucatan.

It was the genius of Cassiodorus which utilized the forces of the Monastic Reformation to preserve something of the continuity of secular culture through the longest and most severe winter which our civilization has suffered. In cloistered gardens the Benedictines culti- vated flowers which would have been nipped by the icy winds of the outside world. Modern writers have at times accused the monastery of being an escape. A twentieth-century bomb shelter is likewise an escape. One of the unsolved problems of our own harassed generation is to find the cultural equivalent of the monastery for the present age. The quest is not promising, for no modern institution possesses the supernatural sanction needed to overawe barbarians bent on devasta- tion.

Cassiodorus' fusion of learning with the ascetic tradition led like- wise to a second result of the greatest importance for the modern world. Benedict had commanded his monks to labor; Cassiodorus had inspired them to be scholars: for the first time the practical and the theoretical were embodied in the same individuals. As we have seen, in antiquity learned men did not work, and workers were not learned. Consequently ancient science consisted mostly of observation and abstract thought: experimental methods were rarely used. The crafts- men had accumulated a vast fund of factual knowledge about nat- ural forces and substances, but the social cleavage prevented classical scientists from feeling that stimulus from technology which has been so conspicuous an element in the development of modern experi- mental science. The monk was the first intellectual to get dirt under his fingernails. He did not immediately launch into scientific investiga- tion, but in his very person he destroyed the old artificial barrier between the empirical and the speculative, the manual and the liberal arts, and thus helped create a social atmosphere favorable to scientific development. It is no accident, therefore, that his ascetic successors, the friar and the Puritan, were eminent and ardent in scientific experiment.

THE CHRISTIANIZING AND CIVILIZING OF NORTHERN EUROPE

Benedict and Cassiodorus formulated the ideal of the monk in the Latin West. Their younger contemporary, Pope Gregory the Great, directed the forces released by the Monastic Reformation to expansion of Christendom into the Teutonic North and incidentally to the civilizing of the converts.

Europe as an historical entity is the product of the seventh to the tenth centuries. While the primary reason for the shift of the focus of history from the Mediterranean basin to the northern plains was a complex of improvements in agricultural methods which lies beyond our present discussion, nevertheless, the monks were the agents of that process of religious and cultural unification which laid the foundation of Europe as we know it today. The Roman Empire had been Mediterranean rather than European; the conversion of the English, Germans, Scandinavians and western Slavs by the Benedictines and the assimilation by these peoples of the culture of Gaul and Italy produced a world which a Roman would not have recognized. The monks were the artisans who made Europe.

In his youth Gregory the Great, himself a Benedictine, had been moved by the sight of English slaves for sale in the Roman forum to vow that he would carry the gospel to that distant and barbarous island. He had started on his mission but was recalled by the ecclesiastical authorities. When at length he became pope, he sent out the prior of his own abbey at the head of a band of monks. They landed in Kent in the year 597, were well received by the local chieftain, and founded the abbey of Canterbury, the first Benedictine house outside Italy.

As one reads the records of the evangelization of the North, cynicism aroused by the methods employed yields to amazement at the results achieved. The usual strategy was to convert the chief man of a region, often through the influence of his wife. Minor notables and the common people would then be commanded or induced to enter the fold of Christ. At times conquered foes were compelled to profess the new faith. The average barbarian baptism would seem to have had little spiritual significance. But the rapid development of the Northern

Church invalidates such a judgment. There is, to be sure, ample evidence that much Christianization was superficial even when the converts were zealous. One recalls the enthusiasm of the ninth-century Saxon poet, endeavoring to tell the gospel story of Peter at the garden of Gethsemane:

Wroth was that ready swordsman Simon Peter. He seethed within, speechless with rage that men should bind his Lord with bonds. Furious he drew the sword at his side and struck the nearest of the foe with his fists' strength, so that cheek and ear burst wide from the sword's bite and blood spurted boiling from the wound.

Here sounds the song of a skald whose heart indeed may have learned to love Christ, but whose harp, like Achilles' heel, has escaped total immersion! Yet, despite such indications of continued unregeneracy, it is clear that Christianity made astonishing spiritual conquests under the auspices of the monks. Within a century of the foundation of Canterbury the English had dotted their land with monastic schools and had produced in the Venerable Bede the most learned European of his time. Swept on by ardor for the faith, the Anglo-Saxons became the greatest of evangelists. In the eighth century they poured across the North Sea, reformed the decadent Frankish Church, and penetrated the swamps and forests of Germany carrying the gospel, founding abbeys, often suffering martyrdom. Almost at once Germany repeated the experience of England: scholars and saints flourished in the monasteries; missionaries set their faces northward toward the Vikings and eastward toward Czechs and Poles. The grandsons of the savage Saxons who had dived into rivers to wash off the holy water after their forcible baptism by Charlemagne became pillars of Christendom.

Indeed, the rapidity with which Christianity took root and flowered among the Teutonic peoples cannot be explained entirely by the devotion of the monks from whom the barbarians received the faith. The tribes surrounding the North Sea and Baltic were in many ways primitive, yet we have examples of their jewelry and woodcarving which are unsurpassed in their combination of bold design and intricate detail. A society which fosters such an art contains tempered and subtle minds. We know little of the religious history of the heathen North, but there are indications that a considerable group among the fair-haired peoples was deeply dissatisfied with the traditional cults.

In a famous passage Bede describes the consultation of an Anglo-Saxon king with his nobles regarding the adoption of Christianity. A chieftain arose and said:

It seems to me, my Lord, that this earthly life is as uncertain as a sparrow which flits in at one window and straightway out another, while you sit at dinner with your thanes and carls in the winter time, the hall being warmed by the fire in its midst, but the land abroad being chilled with rain and snow. For a moment it feels not the sting of icy storm, but only fair weather. Then, passing from winter to winter, it vanishes. Thus the life of man appears for a brief space, but of what follows or of what came before, we know nothing. Wherefore, if this new teaching has brought any greater certainty, it is worthy to be accepted.

Such was the sort of question which the Church answered with an authority which did not stoop to argument. To understand the real significance of revelation we should try to imagine what it meant to the sensitive and groping spirit of this Northumbrian warrior: to him Christian dogma must have seemed a liberation from darkness and ignorance. And, indeed, the acceptance of Christianity meant an immense intellectual advance: it offered to the barbarians the first coherent theory of the nature of the universe, of time, and of personality.

The old Northern religions pictured a world tossed about by the whims of a quarreling and disorderly society of gods, supplemented by clouds of demons and fairies. In the context of pagan mythology no concept of natural law, either physical or moral, could grow up. Under such a polytheism any systematic investigation of natural phenomena would have seemed futile. Christianity, on the contrary, asserted the existence of a single God, the Creator and Governor of the universe, without whom no sparrow falls to the ground nor flits through a hall. This God has, to be sure, permitted a certain autonomy to all spiritual creatures, whether angels, men, or devils, and He himself occasionally performs miracles. But to the Christian, in sharp contrast to the pagan, the universe functions in an orderly and normally predictable manner. Monotheism is the necessary presupposition of a concept of natural law and consequently of any rigorous and wide-ranging scientific research. The preaching of a monk in the fastnesses of the German forests may seem far removed from the modern laboratory; yet the monk was an intellectual ancestor of the scientist. As the triumphant chant, "I believe in one God, the Father Almighty," rang through the new churches of the northern frontier, another foundation stone of the modern world was laid, the concept of an orderly and intelligible universe.

Similarly, the old Teutonic paganism had no explanation of the nature of time or history. It was vaguely believed that all things were in decay and that at last the gods themselves would be destroyed in *ι* universal catastrophe. Christianity, on the other hand, offered a perfectly integrated pattern of history, a pageant of salvation extending from the fall of Adam through the incarnation of Christ to the Last Judgment. Just as the physical world was ruled by divine supervision, so the historical process was a vast pilgrimage of the human race towards the new Jerusalem, an epic of the conquest of sin. As an individual the Christian looked forward to heaven; as a member of the human race he awaited the consummation of history: his eyes were fixed not on the past but on the future. Here again dogma furnished the seed from which a typical modern concept grew: Christian eschatology was the embryonic form of the idea of progress.

Finally, Christianity offered to the barbarians a new concept of human nature. So far as we can judge, the highest ideal of the Northern peoples was the warrior hero who maintained his personal honor through feats of arms and implacable blood feud. To this, Christianity opposed a strange and difficult standard. In the eyes of God, it taught, all men from the mightiest king to the humblest peasant are equal. All are equipped in some measure with both reason and will, and by the right exercise of these faculties all may attain conformity to the will of God as revealed by the Church and thus gain salvation. Naturally peoples whose society was aristocratic and who instinctively thought in terms of human inequality were slow to grasp the implications of such doctrine. Yet every monastery was spiritually a democracy which by its very existence rebuked the world beyond the cloister. Generation after generation the monks intoned the words of the *Magnificat:* "He hath put down the mighty from their seat, and hath exalted them of low degree." They kept molding the conscience of Europe until at long last the unnatural and rationally indefensible concept of the infinite worth of even the most degraded personality, a doctrine based ultimately on revelation, became the cardinal dogma of that Age of Reason and Nature, the free-thinking eighteenth century, and found political expression in the institutions of modern democracy.

Of the major upheavals in the history of Christianity the Monastic Reformation was probably the most far-reaching in its influence. It rejuvenated the apostolic faith and released the expansive forces which during the second half of the first Christian millennium were largely instrumental in preserving the remains of ancient Latin learning. It created modern Europe by uniting the Teutonic peoples religiously and culturally with their neighbors dwelling on the northern shore of the Mediterranean. It implanted among the barbarian ancestors of many citizens of the United States some of the basic ideas and presuppositions upon which our American society is built.

FEUDALISM AND THE MEDIEVAL REFORMATION

Monasticism had commenced as a protest against worldliness and corruption, yet in the ninth and tenth centuries the whole Latin Church, including the monks, became entangled in satanic traps of new design. Feudalism, the social and political system which arose under the Carolingian dynasty, was posited on the assumption that property was merely the endowment of a public function, such as fighting, ruling, or praying; if for any reason the function was not fulfilled, the property was forfeited. Thus function and endowment fused: public office became a form of heritable property, while property became subject to social control.

The effect of such concepts upon the Church was disastrous. If a lord built a parish church on one of his manors and set aside lands for its support, he would naturally think of the parish priest in feudal terms. The lower secular clergy was often married; if a priest left a son capable of filling his father's cassock, the lord tended to appoint the son to succeed the father as he would have done in the case of a military fief. Bishoprics—that of Rome itself in the early tenth century— fell into the hands of powerful feudal families, who filled them with younger sons or sold them to the highest bidder. Religious considerations were secondary. In 925 Count Heribert of Vermandois made his five-year-old son Archbishop of Rheims and thus the greatest prelate of France. An archbishop of Narbonne was consecrated at the age of ten, his family having purchased the office for 100,000 shillings. He then sold all the treasures of his diocese to buy the See of Urgel in

Catalonia for his brother. On one occasion a tough young baron was given the archbishopric of Trier. He was rushed through the various degrees of ordination, until, emerging archbishop, he distributed sixty endowed priestly offices of his church to as many knights to constitute the nucleus of a feudal army. Indeed, the martial prelate was a common figure in the feudal age. Bishop Odo of Bayeux, the half-brother of William the Conqueror, caused favorable comment by his observance of the canonical rule that a priest shall not shed blood. At the Battle of Hastings he was armed not with a sword but with a mace, which would merely mash.

Monasteries were in no way immune from the corrupting influences of feudalism. The great barons either annexed abbeys or, when founding them, retained the privilege of appointing abbots. With appalling rapidity learning and piety decayed. By the tenth century there were few communities where the *Rule* of Benedict was rigorously observed. Many monks lived openly with concubines. At the great Italian abbey of Farfa services were for a time abandoned even on Sunday. In the records of every age scandal looms disproportionately. Nevertheless, one cannot doubt that the feudalization of the Church brought spiritual catastrophe.

Not every part of the Church, however, was similarly affected. Since in theory, at least, church lands and offices were not heritable and since the upper clergy were usually unmarried, the ablest monarchs everywhere tended to use clerics for political purposes and to endow bishops and abbots munificently not simply to support their spiritual functions but in return for the normal feudal obligations. Indeed, in the later tenth and eleventh centuries the German emperor gradually gave up the earlier policy of exploiting imperial lands directly and distributed them among the great ecclesiastics, who thus became in large degree the estate managers and agents of the imperial authority. Naturally the emperor kept close control of appointments to important bishoprics and abbeys since his power depended on the loyalty of the great prelates of the realm. The backbone of his army, as well as the more substantial part of his revenues, came from church lands. Clearly ecclesiastics appointed under such conditions would be selected primarily for their administrative ability rather than because of their dedication to the religious life. In externals the Church would thrive, but its spirit would soon wither. At its best, as in Ottonian Germany or the Norman kingdoms, feudalism proved an efficient and fairly stable form of government. At its worst it degenerated into local despotism and general anarchy. But good or bad, feudalism was a cause of decay in the Church.

The Medieval Reformation began as an attempt to extricate the Church from this mire of feudalism and thus to make possible the restoration of spirituality which clearly could not be accomplished so long as political and family interests dominated the clergy. In the year 910 Duke William of Aquitain founded a little abbey at Cluny and populated it with monks from one of the rare monasteries where the pure Benedictine tradition was cherished. Duke William possessed the valley of Cluny without feudal obligations to any overlord, and in endowing the cloister he did not reserve the right to name future abbots. The pope alone was to be superior to the abbot of Cluny. Thus the monks of Cluny found themselves practically autonomous, entirely withdrawn from the feudal system. During the next two centuries they elected a sequence of six great abbots whose ardor for monastic reform was equalled only by their longevity. During the tenth century they revitalized the monastic life in scores of abbeys; but they found that such reformations were sadly temporary so long as a community of monks remained under feudal control. So in the eleventh century they bent their efforts towards building a monastic empire of Benedictine houses subject only to the abbot of Cluny himself and, like Cluny, free of feudal obligations or baronial suzerainty. At the height of its power Cluny is said to have controlled 937 such establishments, chiefly in France but scattered in Britain, Spain, Switzerland, and northern Italy as well.

As a rule the Cluniac monks were solely interested in reforming monasteries. True to the Benedictine tradition that the religious life can be achieved only in separation from the world, they showed little concern with improving the standards of the Church in general. Cluniacs at times refused bishoprics and even the papacy itself, positions which would have given their reforming zeal wide scope had their concept of sanctity not discouraged the acceptance of such posts.

By the middle of the eleventh century, however, there appeared among the secular or non-monastic clergy, the parish priests, cathedral canons, and bishops, a vigorous movement, undoubtedly stimulated in part by Cluniac example, to free the whole Church from dominance by politically minded laymen. The leadership fell into the hands of Hildebrand, a reforming monk who dominated the policy of the papacy for many years before he himself became pope in 1073 with the name Gregory VII. Gregory was aware that until clerical marriage and the appointment of ecclesiastics by kings and nobles could be suppressed, feudal influences would continue to vitiate the spiritual life of the Church. He therefore started out to withdraw the entire Christian Church, together with its properties, from the dominant social order, feudalism.

Considering the place which the Church occupied in European society at that time, no more revolutionary program can well be imagined. It is doubtful whether any social structure could survive the secession of so important an element. Perhaps fortunately, the so-called "Gregorian Reform" was only partly successful. The German emperors were well aware that their power would be shattered if the movement should gain its ends, and they fought the reforming papacy by propaganda and by force of arms for two generations. At last, the issue was completely clarified in 1111 when the Emperor offered to surrender his right of appointing prelates if the great churchmen of Germany would surrender all lands held of him under feudal obligations. The Pope accepted, but a storm of indignation swept the German clergy, who were in no mood to give up their political and economic power. Consequently, the struggle ended in a compromise which left the Church partly feudalized. But only partly, for the Gregorian Reform dealt a staggering blow to a feudalism which was already being undermined by an even more subversive radicalism, the new capitalist order. While the reformers tried to amputate the Church from society, the burgher communes were growing like cancerous cells in the feudal body.

EARLY CAPITALISM AND THE MEDIEVAL REFORMATION

The first two phases of the Medieval Reformation, the Cluniac and the Gregorian, were efforts to cast off the feudal incubus from the Church. But the more perspicacious reformers were beginning to realize that the Church was rapidly being enveloped in an entirely new social context which offered unforeseen obstacles to the development of Christian spirituality. From the late tenth century onward there occurred an unprecedented increase in the size and number of cities. Population grew rapidly; industry and commerce underwent extraordinary expansion; standards of living and luxury were rising. European civilization was ceasing to be rural and agricultural; more and more it was coming to be urban and dominated by commercial interests. With startling suddenness the bourgeois capitalist had arisen to challenge the supremacy of the feudal aristocrat. Not the temporal power but gold, Mammon himself, was the new adversary of the soul.

Quite naturally the first reaction of the reformers was to attempt to apply the old solution to the new problem and to insist that sanctity involved complete retirement from the world. Paralleling the growth of the new economic prosperity came a series of movements looking towards a revival of the primitive monastic ideal. The Camaldulians and Carthusians repudiated even Benedict's work and reverted to the hermitic life of the Egyptian desert. Far more influential was the order of Cistercian monks, reformed Benedictines, who, led by Bernard, established hundreds of abbeys throughout Europe during the twelfth century. To emphasize their breach with the older black-robed Benedictine communities the Cistercians wore a white habit. Like the Cluniac abbeys Cistercian houses insisted on freedom from feudal obligations or connections. Yet the white monks of Cîteaux are best understood, not as a reaction against the spiritual dangers of feudalism, but rather as a revulsion against the new riches of capitalism. Their life was of the greatest austerity: all elaboration, all beautification, was frowned upon. The ban against towers on Cistercian churches in an age when lofty steeples were rising to cleave the skylines of the burgeoning new cities is but the sign of the Cistercian determination not to drift with the tide of their time.

Yet the followers of Bernard miscalculated the force of the new economic and social order. They were so insistent on the spiritual necessity of manual labor that they forbade an abbey to possess more land than its monks could cultivate with their own hands. Shunning endowment, they tended to build their houses in uninhabited but potentially fertile valleys which by clearing and draining were quickly brought into production. Small groups of laboring monks were established at granges to exploit land not easily reached from the mother abbey. Thus the Cistercians were led by their own concept of asceticism to pave the way in working out capitalistic methods of agricultural management, freed from the restrictions of manorial economy.

Indeed, they occasionally broke up established manors, enclosed the common lands, and turned out the peasants. They rapidly became the greatest wool-producers of Europe and thus furnished the raw material for the chief industry of early capitalism.

The Cistercian flight from the world had failed because the refugees did not understand the complexity of the movements from which they were trying to escape. To take architecture once more as a symbol, their denunciation of the elaborately carved and costly Romanesque churches of the Cluniacs led the reformed monks to cultivate the cheaper and leanly functional type of structural engineering which we moderns call "gothic." The Cistercian movement was one of the chief means by which the gothic style was spread throughout Europe. Little did the monks know that the burghers would seize this novel architecture, would bedeck it with the ornament of both worlds, would crown their cities with vast monuments in the new manner, and would make gothic the first major art form of capitalist society.

The Cistercian experience showed that there was no escaping this new age. A revised ideal of the holy life was needed and was emerging, an asceticism which, to sanctify men, would plunge headlong into contemporary turmoil. Neither the mountaintops of Benedict nor the green valleys of Bernard, but rather the clattering alleys and market places of the new cities were to be the arenas of spiritual combat. The Cistercians had accepted without question the assumption of the Monastic Reformation that the achievement of Christian perfection required physical abandonment of the habitations of men. The mendicant orders of the subsequent period were to insist only that the soul dwell in retreat. As a pattern for saints the world-fleeing monk was yielding place to the world-transcending friar.

A movement contemporary with that stemming from Cîteaux showed the trend of the times. Increasingly the priests connected with a cathedral joined together to live in community under a semi-monastic rule. In a sense the development of these so-called "regular" canons represents a monasticizing of the secular clergy. But in the long view its significance is the exact reverse: it marks the first important step in creating a type of monastic who dwells in immediate and daily contact with pulsating urban life. To be sure, the weight of centuries of ascetic tradition proved strong, and many churches of regular canons appeared in rural areas where they represented a monastic ideal differing little from the Benedictine. But others remained in towns, and it was on these that Dominic based the rule for his order of Preaching Friars in the early thirteenth century.

The middle class was wavering in its religious allegiance. From the Balkans strange cults were carried along the trade routes in the bundles and bales of merchants. The word "weaver" became a synonym for "heretic." Peter Waldo, a burgher of Lyons, started a preaching mission which quickly strayed from the fold of the Church. By the year 1200 it seemed that a strip of territory extending from Bosnia through northern Italy and Provence to the Bay of Biscay might be lost permanently to a revived Manichaean dualism teaching the existence of two equally powerful beings, one good, the other evil. The Church, led by Pope Innocent III, fought back desperately with crusader's sword and inquisitor's stake. But it is doubtful whether coercion would have succeeded had it not been supplemented by a valiant effort to reformulate Christianity in such a way that it could be appropriated by the urban classes. The Medieval Reformation, commencing as an effort to save the Church from feudalism and continuing as an unsuccessful revulsion against the riches produced by early capitalism, culminated during the thirteenth century in the work of the two great orders of friars, Dominican and Franciscan. The former strove to reach the minds of the middle class; the latter, to reach their hearts.

THE DOMINICANS AND THE WORK OF THOMAS AQUINAS

The parvenu burghers were intellectually restless. For long centuries the clergy, and especially the monastic clergy, had monopolized speculation regarding the basic problems of existence. Very naturally they had reached solutions in harmony with their form of life: early medieval thought is saturated with the conviction, drawn primarily from Augustine but ultimately from Plato, that this physical world is the merest transitory and defective reflection of an immutable and perfect hierarchy of ideas contained in the mind of God. Moreover, the human reason was regarded as a blunt instrument indeed for piercing the veil of appearances: only by intuitive illumination could one attain the truth. It was too much to expect that the hardheaded bankers, the shrewd merchants, and practical artisans of the growing cities would long be satisfied with such monkish beliefs. Their lives and interests, the things they saw and did, the problems they had to meet, demanded a very different rationale. The Church had despised the world, whereas the burghers, led by the nature of their occupations, considered it very important indeed. The Platonizing theologians, having deserted the world for the desert, found it easy to regard sensory data merely as a springboard into the contemplation of spiritual abstractions. Not so the shopkeepers and craftsmen. They were very much in the world, intensely concerned with making and selling material goods and with judging their qualities and values. The airy disregard of concrete physical fact, the neglect of the natural for the supernatural, of this world for the next, so typical of the older theology, could arouse only scorn in the hearts of the burghers. Moreover, the city-dwellers were suspicious of the non-negotiable truths perceived under illumination. They lived by their wits; they were professionally sceptical of high-falutin talk, demanding proof, preferably rational proof, of all things, even of the Christian faith.

The old intellectual formulations of Christianity disregarded the very elements which seemed most essential in the new world of the middle class—a healthy respect for human reason and for experience of the natural world. In the twelfth century, failing to find sympathy in the Church, a considerable group of adventurous intellectuals turned to the Orient for satisfaction, and a flood of translations from Greek and Arabic inundated the West. It is significant that the material translated was overwhelmingly scientific and philosophical. It supplied the vitamins which the bourgeoisie found lacking in its inherited intellectual larder. In cultural as in social history, the leaders of revolution are not necessarily born of the revolutionary class but rather of the revolutionary situation. Nevertheless, we may note that in an age dominated intellectually by clerics, even though by clerics of all social extractions, a considerable number of these translators were laymen.

Of the utmost importance for an understanding of this movement is the almost complete neglect of Plato's works. Many of these were known in Arabic, and Byzantium was amply supplied with Platonic manuscripts. But the occidentals were not interested. The one exception only serves to emphasize the point: about 1156 a learned Sicilian translated the *Meno* and *Phaedo*, but his versions enjoyed very limited circulation. Clearly the translators knew what their public wanted, and nobody wanted Plato just then. Plato cared nothing for non-mathematical science; his essentially poetic genius had little patience with the self-imposed limitations of strictly rational thinking, save in geometry. But the new Europe was seeking tangible fact and rigorously disciplined thought in all realms of experience.

Aristotle, on the other hand, was able above all others to supply what the West was looking for. In ancient Greece the Stagirite had represented a reaction against the etheriality of his teacher Plato. He had turned to the minute examination of the natural world and to the formulation of the rules of logic. So, also, in the twelfth and thirteenth centuries he became the symbol of revolt against the older Platonic-Augustinian world-view. Every scrap of his extant writings was translated, usually in several versions, and eagerly read everywhere.

In the thirteenth century the peril to traditional orthodoxy arising from the new philosophy was heightened by the fact that Aristotle appeared in the robes of his Arabic commentators, notably those of ibn-Rushd, called Averroes in Latin. The Averroists took delight in sharpening the antagonism between Aristotle and orthodoxy, especially regarding the eternity of the world and the mortality of the soul. To many intelligent men it seemed that to accept the newly discovered benefits of rationality and of the experience of nature one must reject Christianity with all its inherited treasures.

When in 1215 Dominic established his order of mendicant friars in the teeming city of Toulouse, it was primarily to retrieve the souls of dualistic sectaries and the followers of Waldo. But the friars soon saw that these superstitions were merely symptoms of a deeper discontent of spirit. The real problem was what it has remained ever since: the alleged opposition between science and religion or, to put it into thirteenth century terms, between Aristotle and Augustine. Must we accept the one and reject the other, or is there, perhaps, a middle path preserving the best elements of both? Only in the new universities which had seized educational leadership from the monastic schools was the issue really clarified. So to the universities, especially to Paris, the friars sent their ablest minds. The conservatives were trying to crush the Aristotelian serpent. The Dominicans perceived, however, that in a reconciliation of Aristotle with orthodoxy lay the best hope of making Christianity intelligible to the new age. To this task Thomas

Aquinas dedicated himself. It was a daring experiment by a radical thinker.

A grandnephew of Frederick Barbarossa and second cousin to the Emperor Frederick II of Hohenstaufen, Thomas was destined from childhood to become abbot of Monte Cassino. But he rebelled against his family's ambitions and in the face of their apoplectic rage joined the Dominicans, this new order of begging friars lacking all social position or prestige, in a word, completely unsuitable for a young aristocrat related to the best families of Europe. Thomas, a hulking and taciturn man, equipped with the best brain of his century, evidently realized that these dusty mendicants had a relevance to their age which the Benedictines had lost. Here was the new school for sanctity. Thomas was every inch a saint in the new pattern and there were many inches of him. Throughout his career he moved back and forth across Europe, huge, imperturbable, absent-minded, mixing vigorously in the life of the time, yet carrying his cloister within. Indeed, it must have seemed that a kind Providence had made his frame so large to contain so vast an inner life.

The stakes in the battle between Thomas and the Averroists were high. On the outcome depended whether or not the Christian faith should continue to be a vital part of Europe's thinking and consequently of America's. Thomas' victory was recognized by contemporaries to be of the greatest importance, and in art the saint is generally depicted triumphant over the stricken Saracenic philosopher.

The Averroists followed Aristotle in denying that the material world had a beginning or would have an end. God, they said, did not create the world; indeed, He may not be conscious of its existence. It flows eternally from Him as water flows from a spring. Therefore, according to the Averroists, time is an illusion and history is without a goal. All things, including God and man, are governed by immutable necessity. There is not the slightest element of freedom in the universe. Aristotle was believed to have held that the individual mind is a portion of the cosmic mind, to which it returns at death. The Averroists expanded this idea into the doctrine that all knowledge, all active thinking, comes to the individual mind from this one great cosmic mind. A man does not discover truth; he receives it ready-made. He does not really think; he is thought in. Clearly Averroism was in many ways an ancestral form of the mechanistic materialism of recent generations, with its belief in an inexorably grinding, completely purposeless universe in which the individual has neither freedom nor real significance. It is this which makes Thomistic thinking so vividly pertinent to the twentieth century.

Thomas took his battle position boldly upon the central datum of Christian revelation, the incarnation of God in Christ. He does not discuss it at length; he assumes it to be true; thence his thought issues. Surely, says he, if God Himself assumed flesh and became involved in matter, then physical nature and our sensory perceptions of the world are worthy of reverent attention. Here, indeed, Thomas baptizes Aristotle by incorporating into the Christian faith Aristotle's own feeling for the importance of nature. As we shall see, the new Eucharistic cult on which Thomas' profound piety focused was intimately related to the bourgeois concern for material substance. In his greatest hymn he cries, "Sing, oh tongue, the mystery of the glorious body!" *Corporis mysterium*—here is almost a Christianized materialism. Never again could theology be so over-spiritual, so disdainful of the physical creation, as formerly it had been. It is clear that Thomas, whether consciously or unconsciously, was reformulating the Christian faith in terms intelligible and acceptable to the third estate.

Having affirmed the incarnation, Thomas proceeded to defeat the Averroists by working out the rational implications of his prime axiom, which was admittedly non-rational (as were, indeed, the axioms of his opponents). Christ was a person, thinking, willing, loving. If Christ is God, then God is, at the very least, such a person, acting with intention. God is, of course, far more than a person in the limited human sense, yet His non-human attributes in no way contradict His personality. The affirmation that Christ is God, therefore, is the insistence that personality is the greatest of realities.

With such a God it follows that the universe cannot be thought of as a timeless, necessary emanation, indifferent to human fate. On the contrary, as Dante was to express it in the last and consummating line of his epic, "Love moves the sun and the other stars." A purposive creation at the beginning of time must be assumed, and a culmination at the end of time when a spiritual goal is reached. Since the chief purpose of action motivated by love is to share one's own benefits, the primary intention of God's creation was to bring into being personalities made in God's spiritual image, endowed with the divine attributes of intellect and will. Personality is the highest thing in nature: *Persona significat id quod est perfectissimum in natura.* The individual man, then, is not, as the Averroists thought, a momentary configuration of matter having no active intellect or freedom of choice. On the contrary, the individual is conceived to be the most important thing in the world, and the perfection of his personality through his own right exercise of intellect and will is declared to be the chief end of creation. Never before in all history had the supreme worth of the individual been heralded so loudly as by Thomas.

In fact, Thomas maintains the freedom of human will so stoutly that, in disagreement with most previous theologians, he very nearly gives man a Godlike authority not only over his own destiny but even over the rest of the world. Man is a vice-Providence, enjoying what have rightly been called "subordinate sovereignties and autonomies." Here is the complete negation of fatalism. Similarly, Thomas asserts that a free and active intellect is the very core of personality and that every man has a duty to God to exercise his own reason, preferably in the form of Aristotelian logic. This involves the repudiation of the Averroistic notion that we receive truth passively, predigested, from the cosmic mind. Our minds, said Thomas, "make" truth for themselves, almost aggressively, out of the raw material of experience which comes to us from the natural world through our senses. In maintaining this position, so important for an understanding of modern intellectual history, Thomas had to combat not simply the Averroists but also the old Augustinian theory that truth is received from God by mystical illumination without the mediation of our senses. "There is nothing in the mind," he asserts, "which has not come to it through the senses." Here again Thomas' rationalism is closely linked to his naturalism, to his insistence on the importance of the physical world.

Legend tells us that shortly before his death Thomas rose from prayer and, looking towards the great volumes of his *Summa Theologica,* said to a friend, "It is to me as straw." But a modern scholar has added, "Of that straw European civilization was going to make its bed." For Thomas is, if not the father, at least the grandfather of all bourgeois philosophy, especially in the case of bourgeois who know no philosophy in the formal sense. In the year 1200 the burghers were rapidly drifting away from the Church; in 1900 radical critics sneered at the Church as a bourgeois institution. It was Thomas who formulated many of the basic middle-class Christian attitudes which are today perhaps more firmly entrenched in America than anywhere else in the world. As a people we believe that there is nothing more important than the individual and that the physical world and the historical process are neither meaningless nor alien to us, but rather that they are designed to aid the more perfect development of personality. We believe that each person is endowed in a mysterious way with the power of choice, and that by its use he helps to shape his destiny. Finally, we believe that each person enjoys in some measure the good of the intellect by which he may grow in knowledge through the rational exploration of the world in which he lives. These ideas of individuality, moral progress, freedom, and rational inquiry, which have been dominant in capitalist society, rest historically, be it noted, on the central Christian dogma of the incarnation. It was Thomas and his Dominican brethren who popularized and broadcast his ideas, who first showed the middle class the relevance of Christianity to the tendencies of thought which arose from its type of life.

THE FRANCISCANS AND PIETY

Yet not only the thoughts of the new age but its emotions as well demanded incorporation into, and expression through, the Christian tradition. The piety of the early Church and of the Monastic Reformation had been restricted to a relatively narrow octave of emotion—awe, reverence, fear, exultation. Easter, the celebration of triumph over death, was the great feast of the year. Christ was worshiped as Logos and Judge, but he was distant, enthroned between the cherubim. In such an atmosphere the religious arts were necessarily symbolic rather than naturalistic, impersonal rather than intimate. One who has sensed the cosmic ecstasy of the plainsong of Benedictine liturgy may suspect that most subsequent expressions of Christian emotion have been tinctured with sentimentalism and even vulgarity. But the feverish life of the towns bred different patterns of feeling which were quickly reflected in an immense widening of the range of piety. The Medieval Reformation was permeated with new and unprecedented types of religious emotion. Heaven drew near to earth, and God to man. The crucifix, for example, was too brutal a symbol of God's humanity to be popular in the first Christian millennium. When it was used, the crucified Christ was shown passionless, bearing a regal crown, the new

Melchizedek blessing his people. In the time of Bernard pain began to appear frequently in the visage of Jesus, the Cistercians centered their devotion upon the crucified Christ, and such hymns of the Passion as "Oh Sacred Head Now Wounded" emerged. In the thirteenth century the crown of thorns, the marks of the scourging, contortions of agony, jets of blood, all appear. A completely naturalistic, human, and dramatically moving image, which earlier Christians would certainly have regarded as indecent and even revolting, becomes the chief aid to devotion.

Similarly, the new social atmosphere, with its intimacy and vivid sense of the impact of individual character, led to the effective discovery of another great Christian symbol, the Nativity. That the omnipotent Creator should have cast aside all power in order to win men by love, that He should have lain a helpless infant in a manger— this was no less a marvel than that he should have hung as a bleeding victim upon the cross. From very early times the Church had celebrated both the birth and death of Christ, but it is no exaggeration to say that in the twelfth and thirteenth centuries the average Christian first really found Bethlehem and Golgotha. Thus the tender joy of Christmas and the agony of Good Friday were added to the older gamut of approved religious emotions with incalculably liberating effect upon all the realms of culture.

The Franciscan friars in particular picked up and amplified the vibrations of the new emotions. Francis himself is credited with constructing the first crèche or model of the Nativity. His own devotion to the crucified Christ was so intense that the five marks of the Passion appeared (either miraculously or under extreme autohypnosis) upon his flesh, marking him as the first in the long series of stigmatics who have ornamented the Latin Church. Such a piety appealed to the excitable city-dwellers, and such was the piety propagated among burghers and artisans by the gray friars.

But from the orthodox standpoint there were grave dangers in the new forms of religious expression sweeping Western Europe. Their first manifestations seemed entirely meritorious and were, in fact, eagerly embraced by the Church. Toward the end of the twelfth century the cult of the Eucharist experienced a sudden and extraordinary development. Reservation of the consecrated Host, the body of Christ, became habitual rather than exceptional; the elevation of the Host was introduced; monstrances appeared on altars enabling the faithful to see the very substance of their God. In 1215 the doctrine of transubstantiation was first rigorously defined. It was as though Europe had become populated by a race of doubting Thomases eager to thrust their fingers into the very wounds of Christ.

Clearly the new Eucharistic devotion involved a "personal religious empiricism" (to borrow the phrase of a learned priest) closely akin to the mood of the typical bourgeois. But this was indeed a sacramentalism with a new and peculiar flavor. Inevitably the notion spread that to partake of the Host was unnecessary: to see it exposed, or to say one's prayers before the altar where it lay reserved, became a sufficient means of grace. As symbol gave way before literal reality, sacrament yielded to spectacle.

This quite unconscious process can be traced through changes in the habitual representation in art of sacred scenes. It is perhaps most evident in the crucial case of the Last Supper. The early and monastic churches had depicted it at the moment of the institution of the mass: "This is my body." Then a new representation appears, the sop given to Judas. This is transitional, since it combines both sacrament and drama—the Host given by Christ to his betrayer to the latter's damnation. At last, there is a second mutation, and all sacramental interest is eliminated. The moment illustrated becomes the assertion, "One of you shall betray me." The disciples are thrown into a consternation which becomes increasingly individualized, culminating in the masterpiece of Leonardo. Thus the effort of the Medieval Reformation to keep the burghers in the Church presented two related but very different trends. On the one hand, the sacramental system was so concretized that the later Middle Ages were the period of its greatest elaboration. On the other hand, there is visible a contrary tendency to develop a proto-Protestant religion bringing salvation primarily through introspection and psychological readjustment rather than through objective means of grace.

THE NEW ASCETICISM AND THE PROTESTANT REFORMATION

The implications of this second essentially anti-sacramental movement were considerable. The basic reason for distinguishing clergy from laity was the need for a group of men ordained in succession from the apostles and capable of administering valid sacraments. As sacraments came in many minds to seem less important, so did the division of Christians into clerics and laymen. The next step was to re-examine the whole concept of the religious as distinct from the worldly life. Even the friars had assumed that while the religious life did not require retreat from the world it inevitably involved the traditional monastic vows of celibacy, individual poverty, and obedience to ecclesiastical superiors. But in the later twelfth century, especially in the towns of northern Italy, the seed of the third, or puritan, type of Christian asceticism began obscurely to germinate. Small groups of devout laymen, chiefly artisans, banded together under the name *Humiliati*, "the Humble," repudiating all the formal attributes of monastic discipline in favor of a normal active life and living in conformity with what they thought to be Christ's teaching. They reared families, remained in their businesses, and showed so little obedience that they quickly ran afoul the local spiritual authorities and were often driven from the Church.

The great impulse towards a non-monastic asceticism came from Francis. His preaching at times swept communities with such force that the entire population, men, women, and children, begged for admission to his order of friars. But Francis saw that he could not thus devastate towns, break families, and dislocate economic life. The friar-pattern of sanctity, like the monk-pattern, was vestigially aristocratic in assuming that the great majority of people could not or would not adopt it. Might it be that even the mendicant orders had failed to readjust the ascetic ideal sufficiently to meet the demands of the more democratic society of the new age? It was all very well for the friars to repeat Jerome's dictum that while marriage populates the earth, celibacy populates heaven. But who, pray, would populate either monasteries or convents if everyone espoused the monastic ideal? The popular enthusiasm aroused by Francis forced the issue. Does God will that human society continue? If so, then there is a religious duty to beget children and to labor diligently at one's vocation. The traditional dual standard of a religious and a secular way of life is challenged, and the potential sanctity of lay life is affirmed.

Francis met the problem by reviving the essential idea of the *Humiliati*. He established a Third Order (the first two being for his friars and for his feminine followers, the Poor Clares, respectively) of those who would live holy lives while remaining with their families and trades. The Franciscan Tertiaries expanded rapidly and widely, and a similar movement was soon established by the Dominicans. North of the Alps, especially in the Rhine valley, the ferment spread, and there emerged among laymen a great variety of experiments in religious living, notably the Friends of God and the Brethren of the Common Life. Often ill-defined and amorphous, these movements shared a tendency to exalt the spiritual independence of the individual, to insist upon his right to appropriate divine grace wherever he might find it, in sacrament, Scripture, or mystical ecstasy, and to cultivate a kind of asceticism consisting solely of conformity to God's will. The mendicants had considered riches the greatest threat of capitalism to the religious life and consequently had made the vow of poverty central. But in the fourteenth century Tauler is already asserting that wealth holds no peril for a man truly consecrated to God's service. The emphasis of such devout laymen upon immediate personal experience rather than upon authority in matters of religion often made them suspected by the clergy, who exerted constant and partially successful pressure to bring them into conformity with older monastic precedents. But the new wine could not forever be contained in the old wineskins. A new pattern of sanctity was emerging which was neither Benedictine nor mendicant. It was expressed in its simplest form by Gerhard Groot in the later fourteenth century:

To love God and worship him is religion, not the taking of special vows. If, therefore, one aims to live a religious life, his way of living becomes religious in God's opinion, and according to the judgment of our consciences.

The key to an understanding of the Protestant Reformation, the third of the great upheavals of Christian history, is its repudiation of monasticism. Martin Luther, a renegade friar, marrying Catherine von Bora, an ex-nun, begetting children and establishing a family, is a spectacle which certain writers seem unable either to understand or to forgive. Protestantism is presented as the product of Luther's lechery, ably abetted by that of Henry VIII. But Luther's marriage is only a symptom of the final reformulation of Christian spirituality stimulated by the social context of capitalism. The monk had fled the world and had bound his life with triple vows; the friar had stayed in the world but had retained the vows which separated his existence from the normal human pattern; now at last the Puritan abandoned all rigid forms of the religious life, making the basis of his asceticism the pursuit of his "calling."

In both intent and practice Protestants were ascetic. Tourists have long noted the greater sobriety of the peasant costumes of Protestant villages in Germany as compared with neighboring Catholic communities, and one remembers Calvin's exhortation to his followers to marry homely wives, lest the beauty of their consorts distract them from contemplation of the divine omnipotence. When the Venetian ambassador called Cromwell's Ironsides "an army of monks," he was close to the truth. For if the Puritans rejected the distinction between a religious and a secular life, it was to monasticize the laity; if they destroyed abbeys, it was to make an abbey of the whole world. Only so can one understand Calvin's Geneva, Knox's Scotland, or colonial New England.

The Protestant Reformation may be regarded either as the final phase of medieval or the beginning of modern Christianity. In either case it is clear that puritanism, the most vital expression of Protestantism, is the culmination of the late medieval effort to find a spiritual rationale of bourgeois life more consistent than that offered by the last, or mendicant, phase of the Medieval Reformation. But Americans, in particular, who have so much of the Puritan in their constitution, should beware of assuming that the sequence of the three great Christian reformations is an evolutionary series towards a higher form of spirituality. The soul striving for perfection has in every age beaten for itself a typical path of pilgrimage intimately related to contemporary forms of life. When the age changes, a new path must be found. The history of medieval Christianity consists of a group of such experiments in holiness which it would be rash to rank in order of success, since each was designed to meet the spiritual problems of a particular epoch. We of the twentieth century are heirs of them all and not merely the most recent. Each has left a rich legacy and has helped to mold the minds and hearts even of the millions who are conscious of no debt to them. Like God's rain the merits of His saints descend impartially.

5

The Reformation and Classical Protestantism

THE MEANING OF THE REFORMATION

LIKE EVERY OTHER ELEMENTAL TURMOIL OF THE HUMAN SPIRIT THE Reformation can be and has been interpreted in many diverse ways. Its Protestant champions have maintained with Luther that it was nothing less than the recovery of pure Christianity after a millennium of "the Babylonish captivity of the Church." There have been many variations on the theme of Richard Burton that "Luther began upon a sudden to drive away the foggy mists of superstition and to restore the purity of the primitive Church." At the other extreme, the Roman Catholic critics of the Reformation can find little else in it save heresy and schism, inspired by base motives and led by errant rebels. They readily admit the desperate need of a reform of the Church in the sixteenth century, but they condemn with varying degrees of bitterness both the doctrine and the character of the men who broke with the Roman Church in their reforming zeal. Historians with less creedal bias offer us a bewilderingly generous selection of interpretations of the Reformation from which to choose. To some it was largely a political phenomenon, a product of early modern nationalism. To others it was motivated at bottom by economic factors; they point to the interesting correlations between Protestantism and capitalism. On the one hand, it is heralded as a victory of conscience and the reveille of freedom; on the other, it has been condemned as a mere exchange of the old yoke of tradition for the new yoke of Scripture. Charles Beard was confident that the Reformation was the sister of the Renaissance; Nietzsche was even more confident that it was the mortal enemy of the Renaissance and all its works. The young Goethe believed that the Reformation was

a sorry spectacle of boundless confusion, error fighting with error, selfishness with selfishness, the truth only here and there heaving in sight.

But Guizot saw it very differently.

116

The Reformation [said he] was a vast effort made by the human race [sic!] to secure its freedom; it was a newborn desire to think and judge freely and independently of all ideas and opinions which, until then, Europe had received or been bound to receive from the hands of antiquity.

Perhaps the commonest contemporary verdict on the Reformation is that it was an incident in the cultural revolution which displaced the medieval ethos and in the course of about three centuries (1500-1800) ushered in the "modern world." Certainly it is undeniable that the Reformation was a part of a vast complex of cultural forces which conditioned its career. But one underestimates the strength and relevance of religious movements in history who says with Preserved Smith that "the Reformation was but the consequence of the operation of antecedent changes in environment and habit, intellectual and economic." The Reformation was not merely a derivative affair; it was also a determinative factor, and a very powerful one, in the shaping of modern history. Its ideas and concerns are not only a continuing and significant part of our general cultural heritage; they are likewise the wellspring of some of the most vital and important developments in modern religion.

There is no simple truth about the Reformation. It must always be seen in context, as a revolution within a set of revolutions. There was the geographical revolution, the passage to India and the discovery of America, which was altering man's estimate of the size of his world and rendering obsolete the prevailing static notions of the organization of power among the European nations. In addition to this, there was a political revolution in full course; it was focused in the new concept of nationalism and the new possibilities opened by the idea of a sovereign, omnicompetent state. The divine rightness of political authority (a hoary notion) now gave way, for a time, to the claim of a divine hereditary right of kings to unlimited power, a new thing in Christian Europe. Even more powerful than these, perhaps, was the intellectual revolution which had begun in the Renaissance and would reach its climax in the Enlightenment. On the one hand, this was a return to the past, to the ideals of classical paganism; on the other, it was a critical and creative movement which may be adequately symbolized by its first great scientific monument, *De Revolutionibus* of Copernicus, which appeared in 1543, in time for Luther to fulminate against it before he died in 1546. Still a fourth revolution was occurring in the realm of economic theory and practice. This was characterized by the rise of the bourgeoisie, the expansion and freer circulation of trade and commerce, and a new theory of mercantilism with its premium upon wealth and its rejection of certain medieval limitations upon the acquisition of wealth. Both industry and agriculture were slowly being absorbed into the rising structure of finance capitalism.

Within this concurrence of creation and change came the Reformation. It, too, was a revolution, a radical reorientation of religious faith and ethos. The other revolutions preceded, accompanied, and followed the religious revolt; they conditioned and influenced it in a hundred ways. But they did not determine it, nor do they afford an adequate explanation of it. Over and beyond all its cultural environing, there was something original and creative in the Reformation. Despite its obvious secular involvements, it was fundamentally a religious revival, a fresh and vital recovery of an aspect of the Christian gospel which had been smothered and skewed by the Catholic Church of the late medieval period.

The Reformation was long brewing. The conciliar movement, which had sought to establish a constitutional government for the Church, had failed, and its failure had left an unreformed papacy in control of a decadent and yet uneasy Church. At the turn of the sixteenth century Europe was tense, ripe for radical change. Criticism of the Church was widespread and ineffectual. Rigorists like Cardinal Ximenes of Spain, humanists like Erasmus, mystics like Wessel Gansfort, saints like Catherine of Siena, and fanatics like Savonarola all had a common theme: "The Church must be reformed in head and members."

In the face of all this clamor the See of Peter seemed secure enough. The papacy had met and defeated the conciliar threat to place constitutional limitations on its powers. The Renaissance popes were able administrators and statesmen, and the habit of loyalty and obedience was still strong throughout the body of the Church. Nevertheless, reform, long overdue and hitherto resisted, lay heavy on the conscience of Christendom. When the Fifth Lateran Council, assembled as a sop to the Church's critics, ran its course to a futile close on March 16, 1517, it marked the end of an era. Conciliar and pacific methods had apparently failed. Revolution remained as the alternative and this was shortly to be tried in Germany.

Types of Protestantism: Lutheranism

The external history of the Reformation is too well known to warrant a simple retelling. Who does not know how the flame of revolt, lit by Luther at Wittenberg and Worms, quickly swept beyond the borders of Saxony and Germany, following the lines of least political resistance and finding fresh fuel in those centers where humanist learning had blazed a trail? In Switzerland, Holland, England, France, Sweden, the new-found faith and its freedom stirred the hearts and altered the ecclesiastical allegiance of great blocs of the north European peoples. Within thirty years the so-called "Protestant" movement had won impressive victories against Pope and Holy Roman Emperor and had established itself as an accomplished fact in the religious situation of Europe.

But Protestantism never achieved organic unity. An evil genius of division and variation appeared to dog its course. After a century Bossuet was able to parade a formidable "history of the variations of Protestantism" before the eyes and conscience of Christian Europe. At the same time the diversity of ideas, polity, and ethic within these groups can be exaggerated and misunderstood. A closer look at the Protestant kaleidoscope yields the impression that classical Protestantism is more of a single entity than is commonly supposed. Within it four main types of faith and ethos can be discerned which will include almost the whole of non-Roman Christianity in western Europe in the sixteenth and seventeenth centuries. These types may be listed under convenient labels: Lutheranism, Calvinism, Anglicanism, and Radical Protestantism, often called Anabaptism. An analysis of these variant forms ought to afford us a clearer perspective for an understanding and evaluation of classical Protestantism as a religious and ethical force in the past four centuries.

The first of these Protestant types is Lutheranism. It is quite unintelligible apart from the temperament, character, and faith of Martin Luther. A dozen years before he posted his challenge to debate on the church door at Wittenberg, Luther had entered the Augustinian monastery at Erfurt and had begun with the utmost rigor and self-discipline to seek deliverance from his intense sense of sin and his fear of God's wrathful judgment. What he desired above all was a genuine feeling of inner peace and "righteousness before God." Despite fitful periods of happiness and satisfaction, Luther became increasingly sure that the monastic discipline was a dead end. Terror still choked his spirit, and the brooding pessimism so typical of sensitive men in his age still remained and drove him often to the brink of despair. Despite his good works (and they were considerable), he felt frustrated and denied by the very penitential system which the Church had provided to bring absolution and peace to the hearts of the faithful. Instead, he turned more and more to Scripture and to what he took to be the Pauline version of the Christian message of reconciliation. A new truth spoke to him from the Scripture: a man is "justified," forgiven and accepted by God, not by anything he does or can do but by the freely offered grace and love of God. This grace and love are revealed only to the eye of faith, which sees it embodied in Jesus Christ, the Word of God. To Luther this new way of apprehending the graciousness of God was revolutionary. It brought the peace which had been denied him, and he now felt not only absolved from sin but released from the agony and torment of a rigid legalism, which sought assurance of salvation through merit acquired by good works. Step by step, and often unwittingly, Luther was led first to a headlong attack upon the penitential system, then to a rejection of the papacy, and finally to leadership in a separate movement which sought to give communal expression to this neo-Pauline conception of the Christian life.

The gospel of Luther and Lutheranism turns around the problem of man's status before God and the conditions of man's true blessedness. To begin with, Luther and his followers had no very great appreciation of unredeemed human nature or of the natural powers of human reason. Man not only cannot save himself by striving for virtue or increase of knowledge; his depravity is such that he only succeeds in frustrating and wounding himself still more deeply as he seeks to earn or merit God's favor and grace. God is great, God is good; man is weak, man is sinful. How, then, can man come before God and know of His reconciling pardon? The Catholic Church had sought to serve men in their approach to God by means of an elaborate set of mediatorial rites and ceremonies. Helpful as these were, they were easily abused and often led to a false confidence that they insured man's right relation with God. Although official Catholic theology carefully avoided the pitfalls of legalism, in practice the *cultus* often was taken to imply that man somehow might compel the grace of God, that by sufficient effort and self-discipline one might come to deserve God's approbation. Luther cuts all this away with a careless knife. The message of the Word of God to the Lutheran is the good news that men have their reconciliation with God in Christ apart from the good offices of the Church and apart from deliberate moral striving. Men are justified and made blessed because of a new faith which is itself a gift from God as men wait and hope and pray. True salvation consists in a man's joyous acknowledgement, in faith, of God's headship and control of his life. This is the gist of what has been called "the formal principle of the Reformation," the doctrine of justification by faith alone (*sola fide*).

The complement to this is what likewise has been called "the material principle of the Reformation"—the direct authority of the Holy Scripture (*sola scriptura*). In place of tradition and the papacy Luther set forth the Scriptures as the single objective norm of authority for Christian teaching. He was able, however, to maintain a flexible and critical method in the interpretation of Scripture because of his constant emphasis on the fact that what matters in the Bible is its specific content, which is nothing other than Christ, the Word or message of God's forgiving love:

This is also the proper touchstone for the criticism of all books, if we observe whether they treat of Christ or not, since all Scripture testifies of Christ and St. Paul will know nothing but Christ. That which does not teach Christ is not apostolic even though St. Peter or St. Paul should teach it. On the other hand, whatever preaches Christ would be apostolic, even if Judas, Hannas, Pilate, and Herod should do it.

On this basis he is able to call the epistle of James "a right strawy epistle. . . . for it certainly has no evangelical character about it"; he has similar reservations about other sections of both the Old and New Testaments. Only the believer can truly fathom the real depths of scriptural truth, and hence the Bible exists to minister to faith and not to constitute it. This is at once a more liberal and a more subjective attitude toward the Bible than that which some other types of Protestantism were to take.

It is easy to see how this double principle of *sola fide* and *sola scriptura* led toward an anti-intellectualism which could despise or dispense with the resources of science and philosophy. In the first place, Luther's own implicit metaphysical view was intensely voluntaristic and thus ran counter to the intellectualism of the dominant medieval philosophy. In the second place, human reason, especially in matters of morality and religion, was to Luther "the devil's strumpet," seducing men to a false trust in their own wisdom and powers. Finally, the riches of truth which are accessible to men in the Scriptures, read with the eye of faith, render nugatory any serious dependence upon philosophical ethics or natural science save as they confirm the faith. This anti-intellectualism of Luther was to play an important role in the development of all later Protestantism. Positively, however, his double principle of authority issues in the doctrine of "the priesthood of all believers." Truth is not the exclusive treasure of priests or theologians. Since faith and the Scripture are both freely given to the Christian man, he has in them all the help required to act as priest in his own home and to exercise his private judgment in matters of faith and conscience.

From 1525 on, Lutheranism came more and more under the control of complex political forces which were stirring in Germany. In its relation both to the political and to the social orders Lutheranism was essentially quietist. This was a matter of principle and not merely practical opportunism. The essential thing for the Lutheran ethos is the community of the Word, wherein the gospel is purely preached and the sacraments duly administered. This doctrine of the spiritual nature of the Church means that for Lutherans problems of polity and order are secondary; so, too, are matters of civil and political import. The impact of the Church upon the world is powerful but indirect. This means that the Church will not seek to control the state and society, that it will seek to influence them only by moral pressures. Nevertheless, the Church will resist to the death the abridgment by the state of its own unique spiritual functions.

The Lutheran ideal of the Christian life is nowhere put more succinctly than in the great tractate of 1520, *On the Liberty of the Christian Man.* Luther's paradoxical thesis is that

a Christian man is the most free lord of all and subject to no one; a Christian man is the most dutiful servant of all and subject to everyone.

After explaining the doctrine of justification by faith alone he emphasizes the moral virtues which will naturally flow from faith. In vigorous terms he insists upon this spontaneity of Christian virtue:

This is the truly Christian life; this is faith really working by love: when a man applies himself with love and joy to the works of that freest servitude, in which he serves others voluntarily and for naught, himself abundantly satisfied in the fullness and riches of his own faith.

He may be accused of exalting faith at the expense of good works; what he intended was that faith should issue in good works, inspired by love and without thought of reward.

THE REFORMED CHURCHES: ZWINGLI AND CALVIN

The second main type of classical Protestantism arose in Switzerland, where external conditions were more favorable than anywhere else on the continent. Its own favorite name was "the Reformed Church," but it is more widely called, after its greatest exponent, "Calvinism." This type of religious thought appears first at Zurich under the leadership of Huldreich Zwingli, a Swiss priest who had been influenced greatly by the "Bible humanists" and Luther. Zwingli's reformatory ideas did not come to him as the result of a long, inner travail of soul like Luther's but rather from a fresh and inductive study of the Bible. In Luther he found the principle of appeal to the Scriptures; from the humanists he had received the literary resources for the exegesis and interpretation of them. Probably under the influence of the Dutch "sacramentarians," he attacked the doctrine of transubstantiation and substituted an allegorical conception of the sacraments which denied any notion of real presence in either the elements or the rites of baptism or the Lord's Supper. His religious thought centered around a version of the doctrine of justification by faith which greatly stressed the sovereign will of God, and with it the idea of divine election or predestination and the distinction between the true or "invisible" Church and the "visible" or corrupted Church. The papists obviously belonged to a visible religious fellowship, but this did not mean that they belonged to the *numerus electorum*, "the number of God's chosen ones," who compose the invisible, true Church. These views were not exclusively religious in their inspiration. Zwingli was deeply influenced by humanism; his emphasis on God as sole cause of all events bears the imprint of philosophical monism; his denial of the significance and the authority of the visible Church echoes the secularism of Marsiglio of Padua.

From Zurich the Reformation spread to other Swiss cantons and made rapid progress under the leadership of men like Oecolampadius in Basle and Butzer in Strassburg. These men and their colleagues, all with humanist training, laid great stress upon the direct and literal authority of the Bible, which they regarded as a hitherto neglected treasury of truth. Their own religious experiences show little of the turmoil and agony of Luther's struggle and little of his distinction between the Word of God and the letter of Scripture.

But the man who was to give a normative character to "reformed" thought and its ethos was a Frenchman who spent the greater part of his adult life in Geneva. In his youth and early manhood John Calvin had been deeply influenced by French humanism and by the revived interest in scriptural religion led by Lefèvre d' Étaples. Lefèvre and his disciples were moderates, seeking to purify the faith of Catholic Christianity without altering the cultus; thus they escaped serious persecution or the painful choice of breaking their ties with Rome. Calvin was closely associated with this group—Lefèvre, Briçonnet, Cop—but little by little he came to believe that no effectual reform of the Church was possible without challenging the papal principle of authority and the prescriptive claims of the Catholic cultus. To the former he opposed the authority of Scripture and to the latter the doctrine of justification by faith. By the summer of 1534 he had lost his "reverence" for the Roman Church, and early in 1535 he is out of France, first at Basle, then at Geneva, ready to publish his great theological manual, *The Institutes of the Christian Religion*, and to enter upon his career as the most influential reformer of all.

In seeking to understand Calvin and his work it is important to bear in mind that he represents what we may call the "second generation" of the Reformation. By the time he assumed control of the religious life of Geneva, Protestantism had won a fair degree of security and independence in its struggle with Rome. The Schmalkald League in Germany and the successful revolt of the Swiss cantons from Catholic control had given promise of an assured future for the Protestant cause. Calvin's task was to fill out and organize, in terms of polity and doctrine, the central insights of the pioneers who had cleared the way before him. At the same time, his was a powerful and original mind, and Calvinism is a distinct and autonomous type of Protestant Christianity.

The dominant idea in Calvin's life and theology is that of a sovereign, majestic God whose power and grace give being and meaning to the whole creation and whose glory is the chief end both of man and the rest of creation. This sovereign God is to be understood primarily in terms of His omnipotent Will, which is the ultimate cause of every event in experience and history. Men are naturally self-affirming and sinful, and they are saved, if at all, by the grace of God bestowed upon them, with no preconditions of works or personal merit on their part. God saves whom He wills to save, and there is no rational basis upon which His choices can be explained. God determines the destiny of men. This is the gist of the famous doctrines of predestination and irresistible grace, and it is the very heart of Calvinism. Luther, too, had attributed man's salvation wholly to God, but with him it was mainly a matter of piety and grateful dependence rather than dogma. Calvin makes the notion singularly explicit and literal. This divine determinism is very far from fatalism because God's will is spontaneous and personal. In this connection it is a significant fact that Calvinism has exhibited the most active and effectual social ethic of all the Protestant types. It has been an aggressive movement, bursting across national and cultural frontiers, though it has been generally balked by class lines. Whereas Lutheranism spread no farther than middle Europe and the Scandinavian countries, Calvinism has been the prime mover in the Protestantism of France, the Low Countries, and much of middle Europe, Scotland, England, and America.

Calvin's purpose was to renew the whole of Christian faith and life in creed and character. He proposed to use the Bible as the single and sufficient authority and constitution for faith and order, life and work:

The Scriptures are a school of the Holy Spirit, in which, as nothing necessary or useful to know is omitted, so nothing is taught except what is profitable to know.

The Scriptures are literally inspired:

They [the writers of Scripture] were infallible and authoritative aman-
uenses of the Holy Spirit and are, therefore, to be held as oracles of God.

To guard against eccentric use of the Bible, Calvin taught that it
can only be interpreted by one who is illumined by the Holy Spirit
and that Scripture should be tested not only by private feeling but
by other Scripture as well. It is worth remarking that this attitude
toward the Bible is much more rigid and formal than was Luther's.
Calvin considered the Bible as equally inspired throughout, whereas
Luther had a more discriminative, critical norm in his doctrine of
the Word of God in the Bible.

In Calvin's ethic the "elect" individual has a dignity and a task of
immense significance. Since his "calling and election" is sure, there
is a minimum preoccupation with "inner states," or the effort to gain
assurance of personal salvation, and a maximum concern with the
tasks whereby he may serve the community and glorify God. Like
Luther he emphasized the worth and religious significance of earthly
callings, and far more than Luther he elaborated a positive and
active pattern of Christian living which called for what Max Weber
has termed "asceticism-in-the-world" (*innerweltliche Askese*). This
follows from Calvin's insistent connection of the moral law with the
gospel of grace. Luther had tended to separate the two and to exalt
grace at the expense of the moral law. Calvin identifies the "natural
law" with the Torah of the Old Testament and refuses to see any
essential conflict between this and the Gospel, with its "counsels of
perfection," in the New Testament. The moral law, thus explicitly
defined, is binding on the community and determines the end of all
human acts. Men may work at any useful task and may make moderate and disciplined use of this world's goods. But their chief end
must always lie beyond the economic and the social spheres, "to
glorify God and to enjoy Him forever."

Calvinism has always made much of the idea of a "holy community." The Church is not merely the assemblage of the elect which
endures the wickedness of the world in patience and hope. Rather, it
is the trustee of spiritual insight and moral judgment in the community. Its mission is to Christianize the community "by placing the
whole range of life under the control of Christian regulations and
Christian purposes." This means, obviously, that the Church can
and should exercise moral judgment over the state, although it

should not seek to usurp its political responsibilities. This is another area in which the activist mood of Calvinism contrasts with Lutheran quietism. It is no accident that after the failure to realize its ideal of theocracy Calvinism joined forces with the rising middle classes in their bid for political franchise. Thus it has been a potent factor in the gradual creation of political democracy in England and America.

Finally, Calvin and the Reformed Church in general moved to a middle ground between Zwingli's allegorism and Luther's realism in the doctrine of the sacraments. Calvin agrees with Luther in his emphasis upon the intimate connection between the Word and the sacraments, but he rejects Luther's idea of consubstantiation and the ubiquity of Christ's human body. Sacraments in Calvinism are pillars of faith and mirrors of faith:

The office of the sacraments is precisely the same as that of the Word of God, which is to offer and present Christ to us, and in him the treasures of heavenly grace; but they confer no advantage without being received by faith. . . . They communicate no grace from themselves, but announce and show and, as earnests and pledges, ratify the things which are given to us by the goodness of God.

It may be interesting here to note that, whereas in Catholicism the sacraments tend to be dramatized prayers, in Protestantism of the churchly sort they tend to be dramatized sermons.

ANGLICANISM

The third main type of classical Protestantism arose in England and is generally called "Anglicanism." In both faith and order it stands closer to Rome than any other Protestant group; indeed, it is a standing claim among most Anglicans that their church is truly catholic and apostolic. England achieved its Reformation in quite a different fashion than the Continent and this is reflected in the differences in religious and sociological form between continental Protestantism and the Church of England. In the beginning, at least, there was a minimum dislocation of doctrinal tradition and ecclesiastical machinery. The first formal rupture with the Pope was an act of state, supported by many loyal Catholics who had no idea that it would lead to a repudiation of the Catholic Church. Henry VIII would countenance no major doctrinal alterations, but he abrogated the papal authority over the *ecclesia anglicana,* made the English church subject to crown control, and confiscated an enormous loot from the monasteries and foundations. Once the phalanx of popery was broken, however, it was inevitable that continental Protestant ideas and leaders should find strategic opportunities for exerting their influence. The reign of Edward VI was a field day for the Protestants, in which Cranmer and his colleagues published a second Book of Common Prayer before the first one was generally accepted and promulgated a decidedly Protestant set of forty-two articles just before the young king's death (1553). Queen Mary, half Spaniard and a zealous Catholic, sought valiantly to undo the Protestant mischief but succeeded only in deepening the gulf between Protestants and Papists and earning for herself a tragic sobriquet, "Bloody Mary." With mixed motives and admirable tact Queen Elizabeth moved toward a working arrangement between the contending factions in the kingdom. She was finally able to establish in power the moderates, men who were seeking a broader base for doctrine and polity than the extremes of Wittenberg, Geneva, or Rome. The two great achievements of this party were the XXXIX Articles (1576) and the revised Prayer Book. Together they are Catholic in tone and spirit, but they have assimilated the Protestant emphases upon unconditional grace and the primacy of faith.

But England was not to know religious peace for a century. The Elizabethan settlement was mere frustration to the Romanists on the one side and the Puritans and Radicals on the other. The Puritans hungered and thirsted to purify the English Church after the pattern of Wittenberg and Geneva. They opposed prelacy and the use of vestments and other symbols of the old order, and they insisted upon a presbyterial polity and Calvinist doctrine. The Romanists, of course, were recusant and worked unceasingly for a restoration of "the true religion" to England. This complex struggle dragged England through many bitter decades and deeply marked the complexion and character of the Anglican Church. In the course of it, the so-called "Authorized" or King James Version of the Bible was published; a bloody civil war was fought; a king and his archbishop lost their heads; a vast new impetus was given to the colonization of America; and the country ran the gamut of sovereigns of the most widely varying religious views from Cromwell to James II. At the end of it all the Anglican Church emerged badly eroded in spiritual power but still retaining the general form and standpoint it had achieved under Elizabeth in the last half of the sixteenth century.

Anglicanism is unique among Protestant types for the comprehensive nature of its fellowship. Within the single type there has always been great variety of doctrinal position and interpretation of the cultus of the Prayer Book. Nevertheless, it is possible to discern a fairly constant and dominant tradition in Anglican history. This has been aptly called "central Anglicanism." For the period which we are studying its great spokesmen were Archbishop Matthew Parker, Richard Hooker, John Donne, Bishop Lancelot Andrewes, Archbishop William Laud, and Bishop Joseph Butler. The great literary monument of this tradition is Richard Hooker's *Of the Laws of Ecclesiastical Polity* (1594-97). Although this book was engendered in controversy with the redoubtable Puritans, Walter Travers and Thomas Cartwright, it is wonderfully free from polemical bitterness. It is a rare combination of wide and deep learning and a prose style fit to bear its subtle and profound thought. Like Parker and Andrews, Hooker makes an appeal to the threefold canon of the Scriptures, Christian antiquity, and human reason as the basis for faith and order. This broad view of authority he lays upon a metaphysical basis of divine and natural law. Of the natural law he says, "Her seat is the bosom of God, her voice the harmony of the world." This natural law underlies and supplements the truths which the Bible reveals; thus he refutes the puritan appeal to the *sola scriptura*. Natural law, likewise, is the reality which history exhibits; thus he denies the Romanists their claim to sole possession of Christian tradition developing through history. The human reason which apprehends the natural law is God's image in man: "The law of reason doth somewhat direct men how to honour God as their creator." Of course, reason and natural law are not enough and must be supplemented by divine law or revelation. But Hooker sets his face against all obscurantism; authority must be reasonable and just; positive codes of polity must be adaptable to changing circumstance and conditions. This viewpoint undermines the rigidities of Roman dogma and the Calvinist theory of church order based upon Scripture alone. And its equal cherishing of Scripture, tradition, and reason makes it a *via media* between Protestant and Catholic extremists.

There is no doctrinal novelty in Hooker. But his view of the relation of Church and state is rather significant, although he is only putting into words the ideas of Cranmer and Parker and rationalizing the accomplished fact of the English Church-state. He finds an analogy between the Church of England and the ancient Hebrew religious monarchy:

> Our state is according to the pattern of God's own ancient elect people, which people was not part of them the commonwealth and part of them the Church of God, but the selfsame people whole and entire were both under one chief Governor on whose supreme authority they did all depend.

The King, however, is himself under God's law and must rule by law. This is a denial of the later Stuart and Bourbon claim to hereditary divine right. The Church and state are reciprocals; neither is properly subservient to the other; together they comprise the commonwealth. This kind of political philosophy obviously presupposes an inclusive and powerful Christian culture in the nation, and since this is always partly lacking or corrupted, there is here an ominous tendency toward secularism. Central Anglicanism has always resisted this tendency and has had a measure of success in envisaging a Christian ethic in which the rational and the specifically Christian virtues mutually support the entire life of society.

The typical moderation and inclusive character of Anglicanism were due partly to the continuing medieval traditions of intellectualism and synergism, partly to the close alliance in England between the religious leaders and humanism. But they were also due to the influence in England of such new currents of theology and philosophy as those represented by Arminianism and the Cambridge Platonists. The former denied any such notion as that of irresistible grace and sturdily insisted upon the importance of the human response to the divine initiative and the consequent freedom and responsibility of man's moral and religious life. The Cambridge Platonists—Whichcote, Cudworth, More—sought to reconcile faith and reason, the Christian imperatives and rational morality. These forces became parts of the Anglican theological synthesis and are later to be seen in interesting variations in William Law, John Wesley, and Joseph Butler.

PROTESTANT RADICALISM

There is still one more type of classical Protestantism which has exercized an influence on later religious developments out of all proportion to its original size and weight. This is "the left wing of the Reformation" and includes those ardent souls who were led much further than the Lutherans, Calvinists, and Anglicans and who insisted upon religious primitivism and moral rigorism. These we may call the "Protestant Radicals" although they were more often called "Anabaptists." This general form of religious radicalism can be thought of as a single entity only if it be understood that it comprises a conglomeration of groups and individuals who, while differing widely among themselves, are similar in their radical break with the medieval tradition. They sprang up in Switzerland, Germany, the Netherlands, and England in the wake of the successful revolts of the more conservative Protestant groups against Rome, but were dissatisfied and disappointed over what they felt to be the laxity and compromise of other Protestants.

These Radicals sought to achieve a uniformly high level of moral purity and religious devotion in their Christian fellowship. Thus they insisted upon "believer's baptism" and denied the validity of infant baptism. Many of them even provided a second baptism for adults who had previously been baptized as infants in Roman, or sometimes in Protestant, churches. Hence their nickname, Anabaptists or "rebaptizers." In the teachings and example of Jesus and especially in the Sermon on the Mount they found the truly Christian design for living. The churches of the New Testament they took as patterns for their own "holy communities." Ernst Troeltsch has characterized their ethos in a compact summary:

> Detachment from the state, from all official positions, from law, force, and the oath, and from war, violence and capital punishment; the quiet endurance of suffering and injustice as their share in the Cross of Christ, the intimate social relationship of the members with each other through care for the poor and the provision of relief funds, so that within these groups no one was allowed to beg or to starve; strict control over the church members through the exercise of excommunication and congregational discipline. Their form of worship was a simple service, purely scriptural in character, conducted by elected preachers and pastors who had been ordained by . . . synods representing the local groups.

The sharp contrast between the radical groups and the other Protestants suggests a fundamental difference between two versions of the nature of the Christian community, a distinction made familiar by Troeltsch as that between "church" and "sect." The church ideal is inclusive, aimed at evangelizing and transforming all members and institutions of society toward the Christian ideal, even though the process entails varying degrees of compromise and accommodation. The churchman feels that the church must accept and seek to discharge its responsibility toward the social, economic, and political orders. One of his favorite texts, used to justify the inclusion of worldly or half-worldly persons in the Church, is the parable of the wheat and the tares growing together. The sect ideal, on the other hand, emphasizes the exclusive character of life in the Christian *ecclesia*, "those called out of the world." It insists on a closely knit fellowship of adult believers on a voluntary basis, intensely concerned with the purity of faith and life of the group and prepared to exclude all who fail to measure up to their rigorous standards. The sectarian, too, has a favorite text: "Come ye out from among them and be ye separate." The Church acknowledges the grades and distinctions of social and economic status in any community and tries to ameliorate the resulting tensions and injustices. The sect recognizes the problem caused by these but denies that it is particularly relevant to the primary question of man's personal relation to God. Differences in wealth and class are of minor concern to those who are truly committed to God's rule in their lives. Thus the sect substitutes religious status for social and economic status and maintains within its own exclusive fellowship a very high degree of democracy and mutuality. The churchman's danger is undue conservatism; the sectarian's typical fault is spiritual pride. This basic differentiation of social ethics has in Protestantism given rise to some very complex and confusing developments. For sectarian ideas and ideals have been enormously influential, especially in American Christianity, even upon the so-called "churches." At the same time, many Protestant denominations which began as sects have followed in varying degree the stages of evolution toward "churchliness."

Among the Radicals we can identify at least three main species. The first we may call the "revolutionaries." These were high-spirited men, impatient with Luther's social conservatism and Calvin's bourgeois affinities. They were prepared to hasten, sometimes by force, the apocalyptic advent of Christ and the "New Jerusalem." Exemplars of this spirit are the prophets of Zwickau, the Münster rebels, and the "Fifth Monarchy Men" in England. A second species of the Radicals can be called the "communalists," who sought to establish theonomous communities, constituted by the law of Scripture. Their main concern was a closely knit fellowship, exclusive and rigorous, patterned after the familial ethos of the Christian churches of the New Testament. This ardent primitivism is illustrated in the Mennonites, the Hutterian Brethren, the Schwenkfeldians.

Still a third species are the "spiritual idealists." This was hardly a pure type but a congeries of individuals and small groups who sought to combine the rigorous sect-ethic with concepts of prophetism and Christ-mysticism. Luther, with his peculiar gift for untranslatable epithet, called these people *Schwärmerei*, "fanatics" and *Sakrament-ierer*, "men indifferent to the sacraments." In this group are men like Franck, Hoen, Coornheert, Ochino, and a host of similar temper. Most of them exhibit an indifference to cultus and dogma and put a premium upon humane and tolerant attitudes and upon essentially mystical religious experience. Although naturally individualistic, this type of religion succeeded in producing group fellowships of great significance, as among the Collegiants in Holland and the Quakers in England. Moreover, this compound of mysticism and moralism has had a widespread and continuing influence in later Protestantism. Its ideas of religious intuition and liberty of conscience and its essential optimism about human nature and its improvement have appealed to the minds and imagination of members of all the Protestant types. Its "low-church" polity, with a minimal interest in the authority and continuity of the Church and a great stress on local or congregational autonomy, has been appropriated in varying measure by the Independents, Congregationalists, and Baptists in England and especially in America. Finally, its natural corollary is a theory of separation of Church and state, and this has been a potent factor in the modern struggle for religious liberty.

At the fringe of this Protestant radicalism and beyond the pale of orthodoxy stood the Socinians, unitarians in theology, who substituted an almost pure moralism for the Christian view of salvation by faith in Christ the Redeemer. Their optimistic doctrine of human nature and their estimate of Jesus Christ as ethical teacher later mingled with the larger stream of Protestant thought and has been a very significant aspect of the liberal Protestantism which arose to challenge classical Protestantism in the nineteenth century.

THE EVOLUTION OF PROTESTANTISM

To this brief analysis of the types we must attempt to add an even less detailed summary of the evolution of classical Protestantism from its rise in the early sixteenth century to its decline in the eighteenth. Such generalizations as we can make will perforce telescope and distort the history of the period; their value may be to suggest that classical Protestantism, like other human enterprises, has its own natural history. Indeed, we may distinguish three main stages of development, corresponding roughly to the three centuries of the period. The sixteenth century witnessed the rise of the movement and the emergence of its basic insights and its most creative leaders. In it we see that amazing run of luck or providence which allowed the revolt from Rome to become an accomplished fact. It was the Peace of Augsburg (1555) which inscribed schism on the map of Europe and re-established the old Germanic pattern of *Landeskirchen,* "territorial churches," with its formula *Cuius regio, eius religio,* "The religion of the ruler is the religion of the region." The revolts against the papacy served to stir the Roman Church to new life. The Catholic revival, commonly called the "Counter Reformation," took the form of a spontaneous emergence of many new monastic and missionary orders and the genuine reform of the older orders. In the Council of Trent (1545-63) the Roman Church met the theological challenge of the Protestants by carefully defining and systematizing the Catholic faith with special emphasis upon the points in conflict with the reformers. The Canons of this council, together with the Index Expurgatorius and a reorganized Inquisition, gave the Romanists powerful weapons of propaganda, and by the century's end they had won back much of their lost territory and prestige. But they also had the unfortunate effect of imposing a rigid dogmatism upon Catholicism after Trent which is in contrast to the flexibility and viability of the earlier Catholic tradition. Since Trent there has been no basis of *rapprochement* between Protestants and Catholics save on terms of abject surrender to Rome.

In the closing years of the sixteenth and the first half of the seventeenth century a marked change occurs in Protestantism as it seeks to adjust itself to the exciting and disturbing events of those turbulent times. In the place of the blazing confidence and daring of Luther and Calvin in the reinterpretation of received doctrines, we see a new Protestant scholasticism, far less imaginative and intellectually curious than its medieval prototype. Men like Gerhard, Quenstedt, Heidegger, and their fellow "dogmaticians" were primarily concerned to reproduce the pure doctrine of Luther and Calvin. In so doing their theological method was bound by a rigid Biblicism. By and large, Protestant theology went its way almost oblivious or unappreciative of the epochal events which were shaking the philosophic and scientific world through the labors of men like Kepler, Newton, Descartes, Spinoza, and their colleagues, who made this period one of the most creative in philosophy and science since the apogee of Greece. Thus Protestantism, which already had in itself anti-intellectualist tendencies, failed to come to grips with the thoughtful and critical minds of the age and was consequently driven more and more into dogmatic confessionalism. The result was an arrested development which divorced theology and philosophy. Many of the surviving forms of Protestantism, particularly what is called "fundamentalism," bear the marks of this obscurantist scholasticism. The seventeenth century also witnessed an interesting revival of the otherworldly cult of heaven and hell. It is worth noting that the two great prose classics of English nonconformity—Bunyan's *Pilgrim's Progress* and Richard Baxter's *The Saints' Everlasting Rest*—are both variations on the same theme.

But the seventeenth century saw more than Protestant scholasticism and the great renewal of science and philosophy. It suffered the Wars of Religion, the most terrible wars in European history up to that point. After a long, appallingly bitter, and destructive struggle, the nations of Europe came to the peace table at Westphalia (1648), disillusioned and weary of the struggles about religious opinions and hegemony, and proceeded to consecrate a new secularism in the treaty which they signed there. Political alliances and actions will henceforth be determined by national and secular interests rather than religious allegiance. Also, toward the century's close England finally achieved her emancipation from political absolutism in the constitutional monarchy established for William and Mary by the so-called "Glorious Revolution" of 1688.

In England the century brought new life and power to the Protestant dissenters. These included the Congregationalist and the

Baptist groups, which advocated the general sectarian view of the Church and the Christian life described in the preceding section. They were heroic servants of the cause of religious toleration and freedom. In this they were abetted by quite unsectarian liberals like Locke, Spinoza, and Cherbury. But perhaps the most interesting and influential of these nonconforming groups was the Society of Friends, or Quakers. Under the leadership of their founder, George Fox, and their foremost interpreter of doctrine, Robert Barclay, they sought to combine the extreme subjectivity of "the inner Light," the communion of the private self with the indwelling Spirit of God, with an equally firm insistence on corporate fellowship and love, opposing war and oaths and emphasizing democracy and freedom of conscience. They also took over the puritan idea of "earthly calling," and this powerfully influenced the later evolution of Quakerism in the direction of a predominantly middle-class movement. In America, in the eighteenth century and after, the Quakers found a greater opportunity than they ever had in England to exercise their peculiar gifts and virtues. Here, in Pennsylvania and elsewhere, they made significant contributions to social ethics and were among the pioneers in the anti-slavery movement.

The great gain of the seventeenth century was the triumph of the idea of religious liberty; its great loss was the general, though not universal, erosion of vital religion. The eighteenth century is exceedingly difficult to characterize because it is mainly a time of transition and ferment. Near its beginning the Peace of Utrecht (1713), which ended the War of the Spanish Succession, announced to the world that Catholic Spain was no longer a great power and that the center of gravity in European politics had shifted north and west. England was greatly aided in her colonial ambitions, and the Hohenzollerns were established in Prussia. A new era of expansion now lay before the Protestant North. But it is just in this area that, in the main, intellectual leadership is passing from orthodox Christian preachers and theologians to the enlarging ranks of scientists, philosophers, and moralists, whose work and temper give to the period its usual titles, "the Enlightenment" and "the Age of Reason." The bitter struggles about "truth" in the seventeenth century give place to a calmer enquiry about "nature" in the eighteenth. Many thoughtful men, tired of the "rage of the theologians" (*odium theologicum*), are now interested in a natural religion, i.e., religion based on reason and experience, and common-sense morality. This, they think, is all that is worth saving from traditional Christianity; the claims of "revealed truth" are more and more questioned. The extremists in this trend are the "deists," who hold the general view that God operates the world mechanically by natural processes, and who make much of their claim that theirs is "the religion of sensible men." But rationalism likewise becomes the characteristic temper of the whole century among enlightened and progressive men in the camp of the "theists," who believe that God is personal and manifests Himself in His creation and history in acts of purpose and benevolence. Parallel to this rationalism there is also to be noted a growing formalism in religion which was throttling the fervor and freedom which had made the sixteenth century spiritually enfranchising.

For religion this double tendency toward rationalism and formalism led to a dismal state of affairs. Joseph Butler, a contemporary witness, laments that "the deplorable distinction of the age is an avowed scorn of religion in some and a growing disregard to it in the generality." In reaction to all this, men like Butler, Warburton, and Paley urged the double claim that the Christian affirmations are valid not only because they are revealed in the Scriptures but also because they are reasonable and credible. Butler's *Analogy of Religion* is the classic example of this attempt to hold reason and faith (natural and revealed religion) in a balanced synthesis. Its central thesis is typical of this whole type of apologetic:

The general scheme of Christianity, and the principal parts of it, are conformable to the experienced constitution of things, and the whole perfectly credible.

The century also exhibits a powerful upsurge of vital religion in reaction against the pall of formalism and indifference in the established churches. This movement, called "pietism" on the continent, was led by men like Spener, Francke, Swedenborg, and the Moravians. In England a similar movement under the leadership of John and Charles Wesley emerged to produce a great evangelical revival which was an important factor in the religious life and thought of the century and has been a powerful factor in later Protestant history. This new pietism accepted the main lines of the old orthodoxy but went beyond it in its emphasis upon vivid personal feelings of Christian commitment ("conversion"), an ethic of pure and kindly living, and the goal of Christian perfection ("holiness"). This new and confident gospel, especially in the Methodist revival in England, was tremendously powerful and injected a fresh fervor into Protestantism. It also gave impetus to significant philanthropic and humanitarian enterprises—orphanages, hospitals, endowments, etc. One may here see a mingling of the older puritan concern for man's duty in his earthly calling with a new romantic interpretation of Christian discipleship. This was, indeed, the genius of the movement—its wholehearted insistence upon ardent and personal religious experience and equally ardent and personal moral exertion. This emphasis upon religious sentiment and subjectivity, however, tended to weaken or, at least, to qualify the earlier Protestant claim to objective authority. Thus pietism, especially Methodism in England, represents a transitional phase in the development of Protestantism. It does not conform strictly to the types we have noted, yet it is not in itself a new type. In doctrine it looks backward to classical Protestantism and to the *theologia cordis*, "religion of the heart," of medieval Catholicism. In mood and method, however, it looks forward to the liberal Protestantism of the nineteenth and twentieth centuries.

The end of the eighteenth century marks a period in the development of classical Protestantism. Both the spontaneity of the sixteenth century and the scholasticism of the seventeenth century have been subtly transformed by the rationalists and the pietists. Henceforth a new spirit and new concerns will dominate all but the most conservative Protestant minds. Rational apologetics, originally conceived as a shield for Christian faith, now becomes a spearhead for a new interpretation of Christianity itself; the way is open for the historico-critical method with its revolutionary treatment of the Bible and Christian history. The pietist enthusiasm for "religious experience," originally meant to warm and vitalize the established churches, now affords a new, romantic basis for a subjective doctrine of authority and faith which will, in the nineteenth century and beyond, alter the traditional claim of both Protestant and Catholic to objective and infallible authority. Here we have come to something like the twilight of classical Protestantism. It will be followed soon by the dawn of liberal Protestantism.

CLASSICAL PROTESTANTISM: AN EVALUATION

What should be our estimate of classical Protestantism? The Reformation, for all its involvement in its cultural milieu, was an affair of religion. It can hardly be understood, much less appreciated, apart from its own typical ideas and principles. Naturally, a synoptic critique is not likely to seem wholly adequate or satisfactory either to those who know very much or to those who know very little about the fluctuating and turbulent history of Protestantism. What meaning is there to Chillingworth's phrase, "the religion of Protestants"? How ought classical Protestantism to be differentiated from the Catholicism from which it departed and the newer versions of Christianity which later sought to displace it? The light of partial wisdom is shed on this problem if we seek to summarize the basic principles and insights which constantly appear in its literature and life.

The first of these, in emphasis if not importance, is the principle of unmerited and unmediated grace, the doctrine of justification by faith. Over against all sacramentalism and moralism, both of which tend to regularize and generalize religious experience, Protestantism has insisted upon the spontaneity and particularity of man's encounters with God. "The Spirit bloweth where it listeth"; God is neither coerced nor persuaded by priest, rite, or good deed. Yet in Christ He reveals His love to men freely, directly, effectually. Here is the typical Protestant paradox—a bleak pessimism about "fallen human nature" linked with soaring optimism about the simplicity and finality of man's reconciliation to God. Salvation is a pure miracle of grace, which man joyously accepts but in no sense initiates. It is instructive on this point to compare the canons of the sixth session of the Council of Trent (1547) and Calvin's *Institutes*.

A second basic principle of classical Protestantism is that of the priesthood of all believers, with its corollary, the right and duty of private judgment in matters of religious faith. This was the new dignity and liberty of the Christian man which Luther extolled and all the reformers defended. Every man stands before God as prophet to hear His Word, as theologian to interpret its meaning, as priest to celebrate its truth and power. Save for some of the Radicals, the Protestants tried to hedge this individualism about with doctrines of the Church and Christian unity, but these were rarely strong enough to prevent clashes of mind and will in fundamental matters of faith. For all the variety of church organizations in Protestantism, there is in them all a steady refusal to separate clergy from laity save in function. The Protestant cleric is "minister," "preacher," "rector" of a congregation rather than its "priest." Even in the apparently exceptional case of the Anglicans, there is a wide difference between their view and the Roman view of the hierarchy. This puts a direct responsibility on every Christian to wrestle with Scripture and theology, to be able to explain and defend the faith that is in him. It goes without saying that these egalitarian notions led to results quite other than those intended by the reformers themselves. Nevertheless, the priesthood of all believers and the obligation of private judgment conserve the precious root of individuality, so that uncorrupted Protestantism comports ill with all impersonal collectivism and massmindedness.

Still a third basic principle in Protestantism derives from its emphasis upon the direct authority of the Scripture. Protestant theology is theology of the Word of God. All the Reformers found new truth and new life in the Bible and insisted that in it God spoke directly to the devout and seeking heart. The Bible became and remained, at least in classical Protestantism, the standard and almost exclusive source of religious nurture and the decisive norm for all preaching and teaching. It was pored over, lovingly and thoughtfully, by laymen and minister alike, not with historical or speculative interest foremost, but in an earnest personal search for "a word from the Lord." The typical Protestant could repeat with special meaning the familiar phrase, "the Bible speaks to my condition." Thus Holy Scripture became a powerful focus of religious faith and thought and also staple food for the mind of the age. Acquaintance with its stories and characters was taken for granted as the common knowledge of every professing Christian; sacred and profane use was made of the matchless vigor and concreteness of its style and contents. Moreover, it was agreed that the Bible contained a system of pure doctrine, that this system was coherent and comprehensive, and that

whatsoever is not read therein, nor may be proved thereby, is not to be required of any man, that it should be believed as an article of faith, or be thought requisite or necessary to salvation.

The fact that divergent systems were deduced from the Holy Book did not shake this fundamental notion. It was in the Scripture that the Protestants found a new, objective authority to put in place of the broken rod of Rome. If it be banal to repeat the old saw that in place of an infallible Pope the Protestants put an infallible Book, still something of the sort did happen. As one should expect, however, there was very wide variation in the application of this principle of authority, from the Anglicans, who made the Bible co-ordinate with church tradition and reason, to the Mennonites and other sectarians, who adopted a rigid Biblicism and regarded as improper and forbidden everything not specifically allowed in Holy Writ. Then, too, there was latitude in the interpretation of the nature of biblical revelation, ranging from Luther, who found the Word of God *in* the Bible, to Calvin and the Scholastics, who identified the very *words* of the Bible with the Word of God. Men like Gerhard and Quenstedt carried this to the heroic climax of claiming that the Hebrew vowel points of the original were inspired.

Finally, all the Protestants of every stripe and kidney united vigorously in their rejection of the papal monarchy. It is often urged that Protestantism is a negative affair with nothing to distinguish it save its antagonism to Rome. This is patently false if proposed as the whole truth, but there can be no doubt that much of the motive power of Protestantism came from a deep and thoroughgoing distrust of and enmity toward the Pope and all his works. From the beginning the Protestant movement afforded shelter for those whose spirits had been frustrated and oppressed by the decadent late medieval Church; it also received others with less noble grievances. As the movement developed, the Catholic methods of counterattacking the Protestant revolt drove the fear of popery deeper and deeper into the very soul of Protestants, so that even today, after more than a century of mutual toleration, the typical Protestant is still convinced that the chief aims of Rome are political tyranny and religious absolutism. But the Protestant rejection of the papal hierarchy is not mere prejudice. There is in Protestantism a deep distrust of unlimited personal power in the hands of men who cannot be disciplined by those who delegate the power. Its version of human depravity recognizes in power a corrupting thing and infinite power as infinitely corrupting. No man is good enough to wield, as by right, unchecked control over the lives and fortunes of other men. By and large, classical Protestantism despaired of the conciliar dream of constitutional government in the Church, partly because the same objection to personal power can be leveled against group power. Thus it denied that priestly ordination conferred "an indelible character" and sought to rest its polity on the Scripture which, it fondly thought, was beyond the perversions of the human will-to-power. Its error was discovered too late, after the Stuarts and the Bourbons claimed hereditary divine right and offered Bible verses as proof. The republican principle of checks and balances is not a direct product of the Protestant ideology, but it is entirely congruent with and probably an indirect derivative of the Protestant spirit.

We must list now much more briefly some other significant insights and values which are to be found widespread in various sectors of classical Protestantism. The first of these is the recovery of worship "in the common tongue" and the rebirth of preaching. Preaching came to hold the central place in the typical Protestant service of worship. The Bible in the vernacular, together with liturgies and hymns which the people could use themselves, gave great impetus to piety and religious literature. This is in contrast to the Council of Trent which refused to allow the mass to be said in the language of the people. An incidental fruit of the Protestant emphasis upon public and congregational worship was that it gave a great impetus to adult education. A competent economic historian has remarked that

merely by forcing the individual to learn to read, the Protestant Reformation precipitated and infinitely increased the results of printing, and willingly or unwillingly joined the Renaissance in preparing the way for the revolutions of science.

This emphasis upon a literate constituency in Protestantism has had interesting corollaries, not the least of which is a concern for public education in both its elementary and higher branches. This is another example of the striking congeniality between Protestantism and modern democracy, in that both require an informed and intelligent support for their very existence.

Max Weber had the acumen first to emphasize the fact that Protestantism, particularly of the Calvinist variety, so fostered the self-denying virtues of thrift, diligence, honesty, and sobriety that it provided a moral ally, if not a powerful direct cause, of the rising spirit of capitalism. This thesis has provoked lively discussion by both historical novice and virtuoso. The interested reader can glean the grain of it in the books of Tawney, Robertson, and Fanfani. It is true that Protestantism, with its asceticism-in-the-world of which we have spoken, put a premium upon work and acquisition and frowned upon self-indulgence, luxury and waste. In an expanding economic order such an ethic was bound to result in accumulated wealth which could then be used in the acquisition of more wealth. But no form of the Protestant ethic ever allowed wealth as an end for its own sake, and all of the Protestant leaders laid strict injunction that wealth should be used for the glory of God. Typical of this is Wesley's familiar maxim: "Gain all you can, save all you can, give all you can." Gain for gain's sake, with no ethical limits upon the size and method of acquisition of a fortune or its use in society, and ruthless competition in the economic struggle (a rough epitome of the spirit of capitalism) have no more real sanction in the Protestant ethic than in the Catholic. Classical Protestantism has had only slight success in evangelizing the economic order, but its contributions to the modern Midas have been indirect and unintended.

The really creative contribution of Protestantism to social ethics was the revaluation of common life and labor which it sponsored. A wider connotation and moral significance were attached to the older Christian concept of "vocation." The medieval notions of vocation separated the "religious," priest and monk, from the "worldly," artisan and menial, as has been pointed out in the preceding chapter. The Protestants sought to close the gap between the sacred and the secular; men are called to serve God in their earthly callings, and all useful tasks offer equal opportunities for devotion and Christian discipleship. Men and women, working in their daily round with rigor, self-discipline, and concern for the common good, may glorify God as much as ever a monk telling his beads or a priest intoning the mass. Thus something of the spirit of the monastery was transferred to the home and school and mart. We have seen how this asceticism-in-the-world met and matched the needs of the rising capitalistic ethos. But its moral quality and aims were almost wholly different. The ideal of honest and useful work, having meaning and significance apart from its economic value, is certainly not a Protestant monopoly, but it has received direct and powerful sanction from the Protestant view of earthly calling. Protestantism stressed the principles of stewardship and simplicity of life and depended on these, together with its idea of vocation, to serve as leaven in all the secular orders.

Although Luther and Calvin were chary of natural religion (Luther more so than Calvin), many Protestants retained the older Christian concepts of natural law and a rational ethic which could be derived from it. We have already seen this in Hooker and central Anglicanism. Other interesting variations of it occur in Grotius, Pufendorf, and Locke. This interest in the divine and natural law is essentially an attempt to find a broader and more rational base for moral values and political authority than either the literal words of Scripture or private judgment. There is a moral order in the whole of creation, and man's good here below is to seek and conform to this order. Moral values are rooted in a universal order, even if they are always relatively and imperfectly realized by finite and sinful men. They are, moreover, directly congruent with the divine imperative which speaks in the Scripture. Thus the rational ethic may be collated with, though it cannot displace, the ethic of faith and commitment.

Over against this we must add in equal appreciation the contribution of the radical sect-ethic and its ideals of holiness and religious liberty. If the established churches sought to find the circumference of the circle of religious community, the Radicals were intent upon its center. What in the Catholic ethos was a higher level of renunciation and obedience, incumbent only upon the religious, the Protestant Radical insisted was the plain obligation of every worthy member of the Christian fellowship. Concerns of property and prestige, family and life were subordinated by the sect to the treasured end of holiness. Protestantism as a whole has never been able to assimilate the Radicals into church fellowship, but it has always been stirred somewhat by their insistent call to the holy life which the sect-ethic requires. The other great contributions of the sectarians was their share in the struggle for religious liberty in the modern world. These Radicals, contemned and persecuted by Protestant and Catholic alike, needed and pleaded for toleration, asking only to be left in peace in the existing political order. On the continent, save for the Netherlands, they were brutally oppressed and almost exterminated, but in England the long ordeal of the civil war gave the sects an opportunity they were quick to seize. One of the distinctive features of the final pacification of

England after 1688 was practical toleration for all but the most intransigent sects. The cause of liberty was joined, also, by men of enlightenment so that unsaintly philosophers and unphilosophic saints for once agreed. It may be instructive to reflect upon the mixed soil in which we find the taproot of our "four freedoms."

The evil that men do lives after them. The Protestant Reformation was certainly no unmixed blessing either to the ongoing Christian tradition or to the unity of Western society. In any such titanic clash sweet reasonableness and objectivity are not to be looked for. The Romanists were intent on maintaining their sacrosanct and vested interests, and the Protestants were equally intent on the triumph of their sacrosanct ideas and principles. Yet no merely cynical account of the struggle will suffice: there was less cold-blooded malice and blind iconoclasm in the Reformation than passionate and partisan loyalties to partial truths and goods. It is a prime example of the peculiar bitterness which tends to go with religious controversy. The mischief which has followed in its train was largely unintended by the reformers and their antagonists. Yet we must confess our sins, witting and unwitting, without too much extenuation or complacency. To do so is certainly not to repudiate our Protestant heritage or leave the field to the Romanists. The first and gravest item on the debit side is the divided body of Christendom. The Reformation destroyed indefinitely the possibility of anything like a universal Christian Church. Indeed, it has fostered the belief in many of its adherents that this is not a particularly tragic or regrettable fact. But if one believes that one of the undeniable imperatives of the Christian gospel is a universal communion with valid sacraments and continuity, embracing all believers not in the bonds of a rigid orthodoxy but of common faith and mutuality, it is clear that the Reformation was an appalling tragedy, involving sin on both sides of this fierce civil war in the Christian family. What is worse, the sin has been compounded by the post-Reformation developments among both Protestants and Catholics. Today that schism is at a practical impasse.

The second kind of mischief which can be laid at the door of Protestantism is its internal divisiveness. The whole tendency of the Reformation spirit, with its insistence upon the sovereign right of private judgment, is atomistic and centrifugal, as the dismal record of the divisions and internecine strife among Protestants has proved. The old Church had lain about the people almost like the order of nature and had exercised something of the same sort of integral authority for them. When that authority was broken, the new freedom had no rational integration. The astonishing number of denominations under the general banner of Protestantism bears witness to the tenuousness of its bonds of unity. And the Protestant dichotomy between the visible and invisible Church made it easy to minimize the actual defects in the Church visible by appealing to the ideal perfections of the Church invisible. Only of late have there been impressive stirrings of contrition among Protestants; the contemporary ecumenical movement has tremendous significance and promise. But its like can hardly be found in the three centuries of classical Protestantism.

We have already spoken of the Protestant scholasticism which had the effect of turning the great spiritual intuitions of the reformers into fixed ideas of doctrine (*loci communes theologici*). Religious life was led captive to abstractly conceived doctrine; faith was understood more as assent to truth than trust in a living personal Redeemer. Moreover, this scholasticism was theology without any conscious philosophical undergirding and went its way in almost complete indifference to the intellectual revolution taking place around it. Save for Anglicanism, Protestantism had an anti-intellectualist bias from the beginning; in the hands of the dogmaticians this fideism comes to the verge of obscurantism. Protestantism at its best is always an expression of that deep personal religion of the spirit which cherishes God's private dealings with His children, which denies what Milton called "blank virtue," and which claims liberty for the minds and consciences of men of good will. But Protestantism at its worst has often relied merely upon a new kind of orthodoxy and infallibility and has thus been only the drab and tragic exchange of new shackles for old.

Both Renaissance and Reformation tugged at the foundations of the older, static, intellectualistic views of truth. Both proclaimed the freedom of the human mind. But it is one thing to release a force and another thing to guide it. In this, Protestantism proved recreant or impotent. In the centuries when the modern mind, with its devotion to and dependence upon science, was being molded, Protestantism not only failed to leaven the spirit of science with the spirit of high religion but was often actually antagonistic to science and philosophy. At last, when the triumph of modern learning left it no alternative, a new version of Protestantism sought an alliance with science and philosophy, but it had to do so largely on sufferance. The medieval order is reversed; philosophical theology becomes philosophy of religion, suspicious or contemptuous of theology. Liberal Christian thought often accepts the metaphysical assumptions of naturalism without perceiving the full enmity between it and the *philosophia perennis* of Plato, Aristotle, Plotinus, Augustine, and Thomas, which had been "the old loving nurse" of Christian theology since the second century.

The Revival and Future of Classical Protestantism

The end of the eighteenth century marks the end of the dominance of the general form of religion we have been calling "classical Protestantism." It has now become "the old order." A new cultural transformation, produced by the Industrial Revolution, modern science, and technology, arises to force upon Western civilization radical reorientations of thought and faith. Neither the rational apologetics nor the pietism of the eighteenth century offered an adequate basis for the newer stresses of the human mind and spirit, however valuable service they may have rendered in their heyday. The way is now open for Kant and Schleiermacher and a new kind of Protestantism.

For all this, the Protestantism which we have surveyed is no museum piece. In form it has continued mainly as a conservative, sometimes reactionary, tradition, still powerful in almost every major Protestant denomination and rampant among contemporary Protestant "fundamentalists." In spirit, however, it survives in varying nuance throughout many of the liberal schools of religious thought and is now experiencing a forceful revival under the impetus of the so-called "neo-orthodox" theologians, notably Karl Barth, Emil Brunner, and Reinhold Niebuhr. This spirit is difficult to characterize. The Reformation was a revolution toward and on behalf of personal religion. The Protestant spirit lays unwearied stress on the crucial fact of human individuality and the spontaneity of man's direct, personal faith in response to his decisive encounters with the divine. It focuses its faith and hope in Jesus Christ, God's gracious Word to man, man's indispensable clue to God. The Protestant man's faith in God leads him to do the works of love and mercy among his fellows. God's rule or Kingdom creates a redeemed community which is the bearer of the gospel. The Protestant Church is nourished by its reverence for the Scriptures and the

preaching of the Word. The Protestant ethos is centered in the obligation to respond to this Word of God by sober and useful work in all
the callings of the common life. Here, and properly, faith and works do
unite in a religious elevation of the daily round, the common task.

For all its shortcomings classical Protestantism has still a destiny.
Before the rising tide of totalitarianism it will continue to thrust up the
bulwark of human individuality. Before the pervasive threat of secularism it will continue to cling to its sense of the divine judgment of
the Holy God and the prophetic criticism of all the orders of human
life. Against all man-centered schemes for self-redemption it will continue to proclaim the sovereignty of God. Our proof of all this is
magnificently apparent in the titanic struggle now gripping the whole
of Europe against Nazi racism, statism, and moral relativism. In Britain
there is a forceful resurgence of Reformation emphases. In Germany,
Norway, Holland, and France it is the surviving remnants of classical
Protestantism which are exhibiting the most heroic fortitude and
vitality in the face of persecution and tyranny. It is clear, therefore,
that in the amalgam of the postwar world the older forms of Protestantism will be compounded. Yet it is doubtful if they have the capacity
in their traditional forms to produce a religious culture in the modern
world. It may be that we stand upon the threshold of a new emergence
in the endless inventiveness of the ongoing Christian life. It would be
heartening to be able to believe that a new ecumenical synthesis is
possible which will bring forth things both old and new for the building
of the Church. In any case, we are only philistine if we ignore or deny
the immense debt all modern men, both those who profess and call
themselves Christian and those who do not, still owe to the Reformation and its children.

6

The Nineteenth Century and Today

IT IS OFTEN THE HABIT OF YOUTH, CERTAINLY IN OUR TIME, TO DISPARAGE their parentage and idealize their remoter ancestry. Distance tends to lift great figures and events above their commonplace surroundings and to enfold them in a roseate aura which magnifies their proportions and disguises their limitations. We hark back to the "Founding Fathers" and long for the "Great Ages" of the past.

In a movement so deeply steeped in history as Christianity, this inveterate human tendency is at its strongest. Christians habitually glory in the achievements of the first centuries, the magnificence of medieval Christendom, the triumphs of the age of Reformation, and judge the Church of today and yesterday a poor thing by comparison. For half a century and more, an assumption has been so widespread within intellectual circles as to be almost axiomatic. It is the assumption that Christianity both as a faith and as a force in the world stands in extremity, struggling for some time past in desperate and losing defense against a dominant world-view opposed to it and battling now against the disintegrating effects of a catastrophic world-convulsion.

An assumption so generally held cannot be without a measure of justification. Nevertheless, dispassionate appraisal of the facts does not sustain it. From the point of view of practical vitality—energy for geographic extension and power for transformation of culture— the period which lies immediately behind our own and of which we are heirs must be put down as the "Great Century"[1] in the history of Christianity. For the first time, emissaries of the Christian message carried it to the ends of the earth, penetrating every continent and touching almost every people. Heralds of that message made bold to

[1] The phrase is Professor K. S. Latourette's and is becoming current through its employment in his monumental *History of the Expansion of Christianity*. Any account of the Christian movement in the nineteenth century must lean heavily upon his researches.

149

stake its claim over every aspect of human life, corporate no less than individual. From the point of view of intellectual vigor, the bolder schools of Christian thought drank deep of the intoxicating elixirs of their age—the historical and scientific movements, enthusiasm for social reform, confidence in progress. They rediscovered neglected treasures within the Christian tradition, rephrased its essential tenets in the new universe of discourse, and furnished the Church with an apologetic adequate to sustain its prodigious labors of expansion and permeation.

THE CHRISTIAN MOVEMENT IN THE NINETEENTH CENTURY

The visitor from Mars who had chanced upon this planet at the dawn of the nineteenth century would hardly have entertained good hopes for the future of Christianity. For more than a century, in both faith and life the Christian Church had suffered deepening strain, sterility, and loss. In area after area to which Christian missionaries had ventured in the preceding era of vitality and expansion, their frail young churches sickened and died. In Latin America, the scene of most notable recent extension, adventurers who had sought to subdue a continent under the joint aegis of sword and cross had dissipated their strength through lust and greed and had brought corruption and disrepute upon the missions allied with their conquests. The waning vitality of the ruling nations, Spain and Portugal, infected the Roman Catholic churches which were their spiritual counterparts. Australia, New Zealand, and much of Oceania as yet knew nothing of Western culture and religion. In Japan, Christianity had been driven wholly underground. In China and Korea persecution harassed the weak Christian communities. Here and there, along the littoral of Africa, in India and Ceylon, at a few centers in Malaya and Indo-China, on certain islands of the Pacific, Christian outstations could be discovered. Only rarely, as in the Philippines, had the Church succeeded in winning any considerable proportion of the native populace. Moreover, the Christian outstations were prevailingly spiritual adjuncts to the outposts of European political or economic imperialism. Christianity was still quite definitely a European faith, whose fate as a world religion appeared linked to the future of European conquest. At the same time, its continuance even as the faith of Europeans seemed gravely insecure.

Throughout Europe, the only continent where Christianity had succeeded in establishing itself as the dominant religion, the Church was speedily losing its hold upon the common people; its claim to the convinced allegiance of the educated and worldly-wise appeared already gone. In England and Germany rationalism, the regnant intellectual vogue, had effected an uneasy liaison with Christian faith to yield a thin and sterile deism. In Roman Catholic lands such as France rationalism was frankly agnostic or atheistic. Romanticism, the other great enthusiasm of the age, summoned its devotees to a new religion of nature, of feeling, of the spirit, but was hardly less disdainful of the Christian tradition. Voltaire, Rousseau, Diderot; Hobbes, Hume, Bentham; Spinoza; Herder, Goethe, Kant—these were the great prophets of the mind. None of them acknowledged more than lip-service to the traditional faith. Meantime, the ardor of the masses centered in secular revolutionary movements which, prophetic of the great revolutionary leader of the nineteenth century, dismissed religion as an opiate of the people. This was patently true of the French Revolution, hardly less of Napoleon and those who rallied to his cause.

Moreover, the forces which had undermined Christianity's influence over great thinkers and popular leaders were having their corrosive effect upon leadership within the churches. The result was sterility and even corruption in their worship and practice. John Buchan thus describes the state of religion in Scotland toward the end of the eighteenth century:

Nor was there any compensating vigour of life in that church which had once been the chief voice of Scotland. . . . The dominant party, the Moderates, made religion a thing of social decency and private virtues, and their sober, if shallow, creed was undoubtedly a stabilizing factor in a difficult time. . . . The High-flyers, the other party, were equally void of inspiration, and disputed chiefly on questions of church government. . . . The ministers satirized by Burns in his "Holy Fair" were representative types, but little overdrawn, of the then church in Scotland—a church from which most that was vital in the national life was deeply estranged.[2]

The English parallels were even more disquieting:

A sodden coarseness characterized what called itself the best society. . . . At the opposite social extreme was the great mass of ignorant, restless, half-brutalized population. . . . Drunkenness was almost universal. . . . Every sixth house in London was a gin shop. . . . After nightfall, London was at

[2] John Buchan, *Sir Walter Scott*, p. 15.

the mercy of footpads and desperadoes. . . . The laws were savage but
ineffectual. . . . The prisons were sinks of filth, stench, and disease. . . .
The test of excellence in religion as well as in politics, art, literature, was
reason, moderation, good sense. . . . It is said that the two texts on which
most sermons were preached were "Let your moderation be known to all
men," and "Be not righteous overmuch." [3]

Nor were these conditions confined to Christianity in Europe.
Many Americans of today entertain a false impression of the influence
of Christianity upon the birth and childhood of the new nation. True,
this continent had been settled largely by men and women of profound religious faith. But over large areas the initial impulse had run
down. The livest minds had fallen captive to new modes of thought
flowing freely across the Atlantic, especially from France. The period
of the Revolution and the Constitution was not notable as an age of
faith. Meantime, beyond the scattered white settlements fringing
the Atlantic seaboard stretched a vast Indian population virtually
untouched, and in their midst dwelt a rapidly propagating Negro
race still largely heathen.

Such were the condition and prospect of Christianity at the close
of the Napoleonic Wars. These facts could hardly have failed to paint
the main outlines of the picture for the man from Mars. It is by no
means so sure that his attention would have been caught by certain
other features well-nigh hidden beneath the prevailing currents of
proud intellectualism, of romantic confidence in man and his future,
of revolutionary utopianism, of religious indifference and unbelief.
He might have traversed the length of Germany and heard no mention of a numerically small and culturally inconspicuous sect known
as Moravians. To be sure, in England, John Wesley had stirred to
revival thousands among the underprivileged but few among the
molders of thought or leaders of public life. As for other isolated events
—the launching of a number of missionary bodies in England, the
founding of the Netherlands Missionary Society in Holland, a gather-
ing of five zealous American undergraduates beneath a haystack at
Williamstown—few knew of these; fewer still would have estimated
them as more than inconsequential gestures against the rising tides
of secularism. Yet, in fact, these modest and unnoted beginnings
were to wield a larger determination upon the fate of Christianity

[3] C. T. Winchester, *The Life of John Wesley*, pp. 71-79.

in the nineteenth century and beyond than the speculations of sceptical scholars or the swirling currents of revolution.

At the outbreak of the next great international conflict a century later, Christianity had become the professed faith of the Western Hemisphere. In the Pacific basin the continents of Australia and New Zealand and certain of the lesser islands harbored predominantly Christian populations. In Africa, Christian influence had worked inland from the seacoasts to establish many sizable and vigorous churches among the native tribes. Indeed, at least some beginnings of the Church were to be found in every country on the face of the earth save Afghanistan and Tibet to which alone Christian representatives were still forbidden entrance. Perhaps most noteworthy of all, among the most advanced peoples of Asia, those most deeply rooted in Oriental culture—India, China, Japan—the Christian movement, though counting in its membership an insignificant minority of the populations, was now flourishing under the ever more vigorous leadership of native Christians whose influence upon national thought and life was out of all proportion to their numbers. Christianity was generally recognized as a factor of first importance for the physical, intellectual, social, and spiritual progress of these lands. Thus had emerged the promise of a Christian faith and a Christian community truly representative of all humanity.

These are the most obvious surface facts concerning the expansion of Christianity in the nineteenth century. By any reasonable test which might be proposed, it was an epoch of great vitality and notable advance.

To recount signs of vigor and growth within the Christian movement itself, however, is to note hardly half the story. This was also a period of Christianity's wide influence upon the culture of which it formed a part. The nineteenth century was pre-eminently the century of social advance. It was marked by the greatest succession of crusades for the amelioration of man's life which history records. Beginning with agitation for the ending of the slave trade early in the century, the consciences of men, especially in English-speaking lands, were claimed for one cause after another of human betterment. Prison reform, abolition of chattel slavery, improved factory conditions, the founding of the Red Cross, elimination of child labor, emancipation for women, universal education, temperance, recognition of organized labor, public health, care of the insane and the infirm, social services, agitation for world peace—these are only the more notable instances in the long list. It cannot be said that Christianity alone was responsible for most of them. But it must be said that men and women driven by Christian faith to heroic and often sacrificial exertion in their behalf were vital factors in each. In all but one, the rise of organized labor, Christian leadership appears to have had a determinative influence. John Howard, Florence Nightingale, the Earl of Shaftesbury, David Livingstone, Wilberforce, William Lloyd Garrison, Wendell Phillips, Lincoln, Keir Hardie and the founders of the British Labor Movement, Washington Gladden, Walter Rauschenbusch—the roll of Christian social pioneers might be lengthened indefinitely.

How are we to account for this unforeseen and epochal expansion and penetration by Christianity? The answer is to be found in the marriage of certain forces born of the times with other factors which sprang from the heart of Christian faith itself.

It was an age when the Western world was marked by the loosing of titanic and seemingly inexhaustible energies. These energies poured through varied channels and in many directions. They set some men to plumbing the mysteries of nature; hence the scientific movement with its immense fruitage both theoretical and practical. Others found their minds drawn toward a new disclosure and interpretation of mankind's past; hence the historical movement which altered the perspective of the world of learning. Similar incentives moved others along more practical lines. Some employed the findings of the new science in creating a new technology. Still others pressed out in political and economic enterprise to bring the resources and peoples of the earth into the service of the technical civilization of the West. Above all, the spirit of the times—its discoveries and inventions, its conquests and achievements—bred an immense confidence in the powers of man, that is, of Western man, and an assured assumption of his "manifest destiny."

Christians were children of that age. Inevitably they bore its most characteristic imprints upon them. But they also brought a distinctive contribution of their own from their faith to the creative efforts of the time. Christianity is intrinsically universalistic. From its first decades it had always looked out toward all mankind and through the centuries had followed when it had not preceded explorers and adventurers. Moreover, the vision and energies which Christianity seemed to share with secular enterprises derived less from the spirit of the times than from its own creative genius. When alive, it is forever giving birth to new movements and impelling men to new adventures of the spirit and new crusades for human emancipation. More particularly, the principal secret of Christianity's record of accomplishment in the recent past is to be sought in a series of spiritual renewals and their aftermaths—the pietistic movement of the early eighteenth century, the Wesleyan revival toward its close, the missionary impulses which made bold in the first years of the nineteenth century to launch new and daring programs for the evangelization of the world at the very hour of Christianity's threatened eclipse, and, finally, near its end another spiritual resurgence inspired by those two extraordinary colleagues, Dwight L. Moody and Henry Drummond. Here, always, are the true source-springs of Christianity on the march.

In what follows, we shall be concerned with Christian thought and its interrelations with the intellectual trends of the time. But our account will lose perspective wholly unless it keeps constantly in view developments of the Christian movement in its reaction to and impact upon civilization in the century. To another of these developments we shall return briefly at the close of the chapter in order to indicate the state of the Church in our own time.

The Legacy of Kantian Dualism

In broad generalization, the sixteenth century was a period of religious revival and reformation, the seventeenth of theological and ecclesiastical consolidation and controversy, the eighteenth of theological disintegration and religious sterility, the nineteenth of spiritual revitalization and theological reconstruction.

Professor Walter Horton has suggested that, within this epoch of four centuries, intellectual leadership oscillated, pendulum-fashion, between Continental Europe and the English-speaking world. The great creative currents at the dawn of the modern era arose principally within Switzerland, Holland, and Germany and flowed thence to England and then on to the new continent of the West. But with the congealing of the new inspiration into dogmatism, religious vitality slackened, and scholasticism hardened and sterilized the Continental mind. Many of the new impulses of the late seventeenth and eighteenth centuries originated in Britain, in the scientific discoveries of Newton and Boyle, the daring, if disintegrative, speculations of Hobbes and Hume, the prodigious vitalities of the evangelical movement. With the dawn of the nineteenth century, the pendulum swung sharply again; philosophical and theological leadership returned to Germany and remained there until our own day. Throughout the period of which we are immediate heirs, British and American thought followed, like an enamored and dutiful disciple, in the train of the brilliant, if somewhat erratic, Teutonic mind.[4]

On the threshold of this new epoch stands by common acknowledgment the most formative intellect of the modern period. It is a truism that any discussion of nineteenth-century thought, whether philosophical or theological, must make its start from Immanuel Kant. Completing his work just as the century was dawning, he bequeathed the issues, and the terms for their discussion, which have largely dominated intellectual controversy since his time.

By heritage and early environment Kant was a child of German Pietism. Pietism was the atmosphere in which his impressionable early years were passed; he never wholly escaped from its imprint. It bred in him, by way of reaction, a deep-rooted distrust of emotion in religion. But also, as positive legacy, it left a profound ethical consciousness and an ineradicable sense for personal character. Pietism was the soil of all that was deepest, least consciously rational in Kant's thought—the primacy of moral issues, the categorical claims of conscience, the reality of human freedom. Intellectually, however, Kant has been rightly identified as "a rationalist by education, temperament and conviction." He set forth on his intellectual pilgrimage in allegiance to the premises of rationalism; and though an important result of his work was to emphasize the limits of human knowledge, he remained at heart a rationalist.

The effect of Kant's rationalism upon his religious thinking and especially upon his attitude towards Christianity will be dealt with later in the chapter on Christianity and Modern Philosophy. But there

[4] Cf. Walter Marshall Horton, *Contemporary English Theology*, Introduction.

is one aspect of his theory of knowledge which has had such a profound influence upon the theological thinkers of the nineteenth century that it must be at least indicated here. It is his insistence that no knowledge of ultimate reality, of "things in themselves," can be attained by reason, that knowledge is confined to "phenomena" or appearances. Therefore, we may postulate the existence of God, as a demand of the moral life, but this is a matter of practical rather than theoretical certainty. Thus, as Kant himself put it, he "destroyed reason in order to make room for faith."

This dualism of reality and appearance and of faith and reason suffered serious reformulation in the nineteenth century and led to consequences Kant would almost certainly have deplored. The distinction was defined no longer as a distinction of appearances and reality, but as one of facts and values. Facts, it was held, are the exclusive domain of science, while values are left to philosophy and religion. To Kant the distinction had been between the realm of phenomena of which we have scientific knowledge and the realm of reality of which we may have at least practical certainty. But under the influence of a more thoroughgoing skepticism, thinkers of the nineteenth century contrasted the world of facts of which science gives us our only genuine knowledge and the realm of values which is conceded no validity beyond men's subjective appreciations and feelings. As a result, there developed a tragic conflict between reason and feeling, head and heart, which had incalculable consequences for religious thinking.

This dualism of fact and value, appearance and reality is fundamentally unsound. We know nothing of facts divorced from values or values unrelated to facts, of mere appearances or pure reality. The foremost English-speaking interpreter of Kant has put it thus:

Existences and values do not constitute independent orders. They interpenetrate and neither can be adequately dealt with apart from considerations appropriate to the other.[5]

A somewhat similar statement could be made about reality and its appearances: reality reveals itself in its appearances, and every appearance is a revelation of reality. The net result of Kant's unfortunate dualism was twofold: the skeptical assumption that ultimate reality is

[5] Norman Kemp Smith, *A Commentary to Kant's Critique of Pure Reason*, p. lxi.

forever unknowable, and the conviction that it is to science alone that men are to look for dependable knowledge. In both respects, Kant's influence pioneered the way for the positivism and moral relativism of the modern mind. This was the destructive side of his thinking; the more constructive side, growing out of his emphasis upon the demands of morality, had an equally unfortunate effect upon his interpretation of Christianity, as will be shown in Chapter 9.

As we pass from Kant to the nineteenth-century theologians, it will throw light upon our task if we remember the three faculties in the human mind posited by traditional psychology—intellect, will, and emotion, characterized respectively by thought, volition, and feeling. Whatever our judgment upon this faculty psychology, it is a fact of history that, in their thinking about religion, men tend to follow one of three alternative courses as thought, volition, or feeling predominates. Some, of a reflective cast of mind, hunger for understanding; they turn to religion to query what light it can cast upon the mysteries of human existence; if satisfied in their quest, they discover in religion ultimate wisdom; their approach is primarily speculative. Others, of practical bent and active spirit, seek moral direction and empowerment; they ask not so much what they may believe as how they should live and what they should do; religion wins them through a commanding claim upon their devotion; their response is mainly ethical. Still others yearn for an experience of deliverance from evil which shall unite their souls with the Divine in intimate communion; they desire the assurance of salvation; religion validates itself to their feelings; their interest is mystical or redemptive. In the history of Christianity these three types are clearly distinguished in every age from the early Church to our own day. In any period they furnish one of the most revealing bases of classification of Christian thinkers and one of the deepest causes of division and misunderstanding among Christians in general. By chance, the three most formative theologians of the nineteenth century, each of whom inherited the legacy of Kant but sought to vindicate Christian faith afresh against the prevailing scepticism, brought to their task contrasted temperaments and discovered the root of religion respectively in feeling, in thought, and in will. To glance quickly at Schleiermacher, Hegel, and Ritschl is to sense the main currents of the century in Christian thought.

Schleiermacher and the Theology of Experience

The title of Father of Modern Theology belongs, by universal consent, to Friedrich Schleiermacher. "It was not a school that he founded but an epoch."

E. C. Moore is correct in saying of him, "Of no theologian is it more true that we must understand his background, his temperament, and his experience if we are to understand his theology." Among the forces which formed his life, three merit mention:

1. *The intense Moravian piety of his home.* The parallel to Kant is striking. There is food for reflection in the fact that pietism was the nurturing seed-plot of the minds of the two most influential thinkers in post-Reformation Christianity. The thought of each may be interpreted in terms of reaction from and return to this original pattern. Kant came to distrust its emotion; Schleiermacher, its obscurantism. Kant bore throughout his whole life the impress of its ethical rigor and simple devotion; Schleiermacher, of its deep feeling and religious inwardness.

2. *Romanticism.* Kant found escape from the limitations of pietism in the austerity of rationalism. Schleiermacher, a half-century later, sought refuge from the arid and sterile rationalism of the time in lyrical and subjective romanticism. The opening paragraph of his *Soliloquies* is a classic expression of the romantic mood:

No choicer gift can any man give to another than his spirit's intimate converse with itself. For this affords the highest boon there is, a clear and undistorted insight into a free being. . . . Come, take the gift, ye who can understand my spirit's thought! May my feelings here intoned be an accompaniment to the melody within yourselves, and may the shock which passes through you at the contact of my spirit, become a quickening impulse in your life.

3. *The teaching of Spinoza,* his pantheism, and his vivid sense of the inwardness of religious experience.

Our impression of Schleiermacher would be altogether one-sided, however, if we thought of him only as philosopher and theologian. His interests and activities extended into a dozen fields. His published writings fill twenty-five volumes. Throughout his career he was a preacher of rare brilliance and eloquence. He was an ardent and energetic churchman. His political influence was very considerable. He never surrendered his early artistic interests and associations. Yet to visualize all these public activities is still to see but half the man. His greatest inspiration and his richest happiness were found in deep and intimate friendships.

Everything I do, I like to do in the company of others. Even while engaged in meditation, in contemplation, or in the assimilation of anything new, I need the presence of some loved one, so that the inner event may immediately be communicated, and I may forthwith make my account with the world through the sweet and easy mediation of friendship.[6]

This remained true of his nature, as sensitive as it was powerful, as responsive as it was versatile, all his life through.

It is a signal misfortune that, until a decade ago, Schleiermacher was known to the English-reading public almost entirely through his earliest work, the *Discourses on Religion Addressed to Its Cultured Despisers*. Written contemporaneously with the *Soliloquies*, it reveals the youthful theologian at the height of his romantic infatuation. Directed to his romanticist intimates in the hope of weaning them from their disdain toward religion, the core of the argument is that thorough pursuit of the romantic passion for fullness and variety of feeling should not make one hostile to religion but conduct one within its portals. And what is religion, the completion of the romantic pilgrimage? "True religion is sense and taste for the Infinite. . . . The religious life is found when the whole soul is dissolved in the immediate feeling of the Infinite and the Eternal." God is often referred to in pantheistic terms as "the world," "the universe," "the world and the spirit," "the One and the Whole," "the spirit of the universe." Christianity does not claim to be the only true religion; it is the highest example of the universal religious impulse. Religion is wholly a matter of individual experience; the Church is irrelevant. If the Father of Modern Theology were to be judged by this youthful outpouring, the violence of contemporary polemic against him would have much warrant.

As a matter of fact, Schleiermacher should be studied almost altogether through his great work, *The Christian Faith*, published some twenty years later when his powers were at their highest. Here theology is defined as a discipline the sole purpose of which is to serve the Christian Church. And the Church is central for Christian experi-

[6] *Op. cit.*, p. 37.

ence as well as for Christian thought; strictly, Christian experience is impossible save in and through the Church.

The secret of Schleiermacher's originality and of his revolutionary influence upon Christian thought is his insistence upon making the witness of Christian experience determinative for both the content and the structure of theology. All rests upon the definition of religion and then of Christianity. As in the *Discourses*, religion is defined in the first instance in terms of feeling; but it has now become "the feeling of absolute dependence upon God." This experience of absolute dependence, which is "an essential element of human nature," leads inevitably through need for fellowship to association with people of like experience, and so to the religious community, the church, and the specific religion. Thus we are brought to the definition of Christianity:

Christianity is a monotheistic faith, belonging to the teleological [i.e. active, ethical] type of religion, and is essentially distinguished from other such faiths by the fact that in it everything is related to the redemption accomplished by Jesus of Nazareth.

These preliminary definitions determine the course which the argument must pursue, so different from that of traditional Christian systems. Since religion at its heart is an experience of dependence, and since the distinctive Christian experience is one of redemption through Christ, the materials for theology are furnished by the inner consciousness of the redeemed person; the task of theology is simply the discovery and disclosure of the inner rationale of that consciousness. The great body of *The Christian Faith* is neither more nor less than an exhaustive inquiry into the inmost processes of individual Christian life-transformation and the drawing therefrom of implications regarding God and the world. At first glance, it seems more like a treatise in psychology than in theology. And so, in a sense, it is. Rather, it is a psychological study from which are developed theological corollaries. All of the great themes of faith find treatment. The original feature is that they are discussed incidentally, as it were, and always in relation to the central Christian experience.

What, then, is the experience of redemption which is determinative for Christian faith? It is that process through which a human consciousness, in which the power of sin is dominant and the awareness of God is dormant, is transformed into a consciousness in free and full communion with God. In this changed consciousness the lower impulses, while still present, are passive, and God-consciousness reigns. This substitution in our souls of the rule of the God-consciousness for the present domination of the sensuous consciousness can on no account be achieved by ourselves, but only by divine grace. It is accomplished through communication to us of a God-consciousness we do not possess by one in whom that God-consciousness is already perfect. Such a one is Christ. Thus is the unique redemption which distinguishes Christianity from all other religions effected through Jesus of Nazareth.

The inadequacies of Schleiermacher's thought furnish subject matter for some of the most bitter polemic in present-day Christian discussion. But a man must be judged not alone by his grasp of the full range of Christian faith but also by his sense of the distinctive needs of his own day and his capacity to meet them. Here Schleiermacher stands among the greatest. And there is abundant testimony that he saved many contemporaries from unbelief and despair. Moreover, in at least four respects, he impelled modern theology in new directions and framed premises which will force their challenge upon all serious theological inquiry in this and subsequent generations:

1. His insistence that experience precedes theory and must therefore dictate the limits within which theology should work: the basis of the "theology of religious experience."

2. His conception of theology as the servant of the Church and the handmaid of preaching.

3. His identification of Christianity as the "religion of redemption through Jesus of Nazareth."

4. His interpretation of the fashion in which Christ effects redemption—the source of modern "Christo-centric theology."

The Intellectualism of Hegel

To name Hegel is to call up the thought of a highly speculative and a priori schema of thesis, antithesis, and synthesis into which every datum and phase of reality was artificially forced. Such a basic impression is not wholly incorrect. But we miss Hegel's significance and the extraordinary hold of his thought upon men's imaginations unless we appreciate that this schema arose in the first instance from an unusually acute examination of human consciousness. With all the contrast between him and Schleiermacher, they were akin in one fundamental particular: each developed his theology from a profound analysis of the deeper self-consciousness. In this respect both were prophets of the modern period.

Careful reflection reveals, Hegel pointed out, that at every moment I am more than I appear to be; the self-of-the-moment is organic with its own past and also with its future. Moreover, it is intimately involved with the existence of others, ultimately with all men living and dead and yet to be. Despite this organic unity of experience, however, self-consciousness is inherently plagued by contradiction which can be resolved only by acknowledging the opposites and then reconciling them in a higher synthesis. This in turn yields a fresh contradiction leading to a still more ultimate synthesis, and so on. This process of dialectic is "the logic of passion," the very nature of consciousness by which it advances toward self-realization through a sequence of three successive moments—thesis, antithesis, synthesis.

Turning the same acute powers of analysis and synthesis to the history of the race, Hegel discovers the same triadic process of immanental development to characterize every aspect and movement of human culture. In art the dialectic works itself out from the subjectivity of Oriental art through the objectivity of Greek art to the fulfillment of both in Christian art. In the evolution of political forms the extreme authoritarianism of the Middle Ages gives place, by way of reaction, to the lawlessness of the Enlightenment, and then the climactic synthesis is achieved in the true liberty of the contemporary Prussian state.

This law of development which pervades and dominates all reality finds its highest expression, however, in the history of religious ideas and institutions. Oriental religion, centering all upon the Infinite, finds its antithesis in Greek religion, equally one-sided in stressing the finite, while the synthesis comes to realization in the absolute religion of the God-man, of the Incarnation, the Infinite in the form of the finite—Christianity. In the evolution of the Christian movement itself, Greek Catholicism with its excessive mysticism and subjectivism stands over against Roman Catholicism with its equally extreme insistence upon the objective authority of law and Church, while the union of opposites in true balance is achieved in Protestant-

ism. A similar development in the history of philosophy finds fulfillment in the Hegelian metaphysic. The sum of the whole matter is
that the dialectic of history has been struggling through the ages to
issue in those viewpoints which were central to Hegel's own loyalties
—the contemporary Prussian state, German liberal Protestantism,
Absolute Idealism. It has been suggested facetiously that Hegel
might have paraphrased the Pauline dictum, "The whole creation
groaneth and travaileth in pain together until now, waiting for the
appearance of"—Georg Wilhelm Friedrich Hegel and his philosophy!

It is obvious whither such an analysis of all empirical phenomena—
art, politics, philosophy, religion—points. Just as the logic of passion
within individual consciousness is discovered to furnish a key to the
comprehension of the movement of history, so the inner rationale of
all historical development is discerned to be more than a law of
progress; history is the process of the self-expression, the self-realization of the immanent Infinite Spirit. History is the coming to consciousness of the Absolute, God. As one writer has put it, "The story
of man is the history of God's becoming." Indeed, in his more rigorously logical and self-consistent passages, Hegel does not hesitate to
declare that the Absolute knows Himself only through and within
human consciousness of Him.

God is God only in so far as He knows Himself; His self-knowledge is
His self-consciousness in man, is the knowledge man has of God, which
advances to man's self-knowledge in God.[7]

Thus in Hegel's philosophy religion takes a central position. More
than that, this self-fulfillment of the Absolute which is the very being
of history finds consummation in that religion which is the perfect
synthesis of all imperfect theses and antitheses, Christianity. Christianity alone achieves the true union of subjective and objective, of
Infinite and finite, of spiritual and material, of freedom and law, of
mysticism and order. A supreme expression of this fulfillment is the
central symbol of Christian faith—the God-man, the Christ. But it
requires little perspicacity to guess which of the great Christian concepts would hold strongest fascination for Hegel and confirm him in
his predisposition to acknowledge Christianity as the perfect, the
final religion. It is the idea of the Trinity. What is the historic dogma

[7] *Encyclopädie*, No. 565.

of the Trinity but the inspired intuition of that immanental process which is the very secret of reality? God the Father is pure abstract Idea; God the Son is the eternal going forth of the Idea as Infinite into finite being; God the Holy Spirit is the return of the Idea enriched through self-manifestation in incarnation. Thus it was Hegel's avowed intent to vindicate Christianity, indeed, to establish it beyond challenge as true and absolute.

The appeal of this philosophy in its massive symmetry, its all-embracing comprehensiveness, its confident dogmatism, requires no explanation. To the speculatively inclined its seeming logical coherence and its intellectual assurance offered almost irresistible attraction. To devout believers the centrality it claimed for religion and the final authority it appeared to secure for Christianity made winning appeal. But perhaps its strongest hold was upon those who felt their minds slipping toward insecurity and unbelief. At a time of corroding relativism and scepticism, this was a *Weltanschauung* which, in the name of reason, promised to vindicate the main body of Christian faith.

The inadequacies of Hegel's rendering of Christianity need not delay us. Apart from its highly abstract and speculative structure, its forced reading of history soon discredited by a more sober scholarship, its dubious rebaptizing of great historic beliefs in the interests of a philosophical system, one feature alone must arouse Christian misgiving—the importance attributed to the idea of the Christ as a symbol, the complete unconcern with the reality of the historical Jesus. For Christianity is interpreted as a phase of a world process rather than as a specific historic religion, the child and fulfiller of Judaism. The reality of Christianity is found in its symbolic embodiment of philosophical principles rather than in concrete deeds in human history through which the living Creator God makes known His will for man's redemption.

RITSCHL: TRADITIONALIST AND MODERN

Schleiermacher and Hegel had this in common: both were distinctively "moderns," grateful heirs of humanism. Here Ritschl took stand against them both. In intention, at least, he was a traditionalist. "Back to the New Testament by way of the Reformation"—this was the motto that guided him steadily. Against every allurement of speculation Ritschl affirmed that theology should have no traffic with metaphysics: "in dogmatics, one should take up nothing that cannot be used in preaching and in the intercourse of Christians with one another." Against the subjectivism of mysticism, moreover, he insisted that Christian theology be anchored in the historical and the concrete, the person of Jesus Christ.

Despite this resolve to cleave to New Testament faith as reclaimed by the reformers and to eschew speculative philosophy, in two vital respects Ritschl speaks the language of the contemporary theology and thus shows himself its imperfectly emancipated child. The first of these is his insistence upon prefacing theology with epistemology. Indeed, his entire theology rests upon a particular theory of knowledge. Over against the Platonists who separate reality from appearances, disdain the latter, and encourage man to attempt access to reality via reason and the mystic path, and over against the Kantians who likewise divide reality from appearances but deny that man can by any route attain unto reality, Ritschl followed Lotze in affirming that we may know reality through its appearances in phenomena. This view supplies the foundation for Ritschl's famous theory that theological affirmations are "judgments of value" based on faith, and upon that theory he seeks to erect his doctrine of God. "We know God only in His effects upon us. . . . We know the nature of God and Christ only in their worth for us." We know God to be Christlike because of the sovereign impression of Deity made upon us by the disclosure of Him in Jesus. On the other hand, we affirm the deity of Christ because he attests his identity with God to our souls by accomplishing for us the work which God alone can achieve. Beyond these affirmations concerning either God or Christ, Ritschl held it unnecessary and undevout to penetrate.

The second aspect of the influence of contemporary thought upon Ritschl is to be found in his conception of the nature of religion. Religion arises, said Ritschl, through vivid agony of inner tension as man knows himself at once a part of nature and yet, through his spirit, above nature.

In every religion what is sought, with the help of the supernatural power reverenced by man, is a solution of the contradiction in which man finds himself as both a part of nature and a spiritual personality claiming to dominate nature.

But consideration of Christianity brings Ritschl onto less philosophical and more solidly Christian ground. Christianity is the absolutely ethical religion based on the person and work of Christ, founder of the Kingdom of God. Here the two interests which dominated Ritschl's attention are linked—the religious interest in personal redemption through Christ and the moral and social interest in the Kingdom of God, "the organization of humanity through action inspired by love." These two he spoke of as two foci about which Christianity revolves as an ellipse.

On the side of redemption, Christ's great gifts to men are two, Justification and Reconciliation,[8] which are found to be virtually identical. Both are mediated through the Church not as a divinely authorized institution but as the *communio sanctorum*, the body of true believers. When thus redeemed through Christ, the Christian enjoys dominion over the world, "the freedom of the Christian man." Christ's supreme ethical significance, however, lies in his vocation as "the historical Founder of Christianity." This vocation was accomplished through the complete moral and religious identity of his "self-end" with God's purpose, the Kingdom of God. The kinship of Christ with his Father is one of ethical purpose.

Even so cursory a sketch of the main outlines of Ritschl's thought must convey an impression of some inconsistency and ambiguity. These followed inevitably from the position of the writer, with one foot, so to say, in traditional Christian theology and the other in the outlook of his own day. In making his starting-point in epistemology and in defining religion he follows the pattern in vogue in contemporary theology; on the other hand, in his reading of Christianity, he cleaves to historic faith. Even in his treatment of Christianity, however, ambiguity persists. In his religious doctrine of redemption Ritschl is a loyal child of the Reformation. In his doctrine of the Kingdom of God he breaks genuinely new ground; here he is prophetic of some of the most original and powerful developments of the next half-century, e.g., the social gospel. Ritschl conceived these two emphases as two foci of an ellipse, but he himself never brought them into organic connection with each other. The ellipse is strained. To press the figure, it tends to break asunder and move as a circle with one or the other focus as a center.

[8] Significantly, this is the title of Ritschl's greatest work.

Nevertheless, Ritschl's contribution to subsequent thought was profound and powerful. His insistence upon the fundamentally ethical character of Christian devotion delivered those who heeded from rationalistic or mystical aberrations. His emphasis upon the Kingdom of God furnished the theological premise for the social interpretation of Christianity. Most important of all, his unyielding insistence upon Jesus Christ as heart and norm of all that is vital in Christian faith brought that faith back to its true center and gave the generation to follow a principle of limitless fecundity. Most of what has been fruitful and dynamic in the life of the Church since his time sprang directly from that recovery. We see this clearly as we turn to "liberal theology," the most powerful theological movement of the past half-century. Its principal base, as the pendulum swung once more, was in the Anglo-Saxon world.

LIBERAL THEOLOGY

"Liberal theology" is a cloak whose ample folds have been stretched to cover a variety of viewpoints not always obviously akin. This is implicit in the genius of the movement; to fail of a generous hospitality would be betrayal of the designation "liberal." It is also inevitable in a movement developing during the transition from a dying age to one not yet fully born.

Two distinctions may aid us in understanding liberal theology. The first is the distinction between those employing the term "liberal theology" to denote a temper or spirit, an outlook of open-minded receptivity toward suggestions of truth from whatever source, old or new, and those employing it to designate a more or less determinate theological position. Thus Dr. Coffin says:

By "liberalism" is meant that spirit which reveres truth supremely, and therefore craves freedom to ascertain, to discuss, to publish, and to pursue that which is believed to be true, and seeks fellowship in its discovery.

Such use of the phrase may suggest an attitude but hardly identify a theology; the liberal attitude may grace adherents of almost any theological school. Therefore, the term "liberal theology" should more properly be reserved for a definable theological position.

A second distinction is based upon the fact that, in the modern period, almost all "liberal" theologians have confronted a common

problem, the interpretation of Christianity in the face of new knowledge and new philosophies, but that their response to this common
problem might follow either of two lines. One might take up a
position resolutely within historic Christian faith and experience,
and, from that stance, attempt adjustment to the new and bewilder-
ing modern world. Another might surrender the familiar standing-
ground, launch forth fearlessly upon the new currents, make himself at home within them, and, discovering a position there, reclaim
as much as possible of the old faith. The term "liberal theology" may
more properly be reserved for the former of these alternative courses,
while the latter is the essence of "modernism" and should be so
designated.

With all its variety in detail, it is clear that what is thus properly
called "liberal theology" was determined mainly by two factors. In part,
it was a movement of adjustment, of reorientation, and of accommodation to a new thought-world which was rapidly winning dominance
over men's minds. But, like every other religious development of more
than transient significance, liberalism was also a movement of
advance. It sprang from a vivid and dynamic rediscovery of Christian
experience. Any account of liberal theology badly misses the mark if
it does not stress the religious developments of the time which
paralleled trends of thought and furnished spiritual undergirding for
them. For, as we have seen, energies were being released which carried
the practical enterprises of the Church to far corners of the earth and
into neglected areas of the common life.

Liberal theology, then, was the child of the late-nineteenth-century
intellectual outlook and of the evangelical experience. These two
sources determined its distinguishing characteristics. To the first it
owed its intellectual perspective and certain fundamental presuppositions. We may mention six:

1. *Devotion to truth.* How great a release this basic principle, fidelity
to truth rather than to tradition, brought to eager young minds of
the late nineteenth and early twentieth centuries is difficult for a
generation which has never known any other intellectual climate to
appreciate.

2. *Respect for science and the scientific method.* In the new and
freer quest for truth, it was felt, men had not been left without an
authoritative teacher.

The liberal Christian believes in a thoroughgoing and confident use of scientific method of determining what is fact. . . . For the scientific method is to him one in heart with the Christian method and spirit, the very method and spirit of Jesus Christ.[9]

3. *Tentativeness, if not agnosticism, as to the possibility of metaphysical certainty.* Partly, this was a reflection of the avowed tentativeness of science. More largely, however, it was a direct heritage from Kant and Ritschl. Finding ready alliance with one of the most marked features of the evangelical spirit which we shall note in a moment, it bred indifference to natural theology, disdain of metaphysics, and reliance upon the witness of religious experience as the sole and all-sufficient guide to spiritual truth.

4. *Emphasis upon the principle of continuity.* This was, and is, the major positive principle of the liberal mind.

Running through the whole theology of liberalism there has been the assumption of continuity in the world—continuity between revelation and natural religion, between Christianity and other religions, between the saved and the lost, between Christ and other men, between man and God.[10]

This principle of continuity had received new impetus from the concept of evolution. It found theological expression in the idea of immanence which has been called "the most characteristic theological doctrine of the nineteenth century." It tended to melt the traditional antithesis of natural and supernatural into a rather vague monism. It furnished ground for men's confidence in progress. It bred a new and more sympathetic tolerance toward other religions and toward no religion. It encouraged men to depend upon their own highest experience for the clearest light on the divine nature. It opened the way for a new interpretation of Christ's divinity through his humanity, thus restoring the incarnation to central importance.

5. *Confidence in man and his future.* Above all, liberalism fostered a lofty estimate of man and his potentialities for achievement, both spiritual and material, and high expectancy of the realization of a Christian society in the not too distant future. Indeed, the genius of liberalism may be identified with its confidence in man's God-given capacities to discern truth, in his responsiveness to the highest, in

[9] William Pierson Merrill, *Liberal Christianity*, p. 16.
[10] J. C. Bennett, "After Liberalism, What?" *Christian Century*, Nov. 8, 1933.

the possibility of attaining through "sweet reasonableness" and consecrated effort a loftier fulfillment of individual life and social order.
6. *The liberal spirit.* This inventory of the indebtedness of liberalism would be incomplete without mention of that attitude of dispassionate tolerance, of open-minded receptivity, of modesty in personal profession, of preference for understatement rather than excessive claim, of respect for human personality, of loyalty to justice and honor, which characterizes true liberalism everywhere and always and is one of its most precious gifts to the life of religion.

From its other parent, evangelicalism, liberal theology also drew a rich inheritance which was at least fourfold:
1. *The authority of Christian experience.* When Christians could no longer rest upon familiar orthodoxy for the certitude which living faith requires, the more scholarly might look to the new teacher, science. For the great mass of ordinary folk, this was quite impracticable. Happily there was available to them the needed assurance in a far more accessible and far surer source—in the witness of their own personal religious life. The Romantic movement had prepared the way by centering attention upon inner experiences, as in Schleiermacher. The spirit of the time was subjective and individualistic. For Christians the crumbling of external bulwarks—Scripture, Church, dogma—deepened the mood of uncertainty, of introspection. Now there swept through their ranks a vivid and all-compelling discovery of the presence of God, "the living Christ," within their own spirits. Why trouble about formal and external validation when so intimate and undeniable a certainty ruled their very souls?

Along this nearer and surer pathway liberal theologians followed. It was reiterated in every characteristic confession of the liberal position:

Criticism may assail the historical facts of revelation; rationalism may urge objections to its doctrines; but the surf on our Maine coast might as easily overthrow the granite cliffs against which it breaks as criticism and rationalism disturb the Christian realities which stand firm in the experience of the individual believer and the Church.[11]

Are the doctrines which form the subject matter of theology dogmas to be received on authority, irrespective of their contents; or are they living convictions, born of experience, and maintaining themselves in spite of all

[11] Lewis F. Stearns, *Present Day Theology*, pp. 533 ff.

opposition because of the response which they wake in the hearts and consciences of men?[12]

Religion is the reality of which theology is the study. . . . Theology thus deals only with the realities which make up religion, and with them only as they enter into religion.[13]

This position had been pioneered by Schleiermacher, but it had been most fully worked out by Ritschl who rested the whole weight of Christian faith upon the experience of reconciliation through Christ. And Ritschl was the principal mentor of liberal theologians.

2. *The centrality of Jesus Christ.* At the heart of the experience which furnished both source and norm for liberal theology was the person of Christ. For some, this central place was occupied by the figure of the historical Jesus, made vividly living and contemporary by the studies of biblical scholars and by popular portraits based upon their researches. For others, it was the living Christ, known as a friendly Presence within one's own soul, which was central. For many, the two —the Jesus of history and the Christ of faith—were merged as a single "fact of religious experience." In any case, liberal theology was through and through Christo-centric.

Here, again, illustration might be drawn from the whole range of liberal theological literature.

We are coming more distinctly to recognize the central place of the living Christ in our theological thought. . . . It is Christ himself, in all his living, saving power, upon whom our thought is concentrated, whom we strive to hold up to men, and in whom we find the key to all the problems of religious thought.

. . . We are trying to 'Christologize' our doctrine of God, to set him forth as He is seen in the face of Jesus Christ. . . . So we are learning to Christologize the doctrines of the eternal plan, of creation, and of providence.[14]

In the words of Dr. William Adams Brown, "the new school raises the old cry, 'Back to Christ.' Let no theology call itself Christian which has not its center and source in Him." To the question, "What is the Christian religion?" Harnack, the most brilliant of Ritschl's disciples,

[12] William Adams Brown, *Christ the Vitalizing Principle of Theology,* his inaugural address as Professor of Systematic Theology in Union Theological Seminary, 1898. See pp. 19-20.

[13] William Newton Clarke, *An Outline of Christian Theology,* 1898. See pp. 1, 2, the opening sentences of the first comprehensive and systematic exposition of the "new theology."

[14] Stearns, *op. cit.*

replied: "The answer seems to be simple and at the same time exhaustive: Jesus Christ and his gospel."[15] It was the objective facts of the life and work of the historic Jesus which were to safeguard "the theology of experience" from unchecked subjectivism. Dr. Merrill again voiced the central affirmation of fellow-liberals:

Whatever else may be doubtful about the religion and theology of the liberal Christian, this is sure, that it loses and finds itself wholly in Christ. . . . The Liberal would move, live, and have his whole being in Christ.[16]

And Browning, who served the poetic devotion of liberals somewhat as Ritschl served their minds, could cry:

> I say, the acknowledgement of God in Christ
> Accepted by thy reason, solves for thee
> All questions in the earth and out of it.

3. *Loyalty to the historic faith.* In striking contrast to modernism, liberal evangelicalism was determined to remain fully within the stream of historic Christian development. "The substance of our theology is to be found now, as always, in the great unchanging facts and truths of Christianity accepted in every age of the church."[17] At first, loyalty was secured by use of the principle of growth so congenial to the thought of the time; the new theology was the "fuller flowering" of what had been implicit in traditional beliefs. Later, recourse was had to the principle of "reinterpretation"; modern theology is mainly a translation of the truths of the ancient faith into language familiar and understandable to the present age. Finally, liberalism came more and more to rely upon a distinction given wide currency by Dr. Fosdick—the recognition of "abiding experiences in changing categories."[18] Thus identity with the historic faith was maintained through the "principle of continuity"; and the locus of continuity was discovered in the depths of "religious experience."

4. *Social Idealism.* Liberalism deepened men's insight into the realities of their own corporate life. It quickened their consciences to a thousand social needs and injustices and opportunities which had largely escaped the attention of a more rigid orthodoxy. Above all, it fired them with an unquenchable assurance of what the spirit of

---

[15] Adolph Harnack, *What is Christianity?* 1900, p. 10.
[16] W. P. Merrill, *op. cit.*, p. 48.
[17] Stearns, *op. cit.*, p. 553.
[18] Harry Emerson Fosdick, *The Modern Use of the Bible*, chap. iv.

Christ, through them, might accomplish—here and now, immediately, in this generation, and in every aspect of mankind's life. The result was that, in the short space of half a century, there came forth from it the most remarkable series of movements for the improvement of human life in all history. It expressed itself first as compassion for the underprivileged in great cities, in industrial communities, and in rural and neglected areas. Then it insisted upon the responsibility of Christianity to determine the structure of society as well as the lives of individuals. And, lastly, it deepened conviction of sin over the divisions among Christians and conviction of responsibility to effect a reunion of the Body of Christ.

Whatever the future, this much is sure. The liberal movement in its positive outreach—fidelity to the outlook and faith of the historic Jesus, a vision of mankind's life brought wholly under the ideal of his ethic, reasoned but hopeful expectation of men's response to Christ's faith in them, self-giving compassion for all men everywhere—represents something new in Christian history. In the perspective of later ages it will take its place—with Paul's discovery of the indwelling Christ, with Augustine's comprehension of grace, with Francis' glorification of the whole creation, with Luther's recovery of the freedom of the Christian man, with Tauler's and Fox's awakening to the "inner light"—as one of the great creative advances in the development of Christian thought.

THE REACTION AGAINST LIBERALISM: NEO-ORTHODOXY AND CHRISTIAN REALISM

Clearly, recoil from liberalism is the most important feature of the present situation. It has touched the thinking of every contemporary theologian and is forcing re-examination of the premises and tenets of Christian theology.

We who stand within the shadow of this reaction lack perspective to appraise fairly the justice of its indictment or the validity of the position from which it is recoiling. We can, however, report the alleged inadequacies of liberal theology.

The main burden of the current criticism is a simple one. Recent Christian theology, it is said, has been deeply enmeshed within the dominant secular outlook of its day, sharing its presuppositions, glorying in its utopian anticipations. That outlook is now definitely discredited. Criticism has proven its premises invalid. The passage of events has branded its expectations as absurd. It must be discarded. The prevailing theology, its child, must likewise suffer drastic reconstruction, if not abandonment.

More specific weaknesses are discovered at major points in the liberal position. Christian experience provides no clear and adequate norm for theology; it is too subjective and too individualistic; and, in a day when fewer and fewer people can be assumed to be possessors of such an experience, an appeal to it has little meaning. Hardly less useful as a center of certainty is the appeal to the historical Jesus; advancing biblical studies are changing the lineaments of that figure with baffling and disconcerting rapidity. Nor is liberalism's favorite device to preserve continuity with historic Christianity—the recognition of "abiding experiences in changing categories"—more than a temporary resting-place for a harassed and retreating apologetic. Theological categories should represent objective realities rather than subjective experiences; it is the existence of these realities rather than the worth of religious experiences which is at stake in the modern world. In brief, man's faith requires evidence of the reality of God far more secure and comprehensive than can be furnished by religious experience, his own or that of others.

The deeper dissatisfaction with liberalism, however, has sprung directly out of the public events of today. It concerns those features of the liberal faith which underlie its conception of man and society—its high estimate of man's nature, its confidence in his response to reason and ideals, its utopian proposal to create a "warless world" and a "Christian social order." These assumptions, it is held, are naïve, self-deceived and, in some measure, insincere. And they are without warrant in profounder Christian insight.

The liberal culture of modernity is defective in both religious profundity and political sagacity. . . . It understands neither the heights to which life may rise nor the depths to which it may sink. . . . It is quite unable to give guidance and direction to a confused generation which faces the disintegration of a social system and the task of building a new one.[19]

The reaction from liberalism is revealed also in the positive positions which are offered in its place. These may be divided into two

[19] Reinhold Niebuhr, *Reflections on the End of an Era*, pp. 14, lx. See also, and more fully, his *The Nature and Destiny of Man*.

main types. One may be defined as a movement of "return and recovery"—return to one of the great historic Christian theologies of the past and recovery by this means of authentic Christian faith. Among Continental Neo-Orthodox theologians, the return is directed to the thought of the reformers; Karl Barth, Emil Brunner, and their colleagues and disciples are the principal spokesmen. Paradoxically, this school might take as their own, Ritschl's battle cry—"Back to the New Testament by way of the reformers"; but the result of their retraversing of this well-worn path is a discovery antipodal to Ritschl's in its main features. Others, both Catholics and Protestants, would reach far back behind the Reformation and take their stand with one or another of the great Catholic theologians—Augustine (Reinhold Niebuhr) or Aquinas (Etienne Gilson, Jacques Maritain, and the Neo-Scholastics generally). Even traditional Eastern Orthodox thought is experiencing revival through the persuasive interpretation of it by Nicolas Berdyaev. Still others, less metaphysically inclined, have recourse directly to the New Testament. For all these, the theology of Paul, usually read through one of his classic interpreters, looms with new power.

The alternative school of reaction cannot be so readily defined. Like all developments of thought which have not yet fully found themselves, its meaning is best discovered in the phrases to which it instinctively has recourse. Two are especially prominent in its vocabulary—"realistic theology" and "catholic Christianity." The first expresses the desire to be more realistic both in its certainty of God and in its understanding of man and his society.[20] It acknowledges the indubitable reality, majesty, and priority of the living God. It confesses the inherent willfulness of man and the necessity for drastic dealing with the results both in individual lives and in the body politic. This explains the oft repeated saying that it is moving "politically to the left and theologically to the right."

The second phrase expresses desire for a catholic Christianity, the catholicism neither of the Roman nor of the Eastern tradition but of a more comprehensive and inclusive authority. That is to say, it feels impelled to seek firm grounding, not in the thought-forms of modern culture nor even of the Reformation or the Middle Ages, but in the

[20] Note a number of the essays in *Liberal Theology: An Appraisal*, especially those by John C. Bennett and David E. Roberts.

rich, deep stream of tested certainty which has flowed through the heart of the Church during all the Christian centuries. It wishes to find a place within that truly catholic tradition and to drink deep of its wisdom and its faith. To that end the Church takes a position of centrality, for theology and for personal piety. Thus it makes contact with a parallel tendency of great power in contemporary practical Christianity—the rediscovery of the meaning of the Church.

The Church Yesterday and Today

That the year 1914 dates the end of a period, perhaps an epoch, in human history few would question, though we lack perspective to appraise its permanent significance. It also marks the conclusion of a period in the history of Christianity which we have called the "Great Century." Thirty years of war, respite, regirding, and renewal of war announce a decisive transition in mankind's affairs. Bold indeed would be he who, in the midst of the maelstrom, ventured to forecast its outcome. We can merely record the present situation.

Throughout the three decades since 1914, Christians as always have shared the fate of their civilization, caught in its sequence of catastrophic events, swayed by its kaleidoscopic alternations of mood—bewilderment, humiliation, hope, assurance, apprehension, horror, deepening self-distrust, and desperation. So, likewise, have their churches, save those few small sects which rigorously eschew entanglement with the world. And yet, while involved in the common fate, the Christian Church has in great measure stood apart from and over against the ruling tendencies of the time.

Those whose memories can reclaim the outlook of men as the last war drew toward conclusion will recall its main features. All gloried in a "war to end all wars." Statesmen promised universal disarmament, proclaimed the liberation and self-determination of all peoples. The confident prospect was of a new world society organized into a global league of free peoples. All through the fevered respite between world wars, while the nations vacillated between one and another ineffectual expedient to forestall recurrence of strife, the leadership of the Christian churches of the world (excepting always the Church of Rome) drew closer and closer together in a sequence of important conferences, to hew out common understandings and project united organizations which even the fragmentations of war might not shatter. "Let the Church be the Church" was a watchword proclaimed by the Oxford Conference in 1937 and re-echoed from end to end of Christendom. As a result, when conflict again broke, the churches faced it more nearly one in mind, in mutual trust, and in united provisions to outride its hurricanes than has been true of the Christian movement since the Protestant Reformation.

Today, men of the world again look toward war's end and its aftermath. But with expectations how sharply contrasted with the confident hopes of twenty-five years ago! Today their sober talk is of "World War III" and the meager chances of escaping it. Statesmen project "seven-ocean navies" and a world held in leash by massed military might. They assume the dominance of the great powers. Plans call, not for a league of free peoples, but for a continuing alliance of victor nations—a pattern for peace discredited by the whole weight of the centuries' experience. Over mankind still lowers the darkness of foreboding or desperation. By contrast, Christian leaders today confront the ominous future with sober confidence not only that the Church of Christ will endure through whatever trials the future may threaten but that it may bring to that future greater gifts of wisdom, of reconciliation, of unity than Christianity has been able to offer in any earlier epoch of transition.

This confidence springs, in part, from the record of the Christian churches under war's testings and temptations. That record is not unmixed. But its main outlines have impressed those, within the churches and beyond, who have studied it with some care, perhaps especially those previously most sceptical of the vitality of contemporary Christianity. From that record, two facts stand forth:

1. *The Christian Church has proven the one indomitable champion of human rights.* This is mainly, though not solely, the achievement of churches on the Continent. In country after country—Germany, Czechoslovakia, Norway, Holland, Belgium, France, Jugoslavia, Greece—as one after another of the institutions pledged to maintain and defend liberty, justice, and humanity has crumbled or capitulated, the Church has held firm until today it stands, the only unintimidated voice of truth, the only unshattered protector of the oppressed and persecuted to which all men can turn for guidance in their confusion and for succor and support in their sufferings. The Quisling press of Norway renders its reluctant tribute: "The Christian front is the

most difficult to conquer." Niemöller and Faulhaber; von Galen and Wurm; Berggrav; Kraemer and the Archbishop of Utrecht; Cardinal van Roey; Boegner and Philip; the Metropolitan of Athens—these and dozens more who cannot be named have emerged as spokesmen and leaders of whole peoples. Representative of them all is the Primate of Norway, Bishop Eyvind Berggrav, who today, from solitary confinement, probably wields a larger influence over the populace of an entire nation than any other living man. A Norwegian who escaped a Nazi prison-camp which the Bishop had visited regularly prior to his own incarceration thus describes him:

The Bishop's influence went right through the prison. He almost transformed these men by his influence. He fortified them with something deeper and greater than pride, scorn and hate. . . . He made us realize that in our helpless state our spirit was our only shield and sword. And yet we never heard from him one word of hate, scorn, or reproof of the Germans. . . . No wonder the Church of Norway and the people look up to him and follow his leadership. His spirit is so great that it will lead Norway to victory whatever the Nazis do to him.

The specific issues where human values are most gravely imperiled and where, therefore, the Church has taken its firmest stand vary from land to land. In Norway the major issue has been freedom for school and Church to teach and speak truth. But in Holland it has been the defense of a community almost wholly outside the bounds of the Church, the Jews. In France it has been the menace of moral and spiritual contagion from a corrupt and servile political leadership, and the imposition of anti-Semitic measures upon a reluctant population. In Czechoslovakia it has been the slaughter of innocent patriots; in Serbia, suppression of the Church and murder of its leaders; in Greece, the execution of guiltless hostages. In Germany the offenses against which Christian leadership has not merely uttered its protest but has also taken effective action would require a catalogue—the practice of euthanasia, persecution of Jews, perversion of youth, terrorism by secret police, abrogation of justice, deportations, forced labor, and many more. But the bravest and most significant items of action cannot be recorded until the day of deliverance from the Nazi curse which these German churchmen despise and against which many work secretly, at daily peril of their lives.

Two features of the record of Christian churches under subjugation merit special note. It is a record of Protestants, Catholics, and Orthodox alike; indeed, one of its most remarkable by-products has been unprecedented co-operation of Christian groups heretofore estranged, notably, joint action by Catholics and Protestants in Holland, France, and Germany. Perhaps more noteworthy still, it is a record of churches prevailingly of traditional outlook, steeped in conservative views of the Church's proper relation to government and society, churches which had been widely regarded as comatose, reactionary, perhaps dying. The whole story is well summarized by a young Hollander of world-wide distinction:

The Dutch Reformed Church had become a Church without spiritual leadership and without a voice. . . . It was pastor-centered, largely receptive, often theologically divided and very bourgeois. Traditions of individualism and self-satisfaction have reigned for hundreds of years. As a result, its influence in the country was decreasing. . . .

There is once more a Church in Holland. . . . What most of us in our unbelief had considered impossible has happened. God has sent His breath on the dry bones and we have once more a Mother Church which gives us guidance and consolation, and which holds up our hands in the struggle which is not against flesh and blood, but against the rulers of the darkness of this world. . . .

The barrier between the Church and the people has become transparent. Not only the churchgoer but many who had shown little interest in the Church listen intently and ask, 'What does the Church say?' . . . The Church continues to speak. Indeed its witness has become clearer and richer. . . . Nowhere except in the Church can one hear clear language concerning the present situation. Many who had come to think of the Church as an antiquated institution suddenly find it a central factor in the great national struggle and begin to wonder why the Church stands when so many other bodies fall.

There is a query on the lips of reflective people all over the continent of Europe: "Why does the Church stand when so many other bodies fall?" It has been put in affirmative fashion by Dr. Albert Einstein in words now frequently cited. All his life a deeply religious man but with little use for the institutions of religion, he describes the advent of national socialism in Germany:

Being a lover of freedom, when the revolution came to Germany, I looked to the universities to defend it, knowing that they had always boasted of their devotion to the cause of truth; but no, the universities were immediately silenced. Then I looked to the great editors of the newspapers whose flaming editorials in days gone by had proclaimed their love of freedom, but they, like the universities, were silenced in a few short weeks. Then I looked to the individual writers who as literary guides of Germany had written much and often concerning the place of freedom in modern life; but they too were mute. Only the churches stood squarely across the path of Hitler's campaign for suppressing truth. I never had any special interest in the Church before but now I feel a great affection and admiration because the Church alone has had courage and persistence to stand for intellectual truth and moral freedom. I am forced thus to confess that what I once despised I now praise unreservedly.

2. *The Christian Church has proven the one invincible, indestructible world community.* "Ecumenical Christianity"[21] today is the outcome of nearly a hundred years of yearning, of advance, retreat, advance resumed, and, finally, of steadily growing achievement. Most of this development has taken place among the leaders of the various churches. Much of it has been known only to them. The strength and durability of the unity achieved have been uncertain even to them until it was tried in the fires of the present war.

All through the latter half of the nineteenth century, Christians of different lands and traditions were reaching out toward closer acquaintance and fellowship. These approaches were along many different lines. Some of them involved Christian bodies within nations; others were world-wide in scope. Movements of Christian youth— Y. M. C. A., Y. W. C. A., Student Christian Movement—became linked in world alliances or federations. Christian organizations concerned with particular interests such as religious education, foreign missions, world peace, temperance, held periodic world conventions which authorized continuing committees or councils. By far the most significant of these gatherings was the Edinburgh Missionary Conference of 1910 which brought together over a thousand delegates from every area of the world.

The period following the first World War witnessed a marked acceleration in every type of Christian co-operation and unification. In the decade from 1927 to 1936, fifty-three definite approaches toward Church union were undertaken, fifteen of which resulted in full and final mergers, and these occurred in all parts of the world (seven among the younger Christian churches of mission lands) and involved most of the stronger communions of Protestantism and Eastern Orthodoxy. More notable still, the years since 1936 when the

---

[21] In what follows, "ecumenical Christianity," "the world Church," etc., are terms which embrace virtually all major Christian bodies excepting always the Church of Rome, whose studied aloofness forbids official acknowledgment of, let alone, co-operation with, any other body claiming the name of Christ.

world has been progressively breaking asunder record nearly fifty further advances toward Church unity and at least eight new instances of consummated unification.

Progress in world-wide co-operation was also expressed in a series of great ecumenical conferences—Stockholm (1925), Lausanne (1927), Jerusalem (1928), Oxford and Edinburgh (1937), Madras (1938), Amsterdam (1939). The last two were the most widely representative assemblages of men and women which had ever met in conference under any auspices. There was no sponsorship other than the Christian Church under which they could possibly have come together: at Madras, in the midst of the far eastern conflict, were delegates from every country of the Orient except Korea; to Amsterdam came youth from seventy one countries, while armies were already girding throughout Europe for world conflict. Even more significant, because of more permanent character, were the birth and growth of two new world-Christian organizations conceived on bolder lines than ever before attempted, the Universal Christian Council for Life and Work and the World Conference on Faith and Order. On the very eve of World War II was launched a World Council of Churches which should, when fully constituted, gather up into unity most of the earlier essays toward Christian co-operation and should be empowered within defined limits to speak and act for virtually all non-Roman Christendom. Thus, in the words of a declaration by the Madras Conference of 1938, "the decade since last we met has witnessed the progressive rending of the fabric of humanity; it has witnessed an increasing unification of the Body of Christ."

The present conflict has put ecumenical Christianity to the supreme test. What verdict do the facts return?

Step by step, progress in the uniting of Church bodies presses quietly forward: the two most recent consummations of organic union are reported from Italy and Japan. The World Council of Churches, projected when war already threatened, progressively takes form and reality. Month by month, as the storm darkened and spread and then finally broke, one after another church voted adherence. Today its membership totals more than eighty churches from thirty nations; the two latest additions are from Hungary and Ireland. At Geneva, where most of the world-Christian bodies have their principal headquarters, their leaders are welded in ever more intimate and effective collaboration so that today their organizations function as a single ecumenical Christian movement. From their base there, they are unitedly carrying on, in behalf of all the churches, not only the normal activities of world Christianity, but also many emergency war-time ministries, in behalf of prisoners of war, of refugees, of evacuees, of Jews, of youth. Through the two great neutral oases of Sweden and Switzerland, continuous communication is maintained between Christians of all lands and on both sides of the struggle, with the exception of Japan. Through the several ecumenical war relief funds of the churches, such as World Student Relief, "Orphaned Missions," and War Prisoners Aid, financial contributions flow steadily from Christian groups on every continent into central treasuries and thence are distributed to the distressed and destitute of whatever nation, race, or creed. Finally, much united labor of Christian leaders throughout the world is being devoted to thinking and planning for the future peace. The opinion of Christian leaders as it takes shape in one country is made available, often by secret channels, to colleagues under the iron silence of enemy censorship. Thus is taking place the supremely difficult, yet supremely important, crystallization of common Christian conviction upon the issues of postwar order.

As one resurveys this record in its entirety, three observations may be made in conclusion:

1. It is a record of churches, not of individual Christians, and of individuals only as they speak and act as churchmen. Only a great corporate reality can struggle effectively against demonic corporate might. Only a great corporate reality can stand securely amidst the disintegration of war and revolution. Only a great corporate reality can count significantly in an age of global problems and mass movements.

2. It is a record of Christians and their churches, living, acting, and standing steadfast always in the consciousness of a world community. French Protestants, groping in despondency and uncertainty, are inspired by communications from Christian groups throughout the world to frame their own manifesto of Christian principles which shall command them. They buttress their protest against their government's maltreatment of Jews by direct appeal to the conscience of the world Church. The Catholic bishops of Holland, drafting their indictment of the Nazi regime, find their text in a declaration of the

conference of German bishops. Japanese Christians hold firm to ecumenical Christian vision through awareness of the prayers and faith of fellow-Christians beyond the seas.

3. Finally, it is a record of a world community brought into being as a direct result of the Christian world mission. Here are some words of the Archbishop of Canterbury:

> As though in preparation for such a time as this, God has been building up a Christian fellowship which now extends into almost every nation, and binds citizens of them all together in true unity and mutual love. No human agency has planned this. It is the result of the great missionary enterprise of the last hundred and fifty years. Neither the missionaries nor those who sent them out were aiming at the creation of a world-wide fellowship, interpenetrating the nations, bridging the gulfs between them, and supplying promise of a check to their rivalries. . . . Almost incidentally, the great world-fellowship has arisen from that enterprise. But it has arisen; it is the great new fact of our time. . . . Here is one great ground of hope for the coming days—this world-wide Christian fellowship, this ecumenical movement.

In the light of the record we have sketched—a record of expansion, of reinterpretation, of unification, of heroic devotion to the cause of Christ—who can deny the vitality of the Christian tradition and the Christian Church yesterday and today? Who can doubt that they hold the seeds of promise for tomorrow?

7

The Devotional Literature of Christianity

IN THE DAYS BEFORE THE PRESENT MILITARY STRUGGLE WAS UPON US, there were many disputes in the faculties and state boards of trustees in the land-grant colleges as to the status of military training which originally had been instituted there by agreement with the federal government when the land-grants in aid of the colleges had been turned over to them. The issue under discussion in these prewar years was usually: Is the college under any obligation to see that every male student who attends the college really gets this military preparation, or has the college fulfilled its duty to the government if it formally offers military training? This second interpretation was usually made by those who either disbelieved in military training or who at least were not seriously concerned at the prospect of having it left out in the equipment of their graduates for life. In the breaking down of elaborate arguments of both sides there emerged this basic difference of attitude as to whether, quite apart from the legal aspect, military training mattered in the preparation of the student for life. An understanding of this difference was essential if the issues that really divided these bitterly opposed factions were to be understood.

Similarly, in approaching the teaching of religion in a college it is useless to begin without a clear and unequivocal exposing of the real issue that is at stake there. That issue seems to me to be more than whether or not religious courses shall be offered in the curriculum of a college. For many administrators and faculties are quite happy to have religious courses "offered"—full stop. The real issue, however, is (1) Do they believe that it matters whether or not a student has been moved and won by the Christian religion as an active practicing member? (2) Do they believe that it matters whether the type of Christian religion to which a student adheres is of a conventional sort or whether it is informed by the highest specimens that are revealed in Christian history? If they do believe that both of these

185

objectives matter and matter profoundly, then they may proceed to the questions as to how they can best be accomplished.

Without further preliminaries it may be stated simply here that this essay presupposes these two objectives: (1) that a college has a real obligation to assist a student to come into touch with sources that will increase the likelihood of his being won by the Christian religion as an active practicing member; and (2) that a college is concerned that such adherence shall be to "high" rather than to "low" religion, and to this end the student shall be exposed to the best records of Christian experience which may assist him in the task of discrimination and of adequate interpretation.

CAN RELIGION BE TAUGHT?

When the next question is approached, "How can these two objectives be accomplished?" there is no ready agreement on the means. They are certainly many in number. Here there is opportunity to examine only one type of approach, that of courses in religion, and in detail only one specimen of that type, namely, a course in devotional literature.

Given the concern that young men and women should discover an active practice of the Christian religion, it may at once be queried whether any course in religion could communicate religion any more than a course in the history of art or in ethics could pretend to communicate art or virtue. This is a serious challenge, and almost anyone who has attempted to teach in one of these three fields has puzzled over it in the long hours of many nights.

It is obvious that if it is a question of whether religious devotion or beauty or virtue can be communicated to another person with the logical conclusiveness of a mathematical theorem, the answer is no. It is equally clear that Søren Kierkegaard is completely in the right in his *Unscientific Postscript* and his *Fragments of Philosophy* when he insists that no historical study of the life of Jesus, no matter how minutely accurate in its assemblage of detail about the events of his life, could of itself ever compel commitment to him or to his way of life. In like fashion, no historical survey of types of art or of the principal types of ethical virtue could ever of itself necessarily effect an inward response. To this extent religion, beauty, and virtue cannot be communicated, cannot be taught.

Yet both of these denials come from methods of presentation that presume to expect an almost automatic result from this teaching, a result that is obtainable only with those relatively impersonal, abstractly manipulable data which mathematics, logic, and the physical sciences afford. If there were a more modest expectation where the deeper and more costingly personal ranges of experience in religious devotion, beauty, and virtue are concerned, then the denial of communication might not be so absolute. For sustained exposure to great religious or ethical or aesthetic models, accompanied by a critical attack upon the perversions and hypocrisies of religion or virtue or upon the saccharinely false expectations with which so many approach art, often results in an inward quickening of the religious, the ethical, or the aesthetic response of the student. There are great models in each of these fields capable of awakening many to a prompt response. Moreover, not even in the religious field are these great models so subjectively relative that a teacher need fear personal bias in selecting them.

As for the student's part, Socrates has given every teacher of religion the valuable reminder that the teacher does not do it all. In each student there is a natural capacity of discernment that can be kindled by the right models, the right questions, the right rebukes. The teacher's task is chiefly that of presenting material that may effect an arousal from slumber or from perverse rebellion. The teacher will do well never to forget that in his teaching much has gone on before he begins and that, in George Fox's words, he must only "answer to that of God in every man."

This method of teaching, then, means that the permanently significant must come from the inward response of the native powers of the student. It is to be hoped that this realization may free the teacher from the educational mores of the "precious" liberal period. Then there was severe apprehension over the possibility that the professor might inadvertently be thrown out of solution and be precipitated into a personal judgment. This he might even be inclined to defend, with the result that the student would be exposed to all the dangers of indoctrination. There will never be any effective teaching of religion until this period is behind us, for no person can present the great models of religion or make essential criticisms of the perversions unless he has a point of view in religion and one which he considers important.

The college course in which this is to be done cannot be exclusively factual. It must also be normative if it is to be of worth, and this normative character calls for selection. Each *yes* in it calls for a *no*. This may be presented partly in Socratic dialectic in which the student commits himself and the professor simply asks questions which reveal the untenability of the student's position and point to a more acceptable approach. But if in the hands of Socrates himself Socratic dialectic was never neutral on the status of ultimate values, why need it be so in the hands of the teachers of our time?

THE BIBLE AND DEVOTIONAL LITERATURE

In searching for suitable material in which to present these great models in religion the educator who would teach the Christian religion will naturally turn to the Bible. The popular fashion of beginning the study of religion in college with courses in the history of religion and comparative religions for a time threatened to eclipse the study of the Bible. It was not unassociated with the mood of a period when students who knew little about their own country and culture found it imperative to make a trip to Europe either before or just after their freshman year in college. To one who has begun to know his own tradition a trip abroad is of great stimulus. To one who has not yet become rooted in one culture exposure to conflicting cultures may serve less to clarify than to confuse.

An old botanist who lives on Mount Rainier sat patiently with a friend of mine while the friend told of how many western mountains he had climbed and explored. When he had talked himself out, the old botanist, who knew almost every specimen of plant life that grew on that great mountain, said quietly, "I have been glad for the opportunity to know one mountain well." The Bible, with its great family of Old Testament heroes and prophets, saints and sinners, and the epic New Testament with its parallel accounts of Jesus and its revealing record of the early Christian community, must quite rightly be given first place. It is our home mountain.

Yet the Christian revelation is a continuing revelation. Through the centuries the alluring figure of Jesus and the indwelling power of God's Spirit operative upon men have continued to draw men and women and even whole communities to respond to them. Many of them have responded without conscious reservation, prepared to acknowledge that "who chooseth me, must give and hazard all he hath." To those who would feel the impact of the Christian tradition in its most poignant specimens, this procession of models of total response by temperaments of every type, men and women in different vocations living under the most diverse types of political and economic order, is a most important source of material. Many of these all-out responders to God who have continued the Christian revelation have left behind them testaments of devotion in which they have sought to incite others to leave off their drowsy, lukewarm lip service to Christian living and give themselves with abandon to it.

These devotional writings form a literature of their own. They are usually strongly autobiographical, and yet they contain less diffuse material than most autobiographies. On the other hand, they are not so subject to the temptations of studied eloquence as are sermons. Abbé Bremond, whose masterly study of seventeenth-century French specimens of religious sentiment has been crowned by the French Academy, has written of this uniquely devotional literature:

Every line written by François de Sales or the other great spiritual masters is involuntarily a confidence, a spontaneous witness. One cannot say as much for the majority of sermons. . . . Devotional literature is never platonic; it addresses itself to the imagination and the intellect solely to influence the will. A devotional book in the inner history of the Christian community starts a vibration.

The works of devotional literature nearly always indicate the ways of prayer and of personal discipline which their period has found useful. Often students are convinced of the importance of a scrupulous study of method and laboratory techniques in the physical sciences, and yet their minds may be so untrained and dispersed that they cannot be focused creatively on a half-hour's meditation of some religious or ethical subject. To these, accounts of exacting training and discipline of the mind and will in meditation and prayer may fill a need which is provided for in no other part of the curriculum. Harvard University has recently offered to its undergraduates a course in great explorers which has aroused considerable interest. It is significant that Columbus, Magellan, Balboa, Peary, Scott, and Byrd should become familiar figures to the undergraduates of this generation, while spiritual explorers like Augustine, Eckhart, Catherine of Siena, Theresa of Avila, John of the Cross, George Fox, or William Law should be neglected. It might be a matter of no small interest to students to realize how many of these spiritual explorers and their colleagues were young men and women no older than themselves when they set out on their quest.

Courses in psychology are currently much attended in our colleges. Yet among the names given above are contained some of the most profound psychologists of the human soul of all ages. These men and women knew the soul's heights and its depths and its susceptibility to guidance and its infinite strategy of evasion and retreat. No current questionnaire on religious response has revealed as searchingly the marks of the genuine or the pseudo-religious illumination as Theresa of Avila's two classics of devotion, the *Life* and the *Interior Castle*, written nearly four hundred years ago.

Such devotional works have often been the watersheds out of which the leading schools of theology have risen, and the meaning of some of these great schools of thought remain paradoxical abstractions until illuminated by the devotional spring which gave to the system its unique accent. Religious and social institutions have been revived and often profoundly altered in their course by the appearance of these continuers of revelation, so that their testaments are of great importance in understanding the very course of the history of religious and secular institutions.

Scattered through these devotional classics are passages of great beauty and strength. For they are usually written under an intensity of fervent concern that burns away the conventional expression and proceeds to its theme with a directness and a simplicity that empties its full quiver on the reader's mind. It is a peculiar pleasure for a reader to discover these passages for himself. When this happens, there is a sense of possessing and being possessed by a line or page that is one of the creative aspects of ownership which no second-mortgage anthology can ever supply.

A Course in Classics of Devotional Literature

Apart from the Bible, I know of no material in the Christian tradition which surpasses the field of Christian devotional literature for presenting the great models of religion to students and for analysing the perversions and the hypocrisies indicated in these books. In presenting a course of reading for students that might be called "Classics in Christian Devotional Literature" it is not easy to know how far after the New Testament period to begin. The writings of some of the early Fathers, like Tertullian's *Testimony of the Soul* or certain passages from Clement of Alexandria or Origen, are worthy of inclusion. Much can be said, however, for beginning later and taking off with the first nine books of Augustine's *Confessions*. This classic has opened the lives of so many Christians that it has earned the right to be regarded among the great Christian instruments in history. The *Bible, The Imitation of Christ,* and Augustine's *Confessions*—these three Friedrich von Hügel affirmed toward the end of his life had been his daily diet, and his witness spoke for many.

Readers of Augustine's *Confessions* must be prepared to have the personal narrative interrupted while the writer pours himself out in exalted prayer or gives a religious meditation of some length which has been aroused by some minor incident in his remembered past. For the past, unless it is a mere beaded necklace of discrete events, must, when recovered in memory, give out of its substance some rich meanings that were too covered, too tightly held, too much connected with future revelations to be visible in the original occurrence. Socrates' words that "the unexamined life is not worth living" touch upon the contrast between the chaotic interflow of the original events of most unintentional living and the clarified meaningfulness which these events seem gratefully to yield when examined and pondered over in remembrance.

It is the mature recovery of Augustine's past that emerges from this account—flight from God on the one side, and on the other what Kierkegaard liked to think of as the Great Fisherman with a hook already in Augustine but letting him run year after year with only occasional snubs until he finally gives in and is taken. And the seasoned reader who comes to see the importance of these asides will promptly check any original exasperation at the interruptions to the chronicle of external events.

The *Confessions* are a case study where the much neglected ranges of psychology can be examined and grasped in a way that an abstract presentation can never approach. Sin to a college student is an old-fashioned concept that seems almost as outdated as possession by demons. Yet the picture of Augustine in the throes of sexual habit or vocational patterns of rhetorical flattery that, in spite of all resolutions and impulses for improvement, hold him clamped in the vise of their grip presents a psychological fact that cannot be easily set aside. And beside this aspect of sin is the deeper sense of having by this persistence not only frustrated his own good intentions but wounded a mother who patiently loved and sought after him through it all, as well as One who drew both him and his mother to His way. Here is a further overtone in the psychological phenomenon which could only with great difficulty be communicated abstractly in theological language.

There is in Augustine's *Confessions* a vivid psychological depiction of how in the civil wars we carry on within our breasts the decisive battle is always preceded by many previous engagements, each of which prepares the way for the next. The boyhood experience of the death of his bosom friend who would not come over to Augustine and who died happily acknowledging his Christian baptism; his mother's faithfulness; the progressive disillusionment with the Manicheans, with the academic sceptics, and with the power to heal sin of even the much beloved Neo-Platonic writings; the liberal sermons of Ambrose which taught him that the Old Testament could be freely interpreted; the growing sense of repulsion for his private and professional life; the heroic example of Victorinus and Anthony and of the youthful royal courtiers—the *Confessions* show clearly how all of these harrowed open the soil in his heart to receive the seed of conversion that came to him in the garden scene. Psychology comes alive in these pages, and the student who reads learns better to understand what may be taking place within himself.

Little needs to be said about supplementary material to illuminate this book. The *Confessions* of this native of Tagaste, a little African town that still exists as Souk-Ahras in Algeria, are themselves a biography and tell their own story. Sparrow-Simpson's *Conversion of St. Augustine* is still a sound account of the background. G. Papini's *St. Augustine* is a somewhat flamboyant yet gripping and colorful picture of the saint who was his conveyor to Christ. Two books of interpretative sketches of a number of these devotional classics should be mentioned—Dean Willard Sperry's *Strangers and Pilgrims* and Gaius Glenn Atkins' early book, *Pilgrims of the Lonely Road.* Both

contain chapters on Augustine's *Confessions*. Dean Sperry's book, like
so many books that last, had been "taught over" for a generation before it was set down. Year after year he took a group of his advanced
Harvard Divinity School students, and in what they have always
regarded as an unforgettable series of personal visits he made these
devotional books come alive and tempted his student friends to take
them as lifelong companions.

After Augustine there is much to be said for going at once to
Bernard of Clairvaux. But quaint as some would regard it, my own
students have found a fascination and no small inward profit from a
careful reading and scrutiny of Benedict's *Rule*, which was the pattern for the ordering of the entire monastic movement of the West for
a thousand years. The strengths and the weaknesses of monastic life
are peculiarly revealed in that simple document; and this charter of
the only enduring Occidental experiment in actual communist living
has about it an elevated practicality which seldom fails to impress
the reader. A college president may even derive some comfort in finding at last his own proper designation as he reads the rule which
gives the lowly but exacting duties of the gatekeeper—a man of
sober and trusted life who shall be always on duty at the gate to meet
strangers and transact the business of the monastery so that the others
may continue uninterrupted at their prayers and manual work. Dom
Cuthbert Butler's *Benedictine Monachism* will be useful to help illuminate this little book.

In Bernard of Clairvaux's *On Consideration* the student has an
opportunity to see the twelfth-century spiritual counselor of kings and
popes advising one of his own Cistercian brothers who has just become Pope as Eugenius III on how he may spiritualize that dangerous
office and live as an apostle within it. Although the problem is the
same, Aldous Huxley's *Grey Eminence* might have been less ghastly
had he taken Bernard of Clairvaux instead of Father Joseph as his
subject. Those who, like Gerald Heard, see the future role of the seer
counseling the administrator in government as well as those who
share the intense modern concern over the relation between the
spiritual life and the exercise of great political or social responsibilities will find *On Consideration* of peculiar relevance today. Bernard's
treatise on *The Love of God* and many of the *Sermons on the Canticle
of Canticles* reveal with unusual purity the mystical side of this

dynamic Hammer of God who sought to pound out his century on God's anvil.

Watkins' recent life of Bernard of Clairvaux is the most exhaustive study yet to appear in English. It does not move, however, as does Storr's old *Bernard of Clairvaux*. Mecklin's *The Passing of the Saint* contains two chapters devoted to a critical appraisal of Bernard of Clairvaux and Francis of Assisi. The brief chapters on both Bernard of Clairvaux and Francis of Assisi in H. O. Taylor's *The Medieval Mind* are exquisitely done.

For Francis of Assisi there is no single book to recommend. He wrote none. Yet he inspired legends and stories of the life he and his companions led which are among the great devotional stimuli the Christian world possesses. Students generation after generation are laid low by Francis of Assisi. "He is what we talk about." "Yes, I admit Francis was the real thing." "I doubt if I could resist Francis were he to appear today." His life seems to attack them. No discussion of the status and role of private property in a class in economics could be more fierce and spirited than that provoked by Francis' dedication to holy poverty. The place for the Holy Family which the Third Order of Franciscans provided scarcely placates their attacks on the Franciscan ideal of celibacy. Francis' abdication of control in the order and the century-long struggle between the spiritual and the conventional Franciscans stir up the whole issue of the function of institutional order and of its relation to personal freedom. Yet after this has all been threshed over, students feel the challenge to the life of Christian discipleship to which the joyous dedication of this little five-foot Umbrian merchant's son continues to invite them.

The *Little Flowers of Saint Francis*, the *Mirror of Perfection*, and the *Three Companions* are the best source material to be read by the class. Paul Sabatier's *Francis of Assisi* makes Francis out to have been a little more of an unconscious Protestant than subsequent studies have borne out, but it is still the best biography to put into student hands. G. K. Chesterton's *St. Francis of Assisi* is very brief and impressionistic, but some favor it for this purpose. In order to get the flavor of Franciscan life nothing is better suited than the reading aloud of several of Lawrence Housman's *Little Plays of St. Francis* using selections from both the first and second series. Cuthbert's *Romanticism of St. Francis* and Vida Scudder's *Brother John* and

The Franciscan Adventure all give admirable background for the period. Helen C. White's novel, *Watch in the Night*, gives a vivid picture of second-generation Franciscanism in her portrayal of the life of the great Franciscan poet, Jacapone da Todi, although she takes some liberties with her sources.

Meister Eckhart's *Sermons* and *Tractates* provide an entryway into the wealth of that fourteenth-century outburst of inward religion which is so convincingly described in Rufus M. Jones' *Flowering of Mysticism*. Blakeney has retranslated a selection of Eckhart's sermons and tractates and has rearranged them to suit the interest and needs of one who meets them for the first time. This volume, published by Harper and Brothers in 1941, does not replace but may be considered as an introduction to the more complete two-volume work by C. de B. Evans which was published in England over a decade ago.

The climate of Eckhart's sermons is not temperate. Pascal's cry of "fire" lights up many of the passages in this persuasive volume. These passages proclaim the instant readiness of God to rush into our souls if we will even set the door ajar.

Know then that God is bound to act, to pour Himself out (into thee) as soon as ever He shall find thee ready . . . finding thee ready, He is obliged to act, to overflow into thee. . . . God cannot leave anything void and unfilled. . . . It is one flash the being-ready and the pouring-in: the instant spirit is ready, God enters without hesitation or delay. Thou needest not seek Him here or there, He is no further off than the door of thy heart; there He stands lingering, awaiting whoever is ready to open and let him in. He waits more patiently than thou for thee to open to Him. He longs for thee a thousandfold more urgently than thou for Him: one point, the opening and the entering.—*Sermon IV*

A later sermon confirms this wanton longing in God to give, when Eckhart declares:

God is foolishly in love with us; it seems that He has forgotten heaven and earth and happiness and deity; His entire business seems to be with me alone, to give me everything to comfort me; He gives it to me suddenly, He gives it to me wholly, He gives it to me perfect, He gives it all the time, and He gives it to all creatures.—*Sermon XCI*

This assurance that God is forever ready to bear His Son in our souls is, however, never confused with any automatic redemption. The revolution is and remains a responsible, personal revolution.

If it happen not in me what does it profit me? What matters is that it shall happen in me.—*Sermon I*

Neither are there any bargains here. God's entry cannot be secured at half price. The bargain hunter in us is exposed as Eckhart writes:

Daily we cry, 'thy will be done!' and when his will is done we grumble and are discontented at it.

We would fain be humble; but not despised. We would be poor too, but without privation. And doubtless we are patient, except with the hardships and with disagreeables . . . there are plenty to follow our Lord halfway, but not the other half.—*Sermon XII*

Nowhere in mystical literature is there any more clear-cut questioning of our modern well-intentioned but dispersive religious activism than in Eckhart.

People should think less about what they ought to do and more about what they ought to be. If only they were good [i.e. spiritually good] and their dispositions were good, their works would shine forth brightly.— *Tractate XVII*

We can only spend in good works what we earn in contemplation.

The *Imitation of Christ* has for centuries stood next to the Bible itself as the most widely used book of devotions in the Christian world. It was released to the world in 1441 by Thomas à Kempis, a spiritual follower of Gerhard Groot. But it is Groot's intimate journal that is now generally supposed to have furnished most of the material in the *Imitation*.

Students are both drawn to and repelled by this Christian classic on their first acquaintance with it. "Blessed are those who are glad to have time to spare for God"; "he in whom the eternal word speaks is delivered from many opinions"; the call to take "The Royal Road of the Holy Cross"—these are positive either as reports of inward experiences or as a challenge to take to the road in company with the Master. Yet the strong ascetic note of the *Imitation* puts many younger people off on first meeting. The interpretation of the *Imitation* in its setting of Gerhard Groot's holy fellowship, the Brethren of the Common Life, and of Groot's own life and struggle helps lessen these prejudices. With age there may come a greater tolerance of these ascetic elements and an increasing appreciation of the wisdom of this classic, no matter what extremity life may present. The chapter on the Brethren of the Common Life in Rufus M. Jones' *Studies in Mystical*

Religion as well as in his *The Flowering of Mysticism* is valuable in interpreting the *Imitation*.

The *Theologia Germanica* which had so profound an influence upon the young Luther is a little book born of the mystical mood of this same period and looking to a reformulation of doctrine in keeping with that greatest of all orthodoxies, the orthodoxy of discerning love. "The only thing that shall burn in hell is self-will." "Oh that I might be to the Eternal Goodness what His own hand is to a man." This little book is likely to be prized only by a few. But it is marked by such majesty of statement and is so important as a link between pre- and post-Reformation figures that it is worth including. Gaius Glenn Atkins, Willard L. Sperry, and Rufus M. Jones, in their books previously mentioned, all devote useful chapters of interpretation to the *Theologia Germanica*.

Theresa of Avila's *Life* is a classic of the Counter Reformation. Taken with the valuable supplementary material in her *Foundations* the magnificent life and teachings of this shrewd Spanish religious guide of the sixteenth century are likely to make a deep impression upon those who are exposed to her. The grasp of psychology which this woman possessed will startle those who think such things are a modern discovery. Peers' *Studies of the Spanish Mystics* is a suitable supplementary book in the study of Theresa of Avila, although the first two books mentioned are so complete as to require little more. John of the Cross is a more formidable undertaking and might well be put off for more advanced study.

Of all the better known devotional literature available today, my own students have the opinion that no single work is a match for Francis de Sales' *Introduction to the Devout Life*, another fruit of the Counter Reformation. This little book was written by one who knew the monotonously stereotyped sins of men and women from his long years in the confessional and who, on the other hand, knew from his own life what it was to live in the full flair of Christian freedom. He wrote his handbook not for monks and nuns but for those living in the world. "Christianity is intended to sanctify the world and not to abolish the world; and the world is not and never can be the cloister."

Francis de Sales used Scupoli's *Spiritual Combat*, which had appeared a generation before, as something of a model, but his final product surpassed that of his master. Throughout the book wise instruction is graphically presented on the daily use of silent prayer, on the distractions that disturb such meditation, on the common sins that obstruct growth in the life of devotion, and on the means of overcoming these obstructions. Walter Walsh has suggested that "there is no way of ending sin, except persuading sinners to leave it off." In the *Introduction to the Devout Life* Francis de Sales reveals an unusual power in precisely this area of "persuading sinners to leave it off."

Of the malicious words we say in company about others, Francis convicts us by referring to them as a triple murder. They murder our own souls that utter them. They murder the soul of him who listens to them. And they kill the reputation of him of whom they are related. Or again he persuades us to leave off the sin of self-mutilation in the form of violent impatience with ourselves as we break our resolutions or as we repeat our sins. As he describes these occasions of becoming angry, and then "angry with my proud self for having been angry," the specter of the intense egotistical pride that drives on the mood of anger emerges before us. And as we see the humorous picture of ourselves in a tantrum over having fallen into a ditch, or in abject desolation resigning ourselves to wallow in the ditch forever, because of this unforgivable tumble, he restores perspectives, shows us how useful for humility and God-dependence such experiences may be, and turns them into a form of medicinal healing. This book is as alive today as it was when it was written and will stir any group who will attend to it carefully. The setting for the period is given brilliantly in the first volume of Abbé Bremond's *History of Religious Sentiment in France in the Seventeenth Century*.

Bishop Lancelot Andrewes' *Private Devotions*, translated from the original Greek and Hebrew by the devoted labors of John Henry Newman and John Mason Neale, represents a high watermark in Anglican piety. The cadenced prayers of this little book which Lancelot Andrewes prepared for his own personal use in the extended early-morning vigils to which he dedicated himself are among the most moving in sacred literature. This clean, sharp petition followed by the rhythmic plea for personal establishment, is characteristic of Lancelot Andrewes:

O direct my life towards Thy Commandments
    hallow my soul,
    purify my body,
    correct my thoughts,
    cleanse my desires,
  soul and body, mind and spirit, heart and veins.
  Renew me thoroughly, O God, for if Thou wilt, Thou canst.
I commend to Thee, O Lord,
My soul, and my body.
My mind, and my thoughts,
My prayers, and my vows,
My senses, and my limbs,
My words, and my works,
My life, and my death;
My brothers and my sisters and their children,
My friends and my benefactors,
  My well-wishers
Those who have claim on me;
My kindred, and my neighbors,
My country, and all Christendom.
I commend to Thee, Lord,
My impulses and my startings,
My intentions and my attempts
My going out, and my coming in,
My sitting down and my rising up.

George Fox's *Journal* reveals the springs of strength that kept this titanic witness to inward religion refreshed through nearly half a century of persecution and opposition in middle and late seventeenth-century England. The *Journal* is saturated with a sense of power that communicates itself to the reader. *The Beginnings of Quakerism* by William Braithwaite is a useful supplement to George Fox's *Journal*. Bunyan's *Pilgrim's Progress* may already be well known enough to make its inclusion in such a course unnecessary.

Pascal's *Thoughts* presents a series of aphoristic statements that were to have become the building stones of a great apology for the Christian religion which he was mercifully spared from cementing together. There is no comparable ammunition for blasting loose a complacent intellectual from the securities of his well-reasoned unbelief. Here the mind is turned against its own egotism by the insights and logic of one who is commonly agreed to have been the outstanding genius in an age which Professor Whitehead aptly calls "the Century of Genius." Chevalier's *Pascal* is a useful supplement to the *Thoughts* in fitting this seventeenth-century master into the frame of the age.

The eighteenth century affords an American devotional classic of outstanding worth, John Woolman's *Journal*. Here in the simple, restrained account of a New Jersey Quaker tailor is given the life of a saint who from the age of nineteen, when he records that his heart was made "tender and contrite, and universal love for my fellow creatures increased in me," was shaped and molded until he became a principal instrument in the freeing of the slaves a century before the issue resulted in a national calamity. Students find in this rare blend of spiritual sensitiveness and social responsibility an appealing figure. Janet P. Whitney's recent *John Woolman* presents an excellent picture of the background of John Woolman. Amelia Mott Gummere's *John Woolman* contains essays of Woolman that are an important supplement to the message of the *Journal*. The Whittier edition of the *Journal* is inexpensive and is most suitable for student use.

While I have never used either Jeremy Taylor's *Holy Living and Holy Dying* or William Law's *Serious Call to the Devout Life* with undergraduates, they are both important works and worthy of consideration. An abbreviated edition of John Wesley's *Journal* might also be appropriate with a mature group.

John Henry Newman's *Apologia* presents a portrait of a tender, delicate spirit seeking a corporate religious life deeper than the conventional churches of his period could supply. Held against the background of the Oxford Movement, the *Apologia* can do much to help interpret this revival of the corporate claims of institutional religion. Gaius Glenn Atkins' *Cardinal Newman* may well be held over against Wilfred Ward's standard *Life of Newman* in securing the additional material necessary for placing the *Apologia*. Peck's *Social Implications of the Oxford Movement* presents a neglected side and one which seeks to meet such criticisms of social conservatism as emerge in Atkins.

Søren Kierkegaard's *Purity of Heart* is a particularly striking specimen of his powerful devotional addresses. As the student reads this book, he can scarcely escape the devastating attack on all the folds of gregarious mass-protection in which he has hoped to escape from the divine claim upon him for becoming a responsible individual before God. Much that is central in the great Danish prophet's message on the necessity of becoming an individual is to be found in this work. Walter Lowrie's *Søren Kierkegaard* gives a deeply sympathetic study of Kierkegaard's life and thought.

George Tyrrell's *Autobiography* presents a tragic but ruthlessly frank picture of the development of one of the rare religious spirits of the late nineteenth and early twentieth centuries. The flashes of exposure of the grinding spiritual imperialism of the Roman Catholic Church, while never concealed, do not keep the reader from the book's primary purpose of sharing the brilliant spiritual insights of this scrupulously honest Irish knight of God.

The Selected Letters of George Tyrrell's devoted friend, Baron von Hügel, is a classic that has appeared in our own time and one which never ceases to grip its readers. The biographical essay by Bernard Holland is sufficient introduction to von Hügel. The letters speak for themselves. Written as they are by one of the most vigorous and best informed minds of his generation to meet every sort of situation, they inspire a sense of what can happen when religion and great intellectual gifts are wedded in a single person. Von Hügel's grasp of the threefold place of the intellectual-scientific, of the historical-institutional, and of the mystical-emotional elements in religion shines through and illuminates these letters to the reader's enrichment. It is possible to substitute for Tyrrell or von Hügel, Allen's *Life of Phillips Brooks* or its abbreviated counterpart by Bishop William Lawrence, or to use Forbes Robinson's *Letters to His Friends,* in which the case for intercessory prayer is put with such engaging force. But none of these have the sheer depth of the works which they might be used to replace.

These suggestions of concrete material are only by way of illustrating what has been used several times by the writer in a course for undergraduates, most of whom have no intention of engaging professionally in religious work and who range in age from nineteen to twenty-two. There are infinite variations of it that are possible, and with another teacher undoubtedly desirable. Yet this blend of acquaintance with the continuous revelation to be found in great Christian personalities and with a compelling literature of devotion has proved an effective means of arousing an eager interest in the religious life in college students. And the variety of books used covers enough of a range so that few students are not vulnerable to some work that is met with during the semester. The personal ownership by the student of these books, most of which are inexpensive, provides a continuing invitation to use them and a reserve to return to in the emergency situations that life will visit upon him.

THE PROTESTANT SUSPICION OF DEVOTIONAL LITERATURE

There is one final observation that should be made before concluding. It is not entirely accidental that this valuable devotional literature has been so neglected in the colleges of our country. Quite apart from our overwhelming absorption in the conquest of the external world and our neglect of the inward development of man, in all but a small segment of our higher education where we are not entirely secular we are strongly Protestant in our religious bias. The Protestant tradition, in spite of its individualistic note, has not usually given itself to the personal nurture of souls much past the general level of decency. And it has remained suspicious of all attempts to do so. The fashion was set in Luther's period. For although Luther himself was profoundly influenced as a young man by an outstanding devotional classic, *Theologia Germanica*, yet he feared devotional practice as a work of man and hence as a "filthy rag" that might stay man's utter abandonment to God by faith. This same radical emphasis is continued in Calvin, and we have had it almost savagely enunciated in the Barthian Neo-Calvinism of our time. All "religion" must go. God is all, man is nothing, and no act of man's may ever reach Him. Away with great Christian apostles, away with their writings, away with devotional practices. Destroy them all as idols, props, golden calves. Man's naked soul before God is enough.

This violent opposition to the nurture and discipline of souls was never accepted by the spiritual reformers like Boehme or Schwenkfeld and the other sixteenth-century forerunners of German pietism, nor did a considerable group in the Church of England or later the Quakers and the Methodists fully approve of its harsh extremity. Yet it had its influence even among these groups in its horror of all asceticism and in its suspicious attitude toward set practices of personal devotion and books of devotion. And this influence has held almost down to our own day. George Herbert in the seventeenth century sought to combat this Protestant hatred of fixed devotional practice, of any rules, in his lines in *The Church Porch*:

Slight those who say amidst their sickly healths, 'Thou livest by rule.' What dost not so but man? Houses are built by rule, and Commonwealths. Entice the trusty sun, if that you can, from his ecliptic rule; beckon the sky! Who lives by rule, then, keeps good company. Who keeps no guard upon himself is slack and rots to nothing at the next great thaw.

The result of this distrust of all private devotional aids is that, apart from volumes of sermons, personal records in religious journals like those of Fox, Wesley, or Woolman, and a few unusual specimens like Lancelot Andrewes' *Private Devotions,* John Bunyan's *Pilgrim's Progress,* Jeremy Taylor's *Holy Living and Holy Dying,* and William Law's *Serious Call to the Devout Life,* the greatest classics in this field have come out of the Catholic Christian tradition.

So long as there has been no challenge to its own authority, the Catholic tradition has never feared to acknowledge as God-inspired the totality of abandonment which has marked the lives of so many of the great saints. But for saint and humble lay Christian alike, it has believed that in order to grow to maturity in the Christian life, much daily discipline and daily stimulus are needed. The recorded examples and advices of those who have gone furthest are hence much prized, and in consequence devotional works have flourished under the Catholic tradition.

Yet the greatest of these figures would be acknowledged by most open-minded observers as having transcended all ecclesiastical limitations and as belonging to us all. With their writings the greatest of them form a Christian treasury that we ignore out of some sectarian prejudice only to our own impoverishment. In the face of the present secularism and of the world's bitter need for inward direction, the fact that so many of these devotional classics came from men and women who were devout members of the Roman Catholic Church will not deter any but the most bigoted denominationalist from receiving from them their Christian counsel. And those colleges in America which believe that it matters that their students be moved by the highest type of Christian religion would do well to leave off this neglect and to make use of the precious instrument of devotional literature.

8

The Christian Tradition in Modern Culture

THE COMPLEXITY OF THE MODERN SPIRIT

TO ESTIMATE CORRECTLY THE VITALITY OF A RELIGIOUS TRADITION IN one's own day is all but impossible. The most significant workings of such a tradition elude observation. The operation of leaven, indeed, offers the perfect analogy. In the case of Christianity, for example, the secrecy that marks the divine action in its pure state, that is, in the gospel itself, is only less characteristic of the faith in its cultural amalgams. For though we may be able to identify trends and forces in Christian society, to tabulate the institutional expressions of religion, and, with the aid of retrospect, to assess shrewdly the comparative influence of Christian and secular impulses, our observations and tests must be largely superficial. As the astronomer is surprised by the appearance of comets whose cycles have never been recorded or by other celestial phenomena for which he has no precedent, so the cultural historian knows he is dealing with a field full of incalculable factors, particularly where religion is involved. In our generation there have been those happily surprised by the unexpected powers of resistance of the Church under Nazism and those who have been disoriented by the unexpected collapse of age-old moral and ecclesiastical patterns. Chastened by these observations we may, however, inquire into the role of the Christian tradition in contemporary culture with the hope, at least, of throwing into relief certain dilemmas and certain responsibilities now more fully brought to light by our present crisis.

Several general considerations bearing on the relation of religion and culture must first be mentioned. It should be borne in mind, for one thing, that religion finds cultural expression in both direct and indirect ways. Manifestations of the prevailing faith in direct ways, for example, in the sacred arts or in hymns and liturgy, may be less significant than those that appear more indirectly. A culture like that of the Anglo-Saxon peoples today reflects its basic religious tradition in a very complex way and often obliquely or at a considerable remove from the original impulse. Cultural expressions, as in the field of art or of manners, are unquestionably conditioned by the basic religious heritage, the ultimate fountain of social creativity, but any particular expression may show that conditioning by way of reaction as well as by positive influence or most frequently in ways not immediately observable. Moreover, alien factors complicate the matter. The quality of artistic expression in a given period, for instance, is no simple clue to the vitality of the religious tradition, for a prevailing dearth of taste or curiosity or sensibility or the immaturity of an artistic movement may preclude significant art at the time. Again, a significant literary production that appears reprehensible or scandalous to the orthodox may, nevertheless, have its roots in the religious tradition. The blasphemer often renders doubly clear the ties by which he is held.

A second consideration is the extreme cultural complexity of modern society. Interested as we are in the influence and possibilities of the Hebraic-Christian tradition in our age, we must recognize the variety in both that tradition and the other spiritual traditions running parallel with it and intermingled with it. The variety within it is only formally indicated when we name the three chief religious types, Jewish, Catholic, and Protestant. Each of these, indeed, has its claims as regards its contribution to our social culture. More telling for our inquiry is the distinction that can be made in religious forces or communities between those that have taken on the phase of archaism or crystallization and those that exhibit the power to adapt themselves to new conditions. We should include among the latter those minority movements which by their relevance to the crucial issues of today may be viewed as profoundly potent and as the growing edges of the religious bodies. We shall be wise in times like these, when historical judgments on institutions are in process and when evidently judgment begins at the house of God, to fix our attention on the prophetic rather than the priestly tradition. For the priest is the conserver of the institution, and sometimes his work is too well done, while the prophet is the renewer.

But whether we view our Hebraic-Christian heritage in terms of its institutions or of its spirit, in our present-day society it is deeply overlaid and intimately interwoven with other spiritual traditions or cultural forces. The disorder of our time has even led men to conclude that other outlooks have captured the Western world, outlooks, if not neo-pagan, then at least secularist, and that our hitherto dominant religious tradition has been outlived. In any case, it must be acknowledged that various cultural ideals or world-views hardly reconcilable with Judaism and Christianity have lately multiplied and declared themselves. They may be noted briefly in the chronological order of their origin.

We need to return first to the Renaissance, if not to classical culture, to find the fountain head of a humanist way of life which depreciates the Hebrew Scriptures as anti-cultural if not fanatical. Thence comes an ideal typified by a Montaigne or in certain phases by a Goethe. Combined in various ways with the modern scientific outlook, it constitutes the equivalent of a religion for many of our contemporaries. We do not forget that the Hebraic-Christian tradition itself entered into fruitful relation with the Renaissance, most significantly as regards art and literature in the work of such figures as Milton, Rembrandt, and Bach. But the damaging fact is that the Renaissance tradition has tended to go its own way, particularly in higher education, and to produce a modern attitude deprived of community-building energies. For the mark of the Renaissance was its individualism.

To this cultural tradition we must then add the positivist outlook growing out of scientific empiricism and method. This, too, has constituted a pseudo-religion for many in our day and has impressed itself deeply on all the cultural expressions of our western life. When combined with the characteristic anti-cultural influences of the industrial revolution, it is the chief cause for the spiritual and artistic penury of our society. On the other hand, the co-operation of religion and science when each has recognized its due limits has been of inestimable value to Judaism and Christianity in enabling them to be self-critical, to understand their Scriptures, and to relate themselves more wisely to contemporary need.

A further cultural tradition which has likewise been an ambiguous friend, both an ally and a seducer to our faiths, has been that of the great Romantic movement. Hosts of people in the modern world have lived by it or by a combination of it with other traditions. One has but to think of Wordsworth, Shelley, Emerson, or Whitman to recognize how ambiguous is its cultural relation to Christianity. Many right up to our own day have lived by a dilute aestheticism or transcendentalism or idealism and have supposed themselves with perfect naïveté to be Christians.

We have now, however, to note a different kind of cultural force or outlook, one which in company with the social factors that produced it has made deep inroads on all the older traditions we have described, whether orthodox or not, namely, Marxism. We shall here have in mind rather the actualities of the economic life which gave birth to Marxism and which have continued through its ideology and through their own fatality to destroy older patterns of society and of thought. These economic forces have alienated large parts of the working classes from our older cultural forms and religious loyalties, and they have also shaped a society of conflict and of uprooted individuals for whom the older spiritual traditions appear to be unreal. Add to these persuasions to secularism and these dissolutions of ancient folkways the counsels of relativity that proceed from the recent developments of the sciences, particularly psychology, and we can see to what degree the Christian tradition is thrown on the defensive. Those social patterns which it had created have been widely challenged, and in the wreck of its embodiments it has itself been placed in jeopardy. Evidently its proper course is to dissociate itself from its compromising partnerships.

But just here appears the chief dilemma. Which elements in our contemporary society are compromising? The simplest solution and one chosen by many hasty churchmen is to see no good in our present disorder and to summon the faithful to the monastery or the catacombs. This oversimplification may take the form of arraigning the modern spirit as a whole, the Renaissance, the Reformation, the sciences, and the Enlightenment, and inviting us within the walls of a Church that has never taken the spirit-led risks of man's modern adventure. No such simple solution is possible. The Hebraic-Christian tradition has nourished the modern world despite all its secularism and must not desert those occupied territories and entrenchments in our society where its own effects are operative. There are innumerable and widespread influences of the Christian tradition in Western life today, extensive manifestations of cultural and social health that often rebuke the religious institutions themselves. In identifying them we shall have gone far to answer our question as to the vitality of that tradition today. This aspect of our task is as important as our recognition of the weaknesses or surrenders of the common heritage.

THE REVOLT AGAINST THE BIBLE: RESPONSIBILITY OF THE CHURCHES

To pursue our inquiry within the limits here permitted we shall select two areas in which we can canvass the present power of the Christian tradition. We shall first discuss the role of the Bible itself in our culture and particularly in higher education. We shall then examine contemporary literature for evidences as to the hold of our religious heritage on contemporary life.

Any assessment of the relevance and vitality of the Hebraic-Christian tradition in our culture leads directly to a consideration of the Bible. It is true that the Bible is but one aspect of that tradition. But the attitude taken to the Scriptures by successive generations or by various groups or movements within a given generation furnishes the best test of their adherence to or departure from the spiritual covenant which lies at the foundation of our occidental life. And, though the fate of the Bible in the modern world would appear as yet to be undecided, a fearful dubiety hangs over its claim on the Western conscience.

The jeopardy in which the Scriptures and the traditions based on them stand is not primarily due to external bans and repressions but to pervasive movements of non-biblical faiths. We live in the midst of a world-wide *revolt* against the Bible. It is well to state the fact with all possible forthrightness. The Swedish theologian, Nils Ehrenstrom, went so far as to say at a great interchurch conference that we live in a post-Christian society, that is, one that has outlived the biblical way of life as a real option. It would, of course, be unreasonable not to recognize the favorable factors in the situation—the continuing momentum of Hebraic-Christian institutions and patterns, the growing edges of our religious bodies, and the amazing penetration of Christian influences in the foreign missionary movement. Nor must we overlook the stubborn resistance to neo-paganism on the part of Christian bodies immediately exposed to totalitarian pressure. Yet the total picture, at least of our Western world, forces us to recognize the immense inroads of aggressive anti-biblical faiths and assumptions. The influences we associate with the names of Marx, Nietzsche, Freud, Lenin, and Rosenberg have penetrated far and wide not only on the continent of Europe but in Anglo-Saxon lands. It is true that Hebraic-Christian motives are a component in some of these ideologies or outlooks. Yet their total effect has been to repudiate the insights and relevance of the Bible.

Alongside these overt attacks on the Bible we must place the more subtle destructiveness of certain forms of scientific rationalism which over a longer period of time have challenged the authority of the Bible. We have in mind here influences which have undermined not only dogmatic views of biblical authority but also critical views of its prestige and validity as held by liberal Jews and Christians. The results have been such as to leave the great mass of modern men and women—even those not disturbed by the new ideologies—puzzled and impatient, uncomprehending, and, finally, neglectful and indifferent. The task of clarification of the Bible, indeed, is only less pressing than that of the fundamental defense of the faith.

The role of the Bible in *higher education* illuminates this situation with especial clarity. In a culture based on Hebraic-Christian foundations the Jewish and Christian Scriptures should have a more commanding place in the schools than they actually have. In the college and the university, where the most fundamental thinking concerning society is carried on and where decisive impulses for cultural destiny are set in motion, particularly here should that literature which represents the supreme spiritual tradition of our culture have a central place. In a time when society is in acute disorder both within the nation and in the Western world generally, the relevance of these springs of our spiritual life is the more self-evident.

In the past in the English university and in the early American college there was a natural correspondence between the place of the Bible in education and its importance for the community. Examples can be given of the quickening influences that went out from university centers in times of national or social crisis, influences that arose from the study of the Bible and that shaped the future. It was at Oxford that John Wyclif, Master of Baliol College, first lit the torch of religious freedom. Colet's lectures on the epistles of Paul, likewise at Oxford, gave a decisive impulse to the English Reformation. Puritanism grew greatly in power through its leaders at Cambridge. The origin of Methodism at Oxford is well known.

Yet for various reasons the Bible and its insights have come to have a very restricted opportunity in higher education in America today. The responsibility for this state of affairs should be as fairly stated as possible. It is too easy to utter a jeremiad against modern empiricism, the scientific spirit, rationalism, or secularism. In the curricula and outlook of higher education the Bible and its insights are in one form or another minimized, depreciated, neglected, or excluded. Let us grant this. But Church and society, town and gown, share in the responsibility, and worthy motives are often at work. The obvious factor that our separation of Church and state carries with it a limitation on the teaching of religion in public institutions needs only to be mentioned. Just how far that limitation need go will depend on the co-operation of the religious bodies concerned. Today, in any case, the urgency of the problems of public morality and morale makes such co-operation imperative. Again, even in private institutions religious diversity and sectarianism raise baffling questions with regard to religious emphasis and the role of the Bible. Yet such divergencies would not weigh as they do if men were taught by their faith rather than by their denominational affiliations.

More significant is the fundamental disagreement between Church and Synagogue on the one hand and modern culture as mirrored in higher education on the other. This basic disagreement affects all our educational institutions including the "church-related" colleges. Where does the responsibility for the situation lie?

The responsibility of the religious bodies, in the first place, is very great. If men in the modern world are in incipient or open revolt against the Bible, if there is on the one hand religious eccentricity or fanaticism and on the other disuse or contempt, the fault is in good part with the custodians of the Bible themselves. Those trained in Scripture hardly realize how alien a book it appears or has been made to appear to men of today. Except where its essentials have been made clear and its contents properly explained, it takes on the character of an obsolete assemblage of writings conditioned by outmoded circumstances, a curiosity shop. This is strong language, but it will be worth saying if it makes clear the reaction to the Bible of social radicals, Communists, Fascists, "hard-headed" philistines, pseudo-Hellenists, emancipated college students, and hosts of well-intentioned laymen—extensive groups, all of whom will have a hand in our future. Our religious groups have tolerated and furthered these confusions and raised up enemies to the Bible by four chief errors in their approach to it: literalism, legalism, bibliolatry, and archaism. These root all in a general prose-mindedness, a starved and pinched spiritual life, a blight of imagination, which has afflicted our Western, especially our Protestant, religious life, and which has affected the philistines outside the Church as well as those within.

Literalism ignores the principles of language and of semantics. It turns poetry into prose, figure into fact, gossamer into chains. On the one hand, the liberal involves himself in gratuitous difficulties through his inability to recognize symbol and midrash, i.e., Semitic poetry, for what they are and all unaware pursues his course with plodding ineptitude. On the other, the conservative literalist adds the blindness of dogma to that already described and presents us with a book that either suffocates men or prompts them to reject it.

Legalism ignores the multiple ways in which God fulfills himself, seeks to freeze and congeal the movement of life into static patterns, and turns prophetic injunctions into statutes. Modernists have their own ways of making themselves yokes from the precepts of the Sermon on the Mount, thus escaping the heavier but proper tasks of personal interpretation and application. One writer gives us a book on "the duty of improvidence," *Le Devoir de l'Imprévoyance*. Others carry the prohibition of oaths and divorce over into our later historical situation. Still others feel themselves bound by the injunction on non-resistance even where the domain of public order is involved, thus postulating a philosophical anarchy for which any truly religious assessment of men's hearts should show that the world is by no means ready.

Bibliolatry returns from the highest attainments of the religious pilgrimage to the nethermost gropings of magic. It makes a fetish of the volume itself, whether the paper and the leather, or the version and the typography, or the jot and tittle. Many go so far as to believe that the Bible was first communicated to man in English or at least to teach that the translators of the King James Version were miraculously safeguarded from error or uncertainty, a misconception which a glance at the Preface would suffice to correct.

Archaism would import into our age ancient and obsolete patterns from both covenants, making no distinction between matrix and jewel. There are many points at which the Church acts like a hypochondriac widow who draws down her blinds, sets up the fetishes of her bereavement, never leaves her chamber, for years the victim of a fixation that obsesses her with bygone days and outmoded routines. Archaism is the most fundamental of these distortions, an obsession with formulae, patterns, institutions, however far the spirit has departed from them, and a corresponding insensibility to the contemporary movements of life all about. Thus an institution becomes a cyst or sac in the body of mankind instead of an organ. Walter Hines Page has described certain Confederate soldiers, survivors of the Civil War, who never truly lived on beyond its close. He compares them to clocks on public buildings which had been damaged and stopped during the engagements of the war and whose hands never moved thereafter. Is it any wonder that society sooner or later grows impatient with such groups or that the spirit escapes from them finally to new vehicles? Can we not understand an otherwise regrettable secularist trend or dynamic social movement that reacts in favor of veritable energies of life and nature? In any case, the distaste often apparent for the study of the Bible in the modern university and the disaffection towards the tradition whose norm it is are understandable in the light of such perversions.

Dominant Assumptions in Academic Circles

Over against these responsibilities of the religious bodies for the position of the Bible in higher education today we can state the failings of the academic world even more forcibly. We have in mind, first, a series of provincial modern assumptions typical of our whole Western mentality which operate to the disadvantage of all manifestations of the spiritual life and especially of the Hebraic-Christian tradition.

Particularly in certain departments of our universities and colleges and in certain circles of their constituencies including members of their boards and influential legislators there is a tendency to depreciate the past and to impugn the records of man's experience, especially the classics and religious scripture. "History is bunk" is the axiom here, not always unspoken, though it has not as yet been carved on the lintels of our laboratories or halls of science. It is incredible to many of the quartermasters and sergeants of our modern industry who serve on the boards of our institutions and to many accurate tabulators who have won positions in our faculties that men who lived twenty-five hundred years ago should have had more significant thoughts than themselves. They tend to apply, or misapply, the principle of evolution in the fields of art, literature, and religion where it has little relevance. They are guilty of what has been called "provincialism in time," though they usually compound with it the more commonly recognized provincialisms also. It is perhaps to be expected that those who specialize in their own back yards should magnify their domain at every point.

Accompanying this false assumption we also find a more pardonable one, shared more widely in our college faculties. It is the failure to recognize that the non-precise symbolic and picturesque presentation of reality in poetry, art, and scripture may have merits for certain areas and that in these areas it surpasses the more exact description of scientific statement. In a culture barren of imagination and living under the garish light of our latitudes this works two evils: the fundamentalist insists that the Bible is fact, while the philistine, sophisticated or unsophisticated, knows that it often is not and therefore disallows it. The truth of the Bible, deeper than fact, is thus obscured or discarded.

Even where the values of symbolic presentation are recognized, there has been a powerful tendency to depreciate the Hebraic literary and spiritual genius by contrast with the Hellenic. This has had its corollaries throughout all aspects of our higher education. Thus the classical and humanist outlook has come to have a privileged position alongside, if subordinate to, the scientific outlook, and vested interests now stand in the way of an adequate recognition of the Hebraic-Christian valuations. It is true that the Bible and the classics should not be regarded as competing claimants for place in our schools. These institutions are not churches; and the Bible is more than a work of literature. But the fact is that our secular institutions of learning convey a quasi-religion to their graduates, much of which is founded on classical Renaissance patterns, and the views of man and the world so communicated are not only non-biblical but anti-biblical.

Fundamental to all these false assumptions are basic questions as to the philosophy of history. How and where is the meaning of history to be found? What is the nature of man's higher life? The institution of higher education should be the one place where these crucial questions are insatiably canvassed with all the participants in the discussion fully initiated into the alternatives. That such sporadic inquiry as obtains should go on with so little reference to our chief religious tradition is an anomaly which it is taking a major crisis to expose.

There are more particular vested interests that tend to depreciation or exclusion of biblical influence in our higher education. Chief of these is the academic-intellectual which would see in proposals for stronger departments of religion or the reshaping of the philosophy of the college a danger to the academic *status quo*. Departmental prestige is, of course, involved in any change of emphasis. There may also be in some situations vested interests of a social or economic kind which are satisfied to leave certain pages of the Bible in obscurity. And there are interests of a dogmatic-sectarian character that conscientiously hesitate to have the Bible interpreted by anyone outside their own tradition. It is a tribute to the open Bible that it can still be looked upon as dangerous.

A further reason for the reduced role of the Bible is that the debt of democracy to the Hebraic-Christian tradition has been far too inadequately formulated. As a consequence, our representative institutions of higher education have not been sufficiently concerned to further the study of the Bible as a means of maintaining the liberties by which they themselves exist. No adequate discrimination has been made between democracy in terms of the eighteenth-century Enlightenment, the French Revolution, or English Liberalism and democracy as understood in terms of biblical presuppositions. The all but universal interpretation of liberty in an individualistic sense and the telltale omnipresence of the conception of "rights" as the shibboleth of democracy betray the sub-Christian and the insecure character of our social and political ideals.

CONTEMPORARY RENEWAL AND MODERN APOLOGETIC

But contemporary demoralization has opened the eyes of all but the perverse to the inadequacy of prevailing assumptions. There are many new factors now favorable to re-emphasis on the deeper sanctions of character, conduct, and social motivation. Among educators we see manifestations that run all the way from meditativeness to panic, all indicating a hospitality to suggestions for the renewal of our spiritual heritage in education. With this is to be noted the gradually changing attitude with regard to the scope of science and scientific method. More fundamentally, we are conscious of an epochal cultural transition that carries with it a far-reaching dissolution of established authorities and the shattering of existing molds. Resistances to a new or renewed religious impulse that have until now seemed invincible and vested interests in the intellectual life which have appeared unshakable are on the point of crumbling. It follows that an extraordinary opportunity is open to those who will propose convincingly the claims of the Hebraic-Christian tradition, especially as represented in its classics, as the relevant rallying center for cultural defense and renewal.

Persuasiveness here will rest partly on reminders of the role that this spiritual heritage has had in our Anglo-Saxon life in earlier periods of crisis; partly on clear demonstration of its peculiar relevance to our culture and to the social and moral dilemmas of our contemporary crisis; and partly on general interpretation of the permanent vitality and intrinsic authority of its writings, indeed, their ultimacy as literature and as scripture in all that concerns the deepest life of mankind.

Here it is not sufficient to list the well-known concepts of the Bible which stand in contrast to those of the Hellenic or Buddhist or Hindu or neo-pagan world-view. The hard-won insights of the Hebrew—ethical monotheism, the divine activity in history, the divine goal of history, the biblical anthropology, the social aspects of the Kingdom of God—all such concepts do stand at one or more points in clear contrast with the teachings of non-biblical faiths. It is not to the point to obscure the magnificence or sublimity of non-biblical scriptures and classics, whether they be the Upanishads, the tragedies of Sophocles, or the flowerings of the influence of the Buddha in one age after another in the Orient. We are not merely concerned to argue that the Book of Job as tragedy or the prophecies of Isaiah as literature should have their place beside Aeschylus or Dante or Shakespeare. It is rather a question of fierce need and indispensable resort. A man or woman on the brink of distraction or alienation grasps for that which will guarantee wholeness and centrality. A world once nourished on the Bible can enjoy the luxury of its idolatries, the luxury of experiments with its own liberty, hazardous explorations of the very vitality it owes to its older faith. But the time will come when the stark enigmas of existence will disclose themselves in the midst of the years and a people will desperately seek for its center, as a man blinded in the full light of the sun will reach out for a fixed object; and at that time all the lesser creations of man's spirit, even those most glorious, will be as though they were not.

But to arrest the widespread neglect of, or revolt against, the Bible it will be necessary for the various confessions to agree on a common defense and a common apologetic. The continuing authority, validity, and relevance of the Scriptures must be demonstrated with as much agreement as possible between Jew, Catholic, and Protestant. Precious as are the particular dogmatic convictions of any faith or any sect to its own members, the various communions must be content to join with one another in an apologetic for the Bible grounded on human experience and natural theology. Repugnant as this may be to those who emphasize the incommensurable or unique character of the Word of God or who insist on the finality of one covenant rather than the other, the fate of Synagogue and Church, sect and Bible itself in the modern world may depend on at least a partial recovery of the classics of these faiths, on clarification of the worst confusions regarding them, and on persuasive emphasis on their fundamental values. The alien character of the Bible of which we have spoken, so conducive to error and confusion particularly in a culture like our own, makes such interpretation and simplification imperative.

Such an apologetic would be directed first of all to three non-dogmatic areas in the appreciation of the Bible, namely its depth, its fullness, and its universality of appeal. These can be established both by contrast with other scripture or with the great works of human genius and by positive exposition reinforced by the testimony of the wise and the great.

By the *depth* of the Bible we mean more than Emerson meant when he said that the place which the Bible holds in the world it owes "simply to the fact that it came out of a profounder depth of thought than any other book." We mean more than is suggested by Heine's phrase that it is "rooted in the abysses of the creation." We mean rather that the Bible engages man in the roots of his personal existence, in the inmost citadel of his moral being, at that level where disposition and choice make for character and character makes for destiny. In its concern with this ultimate and crucial stratum of human experience the vocation of Israel manifested itself. It was given to the Hebrews in their wrestling with the enigmatic angel of life, in their desperate exploration of disaster, to receive the classic utterances bearing on the human situation. And we therefore find in the Bible the axioms of human nature, the profoundest intuitions of the race, the inalterable propositions of the moral structure of the world. "Man shall not live by bread alone." "The wages of sin is death." "The heart is deceitful above all things." "The just shall live by faith." "Am I my brother's keeper?" "Shall not the judge of all the earth do right?" To neglect the report of those who sounded these depths is not only frivolous, but it is to shatter oneself on that moral order of the universe which Israel more than any other people laid bare.

By the *fullness* of the Scripture, an old phrase of Tertullian emphasized by the translators of the King James Bible in their address to the reader, we have in mind its plenitude and riches, its diversity of mood and prodigality of forms, its resources for all the protean transformations of the human spirit. To stress the humanity of the Bible is not to disparage it. Where shall men find the Creator and Appeaser of the human heart if not through the whole drama of man's works and days, by the hearth and by the well, at the sheepfold and in the field, at the market place and in the gate, in the shrine and in the council, and, alas, on the battlefield?

The *universal appeal* of the Bible, finally, has reference not only to this scope and diversity but to its form. The truth of the Bible is presented to the heart and to the imagination rather than to the intellect. It is concrete, not abstract; poetry, not prose; narrative and parable, not argument. It is not only that large parts of the Bible offer themselves through sensuous vocabulary, elemental image, and dramatic story to the child and to the unlettered—the literature of a small province penetrating by its universal eloquence to the farthest continents and archipelagoes of the planet—but that the Bible deals with the sublimest truth in its vehicle of symbol, that is, "in the only terms which children and adults, the simple and the wise, can use in common." For, indeed, in these matters all may rightly view themselves as children.

Thus it is possible for Jews and Christians, Protestants and Catholics, to find common ground for a defense of the Bible without invoking the authority of revelation. Few, however, will be satisfied with an apologia in these general terms. In particular the modern Protestant will maintain the *principle of revelation* with regard to the Scriptures and the divine acts they chronicle in ways that take full cognizance of modern thought. Passing beyond the position he can share with the Jew and leaving the Catholic to his own view of revealed authority, the modern Protestant restates the biblical doctrines and more particularly the doctrine of redemption in a form as congenial to the best modern philosophy as is possible without obscuring the scandal of the cross. We do not forget that decision for the Christian faith ultimately engages far more than the reason. But just as in America we would not post the laws of the land in Chinese, neither should we publish the gospel in Ptolemaic, in medieval, or even in seventeenth-century idiom. The later writers of the New Testament showed no hesitancy in taking advantage of the more rational and lucid thought of the Graeco-Roman world to liberate their message. Fortunately, for all its relativism, our contemporary thought-world offers us insights which will confirm rather than contradict the biblical views of man and his moral experience. It stands to reason, moreover, that the literary and historical criticism of the Bible should be conducted with no less rigor than any other historical study. The position of the Bible and the essential teachings of Christianity will suffer thereby only for those whose faith is attached to externals or for those who misconceive the nature of religious authority. To the presentation of religion in these terms the modern university and college should be hospitable.

In a modern defense of the Hebraic-Christian Scriptures the crucial doctrines that center about the person and work of Christ should appear not as matters of embarrassment but as decisive credentials. It is here that the issue as to revelation, its meaning and validity, presents itself most clearly. Traditional theology in its view of revelation may be said to lay its great emphasis on the discontinuity between the operation of God and the context of human experience. Even among many liberal Protestants today there is a vehement insistence on this point, however little inclination there may be to return to the paradoxical antitheses of the reformers. Modern thought, on the other hand, cannot rest content with an unbridged gulf between the creative or redemptive acts of God and the forces resident in human life. Yet even modern thought, save where it is a strictly earthy or reductionistic type of naturalism, is hospitable to the concepts of mutation in history, of emergents in personal development and in general evolution, and of significant cultural or religious myth which focuses in itself wide experience and serves to represent profound truth. If modern Protestantism would boldly interpret the centrality of Christ and the doctrine of atonement in such terms, as Toynbee and others have suggested, a way would be open for commending the truth of revelation to an empirical age. The central transaction of the Christian Scriptures would then be presented as an act of God mediated through the whole human process, but having such novelty or discontinuity as we must necessarily assume for the mystery of life itself.

The relevance of the Bible as a whole appears, finally, when we properly envisage the crisis in which we are living and scrutinize the forces within and without that have brought us to this pass. Not only does the understanding of our situation grow clear, but also the antidote to our disease is made available. The Bible clarifies our situation, for in it we have our best clue to the meaning of *history*. "The Hebrews possessed a secret. They knew which way the world was going." Israel had attained a grip upon those things which the processes of history have most at heart. It is not surprising that these things became partially known to a people whose temper and vicissitudes qualified them. "Verily the Lord will not do anything except he first reveal it to his servants the prophets." A similar understanding of the enigmas of history in any period is possible on the basis of the prophetic insights, but only so. The secularist, the utopian, and the historian of culture misread the signs of the times and the future. Over against their incomprehension of deeper historical principles and forces, the Bible presents the moral order of the world, the purposes of God, and the judgment of the nations.

Indeed, those familiar with the impact of our world crisis on the Church, especially among those peoples that were first the victims of the war, know how pages long obscured in the Hebrew prophets have come into their own. Passages in Isaiah, Jeremiah, and Ezekiel bearing on the responsibilities and destinies of nations have been brilliantly illuminated as by a pencil of light, and the relevance of the Bible to modern bewilderment has been widely felt throughout the religious world. We have in mind passages in which God announces

His inflexible disposition for the peoples grounded on justice—purposes now "to root out and to pull down" and now "to build and to plant." The terrifying horizons are opened to us of a strange God, the Eternal who hath His own purposes, and who is heard to cry out, "I will overturn, overturn, overturn!" Nations today, moreover, are in the mood to acknowledge that "the shameful thing hath devoured the labors of our fathers from our youth, their flocks and their herds, their sons and their daughters"; and to confess that their inhumanity is exposed: "I have set her blood upon the bare rock that it should not be covered."

One aspect of this special relevance of the Bible today is found in its challenge to the false faiths which dispute for pre-eminence in our culture. Where shall we find such armories for the day of spiritual battle as in the doctrine of *man* that is set forth in the Scriptures? All our contemporary foes have here long been understood and disarmed. Over against imperialism the Bible sets its injunction, "Thou shalt not covet." Against nationalism and the pretensions of the master race it states, "The Lord hath made of one blood all the nations of the earth." Over against Marxist materialism it sets its great claim, "Man shall not live by bread alone." And against the mass-man philosophy of both Marxism and fascism it sets its millennial experience and its ultimatums on the inviolable autonomy of the person. Such are not merely oracular aphorisms. They are classic and representative utterances born out of desperate vicissitudes; and the Bible in its totality, by virtue of its eloquence and the qualities we have stressed, has the power to convict men of these truths whenever they are disposed by soberness to hearken.

If such safeguards from social disaster at home and from cultural and international disaster in the world setting are important, the college and the university cannot relegate them to the Church and the Synagogue. Indeed, it is little enough to ask that higher education should at least have the shrewdness to insure its own liberties and should engage the healthful forces of our religious tradition against the irrationalism and violence that threaten their own libraries and that would station a brutal sergeant at their portals. Institutions that have any memory will rather count themselves sluggish and disloyal if in such juncture they do not make every effort to renew what has come to pass in the lecture halls and student bodies of the past. For from such seed beds have gone forth movements of spiritual life that have changed the whole direction of a culture.

CHRISTIAN SYMBOLISM: FROM MILTON TO THE MODERNISTS

The foregoing discussion of the Hebraic-Christian tradition in modern culture viewed with reference to the Bible can now be extended by an examination of the place of that tradition in *contemporary literature*. Here is another area where we can take soundings and so add to the evidence available for our diagnosis. In the imaginative literature of our time how far do biblical conceptions, how far does the Christian drama of salvation, play a constitutive part? We have in mind not the mere use of biblical allusion but the profound operation of the Christian philosophy, the employment of the biblical world-view as framework and the sacred lore as emotional resource of literary creation.

It is a commonplace of criticism today to recognize that literature of any universality employs the "machinery" or the "mythology" of some widely accepted body of symbol, rich in imaginative association and thus capable of giving to a work coherence and depth and resonance. The effectiveness of such a mythology for art or literature requires that it continue to have prestige for faith and to be accepted as living and potent. Once the Greek myths, for instance, become unreal and incapable of winning imaginative assent, they forfeit any power to serve the writer other than as a passing ornament. So it could be with the biblical material.

The situation today of the biblical symbolism in this regard is fully clarified only when we return at least to the time of Milton and trace the factors which since his day have led to its diminishing place in literature. The scientific movement which more than any other was destined to shake the hold of the Christian world-view had found powerful expression already before Milton's time, particularly in the work of Bacon. As time passed, the seventeenth century gave itself with increasing zest to the new "mechanical philosophy," which promised to liberate the minds of men and to bring in the dawn of a new day. Yet it was still possible for John Milton in this period to use the biblical scheme of redemption as the basis of his heroic epic with full conviction himself and, what is more, in anticipation of a reading public prepared to accept this biblical foundation as not merely convenient or decorative but as real and living.

Milton was himself to a great degree a child of the Renaissance and a humanist. His own rationalization of the Scriptures had gone far, and it was no simple matter for him to marry his bold conceptions to the pictorial material of the Bible. Yet the massiveness and ardor, the granite and fire, of his puritan faith lent coherence to the whole. The sublimity of the biblical conceptions found a voice and a language worthy of it, and the resulting work went forth to a generation still close enough to the ages of faith, to the Reformation, and especially to the puritan preachers to hear and to understand. The whole cosmic scheme, the Genesis narrative, Satan and the fall, the angels and the devils, the redemption to come, all these had meaning and authority for Milton's time. He could utilize them. This mythology had not been exploded. The life currents of the age still ran through this body of conception, if not as unconsciously and inevitably as in the time of Dante, yet in some respects with more meaning because of the acute religious throes of the period. The alternative mythology of science, while it had had its unsettling influence on many, as on John Donne, had not yet supplanted it. And Milton's particular power in evoking the Christian metaphysics lay partly in the fact that he had not, like Donne, laid himself open to all the subtle and complex impulses of the new age that was dawning.

As the century wore on, however, the new scientific philosophy took more and more possession not only of men's minds but of their imaginations. The impulses of the Renaissance came into their own and the war upon scholasticism went on apace. This carried with it the supplanting at length not only of the Catholic but also of the Reformation form of the Christian world-assumptions and not only of the Christian imagery but also of that classical imagery which had meant so much to the early Renaissance. For a time men were content with a divorce of reason and faith, but this segregation of religion meant its ultimate withering away before the claims and exuberance of reason. So we are brought to a time in which the poets are permitted no use of the elder world's mythologies save as decoration and ornament.

Here we may take the situation of Wordsworth at the end of the eighteenth-century Age of Reason as instructive. For it was the altogether unprecedented task of Wordsworth to have to read significance into man and the world by the sole power of his own vision, without the resources, hitherto indispensable to poetry, of either the classic or the Christian symbolism. He was "left alone, seeking the visible world."

To animize the "real world," the "universe of death" that the "mechanical" system of philosophy had produced, but to do so without using an exploded myth or fabricating a new one, this was the special task and mission of Wordsworth.[1]

Oversimplification is avoided in picturing the situation at the close of the eighteenth century if we make the following observations. For one thing William Blake's procedure shows us that it was possible then for a poet to draw on biblical doctrine and unite it with esoteric elements to raise a powerful voice against the dominant outlook, though one with a limited echo. Shelley's solution was to construct a personal mythology with the incorporation of eclectic elements from new and old. In the case of Wordsworth himself one should by no means overlook the latent, and in his later period overt, influences of the Christian tradition. It is true that the two most striking positive influences in his work came from the world-view of his time: the sacred quality ascribed to the physical creation, and the romantic view of man. But latent in his work is a nonconformist heritage, working through the handicaps of his situation and acting as a check upon the romantic pantheism then taking its rise.

What has been said about Wordsworth would fit equally the cases of Emerson and Walt Whitman in this country later. In Hawthorne we recognize the last important figure here to do his work as one freely at home in the Hebraic-Christian tradition. Melville illustrates the acute and agonizing stage of the transition and partly for that reason is the most revealing, if not the most significant, figure of the period. But with the work of Emerson and Whitman the Hebraic-Christian tradition goes underground, expressing itself only indirectly thereafter though still powerfully. The departure represented by these writers had its occasion in the general movement known as "romanticism," which in its deeper sources drew from revolutionary optimism and German idealism, the latter taking the form of transcendentalism

[1] B. Willey, *The Seventeenth Century Background*, London, 1942, pp. 298, 299.

in this country. In Emerson and Whitman, particularly in the latter, this romanticism was compounded with the intoxicating self-sufficiency of an expanding new world and the first promise of the industrial age. Yet in both men the religious background still counted strongly.

For the eighteenth-century rationalism and classicism had played havoc with the Christian symbolism, but not necessarily with its deeper assumptions. One way of stating this as regards America may be put in the following words of Howard Mumford Jones:

> The story of eighteenth-century American development is the story of the slow fusion of a culture founded in Protestant dissent with certain of the secular ideas of classicism . . . the result was, on the whole, a secular but not a sceptical victory—that is to say, the transfer of the problem of universal order from the theological to the moral sphere.
> I suggest that the central problem in American thought, at least until late in the nineteenth century, is the problem of the moral order of the universe—a problem so primary as on the whole to subordinate almost all other philosophical and aesthetic considerations to this central question.[2]

Thus we are pointed again to the continuing if disguised operation of the Hebraic-Christian tradition in its Protestant form in American culture.

This retrospect prepares us to understand the situation of the biblical tradition in contemporary literature. That situation continued to change for the worse after the time of the romantic poets. The divinity of nature, the dignity of man, the two affirmations still permitted to Wordsworth or Whitman, evaporated with the march of science and the social disillusionments of the new industrialism. The popularizers of Darwin, Marx, and Freud have further disallowed the biblical scheme and its view of man. But the new situation is due not only to rational or ideological factors. Emphasis should be placed also on the basic changes in human relationships and social forms, in the family and the conditions of livelihood, in neighborhood, status, and class, effected by extensive industrialization and urbanization. It is these that have disposed men to accept counsels of relativism or negation.

In a culture widely characterized by proletarianism, bureaucracy, and impersonality old patterns of faith become unreal, and imaginative creations are suffocated save as they rise from the conflict of classes or from the new irrational ideologies born of despair or social malady.

---

[2] "The Drift to Liberalism in the Eighteenth Century," *Authority and the Individual*. Cambridge, 1937, pp. 333, 336.

The mass-man, "the hollow men," the Teilmensch, the depersonalized laborer or bureaucrat, the robot, the soldier—these represent the human product of a mechanized and rationalized world; and we should not forget the marginal wastage of the antisocial and the neurotic. Even those classes that maintain personal and social health are profoundly affected by the forces that determine the lot of men in such a society, forces of competition, conflict, insecurity, depression, and war. A significant outcome is that many men cannot but see the omnipotent forces that determine their lives as having the impersonal character of fate. For such men the Christian ideology seems untrue to the facts.

What kind of literature will such a society produce? Even recognizing that individual writers of traditional tastes and allegiances write as they will, what kind of literature will it, nevertheless, be disposed to read? Granted that the older traditions survive among us, they are not dominant. As the poet Wallace Stevens has said, ". . . . we live in an intricacy of new and local mythologies, political, economic, poetic, which are asserted with an ever-enlarging incoherence."

If we may take Prometheus as the representative type of the Renaissance and Bunyan's Pilgrim as that of the Reformation, we may note a melancholy outcome of the adventures they have undertaken in the modern world. The exuberance of the former has been humbled, and he has been chained by Zeus like his prototype, while the latter finds himself back where he started in the City of Destruction.

It is understandable, then, that there should be a wide disbelief in Jewish and Christian doctrines and values, disuse or ignorance of their Scriptures, conceptions, and vocabulary, attacks upon their institutions, even blasphemy against their holy things. One or another of these attitudes appears in the brutality and atheism of naturalistic fiction and drama, beginning with Dreiser; in the attempt of Hart Crane to construct a new and secular myth for the interpretation of American destiny; in the nihilism of Robinson Jeffers; in O'Neill's resort to materials from the new psychology as the machinery of his more significant work; in the anti-biblical fastidiousness of Ezra Pound; in the dialectical materialism of the communist literature; and, to go abroad, in the rage for demolition of James Joyce and in the ironic desperation and bitter arraignment of the gods in Franz Kafka.

Over against such signs we may, indeed, remind ourselves of the writers in multitude among us who have sustained the heritage of faith despite all the onsets of relativism and social disorder. Without naming familiar names we can at least suggest the diversity of these "traditional" writers by speaking generally of the regionalists, the classicists, the nature lovers, the social prophets, the lyricists, the religious mystics. They and their following are part of the evidence. It is clear that the older voices of affirmation, of health and vitality, as some will say, continue to speak today amid our confusion of tongues.

But it is just the crux of our modern situation that masses of our contemporaries no longer feel and speak in their terms. The traditionalists and the modernists are like men who in the darkness have been carried far apart by ocean currents and who at daybreak are no longer within hailing distance of each other. Just so, indeed, the modern world has been carried out of range of such voices as those of Wordsworth or Shelley or Browning, not to say of Rupert Brooks, Bridges, and Vachel Lindsay. The life situations are too diverse. Basic needs have altered, the co-ordinates that locate men's existence are no longer the same, and men's assumptions and idioms have changed correspondingly. Yet the modern writers inevitably carry over in varying fashion, consciously or unconsciously, legacies of older convictions. The most profitable way to define and to distinguish in this regard is to scrutinize several of the poets whom the modern spirit has claimed, with particular attention to whatever evidence may appear of influences upon them of a traditional religious character.

CONTEMPORARY POETS AND THE CHRISTIAN TRADITION

It is worth while returning first of all to D. H. Lawrence, not only because so many of the issues of the new period appear in his work but because his mystical attitude can be compared and contrasted with that of Wordsworth. Lawrence suggests to us the recoil of sensitive men of our period from the machine and from a society so mechanized and commercialized as to have lost its roots in nature. He postulated a culture in the best sense primitive because all its functions would be wedded to the cycles and processes of the natural order. In its name he attacked not only mechanism but rationalism. He testified to the stifling of man's instinctive life today, particularly in its social expression. Lawrence's treatment of topics related to the sexes, though often misconceived and antinomian, was serious, and he could be profoundly shocked by frivolity, commercialism, or calculated hedonism in these matters. The fact is, his point of view here was conditioned by his reaction against the faulty attitudes that handicapped his own youth in the stunted nonconformity of his Nottinghamshire home. It is to be noted that his preoccupation with the topic of sex and the paroxysms of his struggle as a youth with its dilemmas, as well as the elements of blasphemy in his work and his concept of himself as a prophet, point in a negative way to the hold upon him of the religious tradition he sought to escape or to transcend.

This observation can be developed into a generalization concerning vast numbers of men today. The Hebraic-Christian tradition, outwardly repudiated, colors their unconscious life, penetrates to the very fiber of their being, and appears unexpectedly in unconscious disguises and parodies of itself. The best in Lawrence, his dynamic personalism, his convulsive striving for abundance of life, his prophetic impulse, these testify to the nonconformist soil out of which he came. In many respects the case of Whitman was similar. And what is true here of Lawrence and Whitman has its general bearing on the Anglo-Saxon type today, so far as it has the Protestant background. Yet in the case of Lawrence it is clear that in his twentieth-century setting no form of traditional ideology offered itself as an available vehicle for his work or his prophecy. He gave expression to a neo-paganism, at some points as in *The Plumed Serpent* highly irrational and dangerous. Though he found nature sacred and man divine, the contrast with Wordsworth's vision is instructive. For the latter read into nature and man and their communion the concepts of mind and spirit. Lawrence, on the other hand, saw only a prodigal life force and a polytheistic world in which all creatures including men are divine and autonomous, with no law but their own self-fulfillment.

The case of Yeats illustrates again the recoil from scientific rationalism. He perceived that it would devastate his imaginative life, and he deliberately ignored it and built up high fortifications against it, including the elaboration of his own symbolic "science" drawn from an eclectic mysticism. What particularly interests us here is his considered refusal of the Christian tradition, which can be documented in certain of his later poems, on the ground that it would deprive him of the richness of his human emotional experience, the *sine qua non* of the artist. The implication is that a Christian so sterilizes his heart that there is no concern left for art and the rich play, the riot and fecundity of life. It is as though the only matter of poetry for Yeats were "the lust of the flesh, the lust of the eyes, and the pride of life." Evidently Yeats perceived in Christianity an ascetic strain which threatened the values he cherished as a man and as an artist. In one of his later poems the following dialogue appears:

> The Soul: Seek out reality, leave things that seem.
> The Heart: What, be a singer born and lack a theme?
> The Soul: Isaiah's coal, what more can man desire?
> The Heart: Struck dumb in the simplicity of fire!
> The Soul: Look on that fire, salvation walks within.
> The Heart: What theme had Homer but original sin? [3]

And in the following poem he bids a reluctant farewell to the Catholic mystic, Friedrich von Hügel, with whom he recognizes that he has much in common, yet

> Homer is my example and his unchristened heart.

The fact is that Yeats was basically right in recognizing the ban that the faith lays on many of the complacencies, not to say idolatries, of the artist. As witness we might summon Gerard Manley Hopkins who for a long time refrained from practicing his priceless talent because of his religious vocation. But we may also say that such Christianity as Yeats found about him was anemic, archaic, or bare, and his resort to other cultural resources is understandable. An ample and passionate Christianity, aware both of its symbolic heritage and of its legitimate humanism, would have made quite a different appeal to Yeats than the forms he knew, whether Catholic or Protestant. As it was, he found a vehicle for powerful work in his own system. But his work suffered from that "numbness to the intricacies of human feeling" which Yvor Winters has shown to be a limitation of all mystical poetry.

In Yeats' case again we have a far-reaching clue to the attitude of many modern men towards the Hebraic-Christian tradition. Christianity has allowed a major ambiguity to remain unsolved in the eyes of generations, of which advantage has been taken by man's "unchristened heart." That ambiguity concerns the affirmation of life. The Christian has not made clear to himself the paradox of world

---

[3] "Vacillation," *The Collected Poems of W. B. Yeats*, New York, 1937, p. 290.

denial and abundance of life. He has often lodged in an otherworldliness that has seemed, whether to a Nietzsche or a Lawrence or a Yeats, a blasphemy against the natural creation, or in a compromise with life that has lost creative appeal and so has deserved the apostasy of those thirsty for reality.

The case of Yeats, however, illustrates another point. The aesthetic type, of considerable influence among our sophisticated groups and incidentally of decisive influence in Latin and Hispanic-American culture, is dominated by a misconception of the biblical tradition. Thus Ezra Pound can write with regard to the Hebrew Scriptures:

> If any one in calm mind will compare the Four Classics [of Confucius] with the greatly publicized Hebrew scriptures, he will find that the former are a record of civilized men, the latter the annals of a servile and nomadic tribe that had not evolved into agricultural order. It is with the greatest and most tortuous difficulty that the Sunday school has got a moral teaching out of these sordid accounts of lechery, trickery, and isolated acts of courage, very fine and such as could be paralleled in the annals of Mohawks and Iroquois. . . . Jehovah is a Semitic cuckoo's egg laid in the European nest. He has no connection with Dante's God. That later concept of supreme Love and Intelligence is certainly not derived from the Old Testament.[4]

Such a passage shows lack of familiarity with Old Testament history and backgrounds and with the sources of medieval theology. Yet such misconceptions with regard to the Scriptures are widespread among writers today. Until they are corrected, any true appreciation of the biblical view of life and of the universal relevance of its culminating drama will be impossible. Fortunately the use of biblical narrative by a thoroughly modern writer like Thomas Mann in *Joseph and His Brothers* and of biblical patterns by a writer like Franz Kafka reassures us that the questions raised and answered in the Scriptures will continually force themselves upon us when we are driven to the profounder levels of experience with which these Scriptures deal.

Yet neither Yeats nor Pound wholly escapes the values of the biblical tradition. Modern man is the creature of that tradition and cannot extricate himself from it if he will. It is true that in his later ripe eclecticism Yeats often comes very close to a pagan transcendence of evil. Yet by and large he gives abundant evidence of his sense of a moral and prophetic task. It appears in his grave rebuke of the passions and violence of the civil strife in Ireland as well as in his refusal to abandon

---

[4] "Mang Tsze," *The Criterion*, London, July, 1938, pp. 617, 618.

his task "of giving more backbone to the high-minded and the high-hearted, to the sweet-minded and the sweet-hearted."

> That were to shirk
> The spiritual intellect's great work . . .
> Nor can there be work so great
> As that which cleans man's dirty slate.[5]

Pound also in his most significant work appeared as a moralist in the best sense, attacking the acquisitive motive in modern society and flaying the philistinism of a world without ritual.

T. S. Eliot with his New England background, his wide culture, his deep initiation into the relativism of the modern outlook and into post-war society, offers us a peculiarly revealing case if not a widely representative one. His earlier work gave a large place to satire on the current types and ethos of Christian bourgeois society. In *The Waste Land*, *Gerontion*, and *The Hollow Men* we have the full expression of the drought of this society. It is this work of Eliot that found in a whole generation its sounding board, that is, those that had the cultural initiation to understand. It was not merely a postwar disenchantment that was expressed here, however, but the famine of spirit, the starvation ration, the anemia and meagerness of our world as a result of its having endured one deprivation after another since nobler days. Yet nostalgia for the past was only one strand among others, and more deeply viewed, the poems describe the human condition at any time.

If we ask now what body of symbolism Eliot employs in *The Waste Land* as framework and resource, we note that he has turned to widespread motifs from primitive religion. With these he uses allusions to the more advanced religions and telling passages from Dante and other poets. This eclecticism, like that of Yeats, indicates again the non-availability of the Hebraic-Christian tradition for any wide communication in our secularized age. When Eliot turned to more direct use of Christian themes with *Ash Wednesday* and *Murder in the Cathedral*, he lost a large part of his earlier following. As is well known, Eliot has now for some time been fully identified with the Christian faith in its Anglo-Catholic form, having also become a British subject. In his case apparently solution of our modern dilemmas in terms of the Protestantism in which he was born was impossible. E. A. Robinson, who belonged to the same background, likewise never found in it the

[5] *Last Poems and Plays*, New York, 1940, p. 83.

resources for a buoyant and positive faith. When Eliot reached beyond the dearth of our age to triumphant affirmation, he had to pass beyond New England nonconformity to do so. Robinson fought the issue out in the framework of his forefathers but could not go beyond an heroic stoicism. Yet in both cases the residual power of the biblical tradition is manifest. If the tradition does not commonly declare itself in overt affirmation or in religious fervor, it is not because it is moribund. It is clear, however, that it must renew itself if it is to hold its talented sons or to furnish them with a system of faith adequate to its modern task and of a dramatic quality conducive to literature and the arts.

When we turn to W. H. Auden, we find again a paradoxical combination of traditional and secular elements. The Anglo-Catholic critic, Brother George Every, after stating that even the blasphemy of extreme moderns like D. H. Lawrence indicates an unsuccessful repression of the Christian faith rather than real apostasy, then adds:

Such distortions of a Christian frame of reference as we find in the work of W. H. Auden seem to be far less sinister, because they betray themselves at every point and indicate suspense rather than bitterness.

Auden affronts and offends all forms of archaism and tabu as well as complacency and softheadedness. He makes continual war on shallow faiths and slogans, the "woozier religions" and unexamined crusades. He startles by his thoroughgoing empiricism, his recurrent tributes to the great scientists and disturbers of men, particularly to Freud:

> Great sedentary Caesars who
> Have pacified some dread tabu,
> Whose wits were able to withdraw
> The numen from some local law
> And with a single concept brought
> Some ancient rubbish heap of thought
> To rational diversity.[6]

Indeed, the significance of Auden lies in the fact that he bridges the gulf between the "mechanical philosophy" and the Christian tradition and weds the conceptions and the language of both, as any outlook must that hopes to speak to the future. The same writer that can appeal to Rimbaud and Baudelaire and quote Voltaire and Nietzsche against Rousseau can also find his themes in the Church Fathers:

[6] *The Double Man*, New York, 1941, p. 40.

O Thou who lovest me, set my love in order,

and can write:

O every day in sleep and labor
Our life and death are with our neighbor.[7]

All in all, the humility, compassion, and responsibility that we find
in the best of the modern poets suggest that the religious reticence
and non-dogmatic character of the modern conscience do not indicate
infidelity but rather a process of restatement. The case of Auden is
the most intriguing as far as future solutions are concerned. For one
thing he is clearly animated by at least the ethical aspect of our
religious heritage, and his interest in such figures as Luther and Pascal
is significant. He combines with this a thoroughgoing social orientation in our complex world. Finally, he is fully initiated into the empirical outlook so determinative for the modern man, and he relates the
data of the sciences, especially psychology, to the field of values in a
way that preserves much of what the prophetic tradition has stood for.
Paul Tillich in discussing the possible solutions today for the dilemma
of Protestantism has distinguished the following: (1) re-Catholization,
(2) dissociation from modern culture altogether, (3) Christian socialism. If Eliot illustrates the first of these, Auden may be said to illustrate the last.

The writers we have briefly scrutinized would point us to the conclusion, then, that the Hebraic-Christian tradition is still a vital force
in contemporary culture but that its witness is indirect, ambiguous,
and at points deeply overlaid with secular or neo-pagan impulses. We
could have called attention to other writers, embittered, nihilistic, and
surrealist, whose work would have strengthened the case for those
who see disintegration. In their respective ways "Oliver Allston"[8] and
Alfred Noyes[9] have recently castigated the pseudo-intellectuals and
the modern writers and artists and have charged them with the
betrayal of our best spiritual tradition. One might point them to the
comportment of the corresponding French groups in face of the Nazi
occupation. Those who have been outstanding for courage and integrity have included Paul Valéry, the heir and ornament of the school

[7] *Ibid.*, p. 71.
[8] Van Wyck Brooks, *The Opinions of Oliver Allston*, New York, 1941.
[9] *On the Edge of the Abyss*, New York, 1942.

sometimes described as "les mauvais maîtres," and André Gide, author of *L'Immoraliste*. The matter is too complex for so sweeping a denunciation as either of those mentioned. Take perhaps the most controversial case, and a writer we have not discussed, James Joyce. The power that is self-evident in *Ulysses* is immediately related to the ambivalence of Joyce's attitude not only to men and women but to Dublin, to the Christian faith, and to the English language itself. He loathes them, and he loves them. And so he breaks them down, and yet despite his savagery he cherishes and broods over and fashions them in such a way as to redeem the very act of disintegration.

Our conclusions with regard to recent literature agree on the whole with those drawn from our inquiry into the role of the Bible in modern culture and education. It is confirmed that for various reasons the biblical tradition has lost its dominant position in the common life and in higher education. The great stream has gone underground, where, however, it makes itself felt in indirect ways. After all, the men and women of our society have been shaped by it in centuries past, and they witness to its power even when they ignore it or decry it. For several generations we have drawn sufficient strength from it to move out on alluring but dangerous explorations of our freedom, experiments with that very spiritual capital it had loaned us. The results of these explorations, whether in the public or private arena, whether in the international or the domestic scene, have brought us close to irreparable disaster. But we may believe that the lesson has been learned. The exuberant and heady adventures in self-sufficiency are now concluded. We have heard the terrible surf beating not far off on a lee shore. And we have forsworn the lying planets by which we chose for a time to steer, to take again the North Star as our guide.

9

Christianity and Modern Philosophy

MODERN PHILOSOPHY, IT HAS BEEN SAID, FREED ITSELF FROM ITS MEDIEVAL bondage to theology only to become enslaved to science. Like most historical generalizations, this statement is far too simple. It is unjust to medieval philosophers such as Thomas Aquinas who used reason to construct a "natural" theology independent of revelation. It is equally unjust to the many modern philosophers from Leibniz to Whitehead who have recognized the importance of religion to philosophy. Nevertheless, the generalization is a useful exaggeration of the fact that science has more and more replaced religion as the dominant influence upon modern philosophy. From the seventeenth century the prestige of science with philosophers has waxed while that of religion has waned; and since the latter part of the nineteenth century the dominant philosophy in many circles has been a naturalism frankly opposed to Christian theism.

What is the fundamental cause of this attitude of modern philosophy to religion? It is to be found, I think, in an uncritical acceptance by modern philosophers of certain assumptions about knowledge and its relation to faith. For these assumptions have given rise to the two methods of attaining knowledge most prized by modern philosophers, rationalism and empiricism; and the exclusive use of these methods, singly or together, has led inevitably to the present dominance of a naturalism which is fundamentally hostile to Christian faith. In order to substantiate this thesis, it will be necessary, first, to examine critically the suspicious or negative attitude of some representative modern philosophers [1] towards Christianity and to show that it has been determined largely by narrow theories of knowledge which excluded the insights of Christian faith. It will then be in order, second, to suggest a more adequate view of knowledge and faith which would

[1] The author is aware of the fact that the selection of only a few philosophers for treatment requires a simplification that is misleading. There is no intention to deny or minimize the importance of the many philosophers who have remained loyal to Christian theism.

make possible once more a positive relationship between philosophy and Christianity. Since philosophy has been impoverished and Christianity has been weakened by the divorce of reason from faith, a new union of the two acceptable to the modern man is desperately needed in a world which is crying out for a reasoned faith to restore meaning to personal and social life. The third part of the chapter, therefore, will discuss the possibility of a Christian philosophy and illustrate its general character by reference to a few philosophical issues.

RATIONALISM

Modern philosophy begins with a vigorous repudiation of authority and an affirmation of the autonomy of the human reason. Perhaps the best example of this is the "systematic doubt" with which Descartes began his search for a true philosophy. Having come to doubt the truth of all he had been taught, he determined to make a fresh start for himself, taking his own reason as his guide. His words are famous:

As for the opinions which up to that time I had embraced, I thought that I could not do better than resolve at once to sweep them wholly away, that I might afterwards be in a position to admit either others more correct, or even perhaps the same when they had undergone the scrutiny of Reason.[2]

If he followed reason rather than custom or authority, he thought, he might hope to gain certainty. The method he laid down for this purpose required, first and foremost, that he should not accept anything as true which was not presented to his mind "so clearly and distinctly as to exclude all ground of doubt," and that he should proceed step by step from "objects the simplest and easiest" to objects more complex. He set out, therefore, to reconstruct his opinions from the very foundations according to a definite plan, beginning with a simple but certain truth and proceeding step by step to deduce more complex truths. In this way, he was convinced, the principles of philosophy could be established with certainty by reason. The truths of the special sciences which depend upon these principles could then be discovered with innumerable benefits to health and happiness.

The modernism of this way of thinking is evident: the distrust of the opinions of the past, the supreme confidence in one's own reason, the reliance upon a single method to discover philosophical truth, and

[2] *Discourse on Method*, p. 14.

the concern for the practical benefits of natural science. But the most important thing to note is Descartes' determination to accept as true only "clear and distinct" ideas which are directly intuited by reason and propositions which can be deduced from them step by step in geometrical fashion. The consequences of following this principle in the natural sciences without supplementing it by the empirical principle defended by Bacon would, of course, have been disastrous. But what is not so well understood is the consequence which actually followed its rigorous application at a somewhat later date to morals and religion.

In the first place the sharp separation of faith from reason meant that all efforts of theologians to make faith intelligible came under suspicion as mere human "opinions" concerning what is beyond the competence of reason. This made it impossible to bring the insights of faith into relation with truths derived from other sources and thus condemned them to the position of irrational and superstitious fancies with no claim to truth. Indeed, there can be no place for religious knowledge in a theory which exalts clear and distinct ideas as the sole means of attaining knowledge. Such a theory can make nothing of the conviction of the man of religion that he "sees" even now, but "in a glass darkly." But religion must be content with glimpses, indications, and bright flashes of divine truth; the clear and distinct ideas of the mathematician, or the rationalistic philosopher influenced by him, are very different from the analogies and symbols of religion which suggest the truth without describing it. The process by which we intuit a truth of the spiritual order, commit ourselves to its reality by faith, and then seek to clarify and confirm it by further experience and reflection is antithetical to the perfect insight into clear and distinct ideas defended by Descartes as the only source of real knowledge. There is a place, of course, for the effort of philosophical theologians to attain such ideas in the field of religion. But it must never be allowed to set itself up as the sole or the original source of religious knowledge. This may be less flattering to the human intellect than Descartes' view, but the finite and fallible reason of man must work in a special way not only in the field of religion but also in every field except mathematics and formal logic. It was a calamity for religion, therefore, when the "father of modern rationalism" divorced faith from reason in the name of the autonomy of pure reason. For it is the death of religion to relegate its beliefs to the realm of incomprehensible faith because they cannot be known in terms of clear and distinct ideas. Significantly, the attempt to do so was to lead in the eighteenth century to a denial of the validity of almost all of the distinctive beliefs of historical religion and the substitution of a purely natural religion based upon reason without revelation.

In the second place, Descartes' divorce of reason from faith was equally calamitous for philosophy. It cut philosophy off from one of the greatest sources of insight into the meaning of nature and human life and tended to narrow its survey to realities which could be brought by pure reason within the focus of perfect vision. The subtleties, the complexities, the heights of aspiration, the depths of mystery illuminated by flashes of meaning, indeed, all of the wonder of nature and of the religious and moral life of man had to be excluded. Without faith it was natural to assume that nature is a mechanical system; that what the poet says is mere fancy, useful only for the adornment of life and the refined pleasure it brings; that the unselfish love praised by moralists is really a disguised egoism; and that whatever religious people believe beyond the essentials of natural religion based on reason alone is "enthusiasm" and "superstition." It was no accident that in the eighteenth century classicism reigned in art and literature, hedonism in ethics, deism in religion, and, in some circles, materialism in metaphysics. It would be foolish to blame Descartes for all this impoverishment of philosophy; but it would be naïve to deny that a rationalism like his had a great deal to do with it.

EMPIRICISM AND SKEPTICISM

Empiricism, though it differs sharply from rationalism with respect to the primary source of knowledge, shares with it a distrust of every authority except that of the natural faculties of the human mind. Whereas rationalism holds that knowledge is restricted to clear and distinct ideas and to what can be deduced from them by pure reason, empiricism holds that knowledge is derived from the "simple ideas" of immediate experience by means of rational processes of abstraction and combination (Locke) or of irrational processes such as the association of ideas in imagination (Hume). The empiricist starts with a mind devoid of all "innate ideas," a *tabula rasa*, or clean slate. His aim is to show that all our knowledge is built up out of the "ideas" or "impressions" bestowed by experience upon the mind, and that reason must limit itself in all its thinking to ideas derived from these or lose itself in arbitrary and fanciful speculation.

The characteristic attitude of empiricism towards Christianity does not become fully evident in the philosophy of John Locke. Despite his empirical theory of the origin of knowledge, Locke has much in common with rationalism and with the Christian philosophy of the Scholastics. Like St. Thomas he believes that the existence of God can be demonstrated rationally, with the help of the causal principle. Accepting the validity of a revelation which goes beyond reason but is not contrary to it, he attempts to show the "reasonableness" of the essentials of Christianity. On the other hand, he tends to simplify Christianity too much by reducing it to a few religious beliefs and moral principles, by following which the believer will attain the reward of immortality. Moreover, he discounts as mere enthusiasm the "revelations" of those who claim to be inspired anew by the Spirit, and he subjects the revelation of the Scriptures themselves to the test of reason. In such ways as these he prepared the way for the deism of the eighteenth century which eliminated or minimized the "mysterious" in Christianity and had little appreciation of the religious as distinguished from the ethical elements in historical faiths.

But it is necessary to go to David Hume to discover the implications of a radical empiricism for religion. Hume derives all knowledge from sense impressions, and ideas are mere copies of these. When analyzed, moreover, each of our perceptions is found to be separate and distinct from the others. Hence all relations between the various items of experience are external and contingent rather than organic and necessary. For example, the relation between cause and effect is not a "necessary connection." The idea of such a connection is due simply to repeated experiences of the succession of two events in the past and the habit established in our imagination of associating them together in a definite order. It is obvious that the logical result of an empiricism and atomism of this kind is phenomenalism, the theory that the only reality knowable is the items of immediate experience and the relations between them as experienced. Hume's skepticism is simply a negative corollary of this view, since it denies the possibility of knowing the ultimate ground of these phenomena and their relations.

Hume's *Dialogues Concerning Natural Religion* must be read with this skeptical theory of knowledge in mind, since it is assumed throughout by Philo, the skeptic, one of the two chief spokesmen for Hume's own views. The book is concerned primarily with the "teleological" argument—the so-called "argument from design"—for the existence of God. This argument, as it was usually stated in Hume's day, proceeds from the analogy between natural order and the products of human design to a supposed analogy between their causes. The order of nature is thus explained as caused by a Divine Mind, which is identified with the God of religion. Hume rightly points out that the analogy between the order of nature and a product of human design such as a machine is weak and that in some ways the order of nature seems to resemble more closely a living organism which has its principle of organization within itself. He argues, therefore, for the possibility that nature has come into being by a process of growth or generation or even by a chance combination of its material elements. Why should the hypothesis of a Divine Mind be regarded as more likely than one or other of these naturalistic hypotheses? When we remember that mind appears only in one species of animal organisms and is thus very limited in extent and power, does not the preference of mind as ultimate cause seem arbitrary and presumptuous? At the most, he concludes, we may be warranted in believing that the cause of nature bears a "remote resemblance" to human mind. Moreover, when we realize that among its effects are the many evils which afflict life so grievously, we are forced to conclude that it is morally neutral or indifferent. At the end of the *Dialogues* one is left with the feeling that whether the existence of such a God is probable or not is, from the point of view of religion, hardly worth quarreling about.

Despite the ingenuity and acuteness with which Philo develops this attack upon natural religion, his argument will convince only those who accept his skeptical theory of knowledge. It is true, of course, that the order of nature, especially at the level of life and mind, does not bear a close analogy to products of human design. For this and other reasons, the eighteenth-century form of the argument from design, which pictured nature as a vast mechanism and God as a great Mechanic or Architect, is today indefensible. But the argument from design is for many strengthened rather than weakened by the fact that the order of nature is more like an organism than a mechanism, with the principles of its order immanent in it. The complexity and creativity, and consequently the wonder, of nature have been shown to be far, far greater than eighteenth-century scientists and theologians realized. Moreover, the probability that the order of nature can best be explained in theistic rather than naturalistic terms may be increased rather than diminished by the knowledge that living organisms have attained their present form as the result of a long process of evolution. For one thing, the countless cumulative variations in a definite direction, stressed by many under the name of "orthogenesis," must be explained. For another, when account is taken of the many ways in which the natural environment is adapted to life, of the rise of life to the level of mind and moral personality, and of the harmony of the beauty and intelligibility of nature with the faculties of the human mind, it seems most probable that Mind has been operative throughout the whole process.

The teleological argument, in short, has become broader since the days of Hume. It does not pretend that the explanation of facts by the hypothesis of a divine Mind is certain like a mathematical demonstration; it claims only that it is far more probable than any naturalistic hypothesis. Of course, if the teleological argument, even in this expanded form, were the only argument for theism, one might hesitate to accept it because its probability is so difficult to assess. But when it is combined with the argument from the moral consciousness confronted with ultimate norms and the argument from the religious experience of communion with a spiritual Reality that transcends the self, it has a strength far greater than it possesses when taken by itself.

Moreover, the plausibility of Hume's criticisms disappears when the assumptions behind them are critically examined. One of these, as we have seen, is that all knowledge is derived from perceptions which are separate and distinct from one another. On this atomistic assumption rests Hume's whole skeptical analysis of the causal relation. Yet the atomistic conception of experience has been abandoned by most psychologists and philosophers, and the reality of relations has been increasingly admitted. It is true, of course, that when we attempt to discover the invisible Cause of the order of nature as a whole, we are involved in the risks that attend all speculation. Those who distrust reason and are more anxious to avoid error than to discover truth with respect to ultimate Reality will prefer, like Hume, to restrict themselves to phenomena. This is the temper which has motivated modern positivists. But the demand for a theory of the ultimate nature and cause of things is not an arbitrary one; it is simply the demand of reason for unity in its knowledge and of will for a good that is ultimate. The danger of applying such ideas as that of causality to ultimate Reality, though real, can be avoided only at the cost of refusing to think philosophically at all. In short, the dogmatism of sense is no more valid than the dogmatism of reason, and it is possible to hold it at all only by ignoring its complete inadequacy to deal with ethical, political, religious, and other problems of human life.

Once we have recognized the falsity of extreme empiricism and the philosophical skepticism to which it leads, the advantages of Creative Mind over natural processes as an ultimate explanation of the order and evolution of nature are obvious. Whereas the movements of matter seem to be blind and purposeless, the principle of organization and adjustment immanent in living organisms demands explanation in terms of purpose. Mind is known to us in ourselves as a source of organization, arranging and adapting materials to the realization of purposes. It is also a cause of development, envisaging possibilities that transcend actuality and moving progressively towards their fulfillment. The appeal of the naturalistic scientist or philosopher to the hidden potencies of matter to explain organization and development is an appeal to the unknown. The appeal of the theist to the creative powers of a Divine Mind, on the other hand, is an appeal to what is at least akin to mind as we know it in ourselves. That neither certain demonstration by reason nor direct perception by sense of the Creative Mind behind nature is possible and that it is necessary to conceive of it by analogy with human mind must simply be accepted with humility as a fact. But the analogy is derived from experience, and its use can be justified by reason as at least more adequate than any analogy drawn from the subhuman world of matter and life.

THE KANTIAN SYNTHESIS AND HEGELIAN IDEALISM

So far we have attempted to prove only that in their extreme forms rationalism and empiricism have tended to be hostile to the Christian faith. It might be supposed, however, that in a synthesis of rationalism and empiricism a more positive attitude to Christian belief would be found. But though this might seem a plausible thesis, it is not borne out by a careful study of the greatest exponent of such a synthesis, Immanuel Kant.

The heart of Kant's "critical" philosophy lies in his confident assertion of the validity of rational principles on the one hand and in his cautious restriction of these principles to phenomena of sense on the other. Thus rationalism is shown to be right in that necessary knowledge is possible by means of principles of reason; but empiricism is vindicated in that such knowledge is possible only in the realm of phenomena. Hence the validity of reason in natural science is justified while its claims in speculative philosophy are disallowed. Reason can know sensible objects, but it cannot know "things in themselves." When it attempts to transcend its limitations and engage in speculation about the latter, it falls into fallacies and contradictions. For religion this means that the traditional proofs for the existence of God and the immortality of the soul must be rejected as unconvincing.

But the influence of traditional theism upon the mind of Kant was too strong to permit this negative conclusion to stand unqualified. What could not be proved by the "theoretical" reason might be "postulated" by the "practical" reason. The "categorical imperative" laid down by the practical reason to govern moral action requires the existence of God, Kant argues, if virtue is to bring the happiness it deserves; and it requires immortality if the attainment of perfect virtue is to be possible. The precise nature and status of these two postulates of practical reason have remained something of a mystery from Kant's time to our own. That postulation is an act of faith is implied by the famous statement of Kant that he had "destroyed reason in order to make room for faith" and by his use of the term "rational faith" for a postulate. Yet the postulates are asserted to be necessary if the claims of morality are to be accepted as valid. In that sense they seem to be rational. But if they are necessary affirmations of reason rather than mere ventures of faith, why does Kant show such hesitation in according to them the status of full knowledge? The reason is to be found in his narrow limitation of knowledge to phenomena of sense, a limitation due to the empirical element in his synthesis. Thus the skeptical habit of mind arising out of his empiricism not only leads to the rejection of the traditional proofs of natural theology but puts his own "ethico-theology" based upon moral postulates in question.

Finally, Kant's rationalism and moralism combine to prevent him from appreciating the distinctive insights of historical Christianity. This is evident in his *Religion within the Limits of Reason Alone*. In this treatise he defines religion as obedience to our duties conceived as divine commands but puts his emphasis upon human duties as such. Duty is to be determined by human reason independently of any supposed revelation of the Divine Will. This is not surprising, since Kant makes so much of the "autonomy," i.e., freedom from authority, with which the practical reason of man lays down universal moral laws. But it makes impossible any real acceptance of faith in the revelation of the Divine Will in Christianity save in so far as it can be shown to accord with the dictates of practical reason. Moreover, the Christian belief that divine grace must strengthen the human will in its effort to do its duty is treated with grave suspicion. Though it is not completely denied, it is regarded as a mere possibility.

This is the more striking since Kant in the first part of the treatise describes the "radical evil" of human nature in terms which would seem logically to require the help of grace to redeem it. But Kant's fundamental skepticism with respect to all which lies beyond phenomena combines with his moralistic insistence upon the autonomy of the human will to make the Christian belief in grace appear to him both a dubious and a dangerous thing.

The concept of a supernatural accession to our moral, though deficient, capacity . . . is a transcendent concept, and is a bare idea, of whose reality no experience can assure us. Even when accepted as an idea in nothing but a practical context, it is very hazardous and hard to reconcile with reason, since that which is to be accredited to us as morally good conduct must take place not through foreign influence but solely through the best possible uses of our own powers.[3]

From the theoretical point of view a mere possibility, from the moral point of view a danger to autonomy—this is Kant's final verdict on the idea of divine grace; and with it skepticism and moralism swallow up one of the most distinctive Christian beliefs. Indeed, it is hardly too much to say that religious belief has with Kant ceased to be necessary in its own right and has become a mere support for moral obligation, anticipating and making vivid the commands of the practical reason. This is not to deny, of course, that Kant felt religious awe in the

[3] *Religion within the Limits of Reason Alone*, tr. by T. M. Greene and H. H. Hudson, p. 179.

presence of "the starry heavens without and the moral law within," i.e., the impersonal natural and moral order, or that the moral postulates whose ambiguous character we have described were sincere convictions with him. But this is, at the most, deism tinged with Christianity. The way is thus open to the moralistic religion of "ethical culture" in our time.

We can refer only briefly to the monistic idealism which followed Kant, although it constitutes an important movement between eighteenth-century rationalism and empiricism and the later naturalism. Nineteenth-century romanticism in literature and idealism in philosophy, despite their differences, have in common a tendency to substitute the immanent, impersonal World Spirit of pantheism for the transcendent, personal God of Christian theism. Unable or unwilling to emancipate themselves from the Christian tradition, however, many idealists sought to assimilate it to their own view. The Hegelian idea of a universal Spirit immanent in nature, the soul, and history is very different from the Christian view of God. But there is a way of minimizing this and other differences. To Hegel, Christian faith is simply the pictorial, imaginative expression of the absolute truth embodied in conceptual terms in his own philosophy. The historical events and beliefs which are fundamental to Christianity are taken as symbols of the eternal, universal truths of idealism and manifestations of them in history. Thus the incarnation of God in Christ becomes simply a notable example of the union of the Divine Spirit with the human spirit as a universal fact. As a result, little is left of the transcendence of God above humanity and of the need of a redeemer and mediator between the Divine and the human. Still less is left of the Christian idea of sin. Since to Hegel the real is rational and necessary through and through, sin becomes merely a necessary stage in the development of man from primitive innocence to spiritual maturity. Is it not obvious that when God has come to be identified with the spiritual principle in nature and especially in man, when Christ has become a mere symbol of the divinity of all men, and when sin has ceased to be a tragic fall of man from his high destiny, the meaning of Christianity has been almost lost? Because of its spiritual view of the world, idealism was more sympathetic with Christian faith than the earlier rationalism and empiricism had been. But it sacrificed some of the most profound and distinctive insights of Christianity by assimilating them to a philosophical pantheism incompatible with them.

NATURALISM AND POSITIVISM

After the Darwinian theory of evolution had triumphed, this idealism and the romantic deification of nature which was its literary counterpart faded away like a dream, and by the end of the nineteenth century naturalism had taken its place as the dominant philosophy. Despite its weaknesses, idealism had nobly stressed the uniqueness and pervasiveness of Spirit in the world and had sought to interpret human nature in spiritual terms. But with the coming of extreme naturalism, which denies the reality of everything but the system of spatio-temporal events we call nature, all of this changed. Naturalistic agnostics like Thomas Huxley could still recognize certain distinctive elements in the nature of man, despite their emphasis upon man's continuity with his animal ancestors and the indifference or hostility of nature to his highest ideals. But the adoption of mechanistic assumptions in biology and the extension of the scientific method to man in psychology and the social sciences led more and more in the direction of reductionism, i.e., the dogma that the higher and more complex is to be explained in terms of the lower and simpler. This resulted in a denial not only of the immanence of Spirit in nature but also of the uniqueness of the spiritual and rational nature of man, which had been insisted upon by classical, Christian, and early modern thinkers alike.

The full implications of reductionism for man and his morality were understood at first only by a few daring thinkers such as Nietzsche. But within the last two generations these implications have been made increasingly clear as Freud and others have attacked the very conception of man as a rational and spiritual being. On the Freudian view, man's personality is largely the product, not of an ideal of the self consciously envisaged and realized, but of the interaction of impersonal biological impulses and social pressures. With this naturalistic reductionism in the ascendency it is no wonder that in totalitarian ideologies the primary driving forces of human life are regarded as irrational, e.g., blood and will-to-power. Nor is it surprising that in democracies like our own the unlimited pleasure and profit and irresponsible liberty of the individual are accepted by many as the ultimate goal of life.

It is true, of course, that naturalism is not always reductionistic in this obvious and extreme fashion. Indeed, the materialistic type of naturalism has steadily lost ground among natural scientists and philosophers alike during the last generation. Its place has been taken by a "higher naturalism." The higher naturalism of Alexander [4] and others attempts to do justice to the uniqueness of the higher levels of nature which have emerged in the evolutionary process. From matter, or "space-time," life has emerged; from life, mind; from mind may not a new level of "deity" emerge? It would be unfair, therefore, to overlook the real distinction between this higher naturalism and reductionistic naturalism and unwise to deny the substantial truth of it as a description of the levels of nature. But if it is regarded as a philosophical explanation, it is subject to the same general criticism as the lower naturalism. To acknowledge the uniqueness of the life and mind which have emerged in nature is not sufficient. An adequate explanation of their emergence is called for. But the new naturalism, like the old, does not postulate the working of Creative Mind in the evolutionary process. It takes it for granted that life and mind have developed in some unexplained way from the lowest level of nature, i.e., matter or space-time. As a scientific description, therefore, it is to be preferred to the older naturalism; but as a philosophical explanation it suffers in some degree from the same error of reductionism.

It is sometimes said that most intellectuals today are not naturalists but positivists, that is, that they believe there are no grounds for a metaphysical position of any kind. Certainly positivism is very prevalent among natural and social scientists, more often perhaps as an unconscious habit of mind than as a consciously held theory; and an aggressive minority of logical positivists is to be found among philosophers. But despite its denial of the validity of all metaphysics, positivism in practice usually leads to naturalism. For positivism holds that truth can be established only by the method of the positive sciences which appeal to sense data to verify their propositions. Accordingly, knowledge is necessarily limited to natural phenomena and their relationships, and we can never get beyond them to their ultimate ground. Subjective events are regarded as concomitants of "objective" events, i.e. physiological processes, and as ultimately describable in terms of these. Thus minds constitute part of the system of physical events in

[4] S. B. Alexander, *Space, Time, and Deity.*

space and time rather than a unique order of spiritual realities with laws of their own. Similarly, all values are regarded as subjective events, satisfactions of desire or feelings, and these are in turn reduced to functions of the organism in relation to its environment.

Apart from its thinly veiled naturalism, the most obvious weakness of this positivism is that it arbitrarily applies methods similar to those of natural science to all fields of knowledge. As we have just noted, this leads to an assimilation of psychology by biology. In the social sciences it results in the accumulation of vast masses of data without an adequate understanding of their significance for human nature and society as a whole. In the humanities it subordinates the revelation of the spiritual life of man, its enduring values, and its varied expression in individuals to the study of biographical facts and historical relations. In consequence, positivism leads to a loss of that philosophical wisdom and spiritual depth which was in the past regarded as the highest achievement of the human mind.

The implications of naturalism and positivism for religion have become very clear in the last generations. The secularism of our society is largely due to the fact that, to minds which have been taught that natural phenomena alone are real, Christian experience and belief appear merely subjective and hence illusory. The only religion which has commended itself to naturalists in any numbers is that of humanism,[5] which seeks to turn the religious impulse to the service of moral and social ideals. Many men and women of Christian spirit who have become convinced of the truth of naturalism have attempted to maintain their loyalty to Christian moral ideals within the framework of that world-view. If naturalism were the only adequate world-view, this position would be a defensible one. But our analysis has indicated that naturalism is simply the late expression of an extreme empiricism which limits truth to what can be verified by sense data, i.e. natural phenomena. This limitation may be necessary in natural science, but it is quite arbitrary in philosophy, and if it were carried out to its logical conclusion, it would lead to complete skepticism in all fields.

Recognition of this fact had led some recent religious thinkers to a synthesis of the higher naturalism with theism. This synthesis may be called "theistic naturalism." It conceives God vaguely as a structure or

[5] See John Dewey, *A Common Faith*, and Julian Huxley, *Religion Without Revelation*.

process of nature, progressively realizing values. Since God on this view is neither personal nor spiritual, He (or It) is incapable of entering into communion with men. Religion becomes loyalty to the immanent, value-producing process in nature. This theory is superior to humanism in asserting the reality of a God of some kind and thus rooting human values in the cosmic process. But its conception of God is so abstract and indefinite as not to provide a satisfactory object of worship, and as a philosophy it represents a compromise between theism and naturalism which has the weaknesses of both and the strength of neither.

We must conclude, then, that the dominant theories of knowledge in modern philosophy are incompatible with rational Christian belief. The fundamental reason we have found to be that divorce of reason from faith which is assumed by all of them. Whether the theory of knowledge adopted be the rationalism of clear and distinct ideas, or the empiricism of impressions, or the synthesis of both in the critical philosophy of Kant, it has no place for a knowledge of supersensible Reality. For such a Reality cannot be apprehended in a clear and distinct idea; it cannot be experienced in a sense impression; and it transcends the categories of our human understanding of phenomena. In the last few generations the ultimate implication of every such theory of knowledge which rules out the intuitions of faith and depends upon the natural faculties of man alone has become clear in naturalism and positivism. For these simply represent, the one in dogmatic and the other in skeptical terms, the logical conclusion to be drawn from any theory of knowledge which rejects the one method by which man may transcend natural phenomena and gain knowledge of a divine, spiritual Being and an order of ultimate values—the intuitions of inspired men and the faith that springs from them.

REASON AND FAITH: A NEW APPROACH

If we are not satisfied with this naturalistic and positivistic conclusion of much modern philosophy, we must discover a more adequate conception of reason and of faith and of their relation to one another. As modern rationalists conceive of reason, it is based upon clear and distinct ideas, and it leads to conclusions as certain as those of logic and mathematics. This rationalism received its death blow at the hands of Hume and Kant, though the skeptical reaction of both went too far. Sober philosophers became more and more convinced that they must follow the method of empiricism which was winning such victories in the natural sciences. The wings of reason were to be clipped, and it was to be assigned to the subordinate role of interpreting experience rather than speaking for itself.

But this empiricism, as we have seen, looked with suspicion upon all ideas which could not be traced back to sense impressions as their origin. According to its narrow view of experience, religious experience of a supersensible Reality must be distrusted. As a result, the breakdown of rationalism in the eighteenth century did not lead to the re-establishment of religious belief by the method of a sound empiricism which could weigh impartially the claims of all kinds of experience. Evangelical preachers like Wesley might appeal to the personal experience of religion, and theologians like Schleiermacher might appeal to the feeling of dependence, as a sufficient proof of religion. But the skepticism engendered by rationalism and empiricism alike had become too strong for most educated people to trust religious experience as a source of truth. That is why deeply religious but intellectually honest writers of the nineteenth century, like Carlyle and Tolstoy, had to accept faith, if at all, only as an affirmation of the will in defiance of reason.

This tragic dualism of head and heart might have been avoided if a broader view of reason and experience had been taken. In the time of Descartes himself, Pascal had warned that a reason dominated by the "spirit of geometry" could not deal with the deeper and subtler realities of human life. In the nineteenth century, Newman insisted that religious belief arises, not out of logical proofs, but out of insight into the meaning of a mass of cumulative and converging evidence. In all the great matters of life—in moral decision, historical judgment, the understanding of man, as well as in religion—the data are various and complex, and a sensitive, discriminating mind is at least as important as logical acuteness in gaining fresh insight. Of course, the claims made by romantics for imagination, intuition, and the like have often been as excessive as sober analysis of their meaning has been deficient. But to deny cognitive value to insights derived from such sources because they cannot be completely formulated in clear and distinct ideas or verified by impressions of sense means to divorce reason from all the substantial realities and values of human life. As the logical positivists have shown, reason can be sterilized in order to insure absolute precision; but the result is to consign moral, aesthetic, metaphysical, and religious beliefs alike to the limbo of the irrational and meaningless.

In short, a broader view of reason than that which is based upon its use in logic and mathematics or upon its use in the natural sciences is needed. The dictum of Aristotle that the method of knowing must be suitable to the field of knowledge under investigation, the method of ethics, for example, differing from that of mathematics, must be taken more seriously. The tendency of a particular method to tyrannize over the human mind [6] by extending itself to other fields than that for which it was developed must be strongly resisted. And this must be done both in the interest of reason and in the interest of the life that it is meant to serve.

Faith, on its side, has also been misconceived. This has been one of the main causes of the attempt of rationalists, empiricists, and even idealists to dispense with it. Christians in the spirit of Tertullian have often defended religion by attacking reason and glorifying faith as irrational. In reaction against the excessive claims of Scholastics like Aquinas in behalf of a rational theology, Martin Luther sought to base faith exclusively upon the revelation by God of His Word in the Bible. The Puritans found in the Bible detailed rules or laws for ecclesiastical organization and moral life. The assumption in both cases was that revelation had been completed in the past and that it consisted of divine truths imparted to virtually passive minds. Spirituals and mystics like the Quakers vainly protested against this conception of revelation on the ground that the Spirit could still speak to men if they would listen. Others, like Richard Hooker and the Cambridge Platonists, insisted that the natural reason of man is also necessary not only to understand and apply the Scriptures but also to supplement them. But the theory of the verbal inspiration and inerrancy of the Bible was very powerful in Protestant circles until the rise of biblical criticism.

Is it any wonder then, that the deists attempted to base natural religion on reason rather than revelation, and that intelligent men like Matthew Arnold have been antagonized by the literalism and narrow-

[6] See the interesting discussion of this tendency in A. N. Whitehead, *The Function of Reason.*

ness of Christians who know only their Bibles? If the work of biblical criticism in the nineteenth century had not made it possible to see the revelation recorded in the Bible as a progressive one, conditioned throughout by the historical situations and the human minds to which it came and requiring to be read discriminatingly as well as devotionally, the Bible might have remained a permanent source of Christian inspiration, but it would have become a hindrance to intellectual progress.

In the Protestant churches the cause of biblical criticism has been won, on the whole, and a more rational view of revelation is now possible. The nature of revelation is one of the most vital issues of contemporary Christian theology, and there is much difference of opinion on disputed points. But there is wide agreement that, while revelation is due to the divine initiative, its form and interpretation are conditioned by the experience of men. There is also general agreement that the revelation recorded in the Bible does not exclude further revelations. Above all, revelation need not be regarded as intrinsically irrational; rather, it is an illumination of the minds of men leading to insights which can and should be verified by further experience and reflection. As a result, faith can now be conceived, not as a blind assent to divine truths imparted to passive minds, but as an affirmation of insights rising out of religious experience and a commitment to the way of life required by these insights. So conceived, faith does not put an end to the efforts of reason to understand ultimate truth. Rather, it provides intuitions which can serve as valuable materials for a religious philosophy.

THE POSSIBILITY OF A CHRISTIAN PHILOSOPHY

This poses a vital question for philosophers: Granting that a more adequate view of reason and faith is now available, how can they be brought into more fruitful relation with one another? The only satisfactory answer to this question is a Christian philosophy in which faith and reason supplement rather than contradict one another. A Christian philosophy may be defined as a philosophy which is developed by reason under the influence of Christian faith. The influence of faith must, of course, be constitutive, that is, it must be of prime importance. For if a philosophy is to be Christian, its first principles must be derived from the Christian faith. But it is equally important that the actual construction of such a philosophy should be carried out by reason freely and that it should take into account evidence derived from all the major fields of experience. Otherwise the result would be a Christian dogmatic theology rather than a Christian philosophy.

The possibility of such a philosophy, it cannot be denied, seems to many philosophers hardly worth considering, indeed, little better than a contradiction in terms. This is largely due to fact that they have unconsciously accepted as final the separation of reason and faith which we have been criticizing. Certain objections must, therefore, be met if the possibility of a Christian philosophy is to be conceded by philosophers.

The first is that philosophy must start without presuppositions and adopt only such first principles as are seen to be necessary after a careful analysis of all the facts. On this view, to accept the first principles of an historical faith as the basis for one's philosophy would limit, if not destroy, the autonomy of philosophy. Did not Western philosophy win its independence in ancient Greece by refusing to start with the popular religious faith? Of course, analysis and reflection upon various kinds of experience may lead to a theistic or other religious philosophy; but no philosopher has the right to start with an historical faith which requires such a philosophy.

This objection assumes that the first principles of a Christian philosophy must be accepted uncritically from the Christian faith without any previous analysis and reflection upon them and upon experience as a whole. But this assumption is due to a misconception of the process by which a Christian philosophy is constructed. Obviously the intuitions of faith can and must be tested before they are accepted as the basis of a philosophy. The fact that in some, perhaps most, cases the intuitions of faith have been accepted by Christian philosophers originally on authority and that the testing has come later is not important. For even if faith usually precedes the process of testing, it sometimes follows it. Augustine, for example, had wrestled long with the problem of Christian faith before he was converted. What alone matters is that the intuitions of faith shall have stood the test of experience and reflection whenever and as often as it was made.

But the objection also raises a more fundamental issue as to how philosophies in general are constructed. Under the influence of scientific method, many philosophers assume that a philosophy must be the result of inductive generalization from a mass of data of various kinds. They assume further that the philosopher is a detached spectator who has a disinterested curiosity but whose personal destiny is not involved in the results of his thinking. Both of these assumptions are false. Philosophy is not science. It is motivated not only by the desire to know but also by a thirst for life in its fullness; and it seeks not merely a scientific description of all phenomena but a general view of reality and its meaning. If it is to attain this end, it must do so from the vantage point of a central, dominant principle, bringing all phases of experience into relation with that principle in order to explain them and their relation with one another. What is the nature of this principle of explanation? It is an intuition or vision of reality. Socrates' dominant principle was Mind seeking to realize Good, and without it the Platonic philosophy would have been impossible. The dominant principle of Christian faith is that a creative, moral, loving Will is the ultimate Reality behind nature and history. Whether it is valid or not depends upon whether it enables us to interpret nature and history more successfully than do rival principles. There is a great deal to be said against it, as every Christian who has had to face squarely the problem of evil knows all too well. Indeed, it can never be proved with certainty. But it cannot be ruled out of court simply because it was discovered by Hebrew men of faith rather than by Greek or modern philosophers.

The second objection to a Christian philosophy is that to accept an historical faith as the first principle of a philosophy is to claim absolute and final truth at the outset and hence to close one's mind to new truth derived from other sources. This objection would be valid if Christian revelation were conceived as a fixed and final body of truth which must simply be held tightly and defended jealously. But, as we have already argued, this is a false conception of revelation. Recent writers on revelation [7] have pointed out that it is not a body of dogma that is revealed but God Himself. Dogmas may be necessary to state as far as possible what this revelation means, but they can never exhaust it. Similarly, it is not propositions of ethics which are revealed in the Sermon on the Mount; it is a kind of life, the life of love. Ethical propositions are necessary to make clear what this love requires, but

[7] For instance, Archbishop William Temple, in *Nature, Man, and God.*

they cannot fathom it completely in all its implications. For this reason the acceptance of the Christian faith should open rather than close, liberate rather than enslave, the mind.

The belief that an acceptance of Christian revelation necessarily leads to conservatism in thought and practice is one of the tragic results of the traditional misconception of revelation as a body of dogmas. But if revelation is conceived not as dogma but as the progressive disclosure of God's will in history, culminating in Jesus of Nazareth but not ending with him, a different result will follow. It will be seen to possess a unity very different from that uniformity so dear to rigid authoritarians. It has the unity in diversity of a growing organism, a piece of music, or a long friendship. As a result, it is open to further investigation and susceptible to reinterpretation as long as history endures. Modern philosophy is, therefore, right in thinking that the acceptance of revelation in the authoritarian sense of the term would frustrate the free investigation of truth by reason. But it has overlooked the fact that Christianity is primarily religion, not dogma; that its beliefs are expressed primarily in concrete and imaginative terms that can never be completely reduced to concepts; and that, in the conceptual interpretation of these as well as in the explanation of other aspects of reality, philosophy is free.

But, it may still be urged, if there is nothing final and absolute in a Christian philosophy, as this would seem to imply, how can it serve as a basis for the kind of commitment religion requires? The answer is simple: the Christian, whether plain man or philosopher, must make his commitment of faith according to the best philosophical formulation of it he can discover. But his Christian faith must not be so completely identified with a particular Christian philosophy as to be dependent upon its acceptance or discredited by its rejection. That would be to forget that even a reasoned Christian faith must always remain faith and that every philosophy is fallible. We have no right to glory in our human wisdom as if it could not simply confirm but take the place of faith. For those who believe that the revelation of God through the Hebrews and especially through Jesus of Nazareth is in some sense ultimate, the Christian faith in its essentials is ultimate; but any Christian philosophy by which they interpret its meaning will be at best only relatively and partially true. This leaves the way open for further developments both in their understanding of the faith and in their philosophical formulation of its relation to other sources of knowledge.

This brings us to the third and most difficult of the philosophical objections to a Christian philosophy. It is the objection against the fundamental assumption of such a philosophy, namely, that God has revealed Himself in a unique way through Christ. If there are no reasons for thinking that this assumption is valid, any discussion of a Christian philosophy, as distinguished from a general theistic philosophy, is academic. The doubts of many modern philosophers run back to the suspicion that faith in the revelation of God through Christ, upon which a Christian philosophy must be based, is irrational and arbitrary.

This is the greatest wave that threatens to engulf our argument, as Socrates would say. Though it is impossible to deal with it adequately here, one or two things about it may be said. The first is that it defines a serious task for the Christian theologians of our day. It has become fashionable for theologians to engage in philosophical discussions of religion in general, based upon evidence derived from science, the moral life, and the like. As a result of this preoccupation with natural theology or philosophy of religion in general, the defense of the specifically Christian faith has been seriously neglected. The study of what used to be called "apologetic" must be revived. It will hardly suffice to tell a philosopher who does not believe in the Christian revelation that he must believe it on the authority of the Bible or the Church, since he does not accept their authority. Nor will it be of any use to tell him at the outset that he might at least accept it as an hypothesis and test it by its fruitfulness in theory and practice. For it must be at least a live hypothesis for him, offering him a "vital option," if he is to accept it even provisionally and go to the trouble of testing it. In a world where there are so many rival hypotheses and where his life is as short as his art is long, he must have reasons for taking it seriously.

Many of the evidences that were relied upon in former times, such as the fulfillment of prophecy, the miracles of Christ, and his bodily resurrection, are at present quite ineffective. The main reason is that they depend upon facts, real or alleged, which are only externally related to the spiritual nature and purpose of that Divine Life which is the source and content of Christian revelation.

For example, even if the virgin birth stories could be shown beyond all doubt to be historical, they would by no means prove that in Christ there took place an incomparable revelation of the nature of God as Father and of the life of love possible for men as sons of God. At most, they would prove that on one side his origin was divine. For this and other reasons the evidence that is most convincing today is the personal experience of events of biblical and Christian history as a whole, as they make their impression upon needy and receptive minds and hearts. The primary evidence for the Christian faith, in other words, is the actual movement of the Divine Life in history, especially in the personality of Christ, and its proved capacity to answer the questions and satisfy the longings of all sorts and conditions of men.

Modern philosophers, on their side, have a special responsibility for examining carefully the reasons which have led so many of them to reject the Christian faith as irrelevant to philosophy. Most of these reasons are relics of the rationalistic and empiricistic theories of knowledge already examined. A good example is the common argument that philosophy can admit as evidence only such data as are accessible to all normal men, whereas the experiences upon which the Christian faith was and is based are limited to some men. Actually data are admitted as evidence by all modern philosophers which are accessible only to those who have met certain conditions of scientific training or moral sensitivity. The special conditions of Christian experience may be hard for many persons to meet since they include moral and spiritual conditions. "Blessed are the pure in heart, for they shall see God," said Jesus; and Paul reminds his converts that only those who "judge spiritually" can judge of "the things of the Spirit of God." But the appeal of Christian preachers since the days of the apostles has always been to all men, and hosts of men have been able, with the help of the divine grace, to meet the necessary conditions. In any case, the fact that only a part of humanity has ever known of the Christian revelation or that many have known without responding to it is irrelevant to the question whether it is true.

An equally common argument is that the very idea of a "special" revelation is arbitrary and arrogant. The orthodox Jewish and Christian view that the Jews were a "chosen people" in the sense of a race selected by God to receive His special favor has given rise to this argument. It is fortified by the interpretation of the incarnation of God in Jesus of Nazareth as due solely to God's will or good pleasure and as wholly discontinuous with His activity in the lives of other men. The answer to this, though one must speak of such mysteries with diffidence, is surely that God's special revelation of Himself to one people and uniquely in one man need not be regarded as arbitrary at all. The greatest Hebrew writers, such as the Second Isaiah [8] and the author of the Book of Jonah, regarded their people not only as the favorites but also as the servants of God with a mission to the Gentiles. From the vantage point of later history we can see that they have been just that. It must also be remembered that historical events and achievements are always unique, human genius always specialized. It is reasonable to suppose, therefore, that the most effective means whereby God could have revealed Himself and His will uniquely was to do so first through one people and finally through one man. Certainly the parallel of philosophy which spread from Athens and perhaps in a special way from Socrates to the whole Western world lends color to this suggestion.

But the traditional way of thinking about God's activity in terms of an arbitrary act of choice or selection is not the only possible way. The revelation to and through the Hebrews and especially through Christ was "special" in the sense of "unique." But we need not regard it as a matter of unconditional and arbitrary choice on God's part. The loftiness of imagination, the moral intensity, and the religious devotion of the greatest Hebrews from Moses onwards, whatever the explanation may be, were surely indispensable conditions of the unique and progressive revelation that came to them. And the Christian who believes that God is the Father of all men can hardly doubt that from the beginning of history He has been ready to reveal Himself to any people or individual who has been able to receive Him.

What are we to say, finally, of the view that philosophy must by its very nature disregard the unique events of every historical religion since its concern is only with the general structure of reality? It is, of course, the primary task of philosophy to deal with ultimate

---

[8] The anonymous prophet of the Exile whose prophecies are to be found in chapters 40-55 of the Book of Isaiah.

reality and its meaning in universal terms. That is why it uses the language of concepts, which embrace many particulars in one idea. The individual event or person, on the other hand, is unique and cannot be apprehended fully by concepts. It is therefore, the proper object of history rather than philosophy. Religion differs from philosophy in that, like history, it is interested in the individual and concrete; but it is like philosophy in that it sees the individual and concrete in relation to the universal and supreme Reality, God. The question, therefore, is this: Granting that the proper language of philosophy is concepts by which alone the general structure of reality can be defined, can it afford to neglect the universal truths which are seen incarnate in individual events and persons by the eye of religious faith?

It seems to me that the answer must be a clear "no." Of course, if the intuitions of the Christian religion were completely discontinuous with truths discovered by other religions and in other ways, it would be impossible for philosophy to deal with them. If there were no universal elements in the revelation of God through the Hebrews and in Christ, there would be no way for the philosopher to understand it at all. But this is not the case, as the traditional interpretation of Christ as the fulfillment of God's revelation of Himself from the beginning has always affirmed. The Christian revelation, though individual and unique, is also the most highly developed expression of a universal revelation. Thus the philosopher will be able to find a preparation for and confirmation of the special revelation recorded by the Bible in the general revelation of nature, history, and experience. Therefore, his acceptance of the special revelation of Christianity will be an act not of blind, but of reasonable, faith. His faith will go beyond what reason can demonstrate, but it need not contradict it. Rather, it will be able to show the path to reason by providing it with first principles to be critically tested and developed into a Christian philosophy with the aid of knowledge derived from other sources.

THE NATURE OF CHRISTIAN PHILOSOPHY: AN ILLUSTRATION

The nature of a Christian philosophy may be illustrated by reference to the perennial issue between monism on the one hand and dualism and pluralism on the other. Broadly speaking, the greatest systems of Greek and medieval philosophy affirmed a plurality of substances and a duality of kinds of being. Plato and Aristotle were both dualistic in that they stressed the distinction between matter and form, body and soul, the world and God. Aristotle avoided the sharpness of the Platonic dualism in certain respects, but his separation of the active intellect from the rest of the soul and of the Prime Mover from the world emphasizes his own fundamental dualism. This dualism was, however, qualified by the theory of a graded scale of forms or kinds in nature, a "great chain of being," reaching up from formless matter to pure Form.

It was this modified dualism which dominated medieval philosophy. While monistic systems like that of Scotus Erigena were regarded with suspicion as pantheistic, dualism, which stressed the vertical dimension by exalting God above His creation and spirit above body, was widely accepted. Thomas Aquinas softened this dualism by means of Aristotle's gradational theory of the creation. In this way continuity was preserved within the framework of a philosophical dualism by placing the various species of creatures in an ascending order from matter up to God, with man occupying a middle position.

Modern philosophy, despite the influence of dualism, has tended towards monistic theories of the nature of reality, especially since the beginning of the nineteenth century. The primary reason for this, apart from its break with the Christian faith which had emphasized the vertical dimension of reality, was its acceptance of rationalism and empiricism. The aim of rationalism was to construct a comprehensive system of propositions concerning reality by deductive reasoning like that of mathematics. Evidence from the senses, imagination, revelation, or any other source which did not fit consistently into such a system was simply rejected or explained away. But it is impossible to construct a completely comprehensive and consistent system by this deductive method unless one reduces the apparent duality of existence to the manifestation of a fundamental unity. For continuity between all the different aspects of reality is necessary if they are to be connected by reason in a coherent system. To admit an irreducible duality of forms of being, such as matter and spirit or nature and God, would make it impossible to deduce either from the other and thus to pass from one to the other without a break in the reasoning.

Therefore, the rationalist tends either to treat matter and spirit as aspects of a more fundamental reality (Spinoza), or to assert the sole reality of matter and reduce mind to movements of body (Hobbes), or to insist upon the sole reality of spirit and view matter as a relatively undeveloped manifestation of spirit (Hegel). In similar fashion, the modern rationalist is unable to admit any irreducible difference between efficient and final causes, necessity and freedom, or the human and the Divine. Naturalistic monism, for example, under the influence of science and the dogma of the continuity of nature, reduces final to efficient causes, freedom to necessity, the Divine to the human. Idealistic monism, on the other hand, elevates all reality to the level of Spirit and virtually deifies nature and man.

Modern empiricism also tends towards monism. Since empiricism assumes with rationalism that all knowledge arises from the use of man's natural capacities, this is not surprising. Radical empiricism traces the origin of all knowledge to sensation. Therefore, it treats the unique spiritual activity at the center of the human self as merely a succession of states or contents of consciousness related to one another by efficient causality like that of the physical world. Thus the uniqueness and freedom of the self as a spiritual being are lost, and spirit is reduced to natural process. For the same reason, radical empiricism regards the experience of a transcendent, spiritual Reality as a figment of imagination projected into reality to satisfy vital needs, and the absolute imperatives of the moral consciousness as mere expressions of individual or social preferences. It leads to a naturalistic monism which reduces all reality to the least common denominator of nature.

What is the position of Christian philosophy on this issue? In the first place, there are obvious elements of monism in Christianity. It rejects the absolute dualism of spirit and flesh and affirms the unity of personality. It asserts the immanence of God in nature and history. Its interest in the eternal life as the ultimate goal of man's earthly pilgrimage does not exclude enjoyment of the relative values of this life. More positively, God is one and every other reality depends upon Him. These monistic elements stand opposed to any absolute dualism which cuts God off from effective contact with His world, treats the spirit as a disembodied wraith, and destroys the organic relationship between man and nature.

But, in the second place, Christianity also includes strong elements of dualism. It is dualistic in its metaphysics, in so far as God is conceived as transcendent, His Kingdom as primarily spiritual rather than material in its blessings. It is more radical in its moral dualism, sharply opposing good and evil, love and selfishness, God and Mammon to each other. The decision of each soul between these opposites is crucial, issuing in eternal life and bliss or spiritual death and misery. Christianity must, therefore, reject any monism, idealistic or naturalistic, which blurs or minimizes these metaphysical and moral distinctions. In short, a Christian philosophy is equally opposed to a sharp dualism, which breaks the connection between God and the world and between spirit and nature, and to the dominant monism of the modern period which blurs all distinctions.

Similarly, the position of a Christian philosophy on the issue between monism and pluralism is distinctive. On the one hand, there is an important element of pluralism in Christianity. The Christian ideal of the harmony of all creatures with God and with one another in love presupposes a plurality of creatures. For the Creation is enriched and the glory of God enhanced by the diversity of individual creatures, especially at the level of human personality. Christianity is therefore opposed to any pantheistic view like that of Spinoza which reduces individuals to mere finite "modes" of one "substance," or to the negative type of mysticism which swallows up individuality in the ecstatic experience of union with God. Moreover, the intensely moral and practical character of Christianity leads to an emphasis upon the freedom and responsibility of each person. Hence every attempt to reduce human acts to mere effects of natural causes or mere manifestations of a universal Spirit is incompatible with Christianity. On the other hand, an extreme pluralism would make the dependence of all creatures upon God for their existence and preservation, as well as the unity of persons in love, impossible. For this and other reasons, pluralism must be affirmed only in so far as it is compatible with an ultimate monism which stresses the sovereignty of God.

We are thus led to three major conclusions. First, modern monism, with its tendency to blur distinctions and to depreciate individuality, must be rejected. Only thus is it possible to do justice to the whole of reality in its height and depth and breadth. For reality cannot be understood by those who have been blinded by a dogmatic rationalism or empiricism to the obvious discontinuities of existence and the bitter struggle between the good and the evil. Second, the duality of God and nature, spirit and matter, good and evil must not be allowed to disrupt the fundamental unity of reality. This duality must be regarded as necessary to the ultimate purpose of the Divine Will and its realization in nature and history. The material then becomes the instrument of the spiritual, and the creation as a whole becomes the manifestation of the Eternal Goodness in time, a "sacramental universe" through and through. Third, the plurality of individuals is necessary in a universal order which realizes the beneficent purpose of one Divine Will in many finite creatures. In this way both duality and plurality may be viewed as necessary to the creative and redemptive work of one God who tirelessly seeks to bring all His creatures to fullness of life in harmony with Himself and with each other.

The Christian View of Man and Personality

The distinctive character of Christian philosophy manifests itself, again, in its view of man and its ideal of personality. For classical and modern humanism, that which distinguishes man is his rationality and his freedom. Almost from the beginning, Christianity was deeply influenced by this humanistic view, but it has never been able to accept it as adequate. For Christians man is a spiritual being, akin to and capable of being moved by the Divine Spirit. Though he is a part of nature, he is also a creature made in the image of God. Through faith he is able to transcend his natural existence and unite himself with the Divine Spirit. He is therefore responsible to God, upon whom he depends not only for his origin but also for his final destiny. If man is thus a spiritual being as well as a creature of nature, his natural capacities should be used for the ends of the spirit. Since God's purpose is a purpose of love, the faith which unites the human spirit with that purpose will give rise to acts of love. As faith is the root, love is the fruit of the Christian life.

But man's nature has been infected by sinful egoism and as a result his natural capacities are in need of healing. This is obviously true of impulse and feeling, for man is always in some measure at the mercy of his passions, and his affections are often stirred by trivial or evil things. But it is also true of the higher faculties which give him his dignity from the humanistic point of view. Not only the will but the reason itself has been perverted by selfishness, so that the self is unable steadfastly to do or even clearly to know its highest good. This is why Christianity insists upon a "conversion" or "rebirth" of the natural self, whether gradual or sudden. The self can escape its self-centeredness only if it is radically transformed by faith and the love it brings. Only so can the natural powers of reason and will, impulse and affection be brought under the control of the spirit and learn to perform their true functions. If man is not thus transformed by faith and love, he contradicts his nature as a spiritual being in his thoughts and acts; made in the image of God, he yet denies his responsibility to God and his neighbor and loves himself first and foremost. His natural powers are thus cut off from their true object and purpose and become instruments of the flesh rather than the spirit, of evil rather than of good purposes. As a result, he falls prey to inner division, strife, and misery, from which he cannot free himself without the aid of the divine grace.

The profundity of the Christian view of man thus lies in its insistence, at one and the same time, upon the higher possibilities of man as a spiritual being and his tragic failure to attain them because of his sin. As Pascal says, it affirms both his "greatness" and his "misery," thus revealing both the heights and the depths of human life. It avoids the reductionistic tendency of naturalism by its emphasis upon the spiritual activity of man, but it also avoids the perfectionistic tendency of idealism by its recognition of the tragic power of sin. It stirs a divine discontent with every partial achievement by its vision of a higher possibility; at the same time it induces a proper humility and penitence in the presence of man's failures. By contrast, modern naturalism has tended to domesticate man in society and make him feel at home with himself as a creature of nature. It has minimized his soaring aspirations which might lift him above his fellows or out of himself, while it has tolerated his shameful egoism—his acquisitiveness, his aggressiveness, his pride—as "natural." It has been able to see neither the saint nor the sinner in him, neither his greatness nor his degradation. On the other hand, modern romanticists have affirmed the natural goodness of man, and idealists have tended to minimize his failure to live up to his spiritual possibilities. Christianity is opposed to this too optimistic view no less than to naturalism.

The importance of the issue between the Christian view of man and these modern views may be shown by a brief analysis of the difference between the Christian theory of education and some of the dominant theories of the modern period. The Christian cannot accept as adequate the technical education prized so highly in our industrial civilization, since it is concerned with knowledge and skill merely as a means to any end desired by the individual or society. The liberal education of humanism is nearer to the Christian ideal since it is interested in the ends as well as the means of human life. But it falls short from the Christian point of view unless it attempts to bring—and how often in our secular age does it fail to do so!—all human abilities and activities into the service of the Kingdom of God. Similarly, integration of the self and adjustment to the group are worthy goals of education, but their value is relative and conditional. Integration is possible at a low level as well as a high one, if it is sought only for the sake of immediate happiness. And adjustment to society may produce willing slaves to the tyranny of a dictator or a majority. From the Christian point of view, therefore, these modern ideals of education are not false, but they are all inadequate. Their defect is that they overlook the most essential thing about man, the necessity that his personality be fulfilled at the spiritual level. By contrast, Christian education subordinates the development of the capacities and skills of the self to the awakening of the spiritual nature and the enlistment of all the energies of the self in the service of the divine purpose of love.

Finally, the ideal of personality, which is an integral part of the Christian view of man, is a distinctive one. The highest secular ideal of the modern world is the humanistic one, the fulfillment of the capacities of the self in a balanced and harmonious manner. But this noble ideal, like the humanistic view of man as a rational being, has one serious defect. Though it develops the powers and enlarges the interests of the self, it subordinates them to no higher purpose above and beyond the self. As a result, the cultivation of intellectual, aesthetic, and other capacities by the humanist often leads to nothing better than pride and self-centeredness. Even when it produces a noble devotion to truth and beauty as absolute values, it lacks faith in an ultimate purpose for human life as a whole which alone can give that devotion its highest meaning. Alongside of this humanism with its tendency to individualism, a more social ideal of personality has also been powerful in modern life. On this view, first developed by idealists like Hegel, the self realizes itself only as it becomes an organ of society, determined in its whole moral substance by the common life. Such a view has value as a criticism of individualism, but it has led increasingly to a depreciation of individuality and, in totalitarianism, to its virtual denial.

The Christian ideal, on the other hand, is found in voluntary devotion of the self to the service of the Divine Will and to that community of love wherein alone fullness of life is possible. The end of man is not only to develop his powers but also to use them as love of God and neighbor dictates. The cultivation of individual abilities and interests is important, for it is necessary to fullness of life. But the primary motive must be the service of the universal, eternal purpose of God for all mankind, rather than the limited and immediate interests of the individual or his society. Can there be any real doubt that the disintegration of Western civilization is in large part due to the submergence of this ideal of personality by the secular ideals of individualism and collectivism? Can Western man ever recover the meaning of life until he makes this ideal once more the goal of all his striving? But can he hope to do so without recovering the Christian faith of which it is an expression and without reconstructing his philosophy in the light of that faith?

10

The Christian Tradition
and
Physical Science

AMONG THE PHASES OF MODERN CULTURE TO WHICH CHRISTIANITY HAS
tried to make an adjustment, physical science is commonly considered
to have presented a formidable obstacle. The vast literature on
science and religion testifies to this fact. Many points of view, to be
sure, have been expressed in this literature. At one extreme is the
assumption that the development of science is providing a substitute
for religion and that ultimately it will entirely replace the influence
of the Christian tradition in the life of the modern world. At the
other extreme is the condemnation of science as an instrument of the
devil, accompanied by a defense of traditional Christian dogmas.
Between these extremes can be found many attempts at reconciliation.

Despite the variety of points of view, there is one assumption which
is generally held. According to the common interpretation of European history, the Christian influence reached its height in the Middle
Ages. Art, literature, and education were under the direct control
of the Church, and religious influence made itself felt even in the
areas of economics and politics. Theology was literally the queen of
the sciences. With the waning of the Middle Ages, there was also a
waning of that form of Christianity which prevailed in medieval
culture. Mathematics and physics replaced theology at the head of
the scientific hierarchy, and the conflict between science and religion
was under way.

It is necessary to admit that in certain types of conflict the scientific
side has emerged victorious, but the result has not always been unfortunate for religion. Christian theology has been purged of many
crude and primitive elements. In the controversy over the Copernican
revolution in astronomy the Church officially adopted a position which
it was forced later to abandon. The Copernican view has, as a matter

of fact, become generally accepted. The more recent controversy over the question of evolution is destined to have a similar outcome.

But there is the further question as to what these so-called "scientific victories" mean. Newton's discovery of gravitational attraction made it possible to describe the movements of the heavenly bodies exclusively in terms of natural law. It was not necessary, from the standpoint of science, to appeal to a divine power guiding the stars in their courses. But does this mean that the existence of God is thereby disproved? Darwin's hypothesis that natural selection is the method by which evolution takes place appears to dispense with God as the guide of the evolutionary course of life. Is this also a demonstration that there can be no God as the ultimate ground of existence?

This is the kind of question which is still pertinent in the discussion of the relation between science and religion. It is not a demonstrated fact that science will replace religion, but an easy reconciliation does not seem to be possible.

SCIENCE AND CHRISTIANITY: CONFLICT OR CONTINUITY?

Before proceeding to analyze the points of conflict, a preliminary word on the contemporary situation may be in order. Although the conflict between modern science and Christianity has held center stage for a long time, it seems now to have been relegated to a position of less importance. There are at least two reasons for this shift. One is that these erstwhile rivals are threatened by a common enemy. The rise of pseudo-religion in the form of nationalism has reached proportions which threaten the very conditions necessary for the growth of both Christianity and science. Science is unable to flourish without a respect for the dignity of the individual scientist and a respect for objective truth. The flower of Christianity withers in a society unless men are allowed to find their supreme devotion in a God who transcends national barriers. Extreme nationalism tends to destroy these conditions. Thus Christianity and science, having been for many years parties to a conflict, are now most accurately seen as partners seeking to destroy a false religion.

The second factor which makes for a revised outlook on the relation between science and religion is a new way of interpreting the transition from the medieval to the modern world. As stated above, the common interpretation of European history makes a sharp break between the medieval and modern periods, although there have been differences of judgment as to whether the change initiated by the Renaissance was good or bad. The Catholic historian tends to look back to the thirteenth century as the time when civilization reached its peak. All that has occurred in the past four hundred years has represented movement on the wrong track. Civilization has gone astray. The historian prejudiced in favor of modernity, on the other hand, looks at the development of the past four centuries as a progressive emancipation from the obscurantism and authoritarianism of the Middle Ages.

From the perspective of the twentieth century the common assumption underlying these contradictory evaluations becomes highly questionable. We can justly acknowledge the break which occurred and at the same time point to certain lines of continuity between medieval Christianity and modern science. The suggestion made above that common conditions are necessary for the flourishing of both Christianity and science is a case in point. The highest ethical ideal of medieval Christianity was that embodied in the life of the monasteries. Man's vocation was understood to consist of complete and unconditional obedience to God's will. It is easy to overlook the similarity between this ethical ideal and that of the scientist. But the scientist also is committed to the ideal of subordinating his own interests and desires to his search for what is actually the fact. It is not unreasonable to assume that the spiritual discipline inculcated by Christianity has been an important element in shaping this ethic of science.

Again, an honest appraisal shows that in the beginning science was not so much a reaction against the notion that God controls the world as a new method that could better reveal the nature of God and the behavior of His world. John Langdon Davies has said that

Copernicus, Kepler, Galileo, Newton, Leibniz and the rest did not merely believe in God in an orthodox sort of way; they believed that their work told humanity more about God than had been known before. If men had not wanted to know about God, it is highly doubtful if they would have worried to know about nature.

These scientists were convinced that nature is written in mathematical symbols and that human reason is competent to interpret the symbols, thereby attaining certainty about the world in which we live. This outlook had a significant meaning for religious thought. Religion is vitally interested in achieving reliable knowledge of the Being who controls nature and of the way He works, in order that lives may be properly adjusted to Him. The desire to have more accurate knowledge of God was an important motivating force in the work of these early men of science.

Moreover, as Gilson has pointed out, the two chief problems of Christian philosophy are those which deal with the nature and existence of God and with the nature and destiny of the human soul. It is of more than passing interest to find that Descartes, who was one of the first to picture the world in terms of physical science, found it necessary to prove the existence of the human soul and God before he could express confidence even in the existence of an external physical world. Although Descartes conceived the physical world after the analogy of a machine, he insisted that the soul of man was something quite different. In a very literal sense, the soul was supernatural if we identify nature with that realm investigated by the physical sciences. Nature was the world of extension, but for Descartes there was another world—the world of thinking substance or mind. This proved to be a very unsatisfactory solution of the body-mind problem, but it does call attention to an assumption which is necessary for the scientific enterprise as it has been understood in modern life, namely, that man must in some sense be superior to the nature which science investigates since it is he who is attempting to understand it and also to control it. Such a view of man is in direct continuity with the Christian tradition which has proclaimed that man is a child of God as well as of nature.

Finally, Berdyaev's suggestion that the mechanistic view of nature was itself made possible by Christianity is at least plausible. He insists that the Christian discipline of faith in God and in the goodness of the creation made it possible for man to lose his fear of nature and thus to envisage it in such terms that he could exercise control over it. One of the more serious problems confronting our own generation is that which results from including the whole of man within the realm of nature mechanistically understood. It was inevitable, of course, that man should eventually turn the searchlight of scientific method upon himself with the result that for many he seems to be, not the master, but the slave of nature. But this problem is more directly concerned with the relation between the Christian tradition and psychology. The point we have been making is that the development of science is not merely a progressive rejection of medieval religious tenets. It is in part a flowering of certain essential ingredients in the Christian faith.

THE CONFLICT OF WORLD VIEWS: MATERIALISM AND DETERMINISM

There are, nevertheless, certain areas in which the tension between physical science and the Christian tradition continues. The two most crucial points of conflict have been in the area of world-views and in the area of reliable methods of achieving knowledge. As to the first, Christianity had believed implicitly in final causes, that is, in the world of nature as primarily an expression of divine purpose. With the growth of the physical sciences, this teleological view was replaced by the notion that the world is governed exclusively by mechanical causation. To many people, therefore, the scientific picture of the world requires a form of naturalism which is in apparent contradiction to the world-view held by Christian thought. As to the second point of conflict, the popularity of science in the modern world has tended to make men believe that the method of science is the only reliable method for attaining truth. Traditional theology appealed ultimately to revelation, while scientific method is based upon observation and experiment. There is no serious doubt concerning the competence of scientific method to understand the world of nature and to institute effective control of natural phenomena. But there is a sharp difference of opinion with respect to its competence to deal with philosophical issues such as those raised by religion.

Let us consider these two problems in order, beginning with the conflict of world-views. The view of the world which is thought by many naturalists to be implied by modern physical science has never been more beautifully expressed than in Bertrand Russell's essay, *A Free Man's Worship*. This view includes the notion that whatever reality lies behind the phenomena investigated by science has no prevision of purposes or goals to be achieved. The causal sequences described by science are the only causes and in their totality form a self-sufficient system. Events in the world are completely determined with no reference whatever to human good or ill and with no reference to final causes. In the light of this point of view, it has seemed obvious to many people that the traditional idea of God can no longer be held. The word God might be used after the fashion of Spinoza to refer merely to the systematic laws of nature, or after the fashion of the religious humanists to refer to ideals which men consider worthy of their devotion. But science makes impossible the validity of a theism which asserts that a personal God is the ground of the universe and providentially guides events toward desirable goals.

It is my contention that the facts of science do not necessitate the rejection of theism or compel the adoption of the world-view described above. I shall not attempt to demonstrate that the facts of science require theism, but shall only show that they do not necessitate the rejection of theism. The question as to whether other facts support the probability of theism may be reserved for later treatment.

Consider first the relationship between scientific facts and the principles or theories which are designed to give meaning to these facts. The history of science is filled with instances where a number of empirically verified facts remain unquestioned and, at the same time, theories of explanation are radically changed. In the field of chemistry, for example, certain facts of combustion have been accepted as true for a long while. On the basis of these facts a theory was propounded that a kind of substance called "phlogiston" existed in inflammable matter and escaped when the matter was in the process of burning. The facts of combustion, therefore, were explained in terms of something escaping from matter into air under the conditions of heat. The generally accepted theory today is exactly the reverse of this. Instead of saying that something goes out from matter into the air, it is said that oxygen is taken from the air into the matter that is being burned. The facts of combustion remain unchanged, but we have had to alter our theory completely as regards the principles at work. We must think in terms of something being taken in rather than something being thrown off. This is but one of many instances of the sort in the history of science. In the field of electricity the flow of a current is an empirical fact. This fact was at one time explained as the result of positive charges, but now the theory is reversed so that negative charges are cited as causing the current. In medicine, also, the interpretation of facts has gone through profound alteration.

If this is true within specific fields of science, it seems clear that the naturalistic view of the world as a whole is not the only possible view consistent with the facts of the physical sciences. It is not true that modern man is presented with the following mutually exclusive alternatives: either the acceptance of science or the belief in God. It is possible to believe in the law-abiding quality of natural processes and the efficacy of scientific method and at the same time consistently to hold to the belief in God and in a providential universe. Moreover, the kind of knowledge which science gives us concerns only that aspect of nature which lends itself to prediction and control. Scientific knowledge has to do with nature only in its orderly and predictable behavior, and we must recognize the fact that this is an abstraction from a much wider context and that there are certain data which are excluded from consideration as a result of this abstraction. Physical science says nothing about religious experiences of human beings or about their experiences of value; yet these are important data to be considered when we are attempting to find an hypothesis which will explain the world as a whole. If, therefore, theism is a possible alternative on the basis of the study of that aspect of nature investigated by science, it may become more than a mere possibility when we consider these additional facts.

Again, consider the change in scientific hypothesis occasioned by the discovery of new facts. Einstein and Infeld show amusement as they look back to the confident prediction made by Helmholtz less than a hundred years ago:

Finally, we discover the problem of physical material science to be to refer natural phenomena back to unchangeable attractive and repulsive forces whose intensity depends upon distance. The solubility of this problem is the condition of the complete comprehensibility of nature.

The simplicity of the problems of physical science as here expressed had its own attractions but has received one jolt after another from the recent developments in physics. Indeed, the work of twentieth-century physics has necessitated the revision of several basic concepts. It is impossible now, even from the standpoint of physics, to picture our world as consisting solely of material particles with simple forces acting between them and depending only on the distance involved. It has come to be realized that the field within which particles move is much more than mere emptiness. The space between the particles has very definite properties of its own, so that in electromagnetics the older mechanical view is completely inadequate. We can go so far as to say that if we wish to know something about the behavior of a particle, it is just as important to understand the field in which the particle is found as to know the nature of the particle itself.

And what about the confident determinism which was allegedly implied by science? Formerly it had been supposed that if one could only know the present positions and velocities of masses, he could predict with complete certainty every item of behavior in the universe. But the actual behavior of electrons does not seem to fit this concept of determinism. Microscopic particles, according to Heisenberg, seem to have broken the stranglehold of fate, for there is something unpredictable about them. Scientific law itself must be thought of more in terms of statistical probability than in terms of strict necessity. Some defenders of religion have been unwarranted in assuming that these changes in physics support positively a theistic view of the universe or that the principle of indeterminacy lays a foundation for human free will. On the other hand, we are justified in pointing out that in the light of these changes deterministic materialism of the nineteenth-century variety does not receive the support of contemporary physics. A materialism consistent with the facts now at our disposal would have to be radically different from its philosophic forerunner.

In general, we can say that science attempts to subject observed regularities to precise analysis. It concentrates attention upon the quantitative or measurable aspects of phenomena in order to determine precisely the degree and amount of regularity in the behavior of nature and the mutual dependence of events. But even this kind of knowledge does not possess the certainty which some people claim for scientific method. If truth is a property which ideas possess after being completely verified in experience, it would seem that certain truth would require complete experience, an obvious impossibility. To affirm that a present scientific hypothesis is a final statement of truth, one would have to make the assumption that no future experience can occur which would invalidate it. The illustrations which we have described demonstrate that this assumption is definitely invalid. It would seem, therefore, not only that scientific knowledge has to do with an abstraction from nature but also that the knowledge we receive even in this area possesses at best a high degree of probability.

As a matter of actual fact, the findings of science have never demonstrated the truth of naturalism. Descartes' assertion that if he were given extension and motion he could make a world was never more than a guiding principle for science to follow. The same is true concerning determinism. At best, it has been an ideal which science has held before itself. During the development of modern culture, as the influence of science became increasingly important, such regulative ideals as these were frequently and unjustifiably assumed to be demonstrated truths. Arguments to the contrary, advanced by theologians and by idealist philosophers, made only a minor impression.

As we have shown, however, both the older materialism and determinism are now being challenged, not only by theologians, but also by scientists and on scientific grounds. The interpretation of the world in terms of matter and motion has been found inadequate technically as well as religiously, and strict determinism does not find support in contemporary physics. We conclude, then, that there is nothing in the body of scientifically ascertained fact which renders untenable the belief in God. In the first place, theism is entirely consistent with scientific facts and may be superior to other world-views, on rational grounds alone, when important data such as religious and value experiences are taken into account. In the second place, the assumptions of early science which seemed most contradictory to the Christian outlook are now being called into question by science itself.

Methods of Knowing: the Decline of Rationalism

Let us turn now to the second area of conflict between Christianity and science: the problem as to whether scientific method is all-sufficient and exclusively valid. On the one hand, there are those who say that the truths of science do not need to be supplemented by another kind of truth. If scientific knowledge appears to be incomplete, the only cure for this deficiency is more science, not some other method. There are, to be sure, some questions habitually raised by man which can never be answered by the method of science—questions relating to ultimate reality, the creation of the world, cosmic purpose, and the like. But such questions ought not be asked because they cannot be answered, and they need not be asked because human beings can get along without bothering their heads over them. Indeed, they will be better off if they do not torture themselves with these meaningless and unanswerable queries. On the other hand, there are those who insist that some of the questions raised by religion and unanswerable by scientific method are of outstanding importance. The fact that the method of science cannot deal with them makes imperative the discovery of some other approach through which satisfactory conclusions may be found.

The significance of this issue as to the proper methods of achieving knowledge is now widely appreciated. Sorokin in his *The Crisis of Our Age* has gone so far as to base an entire interpretation of history on varying systems of truth. He believes that the clue to understanding an historical epoch and the values it cherishes is to be found in its theory of knowledge. There are, he says, three such theories which appear from time to time in history. An "ideational" culture finds its truth in intuition or revelation of suprasensible reality, a "sensate" culture believes only in the truths of the senses, while an "idealistic" culture finds in reason a synthesis of the other two. His analysis of the contemporary situation is that our sensate culture is reaching the last stages of disintegration. One may be much more modest than this in one's generalizations and at the same time recognize the fact that the tone of an entire culture is set to a great extent by the dominant theory of truth. Among the methods which men have employed for getting knowledge, three, roughly corresponding to those mentioned by Sorokin, have been particularly influential. These are revelation, rationalism, and empiricism. The first has commonly been associated with theology, the second with philosophy, and the third with science. It is well to remember, however, that theology has not consistently held to the method of revelation. As a matter of fact, it has been typical of that form of theology called "modernism" to go almost the whole way with science in rejecting revealed truth. Furthermore, philosophy has become less rationalistic and more empirical since the eighteenth century, while the deductive method stressed by rationalism is important in modern science also.

In making a choice of one of these methods rather than another, we tend to use two tests. In the first place, we favor the method which promises the most certain knowledge. In the second place, we want our method to give us information concerning the issues which we consider especially significant. At one time or another, people have given preference to each one of the methods referred to. According to the method of revelation, accepted on faith, the origin of knowledge is in God. This is superior to the other two methods since what is known by faith comes from God's revelation of Himself and therefore is more certain than any knowledge which would result from the activity of man's fallible reason or experience. Revelation is superior, also, because its chief subject matter concerns the nature and existence of God and the destiny of the human soul. These are the most important concerns of human beings, and they can be known only through divine revelation.

If we should favor the method of rationalism, it would be because we have lost confidence in the authenticity of revelation and assume that human reason is sufficient to find answers to all important problems. A rationalist would say that we have to make a distinction between true and false revelations and that the ultimate test must be reason. Thus, to him rationalism is more basic and more certain than revelation. It starts with self-evident truths and builds up a body of knowledge by means of a series of indisputable logical deductions. It is superior to empiricism as well, since it can deal with the ultimate questions of existence whereas empirical science is limited to a description of the surface appearance of things. Also, rationalism is a method which includes among its self-evident truths those which may yield conclusions concerning moral purpose and value. Empiricism may give useful knowledge as to the means for achieving stated ends but is unable to decide whether one goal is more worthy than another.

The dominance of the empirical method, on the other hand, reflects a skepticism not only concerning revelation but also concerning the absolute truths which reason professes to know. It claims that there are no self-evident truths and that what have commonly gone by this name are nothing more than postulates. Empiricism rejects the absolute in favor of the relative and claims that the only knowledge attainable by man consists of ideas verified in experience. It may be modest about the certainty of knowledge achieved in this way but holds that it is the surest type of knowledge available. Empirical science proudly points to the detailed knowledge of nature which it has made possible, with the consequent control of physical forces for human purposes. Furthermore, it confidently assures us that all questions not answered by its technique are unimportant in any case.

Whatever else is true of scientific method, it certainly is not based on revelation. It does, however, include elements drawn from both rationalism and empiricism. The rationalistic phase of scientific method has used mathematics as its model. Mathematics proved to be such a valuable part of science that until the eighteenth century many leading thinkers assumed that all knowledge which made claim to certainty had to be of the mathematical type. Having the faith that the universe itself was a mathematical order, these men believed that if they started with the correct axioms and if they moved logically through a process of deductions, they would arrive at demonstrably true propositions concerning the nature of the world.

Although mathematics has continued as a valuable tool in science, the more recent developments in scientific method have been in a direction away from rationalism and toward empiricism. One reason for this is a new conception of the meaning of mathematical science and a growing doubt as to whether there are such things as axiomatic truths. According to Euclidean geometry, for example, it was assumed that parallel lines can never meet. But there are other geometries, based on the assumption that space is curved, in which parallel lines can meet. Furthermore, there is no objective point of view from which one can decide which geometry is true because the formal character of mathematics does not depend upon physical facts. One inference drawn from this conception of the character of mathematics is that rationalism has lost its self-evident truths, since serious doubt exists as to whether there are any axioms whose truth cannot be questioned. Empiricism is right in its assertion that what were formerly believed to be axiomatic truths are in reality only postulates or assumptions. As we shall show, however, empiricism is wrong in supposing that we can get along without a reasoned faith concerning matters about which rationalism claimed to give knowledge.

THE LIMITATIONS OF EMPIRICISM: MORAL VALUE AND COSMIC PURPOSE

According to the previously stated criteria for judging the relative superiority of one method over another, our problem here must center around two questions. First, is the empirical method of science the only one which can establish knowledge? Second, can this method provide us with all the knowledge we need for a satisfactory life? The most complete verification of ideas results from the use of the empirical method when it takes into account the whole range of experience. At the same time, those beliefs which are not established on scientific grounds are neither meaningless nor mere opinions. Some ideas concerning the ultimate nature of the world ground, or the purpose of the world, have a higher degree of probable truth than others. In the second place, we reject the view that all beliefs not discovered or verified by science are thereby unimportant.

The fact cannot be ignored that man is a purpose-seeking as well as a fact-finding being. He is not only interested in making sure that his ideas on matters of fact correspond with what is the case but is also concerned to know whether his estimate of the goals which he pursues is valid. Since the empirical method of science is particularly successful in the discovery of fact, while tending to ignore questions of purpose, it is inevitable that some doubt should arise regarding the sufficiency of science on this score. It is true that the advocates of scientific method insist that more accurate knowledge in the area of morals can be achieved empirically than in any other way. Instead of being concerned over the fact that empiricism often ends in moral relativism, some of them hail this conclusion as a great improvement over any type of moral absolutism. However, the only empirical technique for judging the superiority of one ideal over another is that of describing the consequences which follow from acting upon it. Many important and relevant data can be ascertained in this way, but there is still the problem of deciding whether the consequences are good or bad. Therefore, it is necessary to supplement the empirical method by a disciplined insight into moral values and a reasoned and tested faith concerning the proper standards of human behavior.

It is possible, for example, to make a scientific analysis of the consequences which follow from political despotism or from a rigid class structure in economic organization. The consequences of the former include the loss of liberty of action and freedom of thought on the part of individual citizens. Under a rigid class structure of society it is inevitable that certain individuals will be virtually instruments or property used by others. Empirical analysis can give us this type of information. But it cannot decide whether it is a good thing or a bad thing for people to be robbed of their liberty, nor can it decide whether some men should be treated as means rather than as ends. If our value judgments should include the Aristotelian notion that some people are by nature fitted only to be slaves, science can help us work out a technique for putting this idea into practice. On the other hand, we would proceed in a different way if we adopted the Christian conviction that all men possess dignity and value in virtue of the fact that they are children of God. If empiricism is the only method of arriving at truth and if it cannot decide between ideals such as these, then the choice would have to be merely a matter of personal opinion. It is evident that the admittedly useful knowledge achieved by science must at this point be supplemented by philosophic reasoning and religious faith.

If we raise the more general question concerning cosmic purpose, we encounter a completely negative reaction from ardent defenders of scientific method. This is just the sort of query which is thought to be scientifically meaningless and unnecessary. But what does it mean to say that it is unnecessary and unimportant to be concerned about the purpose of the world? Does it mean, for example, that people can get along without any convictions on the matter? This is in part a question of fact. The testimony of psychiatry is far from unanimous, but there is a good deal of evidence that the best of mental health is intimately connected with a sense that one can fit his own life pattern into the larger pattern of the universe. People are concerned to make their own values consistent with ultimate value, to integrate their own meanings with an underlying meaning, to gear their purposes into the pattern of cosmic purpose. Whether they can be "cured" of this interest is not a question which is easily answered. Jung informs us that whereas religious factors have played a role in the emotional disturbances of a great majority of his patients, it is also true that health has not been restored until there has been a recovery of religious conviction giving a sense of direction and purpose to life. The patient is looking for something which will take possession of him and give meaning and form to the confusion of his mind.

The analogy of a successful prosecution of war may serve to indicate the possible significance of the conviction that there is an inherent meaning in the course of the world. In fighting a war it is important to have the best of technical equipment and to have vast numbers of individuals trained efficiently to do specific jobs. Granted that some people may do their little tasks without consciously raising the question as to how these fit into the larger purpose of the nation as a whole, it is in general assumed that we must have what is called "morale" as well as trained personnel and superior equipment. "Morale" means, among other things, a deep conviction on the part of the group that the total purpose of the war is worth while and that there is a meaningful connection between specific tasks and the general purpose.

Sensitive individuals are aware of the need of a similar connection between their finite pursuits and the purpose of existence as such. The dynamic of religious living is furnished in no small measure by the certainty that one is moving in the same direction as the divine course of nature and history. The religious passion for doing the right is conceived as obedience to the will of God or to a cosmic demand. It may be that the easy dismissal of the problem of cosmic purpose by the extreme advocates of scientific method has been possible only because the general ideals of Christianity have continued with sufficient force in the modern world to be taken for granted. We find, for example, that although Bertrand Russell, in a recent study of science and religion, has tried to show that wherever religion and science have come into conflict, the latter emerged victorious, he still takes as valuable the ethical doctrine of Christianity, which he summarizes as the

acceptance of Christ's teaching that we should love our neighbours and a belief that in each individual there is something deserving of respect even if it is no longer to be called a soul.

Again, no one has been more partial toward the exclusive use of scientific method than John Dewey, and yet there is no doubt that his ultimate standards of value are derived from the Christian tradition. What are we to do when these assumptions are challenged, when the ideal of mastering is opposed to the ideal of service, or brute conquest to love? Can science decide which is superior, or is there no way of deciding?

Granted, however, that it is no easy task to dissuade people from trying to relate their lives to an ultimate meaning, it may yet properly be asked whether there is any way of knowing that there is a cosmic purpose. We admit, of course, that the truth of this conviction is not susceptible to the type of verification that is used in scientific investigation. On the other hand, there are relevant considerations which make this faith reasonable and not merely arbitrary.

In the first place, it is clear that within nature there are some activities which are purposive. I refer to the behavior of human beings. To be sure, there is a kind of reductive naturalism which attempts to explain away human freedom and purposiveness by analyzing them in terms of physico-chemical laws. It is becoming increasingly clear, however, that human behavior cannot be made completely intelligible in these terms alone. It is not only permissible but necessary to use the category of purpose in explaining human conduct. Mechanical explanation may be entirely adequate in making intelligible many features of inorganic nature. But there are several types of explanation used in the investigation of nature, and their adequacy depends in part upon the kind of subject matter which is being investigated. The category of purpose may safely be ignored in some areas, but it plays an important role in the study of human behavior.

In the second place, if there are several methods used in explaining various phases of nature, the question inevitably arises as to which of these methods is to be the preferred one in attempting to explain the processes of nature as a whole. The choice here must be made by considering which type of explanation renders most intelligible the totality of existence. Since teleological explanation does not exclude the possibility of mechanical processes, and since nature does include some purposive activity which cannot be accounted for mechanically, it would seem that the idea of cosmic purpose is a reasonable hypothesis.

A common objection to this idea is that the presence of evil in the world makes difficult the belief in divine purpose. The fact is, however, that nature does support certain ideals. As F. R. Tennant has pointed out in his *Philosophical Theology*, the world may not guarantee human happiness, but it does provide the conditions for the cultivation of moral character. It is no refutation of cosmic purpose to demonstrate that some human desires are frustrated.

THE NECESSITY FOR A REASONED FAITH

It is evident, then, that we cannot easily dismiss issues as meaningless and insignificant merely because the techniques of empirical science are not adapted to deal with them. It is necessary to go beyond the factual conclusions of science to a reasoned faith. The first step towards such a faith is to recognize that even experimental knowledge must rest upon the assumption that there is at least some sort of reality out of which such knowledge grows and to which ultimately it refers. In the second place, we must make an inference concerning the nature of this reality not only in terms of scientific fact but in terms of all kinds of experience, including considerations of value. The God of religion obviously cannot be established by such inference with the same kind of assurance that we have in empirically verified knowledge, but neither is faith in Him merely an expression of opinion. For at least some postulates concerning the existence of God are grounded in genuine experience, illumine the totality of our experiences, and do not contradict empirically verified fact.

When the further question is raised as to the nature of God and His purpose, the Christian looks to his religious tradition for the answer. He finds himself confronted by what seems to him a revelation of the character of God both in the person of Christ and in the continuing experience of the Christian community. The content of the God-idea is furnished in this way. There is nothing static in such an interpretation of revealed truth. Some people may object to revelation on the theory that we should arrive at our knowledge of the nature of God inductively, but this objection rests upon the belief that we can build up a system of knowledge without any presuppositions or unverified assumptions. One of the most definite results of recent philosophical inquiry, however, is that we can never avoid using unverifiable assumptions in our thinking, whether it be scientific or religious, practical or theoretical. No matter how strictly empirical science attempts to be, it cannot avoid the use of hypotheses that contain some a priori elements and are, therefore, not entirely the result of an inductive process. The method employed by the Christian may be stated in the language of science as starting with the hypothesis of God as revealed in Christ and the Church and then testing this by rational criticism and experience.

For example, one characteristic of God in Christianity is that He is dependable and worthy of man's trust. Experience indubitably points to something in nature which answers to this criterion. Scientific procedure itself rests upon the assumption that nature is law-abiding and therefore trustworthy. Moreover, since a person's religious experiences are a constitutive factor in shaping his world-view, the religious man will go beyond his knowledge of the orderliness of nature to a more complete trust in the dependability of his God. Nevertheless, there are some empirical tests as to the specific ways in which God can be trusted. We have found, for example, that prayer is not a reliable method of bringing rain or delivering us from floods. On the other hand, there is evidence that on condition of proper adjustment what Christians call "salvation" occurs. If, on the basis of such reflection, the religious man concludes that the theistic hypothesis is more likely than any alternative, he is not merely expressing an opinion, nor is he attempting to answer a meaningless question. Rather, he is dealing with an important problem by going beyond empirically verified knowledge to a reasoned faith.

Modern Christianity: Retreat or Affirmation?

In this brief discussion of the relation between Christianity and science we have limited ourselves to three assertions. In the first place, we said that although the prestige of science has been one of the chief obstacles confronted by religion in the modern world, recently there have been signs of collaboration between science and Christianity in opposing the rise of false values or pseudo-religions. Second, we have said that though one of the continuing points of tension between religion and science concerns world-view, there is nothing in the factual findings of the sciences which precludes the belief in Christian theism. Finally, we have explored the question as to whether scientific method is exclusively valid and all-sufficient and shown that there are important questions of human life which cannot be handled by empirical science and that science, therefore, must be supplemented by a reasoned faith.

In conclusion, it may be well to describe some of the reactions of Christian thought to science in the modern world. One reaction is the way of fundamentalism. This has consistently refused to give an inch to the claims of science and has attempted to retain all the items of Protestant orthodoxy. A great many of these items could be defended only by denying outright the central features of the scientific outlook which were becoming widely accepted in the modern world. This was a highly unsatisfactory solution because it meant clinging to forms of belief which at one time had meaning but obviously belonged to a culture which had perished. It, therefore, created an impossibly wide gap between the religious and scientific modes of thought. If religion is going to have any influence in the world, it must have some organic relationship to that world. This was hardly possible under the fundamentalist approach.

Another reaction was that of rationalism. Assuming that revelation was false or unimportant, it took as essential for religion certain basic beliefs which could be defended on scientific grounds. All other features of theology were either ignored or shown to be false. This type of theology was a reflection of what was thought in the eighteenth century to be the method of science. Under the influence of Descartes, Spinoza, and Leibniz the mathematical phase of scientific method had been emphasized. Scientific knowledge was considered a deductive system of propositions which accurately portrayed the nature of the world. Theology attempted to imitate this method by making religion a system of propositions which were capable of verification by human reason. The emphasis in this approach to religion was coldly mathematical, and the God it described was far removed from the vital concerns of men and women. The definition of God which the philosopher or theologian formulates must have at least a remotely recognizable connection with the God of religious experience if it is to be satisfactory. Religion is incurably attached to the heart, but the eighteenth-century theologians were highly opposed to any sort of emotionalism. It is not surprising, therefore, that there was a movement toward evangelicalism in which religious warmth and enthusiasm were given an outlet.

The most important continuation of the reaction against orthodoxy is usually called religious "liberalism." Recognizing the positive contribution of science and wishing at the same time to defend the essential beliefs of religion, liberalism employed the technique of making a series of strategic retreats. Its task was to show that the essence of Christianity does not run counter to scientific fact. As against fundamentalism, the liberal method was concerned with preserving only the permanently valuable parts of the Christian tradition, but it was determined to defend this essential core against the inroads of science. Many liberals followed the empirical procedure of science but laid great stress upon the fact of religious experience as a basis for theistic belief. Both rationalism and liberalism reflect a tendency to imitate science and to make many concessions.

Humanism is the religious view which has accepted most completely the spirit and supposed findings of science. It may be considered as the natural extension of the tendency already present in rationalistic and liberal religious thought. It was inclined to take for granted the naturalistic view of the world and to give up any attempt to find a cogent argument for the existence of God. It boldly accepted the possibility that nature is completely indifferent to man and the values he cherishes and made of religion nothing more than a devotion to purely human ideals. It exhorted men to accept the fact that the human race is psychically alone in a universe which cares little about men and that they alone are completely responsible for the preservation of their ideals.

This movement of thought from rationalism through liberalism to humanism would seem to indicate that modern Christianity has been primarily concerned with the task of making a satisfactory adjustment to modern science. Modern religion has step by step made its retreat, and there have been indications that this would not stop short of complete capitulation. However, the most advanced type of religious thought in our own time is that which makes more positive affirmations of the Christian faith than we have heard for a long time. It is significant that revelation, which until the very recent past appeared to be a dead issue in liberal Christian thought, has now once again come to the fore as one of the most lively topics of discussion. This fact suggests two things. One is that, quite apart from the possible success of the effort to reinstate revelation as an acceptable theory of truth, the fact that even liberal minds are seriously considering this problem means that there is a growing skepticism as to the complete sufficiency of rationalistic and empirical methods. The other is that these positive Christian affirmations have taken on particular vitality at a time when nationalistic movements, such as fascism and nazism, are proclaiming themselves substitutes for religion and preaching ideals antithetical to Christianity. Christian thinkers are now convinced that the chief problem is not that of making proper adjustments to the world, but of persuading the world to adjust itself to Christian principles. This indicates the truth of the point with which we started, that although Christianity still finds a certain obstacle in the prestige of physical science, the scene of its most important battles is on another front. In these battles it may and should find many scientists fighting side by side with it.

11

Christianity and Contemporary Psychology

MAN IS A STRIVING, ASPIRING CREATURE, CAPABLE OF REFLECTION UPON his shortcomings and his possibilities. About this both psychologists and theologians are in substantial agreement, however much they may differ on other matters. The topics dealt with by psychology and by religion, as they try to account for man and his destiny, have much in common, and it is relevant to ask whether or not the answers to common problems as given by psychology and religion are similar. Can modern man accept the Hebraic-Christian tradition without turning his back on contemporary science?

PSYCHOLOGY'S CONCEPTION OF MAN

Recent psychology, conceived as a natural science, has been strongly rooted in biology. This has been especially true in America, where the comparative method, bringing together the lower animals, infants, and human adults, has been widely accepted. Strict behaviorism of the variety advocated most strongly by John B. Watson reached its height about 1925 and was pretty well gone by 1935, but contemporary psychology is still strongly biological, even if not quite so cocksure about its mechanistic position as it was in the heyday of behaviorism. There is a real place for a biological psychology, just as there is for a biological medicine. It would be foolhardy to deny man's mammalian affiliations or to depreciate the values which may come from knowing as much as we are able to find out about man as a physiological organism.

A science is free to narrow its field of inquiry and to make its investigations appropriate to such limitations. But a psychology confining itself to the concepts developed within the biology of infrahuman organisms runs into difficulties when it attempts a more nearly complete account of human psychology. The emergence of speech in man, with the unfolding of possibilities for the manipulation of symbols, poses many new problems. It is not difficult to reconcile the emergence

286

of speech and language with evolutionary theory, since lower animals show primitive forms of reaction to abstract relationships and symbols. Laboratory animals can be taught, for example, to distinguish triangularity from other forms, even though triangularity is presented as three dots after training on three lines. They can also be taught to substitute tokens for food, so that the substitute becomes a symbol to be manipulated. But the reflective thought processes which are associated with man's speech behavior are so complicated and so rich that what man does, while not necessarily discontinuous with what lower animals do, is so far removed as to be essentially different. It is this difference which religion emphasizes in describing man as possessing a spiritual quality—the capacity to transcend his own immediate experience through reflection upon and devotion to ideal values.

Many contemporary psychologists have come to feel that time is lost in the advance of psychology if we fail to take man as we find him, if we fail to study man for himself. They do not turn their backs upon biology or upon the comparative method, but they do pay increasing attention to man as a social person, whose actions are responsive to the behavior of people about him, modified, to be sure, according to the kind of person he is. His biological needs are there to be met, but the ways of meeting them, the postponements of satisfaction, the conflicts and frustrations which develop, are determined largely by the fact that he lives in a community of other persons more or less like himself, who have acquired modes of conduct and of thought which they deem appropriate and which they enforce. These psychologists find their affiliations closer with anthropology and sociology than with physiology and biology.

The development of a dynamic, socially relevant psychology, necessarily concerned with human motives and personality, forces psychology to deal with some of the problems of religious significance. The more narrowly conceived biological psychology could get along without a self because the level of abstraction at which it worked did not require such a concept. Under the circumstances, the neglect of the soul or self need not have caused any conflict with religion, except that an occasional psychologist assumed that his psychology was complete and that anything which he neglected was therefore nonsense. Such a view reflects upon the psychologist, not upon religion. But now that the psychologist proposes theories of the self and of personality, the possibilities of overlap and conflict between psychology and religion become much more real.

The social theories of the self, taking man as he is found, are less constricted than the biological or reflexological conceptions, but they remain naturalistic. Psychology, as one of the sciences, is committed to a naturalistic method, but there is no more occasion for a naturalistic social science than for a naturalistic biological science to be arrogant about its achievements. Such a social psychology may have its place and usefulness without exhausting in its descriptive categories all that may be said about man.

The Conflict Between Science and Religion as Reflected in Psychology

Because religion has sought to make men feel at home in the universe, it has proposed accounts of the nature of the world and man by which men might live with assurance and dignity. As these accounts have been threatened from time to time by new discoveries or interpretations, there has been resistance from established religious authorities. Such resistance arises because the new developments often appear to threaten the security which religious faith engenders. In the end, it has usually proved possible to assimilate the new knowledge and to find the essential religious values unaltered. The struggle recurs on new fronts. The earlier quarrels with astronomy and geology are practically forgotten; the heat of controversy over the Darwinian theory has cooled off. Today it is the social psychologists and anthropologists who are likely to be thought of as threatening religious institutions and beliefs. This is shown to some extent in the reported skepticism of members of various professions in reply to questionnaires about religious beliefs. The physical scientist today is more likely to acknowledge religious belief than the biological scientist, and the scientist most likely to be a skeptic is the one engaged in naturalistic studies of civilized man—the social scientist. This skepticism merely reflects the present frontier of misunderstanding; at another time it would have been the physical scientist who was most in doubt about the religious conception of the universe.

The conflict between science and religion can be reconciled or disposed of in many ways, but there are four main proposals which crop up again and again:

1. The conflict is said to be irreconcilable, and the battle must be fought out. On the one hand, science is treated as heresy; on the other hand, religion is treated as illusion.

2. Fundamental differences between science and religion are denied by trying to show that the teachings of religion are good science, or by attempting to collect naturalistic evidence for the supernatural.

3. A division of subject matter is proposed, some content belonging to science, some to religion. One crude form of this solution is to assign the known to science, the unknown to faith.

4. While both science and religion deal with similar subject matter, they abstract differently from it. Because their tasks are different, according to this view, there is no essential conflict.

1. The problem of reconciling science and religion is not one of squaring a fixed body of theological doctrine with a final or complete body of scientific theory. Conflicts and controversies go on within theology and within science, so that it would be a grave mistake to exaggerate the skirmishes at the borders. In any given religious creed and in any comprehensive scientific theory there may well be elements which are in conflict, so that honest reconciliation can take place only through some elimination and some modification of one or the other position. Thus the Christian Science denial of the germ theory of disease must not be permitted to serve as the prototype of religious belief, any more than the behaviorist denial of consciousness should be taken to represent psychological convictions. Fortunately the areas of free discussion within contemporary religion and contemporary psychology are large enough to permit profitable debate on resolving conflicts between them.

2. To show that religion and science are in fundamental agreement there are efforts made from time to time to show that the Bible contains good science. When the geological controversy was at its height, it was popular to explain the days of the creation story as eras corresponding to those of the geologist. With psychological problems now more in the forefront, there have been attempts to interpret the New Testament to show that Jesus was really a great psychiatrist, the miracles being cures of hysterical conditions. The efforts to make the Bible a textbook on science, while interesting, are not very convincing.

A very different method of demonstrating the fundamental agreement between science and religion is to secure naturalistic evidence for the supernatural. In the effort to make the Bible naturalistic the supernatural elements are toned down; but in demonstrating the reality of spiritualistic phenomena the supernatural elements are incorporated into science.

Research in what is sometimes called "parapsychology" (the study of telepathy, clairvoyance, extrasensory perception) may be carried on within the accepted conventions of science. The proof of powers beyond those ordinarily recognized may be that of material manifestation in one form or another—of scores on a test, of marks on a photographic plate, of other sorts of "materialization" of the psychic. Ordinary canons of scientific caution and control, of statistical analysis and the like, may be accepted. The available evidence is very difficult to evaluate. Experiments by sympathizers secure results which, if not obtained in a field so full of controversy, would be accepted on the basis of the statistical evidence presented. Yet even open-minded psychologists find much to make them skeptical. The best performers seem never to be available for retesting or always to lose their powers in the presence of a skeptic. Phenomena under more rigid controls, if they persist at all, almost invariably are so reduced in amount as to be practically unimportant. Instead of the assay getting richer as the methods are improved, the ore gives a poorer and poorer yield.

Apart from the paucity of results, the question of the religious significance of these experiments remains. In general, spiritualism is the effort of a materialistic age to secure scientific approval for rather primitive interpretations of the nature of the spirit in its survival after death. The demand for a "sign" is atavistic in itself, more appropriate for the time of Moses than for the Christian era. Jesus himself rebuked those who insisted on a sign of his authority.

Neither the attempt to show that religious teachings are good science, nor the attempt to give a scientific demonstration of the truth of religion is likely to succeed. Both place too high a value on science and too low a value on the non-demonstrable aspects of religion.

3. The division of subject matter between science and religion is also little likely to prove a successful solution to the problem, for science will surely encroach more and more on the territory assigned to religion. In the healing arts, for example, medical science encroaches upon prayer. If all diseases which medicine can cure belong to it, and

the medically incurable to religion, religion will gradually be crowded back into an obscure place.

4. The most promising solution of the conflict between science and religion, that most coherent with the logic of modern science, is to recognize that the differences lie not in the subject matter but in the processes of abstraction from that which is given. In other words, both science and religion select their data: a human adult may provide data for a physicist, for a physiologist, for a biochemist, for a psychologist, for a theologian. Each deals with man, but each leaves out a great deal when describing any given man in accordance with its categories of description. The account of man which any given science proposes may be accurate, granting its processes of abstraction, but it cannot be complete, for the possibilities of other kinds of abstraction must also be taken into account. The reason that social science comes most into conflict with religion is that its processes of abstraction are most similar to those of religion, dealing with man as an individual personality among other men. But the similarity has limitations, and if psychology and religion say different things about man, this need not reflect upon the validity of either.

How may the differences in approach between social psychology and religion be summarized? Social psychology, on the one hand, attempts to deal naturalistically with man in his interaction with his physical and social environment in order to form generalizations which will assist in the understanding, prediction, and control of human conduct. Religion, on the other hand, attempts to understand the human being and to regulate his conduct according to a theory of value sanctioned through a conception of the relation of the individual to the universe. The essence of social science is generalizations applicable to man under natural law; the essence of religion is individual man's responsibilities and privileges according to principles of right and wrong which are grounded in a noble conception of his destiny. The values stressed by social science are those of honesty of reporting and consistency of inference; the values stressed by religion are more general, since they include moral goodness and all other values which fulfill human potentialities.

There is no need to press too hard for a clear distinction, for the differences in approach do not require it. Social psychology need not be without a system of values. It need not be without concern for the individual though it seeks generalizations applicable to all men. But on many issues of value it may be neutral without sacrificing its status as science. Correspondingly, religion may well concern itself with immediate and practical social issues, but, as religion, it cannot depart from its concern for the grounding of conduct in a theory of man's participation in the cosmos. Social science, in order to make headway, necessarily limits itself to aspects of human thought and action which can be studied according to the available methods of science. Its limitations are not, therefore, to be charged against it, so long as it continues to evolve new hypotheses and new methods of testing them and is not too boastful of its achievements. Religion, in order to maintain itself as a source of strength and inspiration for men, must continue to proclaim and celebrate values which may or may not be matters of scientific demonstration. Religion is not indifferent to science, but it is different from science. This appears to be the direction of discussion through which clarification of issues between religion and social science will come about.

THE BEARING OF SOCIAL PSYCHOLOGY UPON RELIGION

The similarity in subject matter and the differences in generalizations made may be illustrated through discussion of several concepts appearing in related forms within both psychology and religion. Such a discussion will serve better than a more abstract formula to show how conflict and confusion may occur and yet to indicate that unresolved controversy is not inevitable.

Both psychology and religion deal with problems of human motivation and personality. Hence it is enlightening to compare concepts lying within both of these fields. Three pairs of terms have been selected for consideration, of which the first member of the pair is in each case more reminiscent of religious usage, the second of psychological usage. The pairs are (1) soul and self, (2) sin and guilt, and (3) faith and security.

Soul and self. The sterility of present psychological discussions of the self arises in part because of the many years during which consideration of the self was practically absent from psychological writings. It is no wonder that there is now no consistent theory of the self or personality which is generally acceptable. But interest in these concepts has returned under the influence of widely divergent trends within psychology: through factor analysis, in which the nature of the individual is reconstructed through an assessment of his fundamental attributes as revealed in refined statistical treatment of psychological test scores; through Gestalt theories, in which the emphasis on wholeness properties in perception has led gradually to consideration of wholeness characters in the ego and its value systems; through experimental social psychology, which recognizes the personality as somehow won out of social interaction; through the medical and clinical psychologies, which, in explaining personality maladjustments, arrive at more general conceptions of the personality. There are, in addition, the influences of prewar German characterology, which, distinguishing itself from naturalistic physical science, sought to gain respect for a distinctive treatment of the individual through intuitive processes little familiar in the laboratory.

In spite of lack of agreement on the details of a scientific theory of personality development, most socially oriented psychologists could agree in general on the following account of the growth of personality:

1. The infant is born with potentialities common to all men, but individuals are unlike in their natural endowments. Just how enduring these initial differences are, is a matter of study and conjecture at the present time, but they probably include both intellectual and emotional tendencies which may color much or even all of the life span.

2. Upon these natural tendencies are imposed the skills needed for living in the physical and cultural environment. The family plays a central role in educating and civilizing the child, in transmitting the culture. The child learns how to behave properly; he learns the language; he learns what is permitted and what is prohibited.

The importance of social regulation in the early years of life, much insisted upon by psychoanalysts who follow in the footsteps of Sigmund Freud, is generally accepted by psychologists not affiliated with this school. For the purposes of the present discussion, disagreement among psychologists over the details of the process is unimportant. All agree that ways of acting and thinking, occasions for deep feeling, are to a considerable extent controlled by the approval, disapproval, encouragement, discouragement, praise, and punishment by the adults who provide the important social environment for the child. Other children are important teachers, too, but they tend to re-emphasize chiefly what they have learned from others within the same culture.

It is easy enough to see how the superficial aspects of the culture are transmitted in this manner—how the child learns one language rather than another and how a little girl learns to braid her hair while her brother prefers his hair cut short. But at the same time there is a process of emotionalizing attitudes, of internalizing commands and permissions, so that the content of the conscience or "superego" arises. This is not alike for everyone because each individual experience differs, but within a given culture there are many similarities. People can understand the feelings of one another in part because the occasions for encouraging such feelings have been similar.

Conscience, in these terms, is then largely a result of social pressures acting upon basically pliable biological material. Irrational emotional support is given for certain thoughts and feelings and actions in preference to others. Meaning is given to modesty, shame, propriety, ambition, jealousy, self-assertion, loyalty, and a host of other emotional-motivational dispositions which come to characterize the personality. These meanings are given without full awareness on the part of parents of what is happening to the child, even in contradiction to the verbal precepts which may accompany the social pressures. If religious values are a real part of the child's cultural heritage, these, too, become deeply rooted.

3. While the individual is molded fundamentally by childhood experiences grafted on innate endowments, this is an incomplete story. The mature individual has reflective capacities and can gain a measure of control over himself through self-study and understanding. He need not be a slave to his childhood, even though he cannot completely escape his history. He may choose his own goals and values and, within limits, direct his conduct in relation to them.

Preoccupation with the irrational emotional forces which do so much to shape individuals has tended of late to cause some neglect of the place in personality development of rational thought and reflection, of free choice of goals. The lessons we have learned about the driving force of emotional experiences do not deny the place of reflection; on the contrary, it is a triumph of man's rational nature that he has come to understand himself well enough to know how much of his life is controlled by emotion. This understanding frees intelligence for human reconstruction. With this knowledge our minds are less likely to serve merely to build defenses to justify irrationally grounded conduct, for we are able to see through the fraud and to move on toward realistic and rational conduct.

Selfhood, as won out of the process of socialization just described, is in some ways similar and in other ways different from selfhood as conceived in religion. There is a superficial similarity in the end-product as described in the two cases. Thus Freud's treatment of the personality structure in terms of id, ego, and super-ego is almost translatable into body, mind, and spirit of the early Hebraic-Christian tradition. "The spirit is willing but the flesh is weak" might be a paraphrase of a conflict within the person as described by a contemporary psychoanalyst. There are undoubtedly other deeper similarities, which would be explicable on either of two grounds: on the ground that both religion and psychology are describing aspects fundamental to man's true nature, or on the ground that man as known both to religion and psychology in this comparison is a product of Hebraic-Christian civilization.

The Christian conception of man's spiritual nature does not necessarily conflict with the story of individual socialization through social pressure as described above, but it goes further. It finds in the content of the mature conscience evidence of a deeper affiliation with the universe.

The bolder hypotheses of religion concerning man's nature are hardly such as to be susceptible to scientific treatment. Attempts have been made to do so, by William James and others, through relating man's subconscious to some sort of universal stream of thought, but these attempts become expressions of religious faith rather than of scientific demonstration. The negative experiment is also difficult to conceive, however, so on some of these matters science may as well be neutral. There are natural features of many religious manifestations, such as conversion, mysticism, and the like, and these features are sufficient to provide data for scientific discussions. But there is no way within science to assure that the phenomena have been completely described in its terms; it is of the very nature of science, in fact, that events are incompletely described. All sciences are selective in their descriptions.

The problem of immortality raises similar questions. The discussion is simply not relevant to a naturalistic psychology, for which life remains a puzzle but death creates no problem. Personality is for the psychologist intimately bound up with the biological individual whose nervous system treasures up his past interactions with the physical and social environment. It is not possible to picture a life after death which has continuity with earthly existence within the categories of description used by the psychologist. This, again, is a consequence of his method, and as a psychologist he must be neutral in discussions of the eternal and the everlasting, for he has nothing to say. The psychologist does, of course, have things to say as to why man wishes to believe in life after death. Since many of these reasons are unworthy, and many conceptions of the after-life bizarre, the psychologist, as a man, may come to reject belief in survival after death; or he may find acceptable conceptions of the after-life which satisfy him. But his science does not bear directly on the problem of the possibility of survival.

Sin and guilt. Reflection upon an error committed or contemplated, or upon a duty unfulfilled, may have any of several psychological consequences. In a realm of conduct where mistakes are permissible, there may be a purely matter-of-fact and unemotional acknowledgement of a mistake. Such an error is not a sin. But reflection upon error commonly has emotional consequences in the form of anxiety, shame, or guilt.

Anxiety is the state of vague apprehension lest some wrong has been committed unwittingly or is about to be committed. Shame and guilt are more specific. Shame is felt about acts which are socially disapproved but not so severely that self-punishment is aroused. In shame the penalty arises out of being caught; if not caught, the transgression is forgotten and leaves no emotional residue. To be caught talking to oneself or behaving in some trivial manner unbecoming to one's age arouses shame, not guilt. Shame also is not to be identified with sin. Guilt arises when an act, or even a thought, is so reprehensible that it troubles the person's conscience, whether or not he is caught. Some expiation is necessary before the guilt feeling is expunged; if not, the conscience remains troubled. Here psychological findings come close to the teachings of the Church. Guilt is the psychologist's word for the sense of sin.

The ease with which guilt feelings are aroused in our culture shows the reality for us of part, at least, of what the Church means by the sense of sin. But, we may ask as scientists, are such feelings perhaps a product of our culture? Some anthropologists are convinced that feelings of guilt arise only in a culture like our own where they are encouraged, while some cultures are totally without such feelings. People within those cultures may feel inadequate or incomplete or ashamed, but never guilty. They would never understand the lessons about sin taught in Christian churches.

In its fuller Christian meaning, however, sin refers to a "betrayal of man's higher spiritual destiny," not to guilt feelings aroused through some violation of mere tribal mores. There is, thus, no particular conflict here between science and religion. The guilt feelings easily aroused in our culture have their usefulness in causing people to reflect upon values, to express their loyalties, to dedicate themselves to causes. The Church can state its message in part in terms of sin or guilt. If some peoples are without feelings of guilt, it shows merely the range within which people can be socialized, for the guiltless cultures differ in many other ways from our own.

There are objections among psychologists and among religious workers to undue emphasis upon sin and guilt, in part, because of the therapeutic problems which are often created. Many important lessons may be learned from those whose manifestations of religious interest are essentially neurotic symptoms. While it is a mistake to assign a value to these manifestations in terms of their occasional abnormal origin, care must be taken to avoid the encouragement of religious beliefs and practices which are unwholesome and destructive. The fraudulent must always be distinguished carefully from the real, and caution is needed in religion as elsewhere if sham and self-delusion are to be avoided. All relations between human beings involving deep emotional concern are fraught with possible havoc; religion, though it brings a message of salvation, is not without its dangers. But just as mother-love does not stand condemned because it occasionally stifles a child, so religion should not be criticized for occasional faulty interpretations of its meaning.

Faith and security. Psychological insecurity is reflected in many ways—in timidity, in aggressiveness, in sensitiveness, in vacillation. It arises through too great a disparity between what one would like to be and what one sees himself to be; or, taking another form, it is based on apprehension lest others do not appreciate a person at his full worth. Insecurity thus has two roots: a conflict of values and attainments within the individual as he sees himself, and anxiety about being isolated from the regard and respect of other people. Man struggles to be at peace both with himself and with others. Psychological security means that a person has found satisfactory ways of handling his internal conflicts and has found satisfying relationships with other people.

Religious faith, in its psychological consequences, is above all a source of security. It places in order the values by which the individual lives, thus helping to resolve his internal struggles; it provides fellowship, thus ridding him of the peril of loneliness. To some extent all men seek a faith by which to live.

Security is so important that men will sacrifice much for it, including their intellectual integrity. A return to a once-satisfying authority is always tempting at a time of insecurity and change. The soldier in a fox-hole needs something to which to cling, and he does not go through elaborate discussions before accepting again the God of his childhood. But the religion born of a moment of personal peril is not likely to survive long among thoughtful men: they wish more than an immediate answer to an emotional crisis.

Modern man needs something corresponding to an embracing religious faith to give life meaning, robustness, and fiber. As Erich Fromm has so well pointed out, freedom may mean mere helplessness, and there is a deep despair among the men of our Western world. But in attaining this new faith, man must not lose that which he has gained by freeing himself from blind obedience to authority. Contemporary religion must provide a dynamic faith which will bring security without asking too great a price, without demanding the sacrifice of free intelligence through which high-minded men may help one another toward the goals which they value. A false and irrational security will in the end lead only to disillusionment and despair. In perilous times like these there is little doubt that man needs to renew his conviction that there remain things worth while, that people are capable of living decently together, that civilization is not a farce. The right answer to contemporary bewilderment is of concern both to psychology and to religion.

It is a mistake to discuss religious faith too abstractly, in terms of metaphysical and theological disputation about God. If a common faith rested upon full agreement regarding the nature of God, His powers and His limitations, there could be little hope that a common faith would ever be achieved. But through the historical faith expressed in the Hebraic-Christian tradition there are other grounds for assurance and security than adherence to a formal theological creed. The power of this tradition comes in part, at least, through the depth and breadth of conceptions such as the brotherhood of man and the Kingdom of God on earth, with their high ethical ideas of human dignity and worth, of the importance of the individual, of the possibilities for human social living. Religious faith rests in the confidence that this is the sort of world in which men may hope for a better common life as judged in accordance with lofty standards.

When religious faith is expressed in relation to the possibility of the attainment of values, its message is couched in terms which bear more closely on concerns of the social sciences. It becomes important, therefore, to consider how the social sciences relate to value systems.

Social Psychology and Values

Religion is interested both in a set of beliefs and in a way of life; its essence is to take responsibility for human conduct. In this it differs from science, which is often conceived as limited to honest reporting of what is found out and, in the case of applied science or engineering, to the faithful carrying out of contractual obligations to non-scientific clients. The applications to which society puts its findings have often been thought of as indifferent to science; the airplanes which science develops may serve as well in war as in peace.

Ethical considerations are not really irrelevant; the scientist does care whether his products are being used by friend or enemy. But it is a point of dispute whether he cares only in his role as citizen and not in his role as physicist or engineer. In the social sciences, as in the medical sciences, ethical considerations bear upon the practitioner in ways which are not escapable. The psychologist, dealing with human interaction, cannot hold himself fully aloof from judgments as to the ways in which people ought to live together for their mutual advantage.

From a theoretical point of view, social psychology can play only a secondary role in relation to values, but this secondary role may be a very important one. The basic judgments of value—that life is better than death, that health is better than disease, that tenderness is preferable to cruelty—are made on non-scientific grounds. In our own culture many of these values are so taken for granted that they seem to be validated by the naturalistic methods of science, but reflection will show that they depend very little on the truth or falsity of scientific assertions. Thus the preferences for comfort and survival which seem biologically demonstrable are not sufficient to furnish our ethical standards, for we value acts of heroism and sacrifice which bring pain and death to the agent. In spite of these limitations, social psychology may play an important secondary role in criticizing the presuppositions upon which ethical systems are based and in selecting from possible alternatives those most likely to result in the achievement of accepted ethical values.

The first or critical role lies in the detection and denial of fallacious grounds for ethical beliefs. Thus the excuses of the Nazis for the brutal treatment of the Jews are based on a conception of racial inferiority which can be shown to be false by any test of scientific validity. Ethical systems based on false biology or false psychology cannot be true.

The second or selecting role lies in the guiding of choices into more favorable ways of achieving desired ends. It is possible to show, for example, in groups of children arranged under different types of leadership for purposes of study, that authoritarian and democratic practices have quite different consequences. The democratically controlled groups are generally happier and friendlier than the authoritarian groups; they are more creative and less dependent upon the presence of and orders from the leader. In authoritarian groups there tends to develop either apathy or overt hostility, so that the "scapegoat" treatment of group members is more likely to be found. If one set of values favors mutual understanding, good fellowship, and creativity instead of apathy, hostility, and blind conformity, the results of the experiment favor a choice between the two types of social arrangement. Evidence such as this, as a result of relevant psychological studies, may do much to point the way to social patterns under which accepted values will have greater likelihood of being realized.

When evolutionary theory was at its height and its answers were all clear and straightforward, the hope was commonly expressed of basing an ethic upon the natural course of human progress. Good behavior was thought to be that which favored survival. Contemporary relativism lacks this assurance and leads to a form of ethical agnosticism: everything depends, it is said, upon the frame of reference. This relativism would prove to be hampering to ethical development were it not for many agreed-upon values within differing frames of reference, so that in a broader framework there is common ground. Thus there is widespread agreement that kindness is better than cruelty, that justice is better than injustice, that love is better than hate. Once a few general values are agreed upon, the activities of social scientists become of possible service in showing how the values may be made actual within society as we know it.

Without giving thought to the value judgments involved, practicing psychologists will recommend one kind of handling of a juvenile delinquent in preference to another, one sort of handling of a slow learner in preference to another. As in the case of all other technicians, when they become more confident of their powers, they may become advocates of certain ways of achieving common accepted ends. Thus, as it develops more fully, social psychology will no doubt be in better position than it now is to recommend, in the name of its findings, ways of living by which man can achieve fuller stature. There can be no ultimate conflict between the views of honest men who respect the dignity and worth of the individual and are willing to be guided by reflective thought and interpreted experience in creating conditions under which men may live with freedom and in hope.

12

Christian Ethics and Western Thought

THE TEACHINGS OF JESUS

THE ETHICAL TEACHINGS OF JESUS ARE AN INTEGRAL PART OF HIS religious message and mission. As we have seen in an earlier chapter, this was a proclamation of the gospel or good news that the long-awaited reign of God was at hand, and of the conditions for entrance into this Kingdom. The chief condition was repentance, which Jesus conceived in extremely far-reaching terms. What was necessary was that men should throw themselves with complete devotion and trust upon God, in whose fatherly love and mercy Jesus had absolute confidence. To those who would so repent Jesus held out the assurance of divine forgiveness and the promise of participation in God's Kingdom. These gracious promises were coupled with stern warnings of divine judgment upon all evil. Hence the preaching of Jesus was filled with a sense of imminent crisis. All men face a decision which they cannot evade or long postpone, whether to enter into life or to choose the way of spiritual death.

The repentance which Jesus demanded involved not only the coming into a new relationship of love and absolute dependence upon God but also a thoroughgoing amendment of personal life and social relationships. For the God of Jesus is a Personal Being whose righteous will is the basis of all good, and the very idea of the Kingdom of God is that of a state in which His will is done on earth as it is in heaven.

In demanding obedience to God's will Jesus was in full harmony with the religion of his fellow-countrymen. For Jesus, as for Judaism, the will of God is no mere abstract idea but has been made known in the Law, or the Law and the prophets. In Jesus' day the Law was ascribed to Moses, and its authoritative interpreters were the scribes, most of whom belonged to the organized body of the Pharisees. The Pharisees were especially devoted to a growing body of unwritten law or tradition, the object of which was to apply the Mosaic Torah to the detailed circumstances of daily life. But this essentially progressive enterprise was carried out in an intensely conservative spirit. The Pharisees were devoted to the letter of the Law, and their main object was, as one of their number put it, "to build a fence about the Torah," that is, to hedge it in with a multitude of prescriptions designed to guide the most scrupulous and to safeguard the Law itself.

While Jesus agreed with the Pharisees in regarding the Torah with the utmost reverence and respect as the Law of God, his mode of approach to it was utterly different from theirs. On occasion he could appeal to the text of the Law against what he regarded as a false interpretation or hold that one provision is binding rather than another. But with equal freedom he could go back of the written Law itself to the spirit or purpose which lay behind it and declare by direct intuition what was the will of God. It was his immediate grasp of the will of God and his spontaneous authority in setting forth that will in entire independence of all traditional interpretations which set Jesus apart from and above all his contemporaries. We are told that he taught "as having authority and not as the scribes" (Mark 1:22) and that "the common people heard him gladly" (Mark 12:37).

So he turned to the common people, the despised "people of the land," including even the taxgatherers and sinners, declaring that it is the sick who have need of a physician, and that there is more joy in heaven over one repentant sinner than over ninety-nine righteous persons who need no repentance. This further antagonized the Pharisees who had already been alienated by Jesus' attitude toward the Law and the tradition. Their opposition and that of Herod Antipas, who had put John the Baptist to death and who was suspicious of anything which might arouse messianic excitement among the people, soon forced Jesus virtually to abandon public teaching and eventually to withdraw from Galilee.

As time went on, Jesus also became increasingly critical of the Pharisees, charging them not only with personal hypocrisy, but with "making void the law of God by their tradition" (Matt. 15:6) and with "binding upon men heavy burdens and grievous to be borne" (Matt. 23:4). In contrast he declared, "Come unto me, all ye that labor and are heavy laden. . . . take my yoke upon you and learn of me. . . . my yoke is easy and my burden is light (Matt. 11:28-30). But if there were some who followed him because his yoke was easy and his burden light, they soon discovered that back of his rejection of the pharisaic tradition there was an uncompromising insistence on the will of God. Their righteousness must "exceed that of the scribes and Pharisees" or they could not enter the Kingdom of God (Matt. 5:20).

In one sense, then, Jesus demanded obedience to God's will as the necessary condition for entrance into the Kingdom. But in a more profound sense he realized that perfect obedience is impossible of human attainment. He called upon men to manifest in their own lives the love and forgiveness which they have experienced at the hands of God. In one breath he imposes upon men an absolute obligation and an impossible ideal: "Ye shall be perfect as your heavenly Father is perfect" (Matt. 5:48); and in another he suggests a solution: "The things which are impossible with men are possible with God" (Luke 18:27).

It is frequently said that Jesus rejected the idea of the regulation of life by a detailed *code of laws* and substituted a few broad, *general principles.* Hastings Rashdall argued for the permanent validity of the Christian ethic on the ground that this is what Jesus did and that the principles to which he appealed—"Love thy neighbor as thyself," "As ye would that men should do to you, do ye also to them likewise," (Luke 6:31)—are in full agreement with the enlightened conscience of modern man. There is much truth in this view. Jesus set forth few specific rules for his followers; that forbidding divorce is almost the only rule of any importance. His teachings can be systematized in terms of impartial and unlimited benevolence. The conscience of modern man, where it is enlightened by the Christian spirit, grasps these principles as valid and reasonable and occasionally puts them into practice.

But the key to the understanding of the ethics of Jesus is to be found at a somewhat different point. Most of the reported sayings of Jesus are neither specific rules nor general principles; they are *vivid illustrations of certain attitudes, exemplifications of a spirit* which he sought not only to describe but also to impart. If thy brother offend thee, forgive him (Luke 17:3)—forgive seventy times seven (Matt. 18:22). If thou art offering thy gift at the altar and there rememberest that thy brother hath aught against thee. . . . first be reconciled to thy brother, and then come and offer thy gift (Matt. 5:23-24). Resist not evil; turn the other cheek; go the second mile; love your enemies —these and similar sayings inculcate the spirit of forgiveness and reconciliation. Give to him that asketh; sell all that thou hast and give to the poor—these illustrate the attitude of unfailing good will and sympathy with human suffering. Be not anxious for the morrow. . . . lay not up for yourselves treasures upon earth. . . . but lay up for yourselves treasures in heaven (Matt. 6:19-20)—such sayings teach the attitude of trust in God and dependence upon Him rather than upon earthly riches. If thy right eye offend, pluck it out (Matt. 5:29); whosoever looketh on a woman to lust after her hath committed adultery with her already in his heart (Matt. 5:28)—these set forth the demand for absolute purity of heart and motive. It is absurd to take these sayings as rules to be followed literally, as the laws of a Christian code. Most of them deal with motives, and motives cannot be made the subject of legislation. They call for a transformation of the heart which can come about only when self-centeredness has been left behind and life has become centered wholly in God.

But just as it is a mistake to take these sayings as rules to be followed literally, it is equally false to spiritualize them to such an extent that they lose their edge or become like the salt which has lost its savor. While Jesus was not an ascetic, there is much in his teaching that is heroically rigorous, self-denying, and world-renouncing. He called for a single-minded devotion to the things of God and demanded that his followers unhesitatingly reject anything which comes between themselves and God. He will have nothing of those who would make the best of both worlds: you cannot serve God and Mammon.

It may be observed, however, that some of his most rigorously world-renouncing sayings were directed not to the generality of his hearers but to the immediate circle of his disciples. Sell all that thou hast and give to the poor. . . . and come, follow me (Matt. 19:21); if any man cometh unto me, and hateth not his own father, and mother, and wife, and children, and brethren, and sisters, yea and his own life also, he cannot be my disciple (Luke 14:26)—these utterances and the saying about those who make themselves eunuchs for the Kingdom of Heaven's sake (Matt. 19:12) are probably to be understood as special demands made upon those who felt the call to be enrolled in the group of disciples whom Jesus sent forth to preach the good news of the Kingdom. Some of them may even have been demands made upon particular individuals whose specific moral and spiritual problems Jesus diagnosed.

This is an important consideration because it raises the difficult problem of what is sometimes called a double standard of Christian morality. Traditionally, a distinction came to be made between the ordinary "precepts" of the gospel binding upon all and the "evangelical counsels" for those who "would be perfect." As Dr. Kenneth E. Kirk has pointed out,[1] there is a valid and an invalid form of this theory. The valid form is that which recognizes different stages on the road to spiritual perfection with appropriate precepts for each stage. The ideal is essentially the same for all though admitting of qualifications resulting from differences in vocation. The distinction is simply one of degree. The invalid form of the theory is that which magnifies the differences between vocations to the point where their ends are held to be different and some are declared to be intrinsically higher than others. Here the difference in degree becomes a difference in kind. Under the influence of this invalid form of theory, Christian perfection and the vision of God were held to be open only to those who withdrew from the world and practiced the contemplative life in the narrowest sense, while the layman was confronted with a formalized code which lost sight of the ultimate goal and presented Christian duty as largely a matter of the avoidance of sins.

The rigorist or world-renouncing aspect of the teaching of Jesus, though of fundamental importance, is only one aspect of it. It is balanced by what is called by Dr. Kirk a "humanist strain," in which Jesus manifests appreciation and approval of many of the relative goods of this life. He was sensitive to the beauties of nature. He rejected the regular fasts of the Pharisees and accepted the wholesome pleasures of social intercourse. He showed an appreciation of family life and was fond of children.

Moreover, it is a misunderstanding to think that all of Jesus' sayings spring directly from exalted idealism; some of them are based upon a shrewd common sense and a perspicacious evaluation of consequences. "Agree with thine adversary quickly. . . . lest he deliver thee

[1] *The Vision of God*, pp. 243 ff.

to the judge." This note is particularly evident in some of the parables, for example in Luke 14:28-33. Jesus was not an anarchist, indifferent or opposed to the claims of political authority; he told his hearers to pay their taxes, to "render unto Caesar the things that are Caesar's." But that saying continues, "and unto God the things that are God's." Jesus certainly did not conceive the two realms as co-ordinate. Caesar is subject to God and the things of Caesar must be brought under God's will. Jesus' principle is that of a rigorous putting of first things first, of the subordination of the lower to the higher. "Seek ye first His Kingdom, and His righteousness, and all these things shall be added unto you. . . . Your heavenly Father knoweth that you have need of all these things" (Matt. 6:33-34).

While in important respects Jesus stands in the succession of the Hebrew prophets, one misses in his reported utterances their concern for making political institutions function more justly or for promoting righteousness through bringing about changes in the social structure. Jesus was neither a social reformer nor a revolutionary, though there is much in his teaching which can inspire social change of a far-reaching and revolutionary character. Nor on the other hand was he a conservative, attaching positive value to the institutional arrangements of society. While he recognized the divine basis of the authority exercised by the Jewish religious officials, there is no evidence that he held such a view of the power of the political state. His attitude toward governmental authorities was factual and realistic;[2] they were simply men who possessed power which they often employed with injustice and brutality.

He gave his disciples no instructions as to whether or not they should participate in government or how they should conduct themselves if such responsibilities should ever come to them. The subject status of the Jews and Jesus' own expectation of the imminent end of the age are sufficient reasons why this was not for him a problem. He left one striking saying, however, which bears upon the problem of the Christian's attitude toward the exercise of authority:

Ye know that they who are accounted to rule over the Gentiles lord it over them, and their great ones exercise authority over them. But it is not so among you; but whosoever would become great among you shall be your minister, and whosoever would be first among you shall be servant of all.

—*Mark 10:42-44*

[2] See C. J. Cadoux, *The Early Church and the World*, pp. 34-50.

The direct reference of this saying is not to governmental authority but to leadership in the community of disciples. It illustrates, however, that aspect of Jesus' religious ethic which is most fundamental, his insistence that the thing which matters above all else is that the heart and will should be wholly conformed to God. Jesus did not give his followers a political ethic; what he gave them was a vision of what life would be like if it were centered wholly in God, and therefore a standpoint from which all political ethics can be judged.

PAUL AND THE LEGALISTS

We have seen that the teachings of Jesus do not form as simple a system as is often assumed, and there is a great danger of one-sidedness and over-simplification in interpreting his teachings. This accounts in part for the wide divergences in interpretation which his teachings have received. But we must also take account of the fact that different generations of Christians have tended to interpret his teachings in terms of what they themselves valued most highly. These divergences began in the very earliest times of the Church and may be seen in the New Testament itself. The first generation of Christian disciples was divided by a sharp and protracted controversy over the relation of the Christian gospel to the Jewish Law. At one extreme were those whom we may call Christian Pharisees, who clung to the Law and inherited traditions and simply added the belief that Jesus was the risen Messiah who would shortly return to establish the Kingdom of God. They believed that all the followers of Christ, including gentile converts, were obliged to obey the Law in all its fullness. Was it not the revealed will of God, and had not Jesus said that not a jot or a tittle should be taken from it until all things should be accomplished? Of much wider and more permanent influence were those who declared that Jesus had brought a new Law. The Gospel of Matthew is the great manifesto of this group. They were willing to accept gentile converts without circumcision, but they tended to cling to some residue of Jewish observances and to insist that the moral requirements of the Law must still be upheld. The teachings of Jesus were thought of as supplementing and perfecting the Law, and in that sense as constituting a new Law.

In opposition to both these groups stood Paul, who maintained that Christianity was a new religion, distinct from Judaism and resting on an entirely different basis. In place of an ethic of obedience to an external law—either the Law of Moses or the teachings of Christ conceived as a new Law—Paul taught that life should be lived under the immediate guidance of the Spirit. The Law, he declared, is "holy, just, and for our good," yet men are unable to fulfill it because the power of sin controls their fleshly nature. But those who are "in Christ" are under the control of a higher power and possess an infinitely superior source of moral excellence. For the Spirit of Christ does what no law can do: it breaks the power of evil impulse and habit and strengthens the will toward good; it provides a source of both insight and strength; it produces a veritable transformation of human nature. Thus Paul is the source of what we may call the "conversionist" type of Christian ethics, the distinctive note of which is the insistence upon the moral and spiritual regeneration of the individual as the most fundamental factor in the moral life.

It is important to recognize that Paul safeguarded this position by considerations sometimes neglected by those who have followed this aspect of his thought. In the first place, he emphasized the superiority of moral values springing from love over other "spiritual gifts." His magnificent hymn in praise of *agape*, or Christian love (I Cor. 13), is the most familiar expression of this basic thought. Moreover, the individualism implicit in his opposition to the Law is placed in the framework of his doctrine of the Church as the "body of Christ," whose members are in an organic relation of mutual dependence, forbearance, and love. Thus Paul's position is a profoundly religious and social ethic, and not an example of the religious short-cutting of ethics into which this viewpoint has sometimes degenerated.

Paul's faith that the indwelling Spirit of Christ does away with the necessity of an external moral code was qualified, moreover, by his experience in dealing with practical problems. As he came up against particular difficulties among his converts, he found himself impelled to lay down quite specific rules and to make summary statements of Christian virtues and duties. For there were some who understood Paul's rejection of the Law to be a repudiation of all objective standards of morality, and his inculcation of spiritual spontaneity to be a licensing of human impulse. Against such antinomianism Paul had to insist upon conservative principles and objective standards. Thus even in Paul, as well as in the forms of early Christianity already mentioned, there can be observed a tendency toward "formalism" or rule-making in Christian ethics. There are several examples of this in the literature which comes from near the turn of the first century, e.g., the book known as the *Didache* or *Teaching of the Twelve Apostles.*

Furthermore, with Paul there began a process of conservative adjustment to the existing social order which was destined to go much further than he himself carried it. Paul attached positive value to the state; he declared that its officers bear a divine appointment to hold evil in check and to punish the wrongdoer. Obedience and submission to the state are therefore a matter of conscience and of obedience to the Law of God. The first epistle of Peter likewise declares that subjection to the officials and the law of the state is a Christian duty, and it warns against revolutionary activity. With this recognition of the state as a divinely sanctioned institution which preserves peace and order and cares for justice and external morality went also a tendency to accept institutions of the existing social order such as slavery. It must be borne in mind that Paul's relative conservatism did not always spring from attaching positive value to existing institutions; it was also rooted in his profound indifference to earthly conditions as compared with the disciple's relationship to Christ. Here Paul was clearly influenced by his belief in the imminent return of Christ. But it is also clear that Paul had caught Jesus' spirit of rigorous detachment from all mundane goods. Ernst Troeltsch, the great historian of Christian social thought, rightly says:

The conservative attitude was not founded in love and esteem for the existing institutions, but upon a mixture of contempt, submission, and relative recognition. That is why, in spite of its submissiveness, Christianity did destroy the Roman state by alienating souls from its ideals. . . . It is my belief that . . . the Pauline turn of thought in relation to social matters corresponds to the spirit and meaning of the gospel. . . . A religious doctrine like that of Christian monotheism, which takes religion out of the sphere of existing conditions and the existing order and turns it into a purely ethical religion of redemption, will possess and reveal the radicalism of an ethical and universal ideal in the face of all existing conditions.[3]

The Early Centuries: Christian and Classical Ethics

The geographical expansion of Christianity brought it into contact and conflict with the life and culture of the Graeco-Roman world.

[3] Ernst Troeltsch, *The Social Teachings of the Christian Churches,* I, 82-85.

This is not the place to describe the contributions which Christianity made to the moral life of the ancient world. They were summarized by Lecky in these words:

The high conception that has been formed of the sanctity of human life, the protection of infancy, the elevation and final emancipation of the slave classes, the suppression of barbarous games, the creation of a vast and multifarious organization of charity, constitute together a movement of philanthropy which has never been paralleled or approached in the pagan world. The effects of this movement in promoting happiness have been very great. Its effect in determining character has probably been still greater. In that proportion or disposition of qualities which constitutes the ideal character, the gentler and more benevolent virtues have obtained, through Christianity, the foremost place.[4]

But a brief comparison must be made between the moral teachings and ideals of early Christianity and those which were prevalent in the ancient world, particularly among the philosophers, and we must observe how Christianity dealt with these rival systems and was affected by them.

The philosophical ethics of antiquity was characterized by its scientific or rationalistic method and its humanistic and political temper. Socrates established its basic character through his persistent quest for adequate definitions of such abstract concepts as justice and temperance, courage and friendship. Plato and Aristotle agreed in looking upon ethics as the study of the nature of the good life for man, and they both thought of the good life as the realization of values whose worth seemed self-evident. For Plato there were three primary and intrinsic values—truth, beauty, and goodness, and four cardinal virtues—wisdom, courage, temperance, and justice. Aristotle regarded the good life as an artistic achievement, a life according to rational standards of excellence. He held that each virtue has the character of a mean between extremes of excess and defect; courage, for example, is a mean between foolhardiness and cowardice. His description of the virtues gives us our best picture of the ideals of a Greek gentleman. While both Plato and Aristotle criticized the view that pleasure is the sole or highest good (hedonism), both of them made a large place for it in their conceptions of the good life. Aristotle defined the ultimate good as *eudaimonia,* happiness or well-being. For both of them the

---

[4] *History of European Morals,* II, 100-101. See also C. J. Cadoux, *The Early Church and the World,* pp. 611-619.

good is attained through the harmonious development and rational ordering of the capacities of human nature.

Since the attainment of the good life conceived in this rationalistic and humanistic way depends upon a favorable social and political environment, it seemed evident to Plato and Aristotle that ethics and politics are aspects of a common subject. Both of them sought to show, in opposition to certain tendencies among the sophists, that the life of moral restraint and political organization is natural to man, that it is founded upon human nature and is in harmony with the nature of things. In the *Republic* Plato drew an elaborate analogy between the cardinal virtues of the individual and the classes of the ideal state, while Aristotle based his *Ethics* and *Politics* upon the contention that man is a rational and political animal.

While we rightly think of Greek ethics as humanistic and rationalistic, it was not the product of a pure reason unaffected by social and cultural relativities. Both Plato and Aristotle were thoroughly Hellenic in spirit, loyal citizens of the Greek city-state, aristocrats and intellectuals. Both of them subordinated the individual to the state to such a degree as to leave but little room for liberty, individuality, or privacy. Plato's treatment of sex and marriage in the *Republic,* for example, is strangely insensitive to the claims of personality. Aristotle's description of the great-souled man and of proper pride in the *Ethics* provides a sharp contrast with the Sermon on the Mount. Aristotle justified slavery on the ground of natural inferiority, and both Plato and Aristotle either exclude the common man from citizenship or condemn him to an inferior status. For the common man the good life, if it can be called such, is simply a life of orderly obedience to the constituted authorities and willing service to his betters.

At the time of the rise of Christianity the dominant philosophical schools were not those of Plato and Aristotle, however, but those of the Stoics and Epicureans. Epicureanism was hostile to religion, holding it to be a set of harmful superstitions from which men could be delivered by a rational materialistic philosophy. Its ethical theory was hedonistic, though it counseled moderation in enjoyment and a life of quiet detachment from public affairs. Christianity had little or nothing in common with it except its hostility to the prevailing popular religion. Stoicism, on the other hand, was friendly to religion; it encouraged an allegorical interpretation of the older Greek religious traditions in order to harmonize them with its own more philosophical teachings. In the hands of its later Roman exponents it became even more definitely a religious philosophy; its pantheism took on a theistic tone, and the idea of Divine Providence was emphasized. Its ethics bore a definite resemblance to Christianity at a number of points, though profoundly different in other respects. Like Christianity, the later Stoicism believed that the world is ordered by Divine Providence, that men are children of God, that all men are brothers and fellow-citizens of a world-community. Christianity and Stoicism both had a doctrine of human equality, though they meant different things by it. For Stoicism, men are equal through their common possession of reason, while to early Christianity equality was a purely religious concept: men are equal in the sight of God and equally in need of salvation. The Christian view that men are created in the image of God provided a basis for *rapprochement* with the Stoic conception though the two views were profoundly different in their logical basis.[5] The Stoic doctrine that the virtuous will is the only good bore a more than superficial resemblance to the Christian tenet that God looks upon the heart and demands purity of motive. Its view of the equal guilt of all wrongdoing was similar to the seriousness with which Christians looked upon all sin as violation of the will of God.

But similar as these doctrines might seem, there were yet great differences. The Stoic regarded virtue as entirely a human achievement. Conscious of his own rectitude, he tended to look with scorn upon those who fell below his uncompromising ideals. Not for him was the Christian emphasis upon pity, sympathy, or forgiveness, or the idea of divine grace which is its religious basis. The Stoic philosophy idealized the man of iron will and rational purpose who keeps all feelings under rigid control and accepts the course of events as rationally determined. Its goal was *apatheia* or *ataraxia*, a kind of self-sufficiency and indifference or insensitivity which was essentially individualistic.

Through its influence on Roman law Stoicism led to noteworthy efforts at social reform and amelioration. Its humanitarianism and cosmopolitanism exercised a profound influence on the development of constitutional, and later of democratic, principles in Western political thought. The emphasis on the rights of man has its roots primarily

[5] Troeltsch, *op. cit.*, Vol. I, pp. 71-76.

in Stoic teaching. In spite of all this, however, the predominant influence of Stoicism was essentially conservative. Its ideals of freedom, equality, and brotherhood were frequently regarded as applying to a golden age in the past rather than to the debased epoch of the present. While there were some proletarian Stoics, the typical adherent of the school was an enlightened aristocrat who regarded existing institutions as eminently suitable to the present age, if not wholly rational.

In the early period Christian leaders tended generally to take a hostile attitude toward Greek and Roman philosophy as well as toward contemporary morals and culture generally. They regarded the pagan world as deeply sunk in sin and vice, as indeed it was, and they therefore tended to include all pagan culture under a somewhat indiscriminate condemnation. But there were exceptions to this outlook, and as time went on, they became more numerous. The apologists of the second century dealt with philosophy in a conciliatory spirit, though they were quick to point out its deficiencies, especially its powerlessness to prevent idolatry and sin. As they tried to justify and interpret Christianity philosophically, they found much that was congenial in Platonism and Stoicism. With them there began a fusion of Christian and Stoic ethics which was to have momentous consequences. Irenaeus declared that Plato was more religious than the heretics. Clement of Alexandria taught that philosophy was a gift of God to the Greeks, bestowed upon them for the same reason that the Mosaic Law and the Old Testament revelation had been given to the Hebrews, as a preparation for the gospel. His portrayal of the true Christian Gnostic is strongly suggestive of a Stoic sage, and he drew his list of the cardinal virtues with some modifications from Plato. Origen followed much the same path as Clement and even went so far as to adopt the Aristotelian idea of virtue as the mean between extremes. We should not be misled, however, into exaggerating the extent to which these early Christian writers modified their Christian ideals and principles by their adoption of Stoic and other philosophical concepts. They remained genuinely Christian. What they took over was a philosophical terminology which they employed for purposes of argument and apologetic and as the means of systematizing their teachings. It cannot, of course, be denied that their thought was affected in numerous and subtle ways by their use of this terminology, but it is a mistake to conclude that Christian ideas and ideals were thereby completely obscured or eliminated.

The most important ethical and social idea which patristic Christianity took over from these philosophical sources was the Stoic conception of the *law of nature*. Its fundamental meaning was that there are objective and universal standards for human life in both its individual and collective aspects and that these standards are discoverable at least in part by the human mind. Early Christian thinkers held, of course, that the natural law has its source in God and that it has been made known to men in various ways, through divinely inspired law givers and prophets and, less adequately, through the philosophers. Justin Martyr declared that God "sets before every race of mankind that which is always and universally just, as well as all righteousness. . . ." The Church Fathers commonly identified the decalogue with the natural law, but they differed widely in their views as to the relation between the natural law and the gospel. For Clement and Origen the gospel, including the Sermon on the Mount and the teachings of Jesus generally, was simply a fuller and more perfect statement of the natural divine law; while for others, such as Tertullian, Christ's teachings constitute a new law which is not to be brought within the scope of the natural and rational.

Origen used the natural law as a test for the laws of the state:

One may only obey the laws of the state when they agree with the Divine Law; when, however, the written law of the state commands something other than the divine and natural law, then we must ignore the commands of the state and obey the command of God alone.[6]

It was by means of this argument, as well as by quoting the apostolic declaration, "We must obey God rather than men" (Acts 5:29), that Christians justified their refusal to obey the laws of the Roman Empire directed against their associations and prescribing what they regarded as idolatry.

This line of thinking by itself might have led to a radical social outlook stressing the incompatibility between the natural and divine law on the one hand and existing institutions such as slavery, property, coercive government and war on the other. Some of these institutions seem clearly to be incompatible with the teachings of Jesus in the Sermon on the Mount and elsewhere. Stoicism had faced a similar problem, for the Stoics held that the natural law enjoins equality, freedom, and a kind of communism. But some of them had solved the

---

[6] Quoted by Troeltsch, *op. cit.*, I, 151. See Origen, *Contra Celsum*, v. 37; viii, 26.

problem by making a distinction between the *absolute* law of nature (*jus naturale*), which enjoins these things but which they held to be appropriate only to the golden age of the past, and the *relative* natural law (*jus gentium*) which applies to the present age of vice and sin and by which the existing social order was shown to be fundamentally justified. This distinction was taken over by the Church Fathers with fateful consequences for all later Christian ethics and political philosophy. Ernst Troeltsch states:

This way of thinking inaugurated a method of testing, limiting and establishing the laws, which was gradually followed by all the Fathers of the Church. . . . In the period after Constantine, when the State was Christianized, this point of view became general, and the final acceptance of the State was based upon the ethico-juridical theory that its laws proceed from the Divine Law of Nature, which is identical with the Decalogue. . . . After the State had become Christian, this doctrine made a very conservative attitude possible.[7]

The coercive character of the state and its institutions of slavery, private property, and war represent the necessary adaptations of the law of nature to fallen humanity and the conditions of the present sinful age. They are at once the result of sin and the divinely appointed remedy for sin. The conception of God as Creator and providential Governor of the world strengthened these conservative tendencies, for it tended to sanctify whatever social arrangements happened to exist. Even the harsher aspects of law and government received a relative justification as the consequence of divine punishment for sin.

A somewhat similar development took place in the sphere of *personal* ethics. The Church of the first two centuries was very strict. It considered that Christians were a race set apart from the rest of mankind by their allegiance to the law of Christ, and it imposed a rigorous moral discipline upon its members. Baptism, it was held, washed away the guilt of all sins previously committed, but the problem remained of how to deal with sins committed after its reception. Some thought to meet this problem by postponing the rite until near the end of life, but prevailing opinion condemned this practice as both dangerous and frivolous. As has been pointed out in a previous chapter, it was to meet this problem of post-baptismal sins and to maintain moral discipline that the Church in the early centuries gradually developed the

[7] *Op. cit.*, I, pp. 151-2, and note, pp. 193-4.

system of confession and absolution which came to form the sacrament of penance. At first, confession was public and involved protracted and humiliating penance; later on the system of private auricular confession came into use. But even the severe public penance and confession imposed in early times did not suffice to permit the early Church to pronounce absolution in this life to those guilty of the gravest sins. The Church might forgive venial and even comparatively serious sins, but it was held that the most grievous offenses must be left for divine judgment. By common opinion the capital or mortal sins in the early Church were sexual impurity or fornication, apostasy or idolatry, and shedding of blood or homicide. In the course of the third century it came to be asserted by Callistus and Cyprian that the Church likewise has power to pronounce absolution upon those guilty of impurity and idolatry. These relaxations of the ancient tenets produced schismatic movements of serious proportions among those who thought that the bars were being let down too far. Later those guilty of bloodshed were also admitted to absolution, and by the time of the Council of Nicaea all sins had come to be considered as admitting forgiveness in this life, provided that the requirements for penance were met.

As Christianity gradually became secularized and its teachings accommodated to the standards of the world, a powerful reaction and protest arose in the form of monasticism. The monks tried to retrieve and carry into practice those aspects of the teachings of Jesus which were in danger of being overlooked, the "evangelical counsels" and the rigorous world-renouncing sayings of the Gospels. They did so in the only way which was possible in a decaying world, by turning their backs on the world and attempting to achieve salvation for themselves either in isolation or more often in the common life of a regulated and cloistered community. The excesses of the early anchorites, typified by the so-called "pillar-saints" of Egypt and Syria, have often and with some justification been regarded as casting a dark shadow upon the moral record of early Christianity. And yet it must be borne in mind that the severities of their asceticism were due far more to dualistic ideas which came to them from Greek and ultimately Oriental sources than to the teachings of the gospel. The notion that matter is intrinsically evil and spirit good had great influence in early Christianity, but it came from outside sources and accorded badly with Christian teaching. There is much more of this dualism in Plato than in Paul.

And we must remember also that these men lived in a world that was falling to pieces around them. The rise of asceticism and monasticism is intimately related to the decline of the Roman Empire and the disintegration of ancient civilization. Moreover, it would be hard to overestimate the social value of the labor put forth by the monks of the Dark Ages in clearing the forests and tilling the soil of western and northern Europe and providing for the rude inhabitants of those lands examples of peaceable and industrious living in a violent and barbarous age. But it must not be forgotten that these social values, important as they seem to modern men, were but by-products of monasticism and not its reason for being. For the monk above all else was concerned with the salvation of his soul; it was for this that he left the world and took the vows of poverty, chastity, and obedience. One's judgment of the institution must depend upon one's estimate not only of his goal but of the wisdom of the means he adopted to attain it.

The varied forms of thought which molded Christian ethics in the patristic age may all be observed in Augustine, the greatest of the Latin Fathers. As has been indicated, he shows the influence of Greek philosophical concepts, particularly in a Neo-Platonic form. He was profoundly in sympathy with the monastic ideal and with the discipline of the Church. But the thing that marks his greatness is his ability to hold together these diverse tendencies on the basis of a revival of Paul's conversionist ethics. Augustine, after a profound conversion experience, always insisted that the reorientation of life through divine grace was man's primary need. God's grace or God's love—and for Augustine they are the same—sets men free from the overmastering power of desire and sin,

not only in order that they may know, by the manifestation of that grace, what should be done, but moreover in order that, by its enabling, they may do with love what they know.[8]

In spite of his humanistic and philosophical training, Augustine had scant respect for the natural virtues of the unregenerate man. As a result, he believed that only when man's life has been reborn at its center, can he develop as a truly free and responsible moral being, a child of God. Similarly, his political thought rested upon a largely negative and coolly realistic attitude toward man in society. The state

[8] Augustine, *Rebuke and Grace*, 3.

is the representative of the earthly city, the foundation of which is selfishness. Under God, it has the function of keeping sin in check; but without the moral influence of the Church, which is the representative of the Heavenly City whose basis is love, it could not even exercise this function. And since the Church represents the power and goodness of God, it is destined to triumph, and in God's own time the elect will be gathered into the kingdom of love, the City of God.

MEDIEVAL CHRISTIAN ETHICS

Troeltsch and other writers have laid great stress on the differences between the "church" and the "sect" types[9] of institutional and sociological development in Christian history and the contrasting patterns of ethical and social thought with which they are associated. A church is characterized by an inclusive membership and a tendency to accommodate its teachings and practices to the prevailing standards of the world. It brings its ethical doctrine in general within the framework of a rational pattern, though a particular portion of life may be regarded as the special sphere of religion and be regulated by a code of rules. This combination of rationalism and formalism in ethics is characteristic of the outlook of the church type of religious institution. The sect type, on the other hand, is characterized by a selective, voluntary membership and the maintenance of a sharp contrast between its standards and those of the world. The sect considers itself the faithful remnant which upholds the law of God in a sinful world and remains faithful though all others have fallen away. It normally adheres to the "new law" interpretation of Christian teaching, though conversionist elements are not uncommon in its outlook. In certain circles it is customary to maintain that Christianity began as a sect and only gradually developed into a church and that this development is really a degradation of the original purity of the gospel. There is more than a little truth in this view; yet it should not be forgotten that the sect pays a heavy price in social irresponsibility for its isolation, and the purity of its ideals may represent a great oversimplification of actual conditions and problems. Each of these types and positions needs the corrective which the other can supply, and Christian history is richer because of the interaction between them.

The rise of the medieval sects, such as the Waldenses, represents a

[9] See Troeltsch, *op. cit.*, Vol. I, pp. 331 ff.

reaction against worldliness and ecclesiasticism in the spirit of the rigoristic Christianity of the early Church. They derived their social and moral ideals directly from the Gospels, rejecting both the compromises of the ecclesiastical ethic and the institutional separateness of the monasteries. They renounced the Church's ideal of dominating the world and within their small groups aimed at personal inward perfection and fellowship between the members. Their attitude toward the state and society might be one of indifference, tolerance, or even of hostility; and in the latter case they tried to replace established institutions by a purely Christian order of society. The asceticism of the monasteries was possible only for a kind of privileged minority; it presupposed the life of the world as a general background. But Troeltsch says:

The asceticism of the sects, on the other hand, is merely the simple principle of detachment from the world, and is expressed in the refusal to use the law, to swear in a court of justice, to own property, to exercise dominion over others, or to take part in war. The sects take the Sermon on the Mount as their ideal; they lay stress on the simple but radical opposition of the Kingdom of God to all secular interests and institutions.[10]

But the uncompromising rigorism of the sects was only one of the tendencies of medieval ethics. As in the earlier centuries of the Church, it seemed necessary to accommodate Christian teachings to the ideals of the world. One example of this is the Church's adjustment to the ideals of the barbarians of northern Europe. Many of the practical problems of modern Christian ethics have their source in the difficulty of controlling the turbulence of these northern barbarians. One significant product of this adjustment is to be found in the code of medieval chivalry, which presents an ideal that is both distinctively Christian and vigorously Northern and masculine. It is, of course, clear that the pride and combativeness of the feudal lords and knights is a long way from the humility and peaceableness of the Gospels. We are confronted here with an imperfect combination of disparate values in which profoundly Christian elements are united in a complex relationship with factors of a very different origin and significance. The code of medieval chivalry is an early and typical example of the moral pattern of the modern European civilization which was beginning to take form.

[10] *Op. cit.*, I, 332.

But a deeper and more harmonious synthesis was taking place in the medieval period in the realm of ideas. In the thirteenth century Christian thinkers became acquainted for the first time with the whole range of Aristotle's philosophy and soon adopted it as the framework of a far-reaching adjustment of theology and philosophy, faith and reason, religion and science. The change of fundamental concepts brought about by the influence of Aristotelian categories was particularly marked in ethics and social theory. Aristotle's views of man as a political animal and of the state as a natural institution necessary to the full development of the moral life of man are conceptions very different from the Stoic ideas which had molded Christian thought for a millennium. It was Thomas Aquinas who worked out most satisfactorily a synthesis between the Aristotelian concepts and the traditional categories of Christian thought. Reality was conceived as forming two levels—nature and supernature, the world and God. Though sharply distinguished, they are not opposed, for the world is God's creation, and He made it instrumental to His purposes. Human institutions belong to the world of nature and are adapted to man's fallen state, but they serve, though imperfectly, to further the development of man from nature to God. Aquinas asserted both the divine origin of political authority and the moral end or purpose for which it exists. He wrote:

It belongs to the king's duty to order human life in such a way that men may attain to their true felicity. The true aim of the king should be so to order things that his subjects may live the good life, and the good life is the life according to virtue.[11]

These principles, so different from those of Augustine, furnished Thomas a basis for asserting both the ethical ground and the limitations of political obligation. Christians are bound to obey secular rulers, but not an unjust or usurped authority or one which commands unjust things. Sedition is a grave mortal sin, but a revolt against a tyrannical and unjust ruler is not sedition, for such an authority is directed not to the common good but only to the convenience of the ruler. The relation of the state and the Church is also carefully defined. The Church is the representative of God in the world; it is a universal institution endowed with absolute truth and the power of dispensing grace through the sacraments. The Church recognizes and uses the institutions of the world for its own purposes. Since the natural stage

[11] *De Regimine Principum,* i, 14-15.

of life prepares the way for the supernatural stage, the state should serve the Church. In much the same way, the natural ethic prepares the way for the ethic of grace and miracle; the "natural virtues" of prudence, temperance, fortitude, and justice, conceived in essentially Aristotelian terms, prepare a foundation for the "theological virtues" of faith, hope, and love.

Thomas' thought is nearly always balanced and reasonable. But while in his theological system in general his rational philosophy was supplemented and controlled by Christian principles, in the field of ethics the conservative pattern of Aristotelianism was followed almost too consistently. He even applied the view that virtue is a mean between extremes to the monastic virtues of poverty, chastity, and obedience. He was also, perhaps, too much inclined to claim the sanction of reason itself for social attitudes which were essentially relative to medieval society. This conservative tendency in Thomism often carries over into Catholic programs of social action, as is shown by the high value usually set upon private property and upon order and hierarchy in an organic society. Nevertheless, it is sometimes maintained that the general structure of Thomism lends itself to less conservative social doctrines, and in our own time it has even been made the foundation for radical programs of social transformation.

One of the favorite subjects for medieval disputation in the field of theology was whether God's will is primary or whether it is subordinate to His reason. In ethics the counterpart of this question was the dispute whether a right act is right because God commands it or whether God commands it because it is right. Those who held to the primacy of will in the Divine Nature are known as "voluntarists," and they were likely to hold that God's will is essentially arbitrary. When this position is taken, ethics is usually based upon the superior authority of Bible or Church or possibly upon a non-rational mystical insight into the will of God. Some of the later Scholastics, such as Duns Scotus and William of Occam, took this voluntaristic line of thought. Thomas Aquinas, representing the main trend of scholasticism, upheld the rationalist position, however, and in so doing laid the foundations for modern moral philosophy which declared its independence of theological presuppositions. For if God's will is subordinate to His reason, so that He commands what is right because it is right, it follows that man, since he is a rational being, can attain to a rational apprehension of the fundamental principles of morality. And that he has such rational insight or intuition is the basic assertion with which modern ethical speculation in the seventeenth century made its beginning.

THE PROTESTANT REFORMATION AND MODERN SECULARISM

Luther and Calvin, on the other hand, adopted the voluntaristic view and asserted the total depravity of man, meaning thereby that his reason, as well as his will, is corrupted by sin. Man is, therefore, entirely dependent upon God's revelation of His will and upon His forgiving grace. Salvation is by faith alone. Luther contrasted the revelation of God in Christ with every other source of truth and emphasized the Pauline distinction between law and gospel. Christian liberty means freedom from law and from the necessity of good works as a condition of God's favor, but it also means subjection to one another in love. The Christian ethic is absolute love. And since the law of love reveals the sinfulness of all human life, man is always in need of forgiveness, and sin is inevitable in all human institutions. Yet man should yield willing obedience to the existing powers since they are of God. In its social doctrine Lutheranism returned to a position basically similar to the earlier medieval social theory, which emphasized the relative natural law and the state as an institution appointed by God to hold sin in check. Luther's doctrine of creation and providence also strengthened his emphasis on authority by claiming divine sanction for the basic orders and institutions of society. The close connection of Church and state in the Lutheran system, in combination with these other factors, had the effect, as has been remarked, of "investing Lutheran doctrine with a peculiar tinge of authoritarian conservatism."

Calvin, on the other hand, emphasized the essential unity of the biblical revelation—Old and New Testaments, law and gospel. Believing as thoroughly as Luther in man's sinfulness, he drew the conclusion that man needs not only forgiveness but also constant and unremitting moral discipline. The Church is the instrument of this discipline, and the state is obliged to enforce the law of God, somewhat in the manner of ancient Israel. Calvin was perfectly clear that this intense moral effort is not the ground but the result of salvation; its motive is not the hope of winning God's favor but gratitude for God's free gift. Yet Calvin's conception of Christian holiness in terms of ascetic discipline had larger points of contact with the rigorous ideals of the sects than did the forms of Christian social theory professed by the other great churches. In consequence, later Protestantism has seen the rise of a number of movements which combined elements from Calvinism and the ideals of the sects in a variety of ways. Puritanism was one of the earliest and certainly one of the greatest products of this combination of tendencies. Methodism and the evangelical revival brought consequences in social reform due in large part to this dynamic heritage, and the modern movement of social Christianity based on the social gospel is traceable in large measure to the same historical foundations.

The Reformation roughly coincided with several of the most important developments which gradually transformed the medieval into the modern world. The most important for our purposes were the rise of the modern nation-state, with its accompaniment of nationalism, and the development of the characteristic practices, attitudes, and institutions of economic individualism or capitalism. The relationship between the Reformation and these movements has been long and hotly debated. On the assumption that the Reformation was the causal factor, it has been extravagantly praised and roundly condemned, depending upon the writer's evaluation of nationalism or capitalism. In fairly recent years the thesis of Max Weber has been widely popularized, according to which the spirit of capitalism was the outgrowth of certain teachings of the reformers, particularly of Luther's doctrine that all honest occupations are divine "callings," and of Calvin's "rational methodizing of life." Yet this mode of reasoning seems to overlook the fact that both economic individualism and nationalism were operating as increasingly powerful tendencies even before the Reformation. The truth seems to be that, while the primary motivation of the reformers was purely religious, the movement which they initiated was carried forward and profoundly influenced by these contemporary social forces. Aware as they were of the new forces stirring men's lives, but obviously unable to foresee their ultimate outcome, the reformers swept away many ancient regulations, but they reinforced others and struggled valiantly to deal with the problems created by new conditions. Luther was bitterly opposed to the new capitalism and all its ways. Calvin

of Christian ingredients than is commonly realized. The philosophy of liberal democracy, with its watchwords of liberty, equality, and fraternity, has with justice been described as a secularized version of Christian values. The idealist philosophies revived an organic view of society which is closer to Christian thought in some respects than the extreme individualism from which it was a reaction. The passion for human brotherhood and for raising the lot of the common man which has characterized the socialist movement owes far more than Socialists usually acknowledge to Christian ideals. The history of the influence of Christian ethics in the modern world is the story of both decline and advance, and the very moment of its apparent defeat has more than once been the time for a rediscovery of meaning and vitality in the gospel.

CHRISTIAN ETHICS AND MORAL PHILOSOPHY

Modern philosophical ethics is both a monument to the influence of Christian ethics and an evidence of the increasing sterility of ethical speculation when cut off from religious roots. The problem of modern ethics which distinguishes it from Greek moral philosophy is the problem of the nature and basis of moral *obligation*. The centrality of this problem is itself a product of the influence of Christianity upon the moral consciousness. Its insolubility apart from theistic presuppositions is an indication of the extent to which moral philosophy is bound up with theology. Many philosophers and theologians have followed Kant in holding that if morality, with its sense of unconditional obligation, is to be exhibited as reasonable, it can only be by presupposing or postulating the existence of God. Only the Absolute can be the source of an absolute obligation. This "moral argument for the existence of God," as it is often called, has been advanced in a number of different forms, and competent philosophers have differed widely as to its validity. It is fair to say, however, that those who have denied its force have usually evaded it only by denying that morality presents us with a categorical or unconditional obligation to do the right. This denial is a powerful motive in the so-called "naturalistic" theories of morality which attempt to reduce moral obligation to desire or some other nonmoral aspect of experience. But to deny that moral obligation is what it presents itself to be, a unique fact of experience, is surely an unempirical procedure even if it is done in the name of empiricism. It is possible, of course, simply to take moral obligation as a phenomenon of moral experience and not to seek either to explain it theistically or to explain it away. But this is to leave it as an insoluble problem.

To the plain man ethics is intimately bound up with religion, and the attempt to discuss its problems apart from religious presuppositions and convictions usually seems to him abstract and artificial. And yet this is what theoretical ethics or moral philosophy for several centuries has steadfastly attempted to do. That the attempt has provided an intricate field for intellectual ingenuity, no one can deny. It has resulted in certain abstract problems being isolated and discussed with great acumen but little agreement. The debate has, to a large extent, revolved around the question of the relative merits of the utilitarian and the intuitionist points of view.

Utilitarianism, or teleological ethics, takes the concept of good or value as fundamental and seeks to derive the notions of right and moral obligation from it. It declares that a right act is that which is productive of the best possible consequences of any act open to the agent. In its older form utilitarianism was hedonistic and egoistic; it measured the desirability of consequences solely in terms of the preponderance of pleasure over pain and held that the individual could be motivated only by interest in his own good. First the egoism and then the hedonism of this view were broken down, with the result that more recent ethical speculation of this type has upheld the position known as "ideal utilitarianism," which recognizes other values besides pleasure. It is hardly open to question that the influence of Christian ethics has played a large part in this transformation of utilitarianism from a narrow assertion of self-interest to a broad doctrine based on sympathy with the equal claim of others and on sensitivity to values other than pleasure. Yet it will hardly do to identify Christian ethics with even the broadest form of utilitarianism, for there is in all teleological ethics an attitude of rationalistic calculation which is foreign to the Christian spirit. Furthermore, the broad or ideal form of utilitarianism leaves unanswered the crucial question of the scale of values. It has to fall back on intuition when it attempts to compare one value or pattern of values with another. It is unable to solve the problem of justice in the distribution of values between persons without appealing to intuition again at this crucial point.

And recent criticism of teleological ethics asserts its inability to solve the problem of the basis of obligation and charges it with offering a theory which distorts or even denies one of the fundamental elements of the moral consciousness.

If utilitarianism has to fall back upon intuition at fundamental points, it would seem that a good case could be made for the view that knowledge of right and wrong rests at bottom upon certain self-evident intuitions. This position has been upheld by a still widely influential school of thought which takes the fact of moral obligation as fundamental and assumes that men have direct insight into the rightness and wrongness of at least the basic types of acts. The older *intuitionism* tried to show that the moral law rests upon a limited number of general intuitions or ethical axioms taken to be self-evident, e.g., that promises ought to be kept, that justice is obligatory, and that such acts as lying, stealing, and murder are wrong. The upholders of this theory have generally been rationalists; they believed that the intuition or apprehension of these basic principles was a profoundly rational process. Their ideal of science was geometry, and they sought to capture its rigor and certainty for ethics. But criticism has tended to undermine the claim of rationality for this position by pointing out the inconsistency and relativity of these supposed intuitions. It has also brought out the difficulty of showing any systematic relationship between these intuitions of right and wrong and our experiences of value. Kant, whose position is better described as formalism than as intuitionism, attempted to show that valid moral precepts can be demonstrated by means of the logical rule of non-contradiction, but few have followed him in this contention. He, too, fell back upon intuition, however, in certain of his basic ethical principles, particularly in his assertion that valid principles of ethics must be taken as universal laws and that we should treat our fellow-beings as ends in themselves and never as means only. It is easy to show that these fundamental principles of Kant, as well as the moral axioms of the more typical intuitionists, have in nearly every case been profoundly affected by the deeply ingrained effects of Christian teachings upon him. Thus the relativity of ethical intuitions to specific teaching and experience shows that their claim to complete universality and rationality cannot be taken for granted.

The dispute between the teleological and intuitional schools of ethical theory is likely to continue interminably unless it is recognized that they are different and in some respects complementary approaches to the facts rather than mutually exclusive systems. Either approach without the other is partial and abstract, and it may be maintained that only in the context of Christian thought can the opposition between them be overcome and a proper place be made for the truth that is in each. It is intelligible that God should be the ground of moral obligation if He is also the source and goal of man's true good, as Christianity asserts. Since His will is the expression of His nature, which is holy love, it is not arbitrary. Nor does it merely sanction a general and rational law. It is expressed in the concrete and temporally conditioned personal relationships of a society whose members seek to form a beloved community. Only through reference to the Divine Will of love and the personal relationships of a community of love can judgments of comparative value and decisions as to right conduct be made.

Furthermore, it is only in the light of Christian thought that we can do justice to the element of truth in the philosophy of self-realization and at the same time avoid the pitfalls of this position. *Self-realization* in ethics represents an attempt at the revival of Greek ways of dealing with ethical problems, in that it stresses the fulfillment of the potentialities of the human self as a whole under the guidance of reason. It will hardly satisfy the moral consciousness unless it can show that the self whose realization is sought as the ethical end is both the real self of the individual and a completely social self. Nineteenth-century idealism attempted to maintain this view of the self, but for proof it resorted to the dubious metaphysical doctrine that the real self of the individual is identical with the Absolute. In practice, moreover, the theory fluctuates between an apparent endorsement of self-interest and an undue subordination of the individual to some social whole such as the state.

A direct challenge to the constructive systems of philosophical ethics comes from the many-sided tendency toward *relativism* in modern thought. It is difficult to maintain a rational defense of the objectivity of right and wrong and of judgments of value in the face of the evidence that all such judgments are psychologically and culturally conditioned. The scientific temper of mind leads an increasing number to the conclusion that ethical judgments are purely relative and subjective, that they are mere expressions of preference without cognitive significance. The only way to escape the nihilistic consequences of this conclusion on the humanistic premises of modern secularism is to maintain that while ethics are relative to human nature, human nature at bottom is stable and universal. For only if human nature has these characteristics, is it capable of furnishing an adequate foundation for objective values and moral principles. An ethic built on these foundations would not be absolute, but it can be reasonably maintained that it would be adequate for human needs. It is open to doubt, however, that the thesis of the stability of human nature can be maintained on purely naturalistic or empirical grounds. Radical empiricism seems incapable of discovering irrefragable evidence of such stability because of the diverse and changing expressions of human nature. "Man does not have a nature," says Ortega y Gasset; "he has only a history." If ethics is relative to the preferences of individuals and groups who have no general humanity in common, then justice, as the Sophists long ago asserted, is merely the interest of the stronger. Thus if we follow the modern tendency toward radical empiricism and relativism to the bitter end, we behold the dissolution of human culture. If Christianity goes by the board, humanism will follow.

Far from denying the facts which psychology and anthropology have brought to light, Christianity declares that the relativity of our moral conceptions is the inevitable consequence of human finitude and sin. It asserts that man by his own effort and insight is unable to arrive at complete and objective knowledge of the right and the good, much less to attain them in practice. It does not, however, draw the conclusion that moral terms such as the right and the good have no objective meaning. While warning that our ideals are warped and corrupted by defects in our nature, Christianity also asserts that at their best they approach an objective and absolute standard, the will of God.

Thus Christianity holds out no hope of easy emancipation from the predicament of relativity and partiality in moral thinking, but asserts that its worst consequences can be overcome through persistent, intelligent effort in response to divine love and grace. At this point Christian ethical thought tends to occupy an intermediate position between the rationalism and optimism of much philosophical ethics and the relativism which is often the outcome or presupposition of modern scientific tendencies. It is for these reasons that its analyses of ethical problems often show a depth and richness of perception beyond the range of these simpler and more one-sided theories. For example, its assertion of the possibility and the necessity of conversion is a recognition that the basic moral problem is the radical transformation of human nature.

The objection is sometimes made that the Christian assertion of an absolute though transcendent standard inevitably leads to dogmatism. But this is to overlook the distinction, which is implicit in authentic Christian thought, between our distorted and inadequate ideals and the ultimate meanings of which they are partial reflections. Christian thought at its best is forearmed against the dangers of a closed mind, and the transcendent character of the Christian ideal is the best guarantee against dogmatism. While it must be admitted that Christians have too often fallen into this error through a confusion of the imperfect standards of their group with the ultimate standard of the Divine Will, the fault lies not in their faith but in their inadequate comprehension of it and in their all too human frailties.

On the other hand, it is sometimes said that if the Christian ideal, because of its transcendent character, lies beyond men's grasp, it is useless in illuminating their thought or guiding their conduct. This is a typically academic objection; it could never be made by one who is familiar with the actual life of Christianity in history. For the ideal of Christian love inspires men to heroic conduct through the attractive power of many examples and expressions, and though each one of these is admittedly imperfect, the ideal is partially but fruitfully grasped through them all.

The last two centuries have witnessed a persistent attempt to separate the humanistic and democratic values from their historic roots in Christianity. Sometimes this has taken the form of an assertion that Christian ethics ought to be and can be maintained apart from Christian faith and that the latter may be discarded as an illusion. More recently we have seen the growth of an avowedly non-Christian humanism which contends that humane and democratic values are founded entirely upon present experience and need no support whatever from the Christian tradition. It is, of course, true that values cannot rest merely upon authority; they must maintain themselves in the arena of human experience. They must continually be reverified in terms of the experience of men, on the whole and in the long run. But what that whole and that long run may mean cannot be determined apart from one's faith. It is not the experience of the passing moment, but experience illuminated and sustained by faith, that convinces us that "all men are created free and equal" and that "truth, though crushed to earth, shall rise again." Fruitful ethical insight and analysis always springs from a point of view, not from a mere reflection of immediate experience without the aid of presuppositions. And a point of view, in the last analysis, is a metaphysic or theology, a judgment upon the meaning of life and the totality of its environment. A recent critic has pointed out that Nietzsche's ethic is the consequence of his conclusion that "God is dead." Similarly, we might point out that Christian ethics is the outworking of the proposition that "God is love."

The Christian ideal is not a mere abstraction; it is bound up with the declaration that God is working out His will in history. Thus it supplies a *transcendent* frame of reference which is *relevant* to the values of everyday life, individual and social. But these values are to be regarded as approximations to the Christian ideal, not as its complete substance. For the Christian ideal is neither other-worldly nor this-worldly alone. It is a vision of the world to come which is relevant to this world in that it defines its goal and therefore the direction of man's deepest strivings. It is a pattern of value which serves both to inspire and to judge the intellectual systems and institutional structures of mankind. It is a spirit which requires embodiment in human philosophies and institutions. Yet every such embodiment has a double character; it is both a necessary and an imperfect expression of the Christian ideal. Hence Christianity must in every age rework these relative expressions of its essential character. This is a process which has gone on from age to age, and it would be presumptuous for us to believe that it can stop in our time. It is the task of Christians in this generation to work out expressions of the Christian ideal in terms which are at the same time relevant to the present situation and true to its own historic norms.

Those who are inclined to depreciate the relevance of Christianity to our world sometimes propose a dilemma. Either Christian ethics is a specific social program and pattern of living or it is a mere abstraction. If it is the former, it can hardly be relevant to the present age, nineteen centuries after its beginnings; if the latter, it is too vague and empty to meet our present complexities. To protect themselves against such skepticism, Christians of the present age need to learn both the use of ideals and the limitations of their temporal expressions. But in the final reckoning the relevance of Christian ethics to our age and to every age does not rest merely on the permanent validity of its ideals, as such, but also upon the revealed purpose of God for every age. For it is the Christian faith that in Christ the Word became flesh. God entered into the life of man that man might enter into the life of God. And God's purpose of love stands fast.

13

Christianity and Democracy

IT IS OFTEN ASSERTED IN OUR DAY THAT RELIGION AND DEMOCRACY should make common cause against totalitarianism. From this proposition it is naturally inferred that religion and democracy, despite their obvious differences, are inseparable. At the opposite extreme, many deny an essential connection between Christianity and any form of government. Religion, they say, is concerned, not with political and social institutions, but with worship of God and obedience to His will. Democracy, moreover, numbers among its most loyal supporters men and women who are not religious in any traditional sense of the term.

In view of this serious difference of opinion, it is important to examine carefully the real nature of the relationship between Christianity and democracy. We shall find that, whatever may be said about actual democracy, there is a necessary connection between the democratic theory and certain affirmations of the Christian faith about man and his good. But we shall also find that both democracy and Christianity have been interpreted by many in such a way that this necessary connection has been obscured. We shall need, therefore, to make clear the distinctive contributions of Christianity to democratic theory and at the same time to emphasize the sharp difference between the conception of democracy held by Christians and the individualistic theory of democracy which has been so influential in America for more than a hundred years.

Two Misinterpretations of Christianity

If the distinctive contributions of Christianity to democratic theory are to be understood, however, it is necessary first to deal with two misinterpretations of Christianity. The first is of an historical nature. It asserts that Christianity has from the beginning been indifferent or hostile to democracy. In the Old Testament, it points out, there is no mention of democracy. The Hebrews were governed by kings up to the time of the Exile, and these kings were thought to be responsible to God, not to the people. From the beginning, moreover, there was a theocratic element in Hebrew political thinking: God was the real King and Lawgiver of Israel, and human kings ruled against His will on sufferance, or, at the most, as His agents. This theocratic element became the dominant factor in the government of the Hebrews after the Exile. Since there could be no genuine political autonomy under the great empires which successively ruled them, high priests took the place of the earlier kings as the chief authorities.

In the New Testament, the argument continues, political aspirations and ideals play little or no part. The only concern of Jesus was to prepare men for the coming of the Kingdom of God, a wholly spiritual order to be established by God. While they waited for the Kingdom to be established, his disciples were to support and obey the imperial authority, rendering to Caesar "the things that are Caesar's." Paul goes further. Not only must Christians obey the authorities; they must realize that the authorities have been established by God for the punishment of evildoers and must be accorded respect and honor (Rom. 13:1-7).

Finally, it is only in recent times that the Church has been on the side of democracy. The Catholic Church was associated with Empire from the time of Constantine, and it still supports autocratic regimes like that of Franco in Spain when they are favorable to its own claims. The attitude of early Protestants, with some notable exceptions, was little different. Luther and Calvin urged absolute obedience to rulers, and Protestants in Germany have generally supported absolutist regimes. Is it not clear, therefore, that historically the Hebraic and Christian religions have not shown any affinity with democracy until quite recent times? And in recent European and American history have they not simply adapted themselves to democracies which developed independently of them?

It would be unwise to deny the weight of this evidence. Indeed, there has been a rigid, often reactionary, element in our religious tradition, as well as a creative, prophetic one, and the prophetic element has only very slowly made its way against powerful forces opposed to it inside and outside the churches. It must be pointed out, however, that the prophetic element has been present and has had great influence from a very early date. In the Old Testament absolute monarchy like that which prevailed in other Oriental states was never accepted by the great prophets. David, we are told, entered into a covenant with all the tribes of Israel through their elders when he became King (II Sam. 5:1-3); when he was guilty of taking the wife and causing the death of one of his subjects, Uriah, he was denounced by Nathan the prophet for "despising the commandment of God and doing evil in His sight" (II Sam. 12); and when his son Solomon followed the example of oppression set by Oriental despots, he provoked such discontent that there was a secession of all the northern tribes from the kingdom at the beginning of his son Rehoboam's reign (I Kings 12:20). An even more dramatic case of the prophetic denunciation of tyranny is that of the condemnation of King Ahab by Elijah because of the confiscation of a vineyard and the judicial murder of its owner, Naboth (I Kings 21). Thus, while monarchy was the normal form of government among the Hebrews, as among their neighbors, the best representatives of their religious and moral ideal insisted upon the king's responsibility to God and respect for the rights of his subjects as the people of God.

More important still is the insistence of the prophets upon social and economic justice. From the time of the eighth century, prophets like Amos and Isaiah condemn grasping landlords and harsh creditors for their oppressions, their wives living in luxury off the fruits of exploitation, and their rulers, judges, and priests using political and religious power to enrich themselves at the expense of the poor. Again, debtorship and slavery were accepted by the Hebrews as by their neighbors, but provision was made in the law codes for the release of debtors and the emancipation of Hebrew slaves in the seventh year (Deut. 15:1-18). A high estimate of the rights of the Hebrew as a member of the people of God must lie behind this insistence by the prophets upon political responsibility, economic justice, and protection of the weak and helpless.

With respect to the New Testament and the Church it is necessary to remember the conditions under which the Christian movement arose. For some time the Jews had had no real political autonomy, and every effort to throw off the yoke of the Roman Empire had failed. Even from the point of view of political realism, therefore, it would have been folly to challenge the Empire. But this is not the primary consideration. Jesus had little to say about social institutions. But he had much to say about a purely spiritual order, the Kingdom of God, and this purely spiritual ideal had social implications of a revolutionary kind. It is true that these implications were not at first recognized. But the submission of the early Christians to the imperial authority and the economic and social system of the Empire was under the circumstances natural and necessary. Moreover, the early Christian communities had a marked influence upon social institutions and practices from the first through their more humanitarian attitude towards women and children, their vigorous opposition to the cruelty of the public games, their higher conception of sexual and family life, and their indifference to wealth and power. Finally, the later alliance of the Catholic Church with the Empire and the feudal system, and the dependence of the Lutheran church upon the German princes and of other Protestant churches upon the dominant middle class, must be frankly acknowledged. But this simply indicates that the political and social implications of the gospel can be forgotten and that prophetic Christianity has always had to meet powerful resistance from dominant classes inside and outside the Church.

The chief conclusion to which we are led by this historical analysis is that, while the attitude of rigidly conservative Christianity towards democracy has often been neutral or even hostile, prophetic Christianity from the beginning manifested a deep sympathy with the spirit of freedom which was to express itself later in political and social democracy. Since the middle of the seventeenth century, it has increasingly supported democratic institutions, though it would be a mistake to say that it has won its battle with reactionary conservatism within and without the Church.

This brings us to the second misinterpretation of Christianity, which is closely connected with the first. In its essence, many argue, Christianity is concerned with spiritual rather than temporal things, with otherworldly rather than worldly blessings. Since the form of government of a people has to do only with their temporal welfare, therefore, it is a matter of indifference to Christianity. The Church simply accepts whatever form of government may exist in the earthly city and uses the order it provides for its own pilgrimage to the City of God. On this view the doctrine of the social gospel that a measure of true happiness may be attained in the earthly city under the conditions of a just social order is a heresy due to the influence of modern humanism and the idea of progress.

There are two comments to be made on this interpretation of Christianity. First, it does describe a certain type of Christianity and its political implications. The extreme dualistic interpretation of Christianity, often in alliance with reactionary conservatism in the Church, assumes that spiritual welfare is independent of social conditions and that concern for eternal salvation makes all temporal interests unimportant. If one makes this extreme dualistic assumption, the form of government of the earthly city is a matter of indifference. Submission to the most tyrannical government may, indeed, be justified on the ground that the sufferings and burdens it brings are trials which give an opportunity for faith and fortitude here and greater reward hereafter.

But, second, this dualistic assumption, in the extreme form we have described, is not made in the prophetic religion of the Old and New Testaments. There is a dualistic element in prophetic religion, but it is not so much a philosophical dualism of spirit and matter or other world and this world as a religious and moral dualism of good and evil. It is a dualism which opposes God to the powers of evil, which opposes the service of God to the selfish desire for power and riches. This religious and moral dualism was modified and sometimes almost displaced in the early Church by a pessimistic Greek and Oriental dualism of spirit and matter, supramundane and mundane. The Church was engaged for well over a century in a bitter struggle with this type of foreign philosophical dualism in the form of Gnosticism,[1] and it was branded again and again as unchristian by theologians like Irenaeus. In the milder form represented by Neo-Platonism it is a major element in the Christian philosophy of Augustine; in a harsher form it influenced deeply the monastic ideal of the Middle Ages.

The retention of this overemphasis upon the otherworldly aspect of Christianity by the Protestant reformers and its revival in our own day by a certain kind of orthodoxy should warn us against underestimating its power in Christianity. Moreover, foreign as

[1] Cf. the description of Gnosticism in Ch. III, pp. 58, 59.

dualism is in its extreme form to the thought of the prophets and of Jesus, there is an element of truth in it in its moderate form. There is a real distinction not only between good and evil but also between spirit and matter, the eternal order and temporal existence. Augustine and others have been right in stressing the spiritual rather than the physical life as the center of human personality and in pointing out the instability and imperfection of all natural and temporal goods. Because of this, as well as because of the powerful tendency to egoistic self-love in the human will, man never attains to a state of perfect peace and happiness in this life. One need not draw from these facts the pessimistic conclusions about human nature, history, and politics which were drawn by Augustine and are being drawn by some of his followers in our day. But the incompleteness, not to say the frustration and corruption, of many of the higher efforts of man, intellectual, moral, and political, is too well attested by observation to permit the naïve modern optimism about human nature and progress and the social utopianism which has been based upon it.

But, though we are far from minimizing the truth contained in the dualistic and otherworldly aspect of Christianity, it is only part of the Christian view of life. Christianity, like Judaism, has also affirmed the goodness of the creation, the dignity of man as the lord of creation, and the significance of human history for the divine purpose. World affirmation is doubtless more emphatic in liberal Protestantism than in medieval and modern orthodoxy. But, in one degree or another, all great Christian thinkers insist that nature and its goods are not to be despised, and that society must be organized in such a way as to further the earthly as well as the eternal welfare of man. Human personality and society here and now are not to be denied worth. This world is not the end, but it *is* the beginning, of the pilgrimage of man.

If this is so, the conception of Christianity as indifferent to this life and the kind of community in which men live is false. The spiritual life is no solitary and self-sufficient thing; it is social through and through. All man is and may become is conditioned by the character of his fellowship with others. If, therefore, one form of community is more favorable to moral and spiritual development than others, it is absurd to deny the importance of political constitutions and social structures from the religious point of view. In short, while an extreme dualism in religion may lead to political indifference, the moderate dualism of prophetic religion heightens the importance of good government by making it instrumental not only to happiness and prosperity but also to the moral development and ultimate salvation of man as a spiritual being. At the same time, it prevents the deification of the state by insisting that political institutions are instrumental to the welfare of individuals and must respect their liberties.

THE WORTH OF THE INDIVIDUAL

So far we have been trying merely to show the error in certain misconceptions of Christianity which prevent an impartial consideration of the thesis that there is a genuine connection between democratic theory and prophetic Christianity. Such an effort is not without its value in an age of secularism like our own, when the most superficial statements about religion gain credence because of general ignorance of the facts. But, of course, it is not enough to remove misconceptions; it is necessary also to analyze some of the distinctive contributions of Christianity to democratic theory if a necessary connection is to be shown.

The first of these contributions is the Christian conception of the worth of the individual. Modern democracy rests upon a high estimate of the dignity of the individual. Historically there have been two main sources of this. One is the Greek philosophical view of man as a rational animal capable of controlling his impulses and determining his behavior by principles. The Stoics made this view the basis of a theory that all men are subject to a natural law which is eternal and immutable. The positive laws laid down by earthly rulers must be in conformity with this universal natural law. It is obvious that such a view of man and of natural law is important for democracy both for the dignity it gives to the citizen and for the moral check it imposes upon the ruler. For this reason, recent attacks of Freudians, Fascists, and others upon the rationality of man constitute a peril as deadly to democracy as the excessive claims made by rationalists on behalf of reason.

The other main source of the theory of individual worth is the Hebraic and Christian conception of man as made in the image of God, belonging as a creature to the order of nature but linked as a son of

God with an eternal spiritual Life. On this theory the individual is responsible to his Creator, upon whom he is dependent both for his existence and for his good. As a social being he owes allegiance to his group and its rulers; but as a spiritual being and son of God his ultimate loyalty is to God. This belief has been an invaluable support to democracy by giving individual men a sense of their worth in the eyes of God and by endowing them with courage to defy earthly tyrants in the name of the Divine Will. Moreover, by stressing the direct spiritual relationship between the individual and God, it has rejected the claim of the state to control the religious life and conscience of the individual. Religious liberty was one of the first rights to be won in the modern struggle against arbitrary power, and it logically carries with it the independence of the Church from state control. What is not usually recognized is the extent to which intellectual and political liberty was also bound up with this struggle for religious liberty as early as seventeenth-century English puritanism, e.g. in John Milton.

In the light of the historical record, it is hard to understand the view of those who hold that democracy should rest upon no philosophical theory or religious conviction about the world and man, that it is nothing more than a political and social hypothesis to be tested like other hypotheses by its consequences. On this *pragmatic* view, theories of the state are valid if the forms of government they propose are successful in realizing the values men desire. Thus the liberty established by democracy is justified by the development in the citizens of character and intelligence to which it leads. Similarly, equality is justified by the increase in the contributions made by the citizens to society when they are given real equality of consideration.

There is no objection to this pragmatic argument for democracy as a form of government. But the values democracy seeks and the view of man it assumes are not capable of being established in similar fashion by the pragmatic method. Democracy seeks for all citizens the fullest life, including such values as intellectual and moral development, artistic creation, friendship, love, and happiness. To ask for a further end to which these values are instrumental is to ask a meaningless question. They are intrinsic values in the sense that they bring fullness of life to persons directly. They must be established, not primarily by an appeal to consequences, but by a broad vision of the nature of human personality and of the values which fulfill it. In short, a theory of man and of value forms the indispensable assumption of democratic theory, and it must be based upon religious faith or philosophy rather than upon experimental proof.

The theory that democracy in the full sense of the term can be pragmatically justified without appeal to philosophical or religious presuppositions must, therefore, be rejected as false. The classical conception of man as a rational animal and the Christian conception of him as a spiritual being made in the image of God are basic to democracy; for without the high view of man and his possibilities implied in them democracy as a form of government loses much of its meaning and tends to become an empty shell. This does not mean that one cannot believe in the democratic form of government without accepting these philosophical and religious insights into the nature of man and his good. The existence of ardent defenders of democracy among the positivists and pragmatists would be a sufficient refutation of that claim. But it does mean that if democracy is justified merely by its pragmatic consequences without reference to a general theory of man and value, its claim upon our loyalty becomes far less clear and certain than when it is regarded as the political expression of such a general theory and of the way of life based on it.

LIBERTY AND RIGHTS

The Christian contribution to the democratic theory of liberty is closely connected with this faith. Something like Kant's principle that persons are free and should be treated as ends in themselves, never as mere means, seems to be necessary if the individual or minority is to be guaranteed rights and is to be protected against totalitarian claims of the state. But how are we to conceive of liberty and rights? The question becomes acute when we realize what havoc has been made by the irresponsible assertion of rights in modern democracies. Political rights such as voting have often been exercised in the most careless or selfish way. Civil rights such as freedom of speech have been abused by many who appeal to them most loudly. And economic rights such as freedom of contract have been asserted without any concern whatever for the common good. What, then, can be done to safeguard the rights of individuals and at the same time protect society from their abuse?

An important contribution to the answer is made by prophetic Christianity with its positive and spiritual conception of freedom. The essence of freedom is not the absence of restraint but the capacity to determine one's acts in accordance with judgments of value. It is the power to act according to purposes adopted by the self. This capacity for self-determination is the true meaning of the freedom of the will which has been rightly regarded by philosophers as the basis of all special liberties. But the Christian conception also emphasizes the necessity of opportunities provided by society to make this freedom effective. This means that certain rights of the individual must be recognized by society.

The eighteenth-century theory of natural rights had the merit of stressing this fact. Its error was in conceiving of rights in individualistic terms and in making them absolute. Critics of the theory pointed out that human nature is social as well as individual and that the rights of individuals must be limited by the requirements of the common good. But the nineteenth-century utilitarian theory which based rights upon their social utility is equally dangerous for the opposite reason, since it makes rights dependent for their validity upon social recognition and hence wholly relative to society. In that direction lies the totalitarian denial of individual rights in the name of the "public good." The only escape from this dilemma is to recognize that a right belongs to an individual, as the natural-rights theory held, but that it is justified only as it is used with responsibility, for the good of both the individual and the community. The ultimate moral basis of a right is that it is necessary to the fulfillment of persons in community. Thus a right is neither a natural property of individuals nor a blessing bestowed arbitrarily by a bountiful society, but a requirement of moral personality in community.

If this is the true meaning of a right, it is obvious that a merely formal or verbal right is of no value. Rights must be implemented by external opportunities if they are to be effective. What is the right to vote, without sufficient education and information to understand the issues? What is the right to work, if there are no jobs? Marxists have long insisted that political rights such as the vote, when they are not accompanied by economic opportunities, are without substance. Political liberals have increasingly recognized that the economic and other rights of some must be limited if equality of opportunity is not to be denied to others. The opportunities opened up by education have been more and more stressed by American democracy. Indeed, it has become almost axiomatic with all true believers in democracy that political rights must be accompanied by economic and cultural opportunities if their true end, the fulfillment of personality, is to be attained. The practical interest of Christians in fullness of life for all men has undoubtedly had much to do with the many social measures of the last hundred years for the creation of more opportunities for all classes of men and women.

Finally, and most important, Christianity emphasizes the fact that men as spiritual beings need not simply the *freedom* to determine their own acts and the *rights* and *opportunities* necessary to carry out their purposes, but also an *ultimate goal* to which they can devote themselves. The freedom of a spiritual being must be employed in the service of a common good that transcends the individual and his interest. Service alone is "perfect freedom." In the absence of this, freedom degenerates into irresponsibility and even anarchy, destroying that unity of purpose without which there can be no social health. The appeal of totalitarianism lies in its power to impose unity of purpose upon a divided people and generate heroic devotion to the ends of the state. The only adequate answer to this is the free devotion of individuals to the community. One of the greatest contributions of Christianity to democracy is that it teaches the necessity of a voluntary surrender of the human will to the service of the community under God. Far from being a denial of freedom, such a surrender represents the highest possible use of freedom.

When we compare the Christian conception we have described with the idea of freedom which has dominated modern individualistic thinking in laissez-faire economics and secular democracy, we are struck with the vast difference between them. The individualistic idea of freedom rests upon the assumption that the individual is not only an end in himself but that he determines his own end for himself. Modern economic and political life has shown the danger of this idea of freedom as autonomy. In the absence of genuine Christian faith and love, men have asserted their property rights as if they were absolute and unlimited. They have frankly voted for their own interest and that of their class. Classes have sought their own advantage even when it has led to a denial of the common good and to an open conflict with other classes. Nations have denied their responsibility for the welfare of other nations. In short, the modern man's exercise of his autonomy has all too often been irresponsible and amoral.

Taught by those who banished God from the world and put natural law in His place, the modern individualist has assumed that if each individual or nation would follow his or its own interest without concern for that of others, a harmony of interests would be attained by the beneficent working of quasi-natural laws of supply and demand, balance of power, and the like. But the actual effect of individualism in every sphere has been the very reverse of this. In the economic sphere the irresponsible use of liberty has all but destroyed equality and fraternity and has led to a bitter class struggle. In the political sphere pressure groups representing class or sectional interests have often dominated government. In the international sphere a chaos has resulted which has reached its climax in two world wars within a generation. It should be clear by now that we must return to a more responsible conception of liberty. It should also be clear that Christianity has much to contribute to such a conception in its moral and spiritual view of freedom.

EQUALITY AND JUSTICE

What is the Christian conception of equality, and what has it contributed to democratic theory? It is sometimes thought that the idea of equality is derived primarily from classical and modern sources. The political philosophy of Plato and Aristotle is acknowledged to be aristocratic, the former taking for granted the subordination of manual workers and the latter offering a defense of slavery. But the Stoics stressed the equality of men as rational beings, and after a long period of submergence under Roman imperialism and medieval feudalism this doctrine was revived by eighteenth-century revolutionary thinkers. Nineteenth-century democracy tried to make the claim to equality effective in political life; twentieth-century democracy is having to meet the challenge of inequality in the economic sphere.

There can be no doubt of the importance of these classical and modern roots of the democratic idea of equality. But it must not be forgotten that Stoic rationalism was on the whole a conservative force in the ancient world and that modern humanitarianism has been deeply influenced by Christianity. The truth is that by far the strongest force making for equality in the Western world has been Christianity. The democratic conception of distributive justice, for example, would be inconceivable without it. The highest Greek view of justice, as stated by Aristotle, is that reward should be according to worth or merit, equals to receive equal rewards, unequals proportionately unequal ones. Modern democracy has largely accepted this view, though it has interpreted differences of worth more in terms of contribution to society than in terms of birth. But it has also been deeply and increasingly influenced by the Christian view that human standards of worth or merit are relative and that God's rewards are distributed in accordance with a higher justice.

The parable of the laborers in the vineyard (Matt. 20:1-16) expresses perfectly this view. Those who came to work late in the day received the same pay as those who came early, though the latter naturally expected more. When the early comers murmured against the owner of the vineyard, he answered, "Is it not lawful for me to do what I will with mine own? Or is thine eye evil, because I am good?" This means, of course, that God does not dispense rewards in His Kingdom according to the rather mechanical principle of distribution employed by men in their economic life. Since His will is good, His rewards are dispensed more generously. A somewhat similar point is made in the parable of the prodigal son (Luke 15:11-32) in the difference between the unforgiving attitude of the brother and the joyful welcome of the father. In both parables, of course, it is the perfect love of God which is the source of His more liberal justice.

What is the implication of this teaching for distributive and punitive justice at the human level? It is not that differences of worth or merit are to be denied, but that they are not ultimate. Rewards or punishments based upon such differences according to the principle of retribution, therefore, are not final. For all men are created in the image of God, all as sons of God are precious in His sight, and all as sinners stand in need of His forgiveness. On the one hand, this teaching raises common men to a level of dignity never before conceived. On the other, it humbles the pride of the rich and powerful. For the equality of all men both fosters respect for common men and makes those of superior gifts aware that they have no right to glorify themselves since they have received all they have from God. Moreover, it is the use of whatever talents one possesses rather than the mere possession of great talents that is the test of true worth. Since every talent is a divine gift to be used in the service of God and one's fellows, men of superior ability should not pride themselves on their merits and insist upon special rewards for them, but they should remember that from him to whom much is given much will be required. A poor widow may cast "more than they all" into the treasury if she gives all she has to give. Thus there may be great inequality of ability among men, but all alike receive their gifts from God, and there is no ground for the exploitation of some and the exaltation of others.

Though this is primarily a doctrine of religious rather than social equality, it has important implications for both distributive and punitive justice. It is not equalitarian in the radical sense of the term made familiar by Communists. But it is strongly opposed to all aristocratic theories which justify the existing privileges of a class, race, or nation on the ground that civilization or the higher values of culture depend upon maintaining them. It is equally opposed to an impersonal utilitarianism or collectivism that aims at the maximum attainment of values on the whole without concern for the distribution of them among individuals. For Christian distributive justice demands the realization of values by every person to the limit of his capacity.

To Christians, therefore, the great economic and racial inequality which prevails in modern democracies like our own cannot be a matter of indifference, and the struggle of those who suffer most from it must receive their sympathy and support. Inequality of income and authority may be socially necessary as a means of getting difficult but indispensable work done. But inequality should be functional in the sense that special rewards are justified by special contributions to the common good rather than by accidents of birth and the like. Since much of the economic and social inequality of our democracy is not functional in this sense, it prevents the fullest development of the human capacities and natural resources of the nation.

The conception of punitive justice, like that of distributive justice, has been revolutionized under the influence of the Christian view of God's love and forgiveness. The effect of this view is to mitigate the severity of the retributive theory of punishment. Whereas the justice meted out in a criminal court may be wholly retributive in so far as it simply punishes a past wrong, the higher justice based on Christian love is creative in that it seeks to remove the sources of wrong in the wrongdoer. This does not necessarily mean that the retributive must be replaced by the reformatory theory of punishment. But if the citizens of a society feel towards each other as the brothers of a family do, they cannot be content merely to inflict retribution upon a criminal. They must also have a sense of their own solidarity with him in his guilt and seek to reclaim him. As a result of Christian ideas of this kind democratic penal systems have become more discriminating and humane in their treatment of criminals. Special efforts are made to reform juvenile criminals. Above all, many have come to feel a deep interest in improving the social conditions which have helped to make the criminal what he is.

In short, Christian love has transformed the thinking of the Western world about justice. It has not destroyed the social necessity of distributing rewards according to merit, but it has stressed the fact of religious equality and the implications of this for social and economic equality. It has not taken away the social necessity of punishment, but it has mitigated the rigor of retributive punishment and emphasized the possibility of changing the criminal and reforming the social conditions favorable to crime.

The Nature and Assumptions of Democracy

Even greater perhaps, than the contribution of Christianity to the democratic theory with respect to the worth of the individual, liberty, and justice is its contribution with respect to the *basis of community*. It is at this point, even more than in its view of liberty and equality, that the Christian conception of democracy differs from the individualistic conception. According to the latter, democracy is simply government of the people by representatives of their own choosing under laws to which they consent. Universal adult suffrage, majority rule and minority rights are necessary ways by which the majority may rule without goading the minority into open rebellion. Conflicts of interest between classes and sections are resolved by compromise with the aid of the politician's art. Each group is to be expected to assert its own rights and vote for its own interests, and it must only restrain its egoism sufficiently to make compromise possible and thus preserve the peace. On this view the basis of democracy is simply enlightened self-interest and there is no deep sense of common good. In fact, there is no real community; there are only atomic individuals and conflicting classes.

There are several objections to this individualistic conception of democracy. Not the least of them is the fact that the consent of the people, or of a majority of them, is worth nothing as an expression of the popular will unless it is freely given and based upon adequate information about the issues. Consent can be manufactured by appeals to ignorance and to passions like fear; indeed, in totalitarian countries consent may be won in a plebiscite from 90 per cent or more of the people. In countries like our own, on the other hand, consent is registered only after a process of free discussion in which all classes of people take part. Why is it that we speak of real democracy in the latter case but not in the former? The answer is that democracy is not primarily government based on consent or on the will of the majority; it is government in which policies are determined by means of a process of deliberation in which all citizens participate. A vital aspect of this process of deliberation is *free discussion*. Why? If we can answer that question, we will gain an insight into the nature of real democracy and at the same time into the error of the individualistic conception of it.

The most obvious reason for free discussion is that the interests of all the citizens can be taken into account in the shaping of public policy only if each is given the opportunity of stating what he regards as his own interest. Only the individual citizen, in the last analysis, can know certain effects of an actual policy or law upon his interest, can know whether the shoe fits or whether it pinches at certain points. But this opportunity of the citizen to state his conception of his own advantage and grievance is not the most important aspect of free discussion. More important still is the opportunity it affords him of stating his conception of the common good and of the policy it requires.

This brings us to the heart of the matter. True democracy is based on the assumption that each citizen has a contribution to make to the common good of the community. It need not make romantic claims for the intelligence and virtue of common men. But it is opposed to the views of those from Plato to the Fascists who have urged that public policy should be determined by an elite group, whether a group of noble families or an oligarchy of the rich or an intellectual caste or a single party. It puts its reliance upon the whole people on the ground that their collective wisdom and public spirit are in the long run superior to those of any individual or group. It is only through free discussion that the whole people can speak, that the interests of all and the opinions of all can be expressed. Only in this way can a synthesis be arrived at which is richer and more inclusive than that which any special group would be likely to make. Such a synthesis is the aim of the whole process of deliberation, since the kind of unity which is characteristic of democracy is not the uniformity dear to authoritarians but a unity which reconciles the diversity of interests of the citizens. For the fulfillment of individual persons and smaller associations is an end in itself and is not to be sacrificed for the sake of a rigid uniformity in the state.

It is assumed, however, that in the discussion and the voting the citizens will be motivated by concern for the *common good* rather than by mere self-interest. In one sense, as we have seen, the determination of the common good is the result of the process of discussion by the citizens and their representatives. It is not so much a present reality as a future goal to be attained, and it must be determined afresh from time to time in the light of changing conditions and crises. But in a deeper sense, the common good must be present from the outset and throughout the whole process. For there must be a sense of unity and a fundamental agreement on the character of the ends sought by the nation. Unless argument is to be unconvincing and discussion fruitless, there must be an acceptance by the great majority of certain assumptions and purposes. Without this basic agreement the process of legislation also will be perverted by partisan prejudice and the selfishness of pressure groups. The legislature will become, as Fascists have charged it is, a mere debating society wasting its time in talk without deciding anything.

As Ernest Barker has argued in *The Citizen's Choice*, division of this kind is the greatest threat to democracy. When party spirit becomes stronger than public spirit, several parties may push their principles and proposals to extremes, each making its claims for its program absolute. If opportunity offers, a single party may then seize power, liquidate other parties, and rule the state. Certain thinkers have been so impressed by the apparently irreconcilable conflict of interests between classes which has developed in the democracies that they see no way out of the crisis without the complete triumph of the workers in a socialistic state. It is this way of thinking, whether from the left or the right, that is most dangerous to democracy. It assumes that the economic and other interests of a class are more fundamental than the common good that transcends all class and group interests. Of course, the importance of class and group interests is not to be minimized. Indeed, if the common good is not to be thought of as a mystical entity above and beyond the personal good of the citizens, it must be interpreted so as to include the interest of every class and group. That is why economic and social democracy must accompany political democracy, for there must be economic security and cultural opportunity on the part of all classes if political democracy is to endure.[2] But it remains true that the common good must take precedence over the more limited good of any class, group, or section.

To summarize, democracy is more than a form of government based on consent and compromise motivated by enlightened self-interest. It is a process of participation by all, through free discussion, in the determination of public policy. The assumption behind this process is that all the citizens have a contribution to make to the common good. But this, in turn, presupposes basic agreement on the nature of the common good. If that agreement is lacking, the limited interests of class or group will inevitably be asserted as absolute, and party spirit will destroy democracy.

THE BASIS OF COMMUNITY: LOVE AND JUSTICE

If this is a sound analysis of the nature and assumptions of democracy, it is obvious that the individualistic conception is superficial and that there must be a moral basis of unity in the community. It is at this point that Christianity makes its supreme contribution to democracy. It insists that *the only ultimately satisfactory basis of community is love and the brotherhood it brings.* Though it stresses the worth of the individual and the importance of his freedom, his rights, and his equality with others, it stresses even more its vision of the Kingdom of God, a universal community ruled by love. Paul was the first to see clearly that love was already the source of unity within one community, the Church, the fellowship of those who are living for the Kingdom. For love is a principle which limits the

[2] See Carl Becker in *Modern Democracy.*

liberty of the Christian by making him responsible to others. It creates a unity in the Church so intimate that the analogy of a living organism is used to describe it. We are all members of one body, whose head is Christ, and each of us has need of all the others and is needed by them (I Cor. 12:4-31).

To the Christian, therefore, man is made for community not only through his membership in a particular human group but also by virtue of his membership in the family of God. Nature and history have bound him to his fellows in the group by ties of sex, blood, division of labor, language, and tradition. But over and above these ties there is a spiritual bond which unites him to the universal community of those who seek to do God's will through love of their neighbors. This community is actual in the Church which is its first-fruits, but ideally it should include all humanity. It will, of course, never be realized fully among the kingdoms of this world, for the forces of egoism and pride are arrayed against it. But those whose first loyalty is to it must seek, wherever they are, a form of society which will provide an order of justice and good will and thus approximate in some measure the more perfect love of the Kingdom. It is this principle upon which Christian social philosophy must be based and by which Christians must judge all political questions.

What is the implication of this for democracy? If the argument of the preceding section with respect to the necessity of agreement on the common good is valid, it is obvious that the enlightened self-interest upon which the individualist relies for agreement is wholly inadequate. The willingness to compromise, which is a necessary condition of agreement, can be depended upon only if a basic unity of purpose is already present. Anyone whose motives are egoistic will be tempted on occasion to force or persuade others to serve his interests without equivalent return. He will also be incapable of making the kind and degree of sacrifice that is necessary for democracy, in peace as well as in war. Nor will the natural and historical ties which bind him to his group provide an adequate basis of unity. This is especially the case in the large national states of the modern world. The racial and cultural diversity, the large size, and economic conflicts of national states like our own prevent ties of common race and tradition from creating a deep sense of solidarity and agreement. Modern democracy, therefore, requires a kind of unity which is spiritual as well as natural in its basis. This spiritual basis can only be what Christians call "love."

Christian love, in its purest form as a love for all men without respect to merit or expectation of return, will always seem impractical to those who do not share the high faith of Christians in the possibilities of man. Unless man belongs not merely to the animal kingdom but also to a spiritual and moral realm with distinctive values and blessings of its own, it is idle to expect him to attain such love. Of course, the natural man can achieve a measure of unselfish love in his relations with members of his own family and circle of friends. In times of crisis his social feelings may also impel him to offer his life to his country. But to expect of him a steady application of Christian love to all his social relationships would be utopian. Therefore, since many, perhaps most, of the citizens of Western democracies are not in any deep sense Christian, Christian love in its perfect form can hardly become the sole basis of unity in any actual democracy.

But we should not infer from this that Christian love is practical only in purely personal relations with others and that it is irrelevant to economic and political issues where greed and strife now prevail. In the first place, Christian love is a powerful leaven, winning others to itself by its inherent perfection. By its very nature, it cannot be limited to the personal relationships of the individual. It must seek to express itself at every possible point in the social order, in the kindness and understanding of a school, in the honest service of labor or business, in disinterested political action, and in the support of a foreign policy which seeks the welfare of all nations. The effectiveness of love cannot be measured by the number of those who practice it or by its tangible results. We cannot deny the capacity of men to respond to it if we believe in their spiritual possibilities. Moreover, Christian love has many allies among those who do not profess Christian faith. Many outside the churches have a deep sympathy for Christian love when it is genuinely practiced and manifest a kind of goodness in their own lives not unlike the fruits of that love. Indeed, without a large store of humanitarian good will influenced by Christian love, the liberal democracy of the last hundred years would have been impossible.

In the second place, Christian love can provide a standard of judgment upon every society and social institution, reminding men that they have not taken the perfect way and that their failure to do so has brought evil upon them. It enables them to see the callousness and hardness of our acquisitive economic order, the impoverishment of the lives of millions and the disruption of fellowship between classes which are due to it. It makes clear that nationalism denies the unity of mankind and destroys the possibility of justice between the nations. In ways like these it opens men's minds to the sordidness of habits and institutions they have been taught to take for granted. Moreover, as it judges them, it brings them to repentance and prepares the way for social change.

In the third place, love brings about a gradual improvement of social justice. We have pointed out in a previous section how Christianity has revolutionized the systems of distributive and punitive justice under which Western peoples live. Christians have come more and more to see that the relative and imperfect justice of society should reflect more adequately the absolute and perfect harmony of love. In establishing the rights of individuals under law and in resolving conflicts of interest between classes and nations, justice is the most practical expression of love. For systems of law and relations between groups are not beyond the influence of love. Social justice, unlike love, is concerned primarily with the welfare of the group as a whole, defining rights by law and protecting them by force. But though love is concerned more directly than justice with the welfare of persons, there is no ultimate conflict between love and justice, since justice also seeks the welfare of persons indirectly as members of the group.

It is, of course, peculiarly difficult to resolve the conflicts between classes and nations by means of principles of justice based on love. Every class and nation has many important interests which must be furthered and defended. Its representatives cannot wholly sacrifice vital interests in order to do justice to the interests of other classes and nations but must seek to preserve the interests of their own and of other groups together by a kind of rough justice. So long as the members of each group are egoistic in their motives, moreover, it is inevitable that the force at their disposal will be used to further their own interests. But there is nothing in the nature of group relationships which requires such an egoistic policy or the use of force to support it. If the egoism of the members of a group can be overcome or weakened, a system of justice may be established which will further the interests of other groups as well as their own and use the force of all groups alike to maintain that system.

This brings us back once more to the necessity of Christian love as an indispensable basis of community. Especially in the relations between nations, Christian love is needed to cast out egoism and make possible the subordination of national interests to a world community. Natural and historical bonds of unity are obviously inadequate for the establishment of a *world community* because of its universal scope and the diversity of national traditions it must include. It must arise, therefore, on a spiritual basis of unity, a vision of world brotherhood and a resolute will to realize it. It must also be built, of course, upon tangible foundations of economic co-operation, political organization, and international law sanctioned by force. For the spirit of love must embody itself in habits of collaboration and structures of justice if it is to be effective. It must not exclude concern for the economic and other practical interests of the various nations; it must accept them and weave them together into an harmonious pattern. It must reconcile world brotherhood with national interest, idealism with the demands of the common life.

There is wide agreement among Christians in our time that one of the greatest social tasks of the twentieth century is to establish a stable world community in accordance with these principles. There is not the same measure of agreement as to the best method of accomplishing this task. The most striking difference is that between the Christian pacifist and the Christian realist. The pacifist interprets literally Jesus' injunctions, "Love your enemies" and "Resist not evil." He is convinced that all Christians, or at least those like himself who feel a special "vocation" for it, must follow at any cost the perfect way of love in every sphere of human life, and he interprets this way as incompatible with any and every war. Whatever may be thought about the effectiveness of Christian pacifists in dealing with the evil forces of the present, they are respected by their fellow-Christians as witnesses of the more ideal society of the future and of the creative power of love in the reconciliation of the divided peoples of the world.

Christian realists, on the other hand, interpret their task as requiring them to take responsibility for the establishment of justice in the political and social order and for the use of force if necessary to defend it against attack. They seek to do their best under the imperfect conditions of actual society due to the egoism and folly of men, at the same time bringing to bear the redemptive influences of love. As citizens with a concern for justice, they must move in the realm of relative rather than absolute values, choosing the greater good or the lesser evil open to them. They are aware that many of their acts as citizens, especially in time of war, do not seem to further directly the ultimate end of love and that some of them may even seem to contradict that end. But they are convinced that the refusal to use imperfect means to defend justice in a world of imperfect men simply strengthens the forces of evil and postpones rather than hastens the triumph of love. At the same time, they are repentant for their own share in the evil of the world and stand ready to forgive others. Above all, they are on the watch for every opportunity to realize a higher and more stable justice between the nations which will approximate more nearly the perfect harmony of love.

But differences of method between Christians, such as that which divides the pacifist and the realist, are secondary. The important thing is their fundamental agreement that neither true democracy nor enduring peace is possible without faith in the ultimate sovereignty of God over the lives of men and nations and in His purpose to unite them through love. Without this foundation of faith democracy as a form of government may continue to exist, but it will cease to have a moral purpose. The individualistic conception of it as providing the maximum of liberty and exacting the minimum of responsibility will replace the noble venture of faith in democracy as a free and equal community based on brotherly love. For a time such a secular democracy may be able to bribe the citizens to support it by material gifts of prosperity, comfort, and pleasure. But man cannot live by bread alone. He is a spiritual being, and he can fulfill himself only in a community to which he can willingly devote himself. If he can find no purpose in democracy larger than that of catering to his happiness, if he can find no worthy dream for humanity motivating it, he will cast it aside as a hollow shell from which all life has departed.

But that will not be the end. With no loyalty to the whole family of men and nations to claim him, he will give himself to more limited loyalties of class, race, or state. He will even accept the exploitation or liquidation of other classes or nations as a necessary expression of loyalty to his own. In short, the ultimate alternative to a democracy based upon the religious faith that all men are brothers is not democracy based upon the individualistic conception of liberty; it is totalitarianism based upon a spurious national or class religion. Men cannot live in a spiritual vacuum. Denied a worthy common purpose uniting all classes and nations under one God, they will embrace the lesser purpose of their economic or national group and serve its "divine" Leader with fanatical zeal. If they finally reject the vision of a Kingdom of God embracing all mankind in love, they will substitute for it utopian dreams of their own for the sake of which they will destroy one another.